The Empire of Credit

This publication was grant-aided by the Publications Fund of the National University of Ireland, Galway.

The Empire of Credit

The Financial Revolution in the British Atlantic World, 1688–1815

Edited by

Daniel Carey and Christopher J. Finlay

IRISH ACADEMIC PRESS
DUBLIN • PORTLAND, OR

First published in 2011 by Irish Academic Press

2 Brookside
Dundrum Road,
Dublin 14,
Ireland

920 NE 58th Avenue, Suite 300
Portland, Oregon,
97213–3786
USA

www.iap.ie

British Library Cataloguing in Publication Data
An entry can be found on request

ISBN 978 0 7165 3415 0 (cloth)

Library of Congress Cataloging-in-Publication Data
An entry can be found on request

Typeset by FiSH Books, Enfield, Middx
Printed in Great Britain by Short Run Press Ltd, Exeter, Devon

Contents

Acknowledgements

The project which has resulted in this volume was funded under the Programme for Research in Third-Level Institutions (PRTLI) by the Higher Education Authority of Ireland, as part of the activities of the Moore Institute for Research in the Humanities and Social Studies at the National University of Ireland, Galway. We gratefully acknowledge this support. Daniel Carey would like to thank, in addition, the Irish Research Council for the Humanities and Social Sciences for the award of a Research Fellowship, which, together with the granting of sabbatical leave by NUI Galway, enabled him to undertake research and editing for the volume. The resources of the Columbia University Library and the Bodleian Library, Oxford, were indispensable in facilitating editorial tasks and primary research. Invitations from Jim Moore at Concordia University and John Marshall at Johns Hopkins University afforded invaluable occasions to develop research on Locke's account of money. Christopher Finlay would like to thank Kevin Barry, Nicholas Canny, and Daniel Carey for appointing him as a postdoctoral fellow as part of the project 'Encompassing the World: Networks of Settlement, Commerce & Knowledge' at NUI Galway.

We appreciate the work of the many participants in the project, including Michael Brown, Brian Coates, Silvana Colella, Enrico Dal Lago, Patrick Geoghegan, Patrick Kelly, and Marc Shell. Numerous friends and colleagues have helped in preparing this volume, but in particular we would like to thank Susan Jones, David Rickard, and Carl Wennerlind, and above all our contributors for their efforts and commitment.

At Irish Academic Press we have been fortunate to work with Lisa Hyde, whose support and encouragement have been tremendous. The anonymous reader's report from the press provided crucial advice. Becky Laughner and Kristin Aguilera at the Museum of American Finance in New York kindly offered advice on the back cover image. C. George Caffentzis's essay in this volume appeared in an earlier version in *Eighteenth-Century Ireland*. We thank the editors of the journal for their permission to reproduce it here.

The cover illustration is a photograph of the Bank of Ireland, College Green, Dublin, by Siegried Friesinger. We thank him for granting us permission to use the image. The back cover illustration is the reverse of a New Jersey Six Shillings bill of credit, reproduced by permission from the Collection of the Museum of American Finance.

NUI Galway generously provided a grant-in-aid of publication for the volume which made its appearance possible.

Notes on Contributors

Kevin Barry is Professor of English at the National University of Ireland, Galway. He is the author of several essays on relationships between money and literature in the eighteenth and nineteenth centuries, and editor of James Joyce's *Occasional, Critical, and Political Writings* (Oxford University Press). He is a founder member of the Moore Institute for Research in the Humanities and Social Studies at NUI Galway.

C. George Caffentzis is a Professor of Philosophy at the University of Southern Maine. He has written many essays on social and political themes with special emphasis on the role of money in the history of philosophy. He has written two books on the philosophy of money: *Clipped Coins, Abused Words and Civil Government: John Locke's Philosophy of Money* and *Exciting the Industry of Mankind: George Berkeley's Philosophy of Money*. He is currently writing a book on David Hume's philosophy of money.

Daniel Carey is Senior Lecturer in the School of Humanities at the National University of Ireland, Galway. He is author of *Locke, Shaftesbury, and Hutcheson: Contesting Diversity in the Enlightenment and Beyond* (Cambridge University Press, 2006), co-editor of *The Postcolonial Enlightenment: Eighteenth-Century Colonialism and Postcolonial Theory* (Oxford University Press, 2009) and *Les voyages de Gulliver: mondes lointains ou mondes proches* (Presses universitaires de Caen, 2002); and editor of *Asian Travel in the Renaissance* (Blackwell, 2004).

Roger J. Fechner is Professor of History Emeritus at Adrian College, Michigan. His research focus is on Scottish-American cultural and intellectual relations in the eighteenth-century Enlightenment. He has published essays on Robert Burns, Samuel Miller, Adam Smith, and John Witherspoon. His current projects are a biography of Witherspoon and a monograph on his political ideas and politics during the American Revolution.

Christopher J. Finlay is a Lecturer in Political Theory at the University of Birmingham in the Department of Political Science and International Studies. He writes on just war theory, the ethics of political violence, political theory and eighteenth-century political thought. Recent publications include a monograph, *Hume's Social Philosophy* (Continuum, 2007), and articles in the *Journal of Political Philosophy*, *History of Political Thought*, the *European Journal of International Relations*, the *European Journal of Political Theory*, *Thesis Eleven*, and the *International Journal of Philosophical Studies*. He is British Academy/Leverhulme Trust Senior Research Fellow, 2010–11.

Robin Hermann received his PhD in early modern British history from Washington University in St Louis and is now assistant professor of history at the University of Louisiana at Lafayette. He was awarded a NACBS/Huntington Research Fellowship in 2001. He is currently at work on his first book, entitled *Real Change and Imagined Catastrophe: The Culture of Money in Seventeenth-Century England*, which examines both the reality and the representation of the increasing use and importance of money during England's transition from a moral to a market economy. He is also the author of 'Empire Builders and Mushroom Gentlemen: The Meaning of Money in Colonial Nigeria' (forthcoming in *The International Journal of African Historical Studies*).

Charles Ivar McGrath is a lecturer in the School of History and Archives, University College Dublin. He is the author of *The Making of the Eighteenth-Century Irish Constitution: Government, Parliament and the Revenue, 1692–1714*, of articles in *The English Historical Review, Irish Historical Studies, Parliamentary History, Eighteenth-Century Ireland*, and in several edited collections and reference works. He is the co-editor of *Converts and Conversion in Ireland, 1650–1850* (2005), *Money, Power, and Print: Interdisciplinary Studies on the Financial Revolution in the British Isles* (2008) and *People, Politics and Power: Essays on Irish History 1660–1850 in Honour of James I. McGuire* (2009).

Seán Moore is Associate Professor of English at the University of New Hampshire and the author of *Swift, the Book, and the Irish Financial Revolution: Satire and Sovereignty in Colonial Ireland* (Johns Hopkins University Press, 2010). He is editor of a forthcoming special issue of *Eighteenth-Century Studies* on 'Ireland and Enlightenment' and has published articles in *PMLA*, *The Eighteenth-Century: Theory and Interpretation*, *Atlantic Studies*, and other journals. He was awarded the Richard H. Rodino Prize for the best essay on Jonathan Swift (2009) and has been the recipient of fellowships from the Fulbright Scholarship Board, the John Carter Brown Library, the Folger Shakespeare Library, and other organizations.

Paul Tonks is Associate Professor of World History (principally focusing on the Atlantic World, the United States and the British Empire) at the Underwood International College of Yonsei University (Seoul, South Korea). He is also Chair of the Common (Liberal Arts) Curriculum at Yonsei University's Underwood International College, an elite English-based and multi-disciplinary undergraduate programme.

Hermann Wellenreuther, Emeritus Professor of History at Georg-August University Göttingen, is the author of numerous books, most recently *Von Chaos und Krieg zu Ordnung und Frieden: Der Amerikanischen Revolution erster Teil, 1775–1783* (2006). His *Citizens in a Strange Land: A Study of German-American Broadsides and their Meaning for Germans in North America, 1730–1830*, is forthcoming from Pennsylvania State University Press. Among other volumes, he has co-edited *The Revolution and the People: Thoughts and Documents on the Revolutionary Process in North America, 1774–1776* (2006) and *Jacob Leisler's Atlantic World in the Later Seventeenth Century: Essays on Religion, Militia, Trade, and Networks* (2009).

List of Tables

Preface

This volume appears during a period of economic crisis that began in 2008. Identifying the precise origins of the current situation is far from straightforward. Among the contributing factors were lax financial regulations, the availability of cheap liquidity globally, overheated housing markets, and of course the banks, which served both as conduits and catalysts in the process. In the Irish case, the rising cost of government borrowing, brought about in part as a result of the need to prop up the country's own financial institutions, led to the requirement of a bailout from the European Central Bank and the International Monetary Fund. However acute events became in Ireland, they did not occur in isolation: the pattern was set in the American rescue plan, under George Bush, and the variant pursued by Gordon Brown in expanding public ownership of banks. And it continued in 2010 with the British loan to the Irish government, designed to secure a vital export market, as well to support a country in which its own banks had major 'exposure' on their loan books; or in Europe's decision to extend a massive loan in which it effectively bailed out itself. The details and economic fallout are well known, but at the heart of it lies the dilemma of credit – at once the engine of growth and, as we have discovered, its antagonist when little control over it has been exerted. The integrated world of government debt, banking, taxation, and trade evident in these transactions came into being in the era of the Financial Revolution. This book provides a series of studies of that historical development.

The Financial Revolution has usually been described as an English affair, originating with the founding of the Bank of England in 1694, the creation of new credit instruments, and the emergence of a fiscal-military state, capable of funding extensive military campaigns in protracted wars with France from 1689–1815. Although the scope of this collection follows these chronological parameters, running from the period of the Nine Years' War (1688–1697) to the conclusion of the Napoleonic Wars, we have widened the perspective to consider how the Financial Revolution transpired in Ireland, Scotland, and America. The question is how these different economies negotiated varying levels of access to precious metals, the kinds of credit available for conducting trade, the establishment and role of banks, the development of negotiable instruments and paper money, the provision of taxation, and the funding of the state in its different forms – Ireland under its own parliament but subject to the Crown, Scotland after the Act of Union (1707), and the American colonies engaged in commerce without financial sovereignty or attempting to pay for their war effort and fledgling government during the Revolution and beyond.

The Empire of Credit attempts to describe this complex reality, beginning with a chapter by Daniel Carey surveying the organisation of financial systems in place in England, Scotland, Ireland, and America across the period. The first section of the book, 'Political Economy in Enlightenment Britain', looks at the range of philosophical positions on money and credit held by leading figures. John Locke's outlook, investigated by Carey, was formulated during the Recoinage crisis in England in 1695 brought on by war with France. Locke objected to devaluation and insisted on the sanctity of the monetary standard, not only to defend the interests of creditors but as a realisation of an inescapable reality – the necessity of conducting international commerce through the accumulation of precious metals. Locke's orientation, which downplayed the needs of domestic trade, similarly accorded credit a limited role. David Hume was more open, philosophically, to paper serving as a money form, as Christopher J. Finlay observes, yet he remained deeply unconvinced that it could function adequately in the world of foreign trade. The thinness of ethical and legal obligations between states was an insuperable feature of the international order which collective agreement could not overcome, requiring specie to maintain its traditional role. Some of these assumptions were drawn out in intriguing ways by four later Scottish commentators – Patrick Colquhoun, Sir John Sinclair, William Playfair, and George Chalmers – as Paul Tonks shows in his essay. While committing themselves to notions of freedom bound up with the accumulation of property, they also accepted a basically Hobbesian account of international relations. The twist was to argue that the configurations of the fiscal-military state and its 'modern' provisions in terms of credit and taxation were essential to providing security in such a world, embedding the Financial Revolution in the order of political values.

The second section, 'Change and Exchange in the British Empire', focuses on the challenges experienced by different players constrained by British economic interests. The Royal African Company faced the daunting task of generating surpluses of gold to bolster England's balance of payments (especially given the outflow of precious metals to the East Indies), as Robin Hermann makes clear in his contribution. Difficult though this responsibility was when managing trade on the African coast, it became impossible when selling slaves in America and the Caribbean, where business was conducted largely on the basis of credit. This study shows the distinct limits of the Financial Revolution, even as it demonstrates the intrinsic link between money and empire. In the American colonies, the long lead up to independence saw a transformation of the relationship with the mother country, starting from a position of subservience in which the Navigation Acts set the terms. However, Hermann Wellenreuther explores how the increasing strength of the colonies led to a reversal of fortune. The growth of non-British export markets is part of the story, but this pattern was part of a complex arrangement in which the profits from that trade were needed to offset debts acquired by importing British manufactures. The British concern with sound currency could only be accommodated by allowing American paper currency to pass in internal markets. During the Revolution, the crucial dilemma was how to raise finance and to avoid an excessive note issue that would escalate inflation. Roger J. Fechner's essay on John Witherspoon indicates how his appeal for sound management of government credit was based on a hard-money position congenial to the philosophical outlook of Hume and other Scottish authorities. Witherspoon's views eventually found a sympathetic audience in Alexander Hamilton, in contrast to the precarious experiments conducted by his predecessor, the American financier Robert Morris.

The final section, 'Credit and the Matter of the Irish Public', begins with a chapter by Charles Ivar McGrath on the creation of a national debt in Ireland, which began in 1716. The spike in borrowing followed the pattern of threats posed by Jacobite risings, testifying once more to the intimate relationship between war or war preparations and public finance. At the same time, the Irish arrangements were significant because the cadre of public creditors was composed of an Ascendancy elite which was basically ensuring its own survival through this investment. Seán Moore's essay on the lending practices of Church of Ireland clergy describes an intriguing parallel in which loans constituted a form of debt bondage, in effect, linking the Catholic population to the legal and social authority of the established Church. The scepticism of some of the leading lights about the new systems of credit, notably the provision of a national bank, was in part conditioned by its rivalling of their own financial interests as lenders at high rates of interest.

While the Irish model replicated many features of the English system of taxation and funded debt, the Bank of Ireland was not established by the Irish parliament until 1782 (and opened in 1783). In the earlier period, proposals had been made to establish a bank in 1720–21. The ill-timing of the South Sea Bubble contributed to the defeat of this scheme, but George Berkeley (himself an ordained priest), did not give up his campaign. Following the appearance of *The Querist* (1735–37), Berkeley – now Bishop of Cloyne – attempted to recruit support for a national bank and to place the measure onto the legislative calendar. The effort failed, however, leaving Berkeley, as C. George Caffentzis shows, to make often vituperative accusations against a disparate host of opponents, ranging from private bankers fearing competition, to perverse Irish 'patriots' who preferred poverty to economic development, and finally to the array of insidious libertines responsible for undermining public spirit.

The volume closes with a chapter by Kevin Barry on the Suspension of Cash Payments (1797 to 1821) when the Bank of England no longer agreed to convert notes into hard currency and the Bank of Ireland followed suit. The 'national' novels of Maria Edgeworth composed in the period offer a keen commentary on this episode. Her narratives provide a vision of how the new systems of credit and exchange functioned, in a moral cast defending paper money and a national bank. The vaunted gold standard, whose sacrifice was decried in numerous British contributions of the time, was subjected to critique by Edgeworth, with guineas identified as the agent of expropriation.

The financial world that emerged from this system, underpinned by paper money, banking and government debt, became sufficiently familiar before 2008 to attract limited public comment (with the American withdrawal from the Bretton Woods Agreement in 1971, in the midst of Vietnam War, itself a distant memory). All this has changed with the current crisis, whose end is still not in sight. The merger in practice between sovereigns and banks, and the reassertion of credit as a political tool has brought us back to a point of origin, with the interlinked fortunes that marked the Empire of Credit.

Note on jacket illustrations: the cover illustration is a photograph of the Bank of Ireland, College Green, Dublin, by Siegried Friesinger. The building originated as Parliament House, designed in a neo-Palladian style by Capt. (later Sir) Edward Lovett Pearce and erected 1729–39 (at a total cost of just over £30,000),[1] where the Commons and Lords met until the Act of Union of 1800 dissolved the Irish Parliament. The photograph shows part of the piazza and the Ionic columns of the portico, supporting the central pediment which contained the Royal Arms in the tympanum, sculpted by John Houghton.[2] In 1803, the building was sold to the Bank of Ireland and alterations were undertaken by Francis Johnston, who converted the windows to recesses and closed the central entrance. It opened to the public in 1808. Johnston also commissioned statues to crown the portico 'appropriate to the Building as a National Bank'.[3] Edward Smyth and his son John Smyth sculpted them following sketches by John Flaxman (1809–10).[4] The central figure is Hibernia, seated, with Fidelity to her right and Commerce to her left.

The back cover image is the reverse of a New Jersey Six Shillings note, printed by Isaac Collins in 1776, from the Collection of the Museum of American Finance. The design features a sage leaf, reproduced in a nature printing technique originated by Benjamin Franklin to prevent counterfeiting. Actual botanical specimens were used to create cuts for a variety of note issues.[5] The complexity of detail and tapered lines could not be replicated effectively by contemporary engravers. Franklin developed the method for Pennsylvania paper currency and began using it in his printing of New Jersey currency in 1746. This Six Shillings bill of credit was part of a £100,000 note issue of 25 March 1776, backed by loan office mortgages.[6] The date is printed on the obverse (not reproduced here), with handwritten signatures making it legal by Jonathan Deare, John Hart, and John Stevens, Jr.

Daniel Carey

NOTES

1. E. McParland, *Public Architecture in Ireland 1680–1760* (New Haven: Yale University Press, 2001), p. 188. See also E. McParland, 'Edward Lovett Pearce and the Parliament House', *The Burlington Magazine*, 131, no. 1031 (1989), pp. 91–100.
2. The Knight of Glin and J. Peill, *Irish Furniture* (New Haven: Yale University Press, 2007), 70–71.
3. Quoted in C.P. Curran, 'The Architecture of the Bank', in F.G. Hall, *The Bank of Ireland 1783–1946* (Dublin: Hodges Figgis, 1949), p. 464.
4. Curran, pp. 464–5.
5. For a description of the technique, see E.P. Newman, 'Nature Printing on Colonial and Continental Currency', *The Numismatist*, 77 (February–May 1964), pp. 147–54, 299–305, 457–65, 613–23 (p. 305).
6. See http://www.njarchives.org/links/guides/cgllo001.html; and more generally on the New Jersey loan office system, T.L. Purvis, *Proprietors, Patronage, and Paper Money: Legislative Politics in New Jersey, 1703–1776* (New Brunswick: Rutgers University Press, 1986).

CHAPTER ONE

An Empire of Credit: English, Scottish, Irish, and American Contexts

DANIEL CAREY

The period from 1688–1815 has long been recognized as a crucial era of financial innovation in Britain.[1] The economic strain of war with France (1688–97) and the related crisis in the silver coinage coincided with the founding of the Bank of England (1694), the creation of a national (rather than simply royal) debt, and the emergence of a variety of novel instruments designed to expand credit in different ways. By the end of the period, paper money, which had been traditionally viewed with suspicion, became established by law with the Restriction of Payments (1797) – necessitated by economic conditions in the midst of the French Revolutionary Wars.[2] Some of these innovations may have been 'enforced' rather than elective, but they produced a powerful state capable of funding heavy military commitments.

When P.G.M. Dickson embarked on his ground breaking study of the first part of this period in *The Financial Revolution in England: A Study in the Development of Public Credit, 1688–1756* (1967), he started with the Glorious Revolution and ran through the beginning of the Seven Years' War, situating his account in the transition from longstanding rivalry and conflict with the Dutch in the seventeenth century to a new phase of ongoing English opposition against France. Not only did this time see union with Scotland (1707), but also Britain's emergence, notably after 1713, as a power with new economic and military resources that enabled it to reach unanticipated heights of power, influence and dominion. 'More important even than [its] alliances,' Dickson argued, 'was the system of public borrowing developed in the first half of the period, which enabled

England to spend on war out of all proportion to its tax revenue, and thus to throw into the struggle with France and its allies the decisive margin of ships and men.' The country's capacity to organize itself, not without setbacks or severe challenges, was what distinguished it from its main rival, where, he suggested, 'the fiscal incompetence of the French monarchy was the main reason for its ultimate collapse'.[3]

As these comments suggest, it has been difficult to tell this story without celebrating British achievement and contrasting it with the miseries or mistakes of French absolutism.[4] The first line of John Brewer's *The Sinews of Power* (1989) – a book that is not without critical edge – notes that 'From its modest beginnings as a peripheral power – a minor, infrequent almost inconsequential participant in the great wars that ravaged sixteenth and seventeenth-century Europe – Britain emerged in the late seventeenth and early eighteenth centuries as the military *Wunderkind* of the age.' By the reign of George III (r. 1760–1820), he observes, the country had become 'one of the heaviest weights in the balance of power in Europe'.[5] What made all of this possible, again, was Britain's mastery of its financial potential and the relative inability of its competitors to access revenues on the same scale as those generated from new sources of credit and tax receipts.[6] While the growth of the state under these conditions – its incarnation as *Leviathan* – has provided one focus of critical attention,[7] other scholars (like Douglass North and Barry Weingast) have considered the financial institutions and stability achieved in this period as establishing models of sound financial management.[8] The somewhat selective orientation of this argument has attracted criticism, but even Steve Pincus, who provides a more extensive political analysis, proclaims this moment as one of 'Revolution in Political Economy' in *1688: The First Modern Revolution* (2009).[9]

The classic studies of the Financial Revolution have situated British developments in the context of European warfare and struggles for supremacy.[10] The reorientation of historians around the Atlantic World has offered an alternative trajectory for thinking about these events. Moving beyond a metropolitan discussion in this essay, I describe various ways in which the Financial Revolution played out – or did not play out – in Ireland, Scotland, the Caribbean and America, where conditions of trade, economic development, and politics differed substantially. There are really two aspects of this discussion that must be emphasized.

The first is what might be called the paradox of precious metals.

While Britain was innovating in forms of credit, introducing paper into circulation and creating greater convertibility between different financial instruments, the accumulation of gold and silver remained a priority of international trade (even as mercantilist assumptions were being challenged in some quarters). When these issues are transposed into a wider setting, the paradox deepens. On the one hand, the lack of specie in colonial milieux necessitated financial versatility and innovation. On the other, a conservatism about money form was abiding in the face of worries over financial mismanagement. Thus, from one point of view, the period can be seen as a kind of competition over norms and whether it was possible or desirable to conduct trade without sufficient or regular access to bullion.

The second consideration relates specifically to the emergence of what Brewer has termed the 'fiscal-military state', which developed and exploited the resources of the Financial Revolution through tax regimes, borrowing, and credit arrangements in order to advance its interests during protracted periods of war. There were those in Scotland, as Paul Tonks shows, who supported these measures as essential means of national defense and security,[11] while critics like Thomas Paine disparaged the practice and settled on what might, in another paradox, appear as a more conservative, hard-money solution. Paine complained that 'The funds of other countries are, in general, artificially constructed; the creatures of necessity and contrivance dependent upon credit, and always exposed to hazard and uncertainty.' He proposed a system based on land, as the source of 'natural funds' for America, which could 'neither be annihilated nor lose their value; on the contrary, they universally rise with population, and rapidly so, when under the security of effectual government'.[12]

The task here is to describe the dilemmas associated with scarce precious metals in colonial contexts, banking provisions, the economic and political pressures exerted by the fiscal-military state, and the persistent attachment in some quarters to hard money principles. None of these issues is as straightforward as they might appear when viewed through the prism of what can be called the *Empire of Credit*.

THE ENGLISH REVOLUTION IN FINANCE

Although there were important precedents for the developments that occurred in the 1690s,[13] this decade remained formative in the creation and consolidation of the Financial Revolution. Something of the conceptual leap required to bring this about can be gleaned by considering the remarks of an anonymous contribution from 1672, *A Proposal of Special Advantage to this Nation and Posterity*, which broached the subject of how to establish a system of credit by authority. If properly managed and secured, credit would not only surpass gold and silver as money but would also, by placing public interest at stake, make 'Rebellion impracticable'. The author acknowledged that it was strange to imagine credit having more currency than specie, but he insisted that he affirmed 'no Miracles', even as he refused to spell out what was involved for fear of tipping off England's rivals. The real barrier lay in the understanding, not in any practicalities of the proposal. Yet without 'ocular demonstration', he admitted, 'there is no reason to expect, that those in places of chiefest Government, should presently believe such a thing, so far as to afford time enough from their weighty affairs, to examine the truth of it'.[14]

Circumstances in the 1690s undoubtedly accelerated the process, under the joint pressure of a rapidly deteriorating silver coinage and the urgent need to finance a costly war with France. The variety and inventiveness of schemes to fund government expenditure is remarkable, but we should also remember the precariousness of some of what was being attempted. North and Weingast have stressed the capacity of Parliament to secure investment in different offerings, in contrast with the instability of lending to sovereigns who might seek to escape their debts (as Charles II famously did with the Stop of the Exchequer in 1672, during the run up to the third Anglo-Dutch War),[15] yet, as Anne Murphy has recently argued, this assigns Parliament a much sounder grasp of financial management than was actually the case.[16] What is important is that these measures survived a number of tests of confidence and became established ways of sustaining the needs of government, particularly in wartime.

The most important step was the founding of the Bank of England, but there were other methods devised to engineer long-term borrowing. The complex proposal for a tontine loan was accepted in 1692, but a more successful model was the simpler one of sales of life annuities, which raised £1.3M between 1693–94.[17] Lotteries provided another route for war finance, including the successful Million Adventure launched by the Treasury in 1694. The Malt Lottery of 1697 ran into difficulties, remedied by the decision to circulate the unsubscribed tickets as cash.[18] As Henry Roseveare points out, these schemes 'All appealed to the gambling instinct by injecting a larger chance of a windfall into the normal rewards of lending.'[19] Although the strategy of awarding monopolies was gradually losing favour, the government raised £2M on a loan from the New East India Company (at 8 per cent) in 1698 after awarding it a charter over its rival, the Old East India Company.[20]

As for the Bank, it raised an investment of £1.2M at a return of 8 per cent, delivered over to the government for the most part not in coin but as banknotes or sealed bills since subscriptions in specie were not received immediately.[21] The sealed bills, in large denominations, bore interest and could be endorsed to others. They were given to creditors of the Exchequer and could then be deposited with the Bank or redeemed for cash.[22] The Bank also engaged in the discounting of bills of exchange, made loans to other parties, took deposits, traded in bullion, arranged remittances for the army in Flanders,[23] and issued notes of different kinds, which became a form of circulating credit.[24] All of this was conducted on the basis of a fractional reserve of specie,[25] establishing the grounds for a much wider credit economy.[26] These events were accompanied by an active secondary market trading in lottery tickets, bank shares, annuities, and other stocks and bonds, providing much needed liquidity and consequent support for public funds.[27]

Impressive as this was, the sums pale in comparison with the amounts of money raised through reform of the tax system. Of course there is a symbiotic relationship here, as Brewer has pointed out: the willingness to invest in government debt was shored up by the designation of specific taxes to ensure repayment, which increased the tax burden.[28] Greater amounts of government spending inevitably went towards servicing of debt. Some of these developments were underway in the mid and later seventeenth century but the huge increase of tax revenue belongs to the period after 1688. The key elements included the move away from collection through tax farming towards a specialized cadre of civil servants,[29] and the expansion of indirect taxation in the form of an excise tax on consumption of specific goods.[30] Other sources of taxation included a direct land tax, as well as traditional indirect sources of customs and stamp duties.[31] Given that the increased revenue derived not from economic growth but rises of taxation in real terms,[32] a question remains of how this system was imposed with relatively minimal opposition (other than from the American colonies). Patrick O'Brien has emphasized a 'flexible administration, complemented by an expedient toleration of evasion and a prudent selection of the commodities and social groups "picked upon" to bear the mounting exactions of the state',[33] while Bruce Carruthers has adopted a more socio-political perspective, observing that 'creditors became *politically* obliged to the debtor-regime just as the regime was *financially* obliged to them'.[34]

Near the end of the century, the occasion of another crisis – renewed war with France – resulted in further practical and conceptual developments in the system of money and credit. Amid fears of a French invasion in 1797, the Suspension of Cash Payments was necessitated by the risk of a run on the Bank of England, which had hitherto guaranteed redemption of its notes in gold. The Bank Restriction Act which came into force at this time in fact remained in place until 1821.[35] This moment polarized debate between those who sanctioned the wide availability of credit and stressed the capacity of a paper-based economy to function, and opponents who emphasized the accompanying danger of inflation (associated with the views expressed in the famous Bullion Committee Report of 1810 and the eventual restoration of the gold standard in 1821).[36] Whatever the arguments, the period saw a huge increase in country banks in England and an accompanying rise in issuing of bank notes, in a system that worked to the benefit of foreign trade.[37] At the same time, the Restriction introduced in effect the institution of a central bank and the provision of monetary policy.[38]

THE SCOTTISH CONTEXT

The basic parameters of the situation in Scotland are well known. The final years of the seventeenth century were especially difficult economically, with a series of bad harvests. The founding of the Bank of Scotland in 1695, a year after the Bank of England, but on different principles (in particular it was not formed in order to lend to government),[39] coincided with the establishment of the Company of Scotland (the Darien company), a potential competitor which also engaged in note issue.[40] The Company of Scotland's disastrous venture, in which it attempted to insert itself in colonial economic competition through control of the Isthmus of Panama, resulted in a financial calamity that contributed materially to the decision to sign the Act of Union in 1707.[41] The results of the Union were once thought to have been decisive in transforming Scotland's economic prospects (whatever the political assessment or reaction to these events). More recent research has led to a re-evaluation in which a mixed record is apparent. On the one hand, this arrangement allowed free access to English and colonial markets. Scotland was afforded the benefits of inclusion under the Navigation Acts and the support of the Royal Navy. In a trade off, compensation for shareholders in the failed Company of Scotland was arranged, while a share in Britain's national debt fell to Scotland.[42] On the other, it is clear that the tax burden rose substantially as a result of incorporation within the more efficient and extensive system that had been devised in England. The effects, however, were mitigated, as Tom Devine observes, by the spending of much of this revenue in Scotland rather than outside the country.[43] If the economic benefits of Union were not necessarily immediate, there is little doubt that after 1740 they became emphatic, particularly in the linen industry and the remarkable tobacco trade.[44]

1707 also created monetary union with England, stabilizing what had previously been variable exchange rates and sometimes heavily discounted bills of exchange.[45] But innovations in Scottish finance and banking developed separately, including, among other things, provisions for limited liability, the issuance of notes to the point where, as S.G. Checkland points out, 'gold and silver virtually disappeared', a system of branch banking, and overdrafts, among others.[46] The springs of this seem to lie, if anything, in the response to the historic scarcity of bullion and the need for alternative means of sustaining and stimulating economic activity.[47]

When considering the issue of money and finance it is striking that Scotland produced such different theoretical positions during the eighteenth century, in a spectrum of views from John Law and Sir James Steuart to David Hume and Adam Smith.[48] Law, developing insights that can be traced back to the Restoration, separated money from bullion. This was a theoretical advance of far-reaching importance but its practical implications and implementation in France were much more problematic. Murray Pittock has emphasized Law's Scottish familial tradition (as goldsmiths) and wider cultural inheritance in the formulation of his system in *Money and Trade Consider'd* (1705) and his unpublished 'Essay on a Land Bank' of 1704.[49] The shortage of reserves in specie limited the capacity of the Bank of Scotland to extend credit, which led Law to propose land as a more suitable backing and security. The precarious currency of Scotland – composed of a mixture of foreign and domestic coins of variable fineness – could be remedied by land with more certain value. Ironically, he criticized the Bank of England for its limited reserve of 20–25 per cent in silver against its bank notes, on the grounds that this would expose it to the risk of a run.[50] When he introduced his scheme in France it was elaborated in considerable detail in terms of the structure and resources of his bank, which weakened it fatally, in part due to the assumption of the national debt and the complex relationship to different trading companies it incorporated and obligations to shareholders.[51] Adam Smith's critical discussion of Law in his *Lectures on Jurisprudence* accused him of the mistaken view that 'opulence consists in money' and that the value of gold and silver was arbitrary and dependent on agreement, a conviction that allowed Law to imagine that 'the idea of value might be brought to paper'. Smith traced this notion to the absence of precious metals in Scotland which might be substituted by paper and an Edinburgh land bank. In his account of the French career of Law, Smith seems to have regarded the scheme as viable up to a point had Law quit when he was ahead, but he ended up, unfortunately, 'the dupe of it himself'.[52]

David Hume's evaluation of paper credit led him to the conclusion that it amounted to 'counterfeit money', which he rejected on the basis that it could not be made acceptable to foreigners in payment, but it also posed a risk to national wellbeing since, as he put it, 'any great disorder in the state will reduce [it] to nothing'.[53] As Christopher Finlay argues, Hume was in some sense philosophically open to the concept of credit and paper replacing specie, but in practical terms the necessary relationships of trust and compulsion could not be brought to bear internationally for such a system to work.[54] John Witherspoon, the Scottish-born and educated head of the College of New Jersey, brought similar convictions with him to America, and advocated a hard-money position in the difficult circumstances of Revolutionary finance.[55] During Congressional debates he lamented the damage done to national credit by the depreciation of Continental Loan Office Certificates, appealing instead for a specie-based currency, and set out his philosophical position in an *Essay on Money, as a Medium of Commerce; with Remarks on the Advantages and Disadvantages of Paper admitted into general Circulation* (1786).

THE IRISH PREDICAMENT

The situation that prevailed in Ireland was different for a variety of reasons. There was no Union of 1707 – Ireland's incorporation would wait until 1801 after the failed Uprising of 1798. With its own parliament, Ireland ostensibly had greater political independence, but ongoing dispute over the right of legislation was only resolved legally in 1720 with the Declaratory Act, which established the authority of the British parliament.[56] Thus, unlike Scotland, Ireland did not benefit from the Navigation Acts and could not trade directly with the American colonies. By law the landing of American goods was disallowed in 1696, and only after 1731 was it possible to import non-enumerated goods.[57] This meant that Ireland could not benefit as Scotland did from the re-export of tobacco and sugar.[58] But it is now accepted that whatever additional economic boost Ireland might have gained from this arrangement, it was far from crushed by the ostensible exclusion. In part this is because a healthy trade with the American colonies continued anyway (notably in provisions and linens), but more especially because the dominant trading relationship was with Britain.[59] However, there would be nothing to match Scotland's industrial transformation in the nineteenth century; for Thomas Bartlett, the contrast speaks to Ireland's 'insidious colonial legacies of cultural conflict, religious disharmony, and political division' rather than to 'the effects of the Laws of Trade and Navigation'.[60]

In terms of revenue collection in Ireland, the period before the 1688 has parallels with England. Traditional sources of crown income, the so-called hereditary revenue, came from rents, duties of different kinds (e.g., on wine, lighthouses, woollens), and poundage, which was greatly supplemented by the introduction of excise taxes in the 1660s.[61] These measures made for what one historian has described as 'drastic additions to the permanent taxation of the country'.[62] Writing in 1930, the same historian complained that the Irish parliament had surrendered 'its duty to itself and its successors' in facilitating 'the government of England, while retaining the trappings of parliament in Ireland, to use the parliament only as a catspaw to rake to the royal coffer additional duties'.[63] New excise taxes were introduced after the defeat of James's armies and the establishment of Williamite government, in part to fund a substantial standing army.[64]

The creation of a national debt belongs to the period of 1715–16, in the context of the Jacobite threat, in which the sum of £50,000 was loaned to government at interest of 8 per cent. By 1729, the debt had risen to over £220,000. In 1745, during the next Jacobite rising, a further £70,000 was voted to fund defences.[65] Subscribers for these loans (and one in 1731–2) were not difficult to find, suggesting a strong position for public finances and confidence, based on the meeting of debt obligations over the previous decades.[66] But ongoing disputes over the rights of parliament and the privileges of the crown in controlling matters of finance came into play when opportunities to pay off the debt arose after 1749, which put public credit at risk.[67] The financial and political relationship with Britain entered a new phase, according to Thomas Bartlett, on the conclusion of the Seven Years' War in 1763, with a tightening of legislative authority and control by the Lord-Lieutenant, with a hike in hereditary revenue to sidestep parliament, and increased financial support for the cost of troops in Ireland.[68]

The fitful attempts to establish a national bank in Ireland in the 1720s and 30s, with a pattern of hopeful agitation followed by failure, have led Eoin Magennis to conclude that the Financial Revolution in the country was a limited affair, restricted to the creation of a national debt.[69] The reasons for abandoning the scheme to create a bank in 1721, after a promising start to discussions, have been the subject of considerable critical discussion, but the main factors seem to relate to the collapse of South Sea Company shares and other economic pressures, combined with the political influence of country rather than mercantile interests.[70] The private banks that operated in Ireland were often dominated by the needs of the gentry in remitting rents, either to Dublin or, for absentees, on to London, rather than commercial concerns with discounting bills of exchange. Thus, as Louis Cullen puts it, 'transfer in space not in time was the main activity of Irish banking'.[71] Merchant banks did engage in note issue, sometimes on a significant scale, but the system as a whole largely revolved around specie, according to Cullen.[72]

George Berkeley's unsuccessful attempts to secure political backing for his plan for a national bank in the 1730s came in the midst of competing definitions of the nature of money and the perpetual shortage of coin to serve as a circulating medium. He famously stressed the role of money as token, departing from the Lockean dictum that bargains were always made in silver by weight, making precious metal all important for Locke in the definition and function of money.[73] The difficulty for Ireland was the outflow of silver caused by overvalued gold and undervalued silver.[74] Locke's position during the Recoinage crisis had been partly justified as a way of preventing arbitrage opportunities that resulted from the fact that too high a value was placed on gold because of the depletion of silver from coins in circulation (due to clipping). Restoring the lost silver would at the same time eliminate the differential between the bullion price of silver and its rating at the Mint. The irony is that when efforts in Ireland were made to address a situation with some parallels (i.e., importing of gold and exporting of silver due to differences of valuation between Britain and Ireland), Lockean arguments were used to counter them, indicating that Locke's stand against alterations of official value in coinage had become normative.[75]

The eventual founding of the Bank of Ireland occurred in 1783, in the context of Grattan's parliament, with a capital stock of £600,000 delivered in its entirety to the Treasury in return for an annuity of £24,000 (on the model of the Bank of England's establishment).[76] The bank provided commercial services, most importantly the discounting of trade bills, and engaged in note issue, but its major role was in financing government debt, especially during the troubled years marked by Britain's war with France (starting in 1793) and the Irish Rebellion of 1798. This period saw massive budget deficits and a huge increase in the national debt.[77]

The situation was further complicated by the suspension of cash payments in Britain in 1797. The suspension also applied in Ireland, a matter of prudence due to the potential outflow of gold had this provision not been in place. A difficulty arose, however, after the Irish government raised additional funds in London through a stock issue that yielded 1,500,000 in sterling. The question was how to transfer the funds to Ireland, with pressure exerted on the Bank of Ireland to exchange the Bank of England's notes for its own, but this raised the prospect of the Irish bank's failure if payments in specie were resumed and demands were made on it for coin.[78] In 1804, the spike in the premium paid on Irish bills of exchange in London led to an investigation by the British parliament which concluded that the rise had come about as a result of an overissuing of paper by the Bank of Ireland during the suspension period. The solution of making Bank of Ireland notes convertible with the Bank of England's was again proposed since the latter institution had shown greater restraint in circulating paper, together with an amalgamation of the two currencies as soon as par between them could be achieved.[79] In fact in Ireland itself, the peculiarities of the situation had resulted in a differential rate of exchange between Dublin and Belfast. In the North, gold remained the dominant circulating medium, with bank notes routinely refused in payment.[80]

THE AMERICAN SCENE

The complex trading and political relationship between the American colonies and Britain developed in various ways over the course of the eighteenth century, beginning from a position of relative subservience to a more assertive role in which American interests became predominant, underlined by the successful move to independence. The part played by money, credit, and finance was crucial to the story. The prohibition on establishing a Mint in America made the different territories reliant on a variety of coins, mainly Spanish, for supplies of specie. To maintain a circulating medium there were few options other than to overvalue coins in order to prevent them from leaving the country, but this resulted in conflict with the mother country, which wished to enforce a uniform standard for understandable if self-interested reasons.[81] Thus there were added pressures in an American context that led to innovations in introducing paper credit.

As early as 1691, Cotton Mather intervened on the side of paper credit. Writing to the treasurer of the Massachusetts colony, he noted that silver was in short supply and wondered why his countrymen would not accept

> that, which they call *Paper-mony*, as pay of equal value with the best *Spanish* Silver. What? Is the word *Paper* a scandal to them? Is a *Bond* or *Bill-of-Exchange* for 1000 l, other than Paper? And yet is it not as valuable as so much Silver or Gold, supposing the Security of Payment be sufficient?[82]

The security he proposed was nothing other than the '*Credit of the whole Country*', backed by the provision of taxes. The alternative, entertained by people with 'Heads Idly bewhizled with Conceits that we have no *Magistrates*, no *Government*', was tantamount to imagining that everyone existed in a Hobbesian state of nature, the equivalent of a state of war.[83]

In terms of public finance, control rested with colonial legislatures (and ultimately the Crown, of course), and these bodies engaged in a familiar series of arrangements, including the equivalent of exchequer bills. They also issued bills of credit, to which Mather alluded, that often served as legal tender for public and private payments.[84] It is worth stressing the scale on which paper money in the form of bills of credit circulated. By 1715, most of the colonial assemblies had introduced these measures, and eventually all of them did so (with

Virginia the last hold out). The issue of such bills (some of which bore interest) was guaranteed by tax levies, but in practice the collection of taxes could be deferred and bills reissued, or inadequate provision might have been made for redeeming them in the first place. The challenge therefore was to maintain a circulating medium without it depreciating, a task that became more difficult once the basis for issuing paper expanded from a source in tax revenues to private land securities.[85] Critics like Adam Smith and David Ricardo would later provide alternative explanations for the depreciation of colonial paper currency, but the practice also had defenders who have pointed out that these arrangements proved successful in the middle colonies, even if New England and some of the southern colonies over-issued paper with inflationary consequences.

Disputes over the merits of paper money were not confined to the American colonies, as events in Barbados make clear. Attention to this episode gives some sense of the conflicting interests at stake in such a scenario. In 1706, the colonial assembly passed an Act to create bills of credit that were made current by forcing anyone who refused them to forfeit half the debt on which they were receiving payment. The bills were raised against the value of planters' estates, requiring them to pay 5 per cent interest to keep them in circulation (with this sum used to support the establishment of a bank on the island). The resulting outcry led to a suppression of the Act by the Crown and the replacement of the lieutenant-governor, Sir Bevill Granville, who was behind it (supported by various indebted planters who wished to raise cash). Particular protests came from the Royal African Company, which complained to the Council of Trade and Plantations that paper credit would 'inevitably' pass at a discount. Indeed, one of the original backers of the proposal, William Sharpe, president of the Council, later acknowledged the failure of the scheme since paper notes had suffered a 40–50 per cent loss in value relative to silver (not helped by the fact that the bank rather than holders of notes received the interest premium). Creditors who were obliged to take notes at par found themselves 'discharged with imaginary payments', which delivered a 'dangerous blow to our reputation in all parts of our commerce'. Sharpe and others behind the Act were subsequently turned out of office, but they responded by emphasizing the difficulties that Barbados was facing: the 'want of cash' on the island had depressed prices by half, they claimed, obliging them 'to erect some other measure of trade in the room of silver, of which we were drained'.[86]

Matters did not end there, however. In 1724, with accumulated debt of £24,000, the governor of Barbados proposed once again to introduce paper currency. The backing was a tax levied on slaves at 12d. per head. To ensure the currency's acceptance, the law penalized anyone who would not take it with forfeiture of their debt, even if repayment had been agreed long before in specie.[87] Reporting on these developments with alarm to the Duke of Chandos, his factor proclaimed it 'an Infingement upon the Liberty of the Subject as the Parliament of England never attempted when they past a Law for issuing of Exchequer Bills'.[88] To make the proposal more attractive in Barbados, an amendment to the bill made provision for interest of 6 per cent on £18,000 of the paper money while the other £6,000 would carry no interest. But this plan, the factor complained, 'puts it in the Power of the Person who is to issue them to pay who he pleases with the Bills that carry Interest & others with those that carry none, so that there will be Room for Corruption even at their first setting out'.[89] The duke's interest in the matter came from his leading role in the Royal African Company, whose fortunes he was actively attempting to regenerate. The Act would have removed a potentially vital source of specie, as his agent made clear. Chandos was also well placed since he had become a member of the Privy Council in 1721, which had stopped the 1706 proposal.[90] Merchants also objected, pointing out that while the Act contained a provision that declared counterfeiting of bills a felony, the Treasurer could continue to issue paper in excess of what was agreed without penalty.[91]

When the American colonies declared their independence, they immediately faced the difficulty of arranging finance during the Revolutionary War, which resulted in the creation of various credit instruments and debt to European allies, especially France. Desperate measures to fund armies and other expenses with government paper nearly failed. Continental currency issued by the Continental Congress quickly depreciated in value, trading at a huge discount. This lead to the creation of Continental Loan Office Certificates, bearing interest of 4 per cent (later 6 per cent), but they too collapsed in value and interest payments eventually ceased.[92] French support became crucial, with an interest-free loan and a series of generous restructuring arrangements.[93] Promissory notes of various kinds (to soldiers, army officers, and suppliers) were converted into so-called 'final settlement certificates' which also bore interest, often paid in 'indents' (yet more promissory notes), though these found a market in Dutch investors.[94] It was not until Alexander Hamilton became

Treasury Secretary in 1789 that matters were brought under control.[95]

Given the importance of taxation in spurring the American Revolution, it is worth considering how Hamilton reconfigured public debt while negotiating the issue of the tax burden. As research by Max Edling and Mark Kaplanoff indicates, there are several salient features to Hamilton's plan. First, the assumption of 70 per cent of the states' accumulated debt into the federal debt eased the requirement of the states to impose heavy taxes. Second, he reduced costs by adopting an English approach to public debt, in which tax provisions covered interest charges rather than paying down the principal (with added benefits if interest rates went down). Finally, the major source of tax revenue was indirect, in the form of customs duties (94 per cent of the total), which was more acceptable than direct taxation.[96]

Banking in the new country was established at the national level with the Bank of North America in 1781, under the tenure of Robert Morris as superintendent of finance. The bank's capital of $400,000 came from a share offering in which holders of collateralized debt converted it into stock, enabling Morris to cover pressing cash requirements while essentially playing for time.[97] The intention was for the bank's notes to be accepted in payment of taxes and duties, with the aim of supplying a sounder circulating medium.[98] Hamilton's successor institution, the first Bank of the United States, was founded a decade later, in 1791, with authorized capital of $10,000,000. Shares of $8,000,000 available to the public were quickly subscribed.[99] Hamilton's model was the legal set up of the Bank of England, although in the case of the latter the state did not have a proprietary interest.[100] Yet the role of the American bank was the familiar one of providing government loans, therefore perpetuating the terms of the Financial Revolution.

The rapid growth of American banking in this period (with 22 chartered institutions by 1799) mainly served the interests of merchants. In part this growth was achieved by enabling them to convert book debts, which had been non-negotiable, into tradable instruments, that is, promissory notes that could be discounted with the banks, creating a considerable volume of commercial paper. It was in this context that an ironic transformation occurred in the meaning of the phrase 'scarcity of money'. In the seventeenth century it referred to the want of specie (ostensibly remedied through mercantilist prioritizing of the balance of trade), but it came to mean the unwillingness, on occasion, of banks to discount sufficient quantities of commercial paper to satisfy merchant demand.[101] The emerging financial system underpinning commercial activity still required funds that came from British sources ready to extend credit for substantial periods, whether merchant banks, commission agents, or tobacco magnates.[102] Thus an Atlantic zone of credit remained crucial in the period, even after independence.

The traditional understanding of the Financial Revolution as an English affair, arising in the context of funding warfare on the Continent, takes on a different air when viewed in connection with events in Ireland, Scotland, America and the Caribbean in an Atlantic context. Not only did these countries contribute to the wealth and military viability of the mother country, they also engaged in their own financial innovations and experiments, sometimes through force of economic circumstance. To a certain extent, the luxury of specie was available only in a relatively narrow metropolitan setting, but even the Bank of England was obliged to suspend its promise to pay at the end of the eighteenth century. The vicissitudes of public debt, levels of taxation, and the role of banks, gave rise to a shared history, in the midst of divergent experience of rebellion, union, and independence. Across the century, the emergence of an empire of credit was not only a practical, political, and commercial achievement, but also a continued source of intellectual ferment and dispute.

NOTES

1. See esp. P.G.M. Dickson, *The Financial Revolution in England: A Study in the Development of Public Credit 1688–1756* (London: Macmillan, 1967); revisions to this chronology appear in P.K. O'Brien, 'Fiscal Exceptionalism: Great Britain and its European Rivals from Civil War to Triumph at Trafalgar and Waterloo', in D. Winch and P.K. O'Brien (eds), *The Political Economy of British Historical Experience, 1688–1914* (Oxford: Oxford University Press for The British Academy, 2002), pp. 245–65; and A.L. Murphy, *The Origins of English Financial Markets: Investment and Speculation before the South Sea Bubble* (Cambridge: Cambridge University Press, 2009).
2. The key issue at this time was whether the Bank of England's notes, which had become inconvertible into gold, should be recognized as legal tender. See J.K. Horsefield, 'The Duties of a Banker. II: The Effects of Inconvertibility', in T.S. Ashton and R.S. Sayers (eds), *Papers in English Monetary History* (Oxford: Clarendon Press, 1953), pp. 16–36.
3. Dickson, pp. 9, 11.
4. See E.N. White, 'France and the Failure to Modernize Macroeconomic Institutions', in M.G. Bordo and R. Cortés-Conde (eds), *Transferring Wealth and Power from the Old to the New World: Monetary and Fiscal Institutions in the 17th through the 19th Centuries* (Cambridge: Cambridge University Press, 2001), pp. 59–99.
5. J. Brewer, *The Sinews of Power: War, Money and the English State, 1688–1783* (London: Routledge, 1989), p. xiii. See also B.G. Carruthers, *City of Capital: Politics and Markets in the English Financial Revolution* (Princeton: Princeton University Press, 1996), pp. 90, 108, 112.
6. For Brewer (p. xvii), the 'radical increase in taxation, the development of public deficit

finance (a national debt) on an unprecedented scale, and the growth of a sizable public administration devoted to organizing the fiscal and military activities of the state' was crucial to Britain's new position.

7. See J. Hoppit, 'Checking the Leviathan, 1688–1832', in Winch and O'Brien (eds), *The Political Economy of British Historical Experience, 1688–1914*, pp. 267–94; J.G.A. Pocock, 'Standing Army and Public Credit: The Institutions of Leviathan', in D. Hoak and M. Feingold (eds), *The World of William and Mary: Anglo-Dutch Perspectives on the Revolution of 1688–89* (Stanford: Stanford University Press, 1996), pp. 87–103; P. Tonks, 'Leviathan's Defenders: Scottish Historical Discourse and the Political Economy of Progress' in this volume.
8. D.C. North and B.R. Weingast, 'Constitutions and Commitment: The Evolution of Institutions Governing Public Choice in Seventeenth-Century England', *Journal of Economic History*, 49 (1989), pp. 803–32.
9. Pincus's argument stresses that the Financial Revolution in fact emerged from a 'prior revolution in political economy'. *1688: The First Modern Revolution* (New Haven: Yale University Press, 2009), p. 366; see also p. 393.
10. See Dickson, *Financial Revolution*; Brewer, *Sinews of Power*; and D.W. Jones, *War and Economy in the Age of William III and Marlborough* (Oxford: Basil Blackwell, 1988).
11. Tonks, 'Leviathan's Defenders'.
12. Thomas Paine, *Public Good* (Philadelphia, 1780), p. 35. The context was his proposal for a colonial settlement in the Ohio Valley, in opposition to claims by Virginia to the territory. The land would fund the war with Britain, which no individual state could sustain. For some clarification of Paine's position on money and credit, see A.O. Aldridge, 'Why Did Thomas Paine Write on the Bank?', *Proceedings of the American Philosophical Society*, 93/4 (1949), pp. 309–15.
13. These include the banking services provided by goldsmiths. See S. Quinn, 'Goldsmith-Banking: Mutual Acceptance and Interbanker Clearing in Restoration London', *Explorations in Economic History*, 34/4 (1997), pp. 411–32; and Murphy, *Origins of English Financial Markets*, pp. 44–5.
14. *A Proposal of Special Advantage to this Nation and Posterity* (London, 1672), pp. 3, 5–6. On the development of attitudes to credit and banking during the Interregnum, see C. Wennerlind, 'Credit-Money as the Philosopher's Stone: Alchemy and the Coinage Problem in Seventeenth-Century England', *History of Political Economy*, supplement to vol. 35 (2003), pp. 234–61; and Wennerlind, *Casualties of Credit: The English Financial Revolution, 1620–1720* (Cambridge, MA: Harvard University Press, forthcoming).
15. North and Weingast, 'Constitutions and Commitment'.
16. Murphy, *Origins of English Financial Markets*, pp. 55–7.
17. Dickson, pp. 52–4; Murphy, *Origins of English Financial Markets*, pp. 40–1, Table 42. On the problem of British annuities in the earlier eighteenth century, see Brewer, pp. 122–3. On the subject more generally, see J.M. Poterba, 'Annuities in Early Modern Europe', in W.M. Goetzmann and K.G. Rouwenhorst (eds), *The Origins of Value: The Financial Innovations that Created Modern Capital Markets* (Oxford: Oxford University Press, 2005), pp. 207–24.
18. On these and other schemes in the eighteenth century, see R.D. Richards, 'The Lottery in the History of English Government Finance', *Economic History*, 3, no. 9 (1934), pp. 57–76.
19. H. Roseveare, *The Financial Revolution 1660–1760* (London: Longman, 1991), p. 35. See also R. Dale, *The First Crash: Lessons from the South Sea Bubble* (Princeton: Princeton University Press, 2004), pp. 24–5.
20. W.R. Scott, *The Constitution and Finance of English, Scottish, and Irish Joint Stock Companies to 1720*, 3 vols. (Cambridge, MA: Harvard University Press, 1910–12), ii, 163–5. The two companies finally merged in 1709.
21. R.D. Richards, *The Early History of Banking in England* (London: P.S. King & Son, 1929), p. 149. By the end of the seventeenth century the capital stock had risen to £5,418,801 10s. (pp. 146–8).
22. On the sealed bills and running cash notes, see Richards, *Early History*, pp. 156–8. Richards points out that the Bank did not necessarily exchange sealed bills for specie but might issue running cash notes or new sealed bills (p. 156). These notes then entered circulation. For an interesting complaint about the bank's notes effectively preventing

payments in specie, see *A Reply to the Defence of the Bank: Setting forth the Unreasonableness of their Slow Payments* (London, 1696), pp. 13–14.

23. See J.K. Horsefield, *British Monetary Experiments 1650–1710* (London: G. Bell and Sons, 1960), pp. 130–1.
24. For a summary of these different notes, see R.D. Richards, 'The First Fifty Years of the Bank of England', in J.G. Van Dillen (ed.), *History of the Principal Public Banks* (The Hague: Martinus Nijhoff, 1934), pp. 219–30. On the bank's private business, which was fairly limited, see Horsefield, *British Monetary Experiments*, pp. 135–7; and H.V. Bowen, 'The Bank of England during the Long Eighteenth Century, 1694–1820', in R. Roberts and D. Kynaston (eds), *The Bank of England: Money, Power and Influence 1694–1994* (Oxford: Clarendon Press, 1995), pp. 14–16.
25. In fact there was a run on the Bank on 6 May 1696, during the Recoinage, forcing a partial suspension of cash payments. Two days earlier, clipped coins had ceased to be accepted by law but the Bank had insufficient stores of reminted money to answer demand. See Sir J. Clapham, *The Bank of England: A History*, 2 vols. (Cambridge: Cambridge University Press, 1944), i, 32, 35–6. This episode was recalled by Adam Smith in his critique of paper credit. See *An Inquiry into the Nature and Causes of the Wealth of Nations*, gen. eds R.H Campbell and A.S. Skinner, textual ed. W.B. Todd (1976; Indianapolis: Liberty Fund, 1982), II.ii.80.
26. During the Restoration period, the Treasury had introduced Treasury Orders (i.e., tallies payable when tax receipts arrived), which were negotiable instruments. Murphy, *Origins of English Financial Markets*, p. 45. Under the tenure of Charles Montagu at the Treasury they became known as Exchequer Bills, bore interest, could be redeemed for cash and used in tax payments. See R.D. Richards, 'The Exchequer Bill in the History of English Governmental Finance', *Economic History*, 3, no. 11 (1936), pp. 193–211. They were supported by the Bank of England (see Clapham, i, 54). On personal credit, which was well-established, see C. Muldrew, *The Economy of Obligation: The Culture of Credit and Social Relations in Early Modern England* (Basingstoke: Macmillan, 1998); elsewhere, the problem of chronic shortages in small coins had already led to substantial circulation of tokens. See J.R.S. Whiting, *Trade Tokens: A Social and Economic History* (Newton Abbot: David and Charles, 1971).
27. Murphy, *Origins of English Financial Markets*, pp. 58–61. On social experience, see D. Valenze, *The Social Life of Money in the English Past* (Cambridge: Cambridge University Press, 2006).
28. Brewer, pp. 88–9, 119; see also P.K. O'Brien, 'The Political Economy of British Taxation, 1660–1815', *Economic History Review*, 2nd ser., 41/1 (1988), pp. 2–4.
29. On the history of tax farming, see P.K. O'Brien and P.A. Hunt, 'England, 1485–1815', in R. Bonney (ed.), *The Rise of the Fiscal State in Europe, c.1200–1815* (Oxford: Oxford University Press, 1999), pp. 70–73; on the shift away from tax farming, Brewer, pp. 92–4. See Brewer, pp. 64–87, on the growth of the civil service.
30. Brewer, pp. 100–14.
31. On additional sources of tax revenue, see M.J. Braddick, *The Nerves of State: Taxation and the Financing of the English State, 1558–1714* (Manchester: Manchester University Press, 1996), pp. 101–6.
32. O'Brien, 'The Political Economy of British Taxation', pp. 6–7.
33. O'Brien, 'The Political Economy of British Taxation', p. 7.
34. Carruthers, p. 10.
35. The Bank Restriction Act (37 Geo. III. c. 45) also provided that the Bank of Scotland 'could not be sued for payment of any of its notes for which it was willing to give other notes'. J.W. Gilbart, *The History, Principles, and Practice of Banking*, rev. A.S. Michie, 2 vols. (London: G. Bell & Sons, 1882), i, 49.
36. See Clapham, ii, 1–74; Horsefield, 'The Duties of a Banker'; F.W. Fetter, *Development of British Monetary Orthodoxy 1797–1875* (Cambridge, MA: Harvard University Press, 1965); M.C. Marcuzzo and A. Rosselli, *Ricardo and the Gold Standard: The Foundations of the International Monetary Order*, trans. J. Hall (Basingstoke: Macmillan, 1991). The text of the Bullion Committee Report is reprinted in E. Cannan (ed.), *The Paper Pound of 1797–1821* (London: P.S. King & Son, 1919), pp. 1–71.
37. P. O'Brien, 'Merchants and Bankers as Patriots or Speculators? Foreign Commerce and Monetary Policy in Wartime, 1793–1815', in J.J. McCusker and K. Morgan (eds), *The*

Early Modern Atlantic Economy (Cambridge: Cambridge University Press, 2000), pp. 250–77; L.S. Pressnell, *Country Banking in the Industrial Revolution* (Oxford: Clarendon Press, 1956); R.C. Nash, 'The Organization of Trade and Finance in the British Atlantic Economy, 1600–1830', in P.A. Coclanis (ed.), *The Atlantic Economy during the Seventeenth and Eighteenth Centuries: Organization, Operation, Practice, and Personnel* (Columbia: University of South Carolina Press, 2005), p. 128.

38. J.H. Wood, *A History of Central Banking in Great Britain and the United States* (Cambridge: Cambridge University Press, 2005), ch. 2.
39. S.G. Checkland, *Scottish Banking: A History* (Glasgow: Collins, 1975), p. 24. The bank could not lend to the king without parliamentary approval and a specific tax supporting the fund (p. 26). The Act is printed in R. Saville, *Bank of Scotland: A History 1695–1995* (Edinburgh: Edinburgh University Press, 1996), pp. 819–25. For the relevant passages, see pp. 824–5.
40. C.H. Lee, 'The Establishment of the Financial Network', in T.M. Devine, C.H. Lee, and G.C. Peden (eds), *The Transformation of Scotland: The Economy since 1700* (Edinburgh: Edinburgh University Press, 2005), p. 104; Saville, pp. 34–7; Checkland, pp. 33–4.
41. See J. Robertson (ed.), *A Union for Empire: Political Thought and the British Union of 1707* (Cambridge: Cambridge University Press, 1995); D. Watt, *The Price of Scotland: Darien, Union and the Wealth of Nations* (Edinburgh: Luath Press, 2007).
42. T.M. Devine, 'The Modern Economy: Scotland and the Act of Union', in Devine, Lee, and Peden (eds), *The Transformation of Scotland*, p. 22.
43. Devine, 'Modern Economy', pp. 23–4, notes a fivefold increase in tax takings between 1707 and the 1750s, yet he also observes that 'Modern estimates suggest only about 15–20 per cent of the increased tax burden actually left the country in the five decades after 1707, the rest allocated to civil and military expenditure in Scotland itself' (citing R.A. Campbell, 'The Union and Economic Growth', in T.I. Rae (ed.), *The Union of 1707: The Impact on Scotland* (Glasgow: Blackie, 1974), p. 61. Vigorous Scottish smuggling did something to offset the impact of excise taxes.
44. Devine, 'Modern Economy', pp. 29–30. Devine stresses that 'the Union did not *cause* growth in the Atlantic trades; it simply provided a context in which growth might or might not take place. Ultimately the decisive factor was the Scottish response' (p. 30). See also the review of evidence in T.M. Devine, 'Colonial Commerce and the Scottish Economy, c.1730–1815', in L.M. Cullen and T.C. Smout (eds), *Comparative Aspects of Scottish and Irish Economic and Social History 1600–1900* (Edinburgh: John Donald, 1977), pp. 177–90.
45. On these patterns, see Checkland, pp. 11–12.
46. Checkland, pp. xvii–xviii. The scale of the note issue was what set the Scottish experiment apart. See Saville, pp. 21–3.
47. Lee, p. 101; Saville, p. 16.
48. A. Dow and S. Dow (eds), *A History of Scottish Economic Thought* (London: Routledge, 2006); C. Wennerlind and M. Schabas (eds), *David Hume's Political Economy* (London: Routledge, 2008); A.E. Murphy, *The Genesis of Macroeconomics: New Ideas from Sir William Petty to Henry Thornton* (Oxford: Oxford University Press, 2009).
49. M.G.H. Pittock, 'John Law's Theory of Money and its Roots in Scottish Culture', *Proceedings of the Antiquarian Society of Scotland*, 133 (2003), pp. 391–403.
50. Pittock, p. 398.
51. See A.E. Murphy, *John Law: Economic Theorist and Policy-Maker* (Oxford: Clarendon Press, 1997); Murphy, 'John Law: A New Monetary System', in Murphy, *The Genesis of Macroeconomics*, pp. 43–71.
52. A. Smith, *Lectures on Jurisprudence*, ed. R.L. Meek, D.D. Raphael, and P.G. Stein (Oxford: Clarendon Press, 1978), pp. 515, 517, 519. For some discussion of Smith's views on Law, see A.E. Murphy, 'John Law and the Scottish Enlightenment', in Dow and Dow (eds), *A History of Scottish Economic Thought*, pp. 9–26.
53. D. Hume, *Essays, Moral, Political and Literary*, ed. E.F. Miller (Indianapolis: Liberty Fund, 1985), p. 284.
54. See C. Finlay, 'Commerce and the Law of Nations in Hume's Theory of Money' in this volume; see also C. Wennerlind, 'The Link between David Hume's *Treatise of Human Nature* and His Fiduciary Theory of Money', *History of Political Economy*, 33/1 (2001), pp. 139–60.

55. See R.J. Fechner, '"The sacredness of public credit": The American Revolution, Paper Currency, and John Witherspoon's *Essay on Money* (1786)' in this volume. See also D.W. Howe, 'John Witherspoon and the Transatlantic Enlightenment', in S. Manning and F.D. Cogliano (eds), *The Atlantic Enlightenment* (Aldershot: Ashgate, 2008), pp. 61–79.
56. See I. Victory, 'The Making of the 1720 Declaratory Act', in G. O'Brien (ed.), *Parliament, Politics and People: Essays in Eighteenth-Century Irish History* (Dublin: Irish Academic Press, 1989), pp. 9–29.
57. On the provisions of the Navigation Acts and the economic philosophy behind them, see K. Morgan, 'Mercantilism and the British Empire, 1688–1815', in Winch and O'Brien (eds), *The Political Economy of British Historical Experience*, pp. 165–91.
58. T. Bartlett, '"This famous island set in a Virginian sea": Ireland in the British Empire, 1690–1801', in W.R. Louis (ed.), *The Oxford History of the British Empire*, vol. ii, P.J. Marshall (ed.), *The Eighteenth Century* (Oxford: Oxford University Press, 1998), pp. 255, 257–8; T.M. Devine, 'Irish and Scottish Development Revisited', in Devine, *Clearance and Improvement: Land, Power and People in Scotland, 1700–1900* (Edinburgh: John Donald, 2006), p. 37.
59. Bartlett, pp. 255–8; T.M. Truxes, *Irish-American Trade, 1660–1783* (Cambridge: Cambridge University Press, 1988); R.C. Nash, 'Irish Atlantic Trade in the Seventeenth and Eighteenth Centuries', *William and Mary Quarterly*, 3rd ser., 42/3 (1985), pp. 329–56; on Irish intermediaries in London in the colonial provisioning and linen trade, see Truxes, 'London's Irish Merchant Community and North Atlantic Commerce in the Mid-Eighteenth Century', in D. Dickson, J. Parmentier, and J. Ohlmeyer (eds), *Irish and Scottish Mercantile Networks in Europe and Overseas in the Seventeenth and Eighteenth Centuries* (Gent: Academia Press, 2007), pp. 271–309.
60. Bartlett, p. 259.
61. C.I. McGrath, 'The Irish Experience of "Financial Revolution" 1660–1760', in C.I. McGrath and C. Fauske (eds), *Money, Power, and Print: Interdisciplinary Studies on the Financial Revolution in the British Isles* (Newark: University of Delaware Press, 2008), p. 160.
62. T.J. Kiernan, *History of the Financial Administration of Ireland to 1817* (London: P.S. King & Son, 1930), p. 86.
63. Kiernan, pp. 102–3.
64. See C.I. McGrath, *The Making of the Eighteenth-Century Irish Constitution: Government, Parliament and the Revenue, 1692–1714* (Dublin: Four Courts Press, 2000); McGrath, 'Irish Experience', pp. 161–5.
65. For details and analysis, see C.I. McGrath's contribution to this volume, '"The Public Wealth is the Sinew, the Life, of Every Public Measure": The Creation and Maintenance of a National Debt in Ireland, 1715–45'; Kiernan, pp. 144–9.
66. McGrath, 'Irish Experience', pp. 176–8.
67. See Kiernan, pp. 149–58; and McGrath, 'Irish Experience', pp. 178–80.
68. Bartlett, pp. 262–4. After nearly being paid off in 1759, the national debt ballooned over ensuing years, reaching a figure of £1,919,386. McGrath, 'Irish Experience', p. 180.
69. E. Magennis, 'Whither the Irish Financial Revolution?: Money, Banks and Politics in Ireland in the 1730s', in McGrath and Fauske (eds), *Money, Power, and Print*, p. 204.
70. M. Ryder, 'The Bank of Ireland, 1721: Land, Credit and Dependency', *The Historical Journal*, 25/3 (1982), pp. 557–82; McGrath, '"The Public Wealth is the Sinew"'.
71. L.M. Cullen, 'Landlords, Bankers and Merchants: The Early Irish Banking World, 1700–1820', in A.E. Murphy (ed.), *Economists and the Irish Economy from the Eighteenth Century to the Present Day* (Dublin: Irish Academic Press, 1984), p. 30. See also T.K. Whitaker, 'Origins and Consolidation, 1783–1826', in F.S.L. Lyons (ed.), *Bank of Ireland 1783–1983: Bicentenary Essays* (Dublin: Gill and Macmillan, 1983), pp. 16–18.
72. Cullen, pp. 36, 38, 39. For note issues in the period, see B. Blake and J. Callaway, *Paper Money of Ireland* (Sutton, Surrey: Pam West, 2009).
73. J. Johnston, *Bishop Berkeley's Querist in Historical Perspective* (Dundalk: Dundalgan Press, 1970), p. 162. Johnston reprints *The Querist* in its different forms.
74. Magennis, pp. 191, 200.
75. For some discussion, see Magennis, pp. 190–94, 202, 204. On the condition of Irish coin, problems of valuation, and engagements with Locke's economic writings, see P. Kelly, 'The

Politics of Political Economy in Mid-Eighteenth-Century Ireland', in S.J. Connolly (ed.), *Political Ideas in Eighteenth-Century Ireland* (Dublin: Four Courts Press, 2000), pp. 105–29. On coinage, see also J. Johnston, 'Irish Currency in the Eighteenth Century', in Johnston, *Bishop Berkeley's Querist*, pp. 52–71.

76. F.G. Hall, *The Bank of Ireland 1783–1946* (Dublin: Hodges Figgis, 1949), pp. 32, 35.
77. Hall, pp. 37, 53–4 (on note issue); p. 50 (on discounting); p. 63 (on deficits and national debt).
78. Hall, pp. 67–8 (on the London loan and transfer); pp. 65, 78–83 (on the suspension). On Irish currency in this period, see J.W. Houghton, *Culture and Currency: Cultural Bias in Monetary Theory and Politics* (Boulder, CO: Westview Press, 1991), ch. 3.
79. Hall, pp. 83, 96; Horsefield, 'Duties of a Banker', p. 31. One of the commission witnesses in 1804 even proposed the amalgamation of the Bank of Ireland and the Bank of England. Hall, pp. 93, 96.
80. Hall, p. 85. For further discussion, see Kevin Barry's contribution to this volume, 'The Suspension of Cash Payments and Ireland's Narrative Economy'.
81. See C. Nettels, 'British Policy and Colonial Money Supply', *The Economic History Review*, 3/2 (1931), pp. 219–45.
82. C. Mather, 'Some Considerations on the Bills of Credit Now passing in *New-England*' [1691], in A. McFarland Davis (ed.), *Colonial Currency Reprints 1682–1751*, 4 vols. (Boston: Prince Society, 1910–11), i, 189–90.
83. Mather, i, 190, 191–2. For further discussion, see M.E. Newell, *From Dependency to Independence: Economic Revolution in Colonial New England* (Ithaca: Cornell University Press, 1998), ch. 7.
84. See C. Nettels, 'The Origins of Paper Money in the English Colonies', *Economic History*, 3, no. 9 (1934), pp. 35–56; and J.R. Hummel, 'The Monetary History of America to 1789: A Historiographical Essay', *Journal of Libertarian Studies*, 2/4 (1978), pp. 373–89, for useful clarifications and a review of critical positions.
85. Nettels, 'Origins of Paper Money', pp. 46, 53–4.
86. *Calendar of State Papers, Colonial Series: America and the West Indies, 1706–1708, June* [vol. 23], ed. C. Headlam (London: HM Stationery Office, 1916), pp. 261, 322, 559 (docs. 529, 632.ii, 1133). The offending council members were reinstated after it became evident that the new lieutenant-governor, Mitford Crowe, had misinterpreted his instructions. The adoption of paper credit was attributed to an 'error of judgement' (*Calendar of State Papers...1706–1708*, p. 531; see also pp. 573, 650, 732, 769). On the context, see Nettels, 'British Policy and Colonial Money Supply', pp. 241–2. In the aftermath, Queen Anne wrote to governors in the American colonies (New Hampshire, New York, New Jersey, Maryland, Virginia, and Massachusetts) and in the Caribbean (Jamaica, Bermuda, and the Leeward Islands) notifying them of the repeal of legislation in Barbados that had forced residents 'to receive bills instead of money in satisfaction of all debts and contracts whatsoever' and instructing them to pass no legislation of this kind without submitting it first for approval by the Crown. *Calendar of State Papers...1706–1708*, pp. 293–4 (doc. 583).
87. Defending this policy, the governor, Henry Worsley, noted that the same had been adopted in New York in 1715. *Calendar of State Papers, Colonial Series: America and the West Indies, 1724–1725* [vol. 34], ed. C. Headlam (London: HM Stationery Office, 1936), pp. 37–8 (doc. 70).
88. Bodleian Library MS Gough Somerset 7, pp. 243–4.
89. MS Gough Somerset 7, p. 249.
90. Robin Hermann's essay in this volume, 'Money and Empire: The Failure of the Royal African Company', provides the background for the Company's currency dilemmas in trading between the African coast and the Caribbean.
91. *Calendar of State Papers...1724–1725*, p. 89 (doc. 162).
92. See E.J. Perkins, *American Public Finance and Financial Services, 1700–1815* (Columbus, OH: Ohio State University Press, 1994); E.J. Ferguson, *The Power of the Purse: A History of American Public Finance, 1776–1790* (Chapel Hill: University of North Carolina Press, 1961).
93. The French loan made it possible to shore up Continental Loan Office Certificates, but interest payments in specie (Spanish silver dollars) had to be guaranteed. On these arrangements, see N.W. Downing, 'Transatlantic Paper and the Emergence of the

American Capital Market', in Goetzmann and Rouwenhorst (eds), *The Origins of Value*, pp. 276–8.

94. Downing, p. 294.
95. There are numerous studies on this subject. See, e.g., Ferguson, *Power of the Purse*; Perkins, *American Public Finance and Financial Services*; R.E. Wright, *Hamilton Unbound: Finance and the Creation of the American Republic* (Westport, CT: Greenwood, 2002). For a valuable account of Hamilton's vision, which coincides with the strategies of the English Financial Revolution and fiscal-military state, see M.M. Edling, '"So immense a power in the affairs of war": Alexander Hamilton and the Restoration of Public Credit', *William and Mary Quarterly*, 3rd ser., 64/2 (2007), pp. 287–326.
96. M.M. Edling and M.D. Kaplanoff, 'Alexander Hamilton's Fiscal Reform: Transforming the Structure of Taxation in the Early Republic', *William and Mary Quarterly*, 3rd ser., 61/4 (2004), pp. 713–44, esp. 736–41. See also F.A.B. Dalzell, 'Taxation with Representation: Federal Revenue in the Early Republic' (PhD thesis, Harvard University, 1993).
97. Downing, p. 286.
98. B. Hammond, *Banks and Politics in America from the Revolution to the Civil War* (Princeton: Princeton University Press, 1957), ch. 2.
99. Hammond, pp. 123–4, nicely observes that the government's $2,000,000 share was paid for, effectively, by borrowing it from the bank.
100. Hammond, p. 134.
101. Nash, 'The Organization of Trade', pp. 131, 132. For the earlier notion of scarcity, see, e.g., Thomas Mun, *England's Treasure by Forraign Trade* (London, 1664), ch. 5; and for discussion, Wennerlind, *Casualties of Credit*, ch. 1.
102. Nash, 'The Organization of Trade', pp. 131–2.

I: Political Economy in Enlightenment Britain

CHAPTER TWO

John Locke, Money, and Credit

DANIEL CAREY

Critics of John Locke have often regarded his intervention in the crisis over English currency in the 1690s as misguided. His involvement came in the midst of severe economic conditions caused by a long-term war with France, which required the exportation of high levels of bullion to fund England's armies and allies on the Continent. Partly as a result of this pressure, silver coins had come under criminal attack by clipping; by 1695, they were underweight by an average of 50 per cent.[1] Action by Parliament to remedy the situation became urgent. Locke advocated a recoinage plan based on restoration of the missing silver while retaining the existing standard of weight and fineness of coins and their rating in terms of the unit of account. The main alternative, as set out by William Lowndes in a *Report* written for the Treasury in 1695, was to devalue the currency by 20 per cent, a proposal which would have introduced a number of new coins with an increased rating of their silver content.[2] Both schemes had powerful backers in Parliament, but Locke's side prevailed, and the Great Recoinage began in 1696 on the principle of an unaltered standard.

Objections to Locke's position have taken different forms. Some have held him responsible for the deflationary effects of the recoinage, the disruption to trade, and the social impact, which was disproportionately hard on the poor who had limited resources for avoiding the loss as the currency was gradually demonetized.[3] The rich had several options for maximizing the value of lightweight coin: during a government-authorized grace period they could use it to pay taxes; they could invest in government loans in lightweight coin; or they could sell their clipped coins to dealers without bearing the full brunt of lost value. Yet the problem with blaming Locke for these arrangements is that he did not favour the plan that allowed this to happen. On the contrary, under his proposal a proclamation would have made silver coin circulate immediately by weight, not by tale (i.e., only in terms of the silver content of individual coins, whatever that might be, rather than in terms of the stamp's indication of its ostensible value). This plan was no less deflationary, but it would have imposed a greater loss on holders of clipped coin whom Locke suspected of engaging in speculation; furthermore, his plan avoided the problem endemic in a protracted (rather than immediate) demonetization of clipped coins – that of simply encouraging additional clipping until the deadline finally came and light coin was no longer accepted by the Mint.

Others have doubted Locke's grasp of the economic factors at stake in the discussion, either for his inability to recognize the merits of devaluation under the circumstances, or his less than dynamic conception of economic forces, and the equilibrating effects of bullion flows.[4] These points are not without justice, but William Shaw's depiction of him as a meddling philosopher, ill-informed yet intent on imposing his views on more accurate observers, distorts the case.[5] Certainly it makes a puzzle of the credit Locke received in the eighteenth and nineteenth centuries and beyond as the figure whose principles effectively made the case for adoption of the gold standard.[6] How to position Locke ideologically has also been difficult to determine. On the one hand he appears to take a conservative approach during the crisis of the 1690s, remaining doubtful about the role of credit, insistent upon the sacrosanctity of the monetary standard, and concerned, above all, by the impact of devaluation on creditors, especially landowners with fixed contracts for rents. On the other hand, he has been identified as a liberal defender of markets against the manipulation of the state, a spokesman for a new conception of government that distanced itself from royal prerogative in matters of coinage.[7]

As these points would suggest, placing major philosophical figures in relation to great events of their day can sometimes result in caricature as we attempt to fit their work into available critical parameters. In this essay I propose to reinvestigate the position Locke set out on its own terms, to consider some of the alternatives and objections raised by his contemporaries, and to complicate the story of Locke's philosophical commitments. To do so we need a better sense of historical context and the competing priorities of domestic and foreign trade; the implications of restoring the lost silver to the coin; the problem of managing a bimetallic system in which silver *and* gold circulated; and finally the role of credit as an alternative to a specie-based monetary system. Locke emerges as a figure who developed a consistent approach but one that was often based on rigid assumptions. Yet he was far from being alone in these convictions, even in a moment of financial innovation and experiment.

I

Locke made two substantial published contributions to the debate over money in the 1690s. The first of them, *Some Considerations of the Consequences of the Lowering of Interest, and Raising the Value of Money* (1692), was principally concerned to address recent attempts to reduce the rate of interest, but Locke closed the book with a discussion of suggestions, gaining momentum in Parliament at that time, which argued that England should introduce a devaluation of its coinage by 5 per cent in order to address the problem of clipped coins (or, in contemporary parlance, to 'raise' the rating of money). Legislative measures in support of devaluation failed in Parliament in late 1690 and again in late 1691, but the process of clipping continued apace as William's war effort put yet more demand on bullion in the form of remittances to the Continent. In 1694–95, the rate of exchange with Holland fell, and the price of silver bullion reached 6s. 5d. per ounce by September 1695, far above the Mint price which remained at the official rate of 5s. 2d. Full weight coins were largely hoarded, whether they consisted of hammered coins or milled money (which had begun to enter circulation in 1662).[8] In the meantime, gold had spiked by 40 per cent in price as an alternative store of value, rising to 30s. for guineas in June 1695.[9] These developments created arbitrage opportunities. Imported gold realized a substantial profit when settling accounts and paying for English goods. Where lightweight coins had once circulated by tale or face value (in a semi-fiduciary arrangement, in effect),[10] a premium became payable in exchange with heavy money. The threat of economic collapse made action by Parliament imperative. With the support of Charles Montagu, Chancellor of the Exchequer, Lowndes's *Report* advocated a substantial devaluation in September 1695.[11] Opponents, led by Lord Somers, Keeper of the Privy Seal, enlisted a reply from Locke which appeared as *Further Considerations Concerning Raising the Value of Money* (1696).

The seriousness of the situation did not escape Locke. In *Further Considerations*, he described clipping as 'the great Leak, which for some time past has contributed more to Sink us, than all the Force of our Enemies could do. 'Tis like a Breach in the Sea-bank, which widens every moment till it be stop'd'.[12] To a large extent, Locke's approach was framed around a series of definitions and principles from which he made deductions, rather than taking a more empirical or historical approach. Although this has surprised some commentators,[13] as well it might, given certain aspects of his theory of knowledge in *An Essay concerning Human Understanding* (1690), his strategy was consistent with the need to define terms carefully. As he put it in *Further Considerations*, this 'mysterious Business of Money' was cluttered with 'hard, obscure and doubtful Words, wherewith Men are often misled and mislead others'.[14] Locke's concern about the slipperiness of language, which he tackled especially in Book III of the *Essay*, surfaces once more in this context. In his works on money, Locke concentrated on defending the current legal standard while pointing out a number of negative consequences of the alternative proposal: e.g., the defrauding of creditors, the loss to the king's revenue, and the inflationary impact of devaluation. In *Further Considerations*, he added a point-by-point refutation of Lowndes's proposals.

Locke's principles start with the key claim that money takes its value from the quantity of silver contained in the coin, defined as its intrinsic value.[15] The amount of silver also enables it to serve as the medium of exchange, measuring the relative value of different commodities like wheat, lead or linen. But unlike other measures (e.g., quarts or yards), silver is not an arbitrary unit: silver 'is the thing bargain'd for, as well as the measure of the bargain; and in commerce passes from the buyer to the seller, as being in such a quantity equivalent to the thing sold'.[16] In other words, Locke regards the exchange function of money as dependent on its quantity by weight. He acknowledges that this role came about through 'common consent', that is, as a result of a shared decision to place an 'imaginary' value on silver (the rarity, durability, and divisibility of which makes it particularly suitable for carrying out the role of medium of exchange and store of value). As for the stamp on the coin, this adds no additional value but merely serves as a 'publick voucher' indicating the amount of silver in the coin in terms of weight and fineness (i.e., the alloy).[17] Furthermore, according to Locke, when people make contracts, they do so not on the basis of the denomination of coins but rather in reference to their silver content. Locke's suspicions about the abuse of language surface in his expression of concern that the denomination itself is an empty sound if it becomes detached from the actual silver promised by words like 'crown' or 'shilling'.[18] Silver alone makes for riches, not arbitrarily assigned names for different units of currency.

All of this is predicated on the view that once the standard has been settled by 'publick Authority', it should remain invariable, unless a change becomes absolutely necessary. But Locke believes that no such situation of necessity could ever occur.[19] Even though alterations of the standard had taken place from time to time historically – rising most recently near the end of Elizabeth I's reign in 1601 – he argued that the existing standard was now well-established in everyone's minds, enabling them to make bargains, reckon accounts, and conduct their affairs. In short, the combination of law and custom made it, for all intents and purposes, inviolable.

Despite Locke's insistence that his principles have their 'Foundation in Nature',[20] there are many debatable points here. Be that as it may, his convictions provide the basis for replying to those who wished to remedy the crisis in English coin by devaluing the currency. First of all, he argues that devaluation would defraud landlords and creditors by the amount proposed (20 per cent), which in Locke's view constitutes 'a publick failure of Justice, thus arbitrarily to give one Man's Right and Possession to another, without any fault on the suffering Man's side'.[21] This is because contracts are made, he alleges, on the basis of full weight coin, i.e., legal money. Likewise, the king would lose in tax revenue,[22] as would the church, universities, and hospitals whose income depends on payments from tenants.[23] Public faith would suffer when investors in parliamentary schemes such as the Million Lottery and Bank Act, or those who provided loans, were cheated of 20 per cent.[24] There is no reason to doubt Locke's sincerity or the public concern registered in his arguments, but it is worth noting that part of his revenue came from rent on family lands in Sussex; he purchased an annuity from the Earl of Shaftesbury in 1675; and he had invested substantial sums in the Bank of England.[25]

In Locke's estimation, 'raising' the coin was a specious notion, a tactic designed to convince the unwary that five grains of silver on one day was equal to four the next because both happened to be called a penny. He lampooned this as the equivalent of lengthening a foot by dividing it into 15 parts instead of 12 while still calling the division by the name of 'inches'.[26] Against this he maintained the intuitive idea that bargains were made in silver by weight (not by tale) and that anyone parting with a hundred pounds, which used to amount to 400 ounces of silver, would be cheated if he received 320 ounces as the equivalent in return.

As far as clipping was concerned, Locke identified it as a form of devaluation. As in a devaluation, the coin no longer contained the same amount of silver as compared with the standard guaranteed by the stamp. This unauthorized practice constituted robbery, but everyone still had the right to refuse lightweight coin, whereas an official devaluation would have imposed acceptance of it by law. Locke's remedy to the problem of clipping was for money to pass solely by weight until it could be gradually recalled and reminted through the milling process. His scheme would not disrupt trade, he believed, and it would immediately bring hoarded money back into circulation since full weight coins would no longer be held as a hedge against a prospective devaluation. This source of currency would bolster the money supply and offset the deflationary contraction of recoining according to the existing standard.[27]

Locke largely left gold out of the equation in his analysis, a serious limitation of his argument.[28] Although silver remained the official currency, in reality England operated on a bimetallic monetary system, and it is arguable that gold had in fact become the effective standard of value.[29] When he did address the issue of gold, Locke stated that there could not be two measures of commerce. Silver alone should play this role. Competing sources of value would distort the function of money in regulating exchange because the price between them continually fluctuated. He had no objection to the Mint stamping guineas to indicate their weight and alloy, but the market should determine their price, as with any commodity. Locke's position may have been consistent with his other views, but he ignored the extent to which gold had become the de facto standard. Interestingly Locke seemed to believe that 'very little varying' in the price of gold would occur as long as the Mint's price remained below the market's. Thus all was well when guineas had a Mint price of 20s. but were current in the market at 21 or 22s.[30] Occasional adjustments would be needed to ensure that if the market rate fell, then no one was forced to take a loss in payments to the government.

II

Locke drew on these statements of principle in fashioning his response to Lowndes's *Report*, which preoccupies the greater part of his *Further Considerations*. The strengths and weaknesses of his approach become apparent in this context. The definitional rigour that he achieves in the opening section of the work supplies him with strong criteria for rebutting the devaluation proposal, but Locke's reasoning occasionally comes across as jejune as he wilfully overlooks certain economic realities or distorts the rationale behind the remedy offered by his opponent.[31]

Locke begins by denying a proposition he associates with Lowndes to the effect that silver can 'rise in respect of itself'.[32] Locke responds by arguing that silver is a substance, identical to itself, and therefore cannot be 'raised' strictly speaking. It is interesting that Locke does not engage here in the kind of sceptical reasoning about substances that characterizes the *Essay*.[33] The benefit of stabilizing silver as a substance in this way is that Locke can vest all the value of the coin in its weight, which makes talk of 'raising' its value improper. But he either misunderstands or deliberately overlooks the fact that what is at stake is the unit of account, i.e., the intervention proposed by Lowndes would alter the official rating of silver to respond to particular economic circumstances.[34] For Locke, such manipulations ignore the salient fact that the weight of the substance alone determines its value.

Lowndes was trying to find a solution to the problem of overvalued silver bullion which had risen to 6s. 5d. per ounce.[35] This high price, caused by the demand for silver fuelled by the war, the deteriorating exchange rate with Holland, and by ongoing clipping, made it very attractive to melt down domestic plate and full weight coins, and of course to continue the clipping process. By raising the rate of silver, a wide disparity would no longer exist, eliminating the sizable premium.[36] Locke answered with several objections. He granted that *clipped* coins might be worth 6s. 5d. an ounce, but the same could not be true of 'weighty mill'd money' since this would mean that an ounce and a quarter of silver (the amount represented by 6s. 5d. of milled money) was equal to a mere ounce of the same substance in bullion form.[37] According to Locke's definition of money as silver by weight,[38] such a conclusion was of course perverse, leading him to comment: 'This I not only deny, but farther add, that it is impossible to be so.'[39] But this was really just another way of stating that if the currency had remained at full weight according to the existing standard, then the disparity with the bullion price would not have come about.[40] Whether Locke was right about that is open to question, given the pressure of wartime finance which would have likely driven up silver regardless of the condition of the coinage.[41] In any case, pointing out Lowndes's alleged inconsistency did not make it any easier to choose between a devaluation or revaluation of the lightweight currency as a remedy to the situation.

The fact of the matter, as Locke later acknowledges, is that prices and values had become 'confounded and uncertain',[42] in his words, due to the absence of legal (i.e., full weight) silver money in circulation. Despite this recognition, Locke tended to treat the devaluation proposal as if it were aimed against a full-weight currency rather than one that had already, in effect, been devalued. Lowndes was attempting to find a rating of silver that corresponded to the average weight of money in circulation.[43] But from Locke's perspective, Lowndes proceeded as if clipped coins represented 'the lawful Money of *England*'.[44]

Locke's insistence had the advantage of giving force to the complaint that a devaluation defrauded landlords and creditors by 20 per cent, but his argument on this subject should be considered more closely. His position had some plausibility in relation to contracts covering long-term tenancies that had been in effect for a considerable period of time.[45] Contracts of more recent vintage raised a different problem for Locke, regardless of how short or long the period they covered. In this case, it was hard to be quite so categorical in asserting that people made such agreements in silver according to its weight. In fact, the silver content of coins had already depreciated in the 1680s by figures ranging from c. 11–19 per cent.[46] The process accelerated considerably in the 1690s but it was already a fact of life. Milled money, which protected against clipping, represented a very small amount of the circulating medium.[47] Thus it is more likely that bargains were made in lightweight coin since the circulating medium was so depleted.[48] In fact Locke ended up acknowledging this phenomenon in *Further Considerations* when he remarked that 'our clip'd Money retains amongst the People (who know not how to count but by Current Money) a part of its legal value, whist it passes for the satisfaction of legal Contracts, as if it were Lawful Money'.[49] He attributed the public's willingness to accept it by tale not only to the government's receipt of lightweight coin in payment of taxes, which he deplored, but also, significantly, to landlords who accepted it for rent.[50] Under these circumstances the fraud argument loses its conviction. Locke's statement elsewhere that 'we have now no lawful Silver Money current among us'[51] would seem to indicate, inadvertently, that contracts made in full weight coin were a mere fiction; the more likely scenario was that people had already priced in the reduction of silver content and would thus not suffer the kind of loss Locke was suggesting. Nicholas Barbon pointed out that if Locke's assertion about contracts being made in silver grains were true, then people should have made their agreements according to the date of the year in which the money was actually coined since, by virtue of wear and tear alone, 'the old Unclipp'd Broad Money of England is worn Ten per Cent. lighter than the new-Mill'd Money'.[52]

Locke seems to be sticking in the end to a point of principle about how governments should operate in respecting property. This conclusion is suggested by the fact that on the basis of some of his other premises he could have regarded devaluation as *not* having a negative impact on landlords; conversely, he could also have concluded that a *re*valuation of the kind he proposed would actually harm their position, again in reference to his own arguments. On the first point, Locke emphasizes a price rise under a devaluation, but he does not take into account the fact that rents tend to go up as prices climb, thus compensating landlords for their losses.[53] On the other hand, revaluation would have caused damage according to Locke's own analysis. Commenting in *Some Considerations* on the role of the proportion between money and trade in determining prices, Locke imagined a situation in which England lost half of its money over a seven-year period while other economic factors remained constant. Among the effects, Locke predicted, ''tis certain, that either half our *Rents* should not be paid, half our *Commodities* not vented, and half our *Labourers* not imployed, and so half the *Trade* be clearly lost'.[54] The contraction caused by the recoinage, on this account, would therefore have a negative effect on landlords, reducing their rental income, among other economic outcomes.[55] In light of these considerations, Locke's tenacious defense of the existing standard makes sense less as an economic argument than it does as a political one. Nor should we disregard the size of the proposed devaluation. Locke mentioned the defrauding of creditors argument in 1692 in *Some Considerations* when the amount of the proposed devaluation was 5 per cent, but he laid far more stress on this point in *Further Considerations*, written when Lowndes's plan was to devalue by 20 per cent. At the lower level of devaluation, it could be maintained that the loss to creditors was not so substantial as to be insupportable, especially with the good of the country at stake. Locke's argument became more persuasive when the potential loss was four times higher.

Among his objections to Lowndes, Locke also rejected the proposition that a devaluation would encourage people to bring coin to the Mint. In his view the only change that Lowndes's proposal would create was to the denomination of the coin, declaring a crown piece, for example, to be worth 75 pence when it previously went for only 60. Such a scheme amounted to an assignment of 'imaginary parts' to the denomination, but it had no 'Charms in it to bring Bullion to the Mint to be Coin'd'.[56] Rather than acknowledge Lowndes's goal of enhancing the domestic price of silver to match the existing bullion rate,[57] Locke stresses the fictive manipulation of a settled standard and the fact that this intervention would not enable anyone to buy more commodities with raised coin than they could before. Again, he simply finds himself at cross purposes with Lowndes. Part of this stems from Locke's strongly held conviction that what brings silver to the Mint is the existence of a favourable trade balance with other countries.[58] When money is in surplus in this way, it will be taken to be coined, but for no other reason. In other words, he denies that silver might have a market price at odds with full weight coin under certain conditions (like war, in particular, or in light of different levels of demand by Continental countries, or devaluations that had taken place in France).[59]

Perhaps Locke's strongest argument – certainly the one that was the most difficult to answer – questioned where the elevation of the coin would all end:

> For if raising the Denomination can thus raise the value of Coin in exchange for other Commodities One fifth, by the same reason it can raise it Two fifths, and afterwards Three fifths, and again if need be, Four fifths, and as much further as you please.[60]

Again Locke relied on ignoring or denying a key objective of the devaluation, namely to set a value commensurate with the bullion price of silver, while stressing the unchanged purchasing power of the coin despite the manipulation of names. Locke replied here to Lowndes's claim that devaluation would make money 'more commensurate to the general need thereof',[61] a somewhat oblique way of saying that the alternative proposal would have deflationary consequences while his would not reduce the money supply.[62] For Locke, this comment by Lowndes merely provided an occasion for ridiculing the notion that the purchasing power of money was somehow subject to fiat.[63]

Locke took the occasion to make a witty comparison at the expense of his opponent. He deemed Lowndes's plan equivalent to the actions of the boy who wanted to cover his ball with leather – when he found that cutting the leather into four quarters would not do the job he tried cutting it into five.[64] This example exposes the bias of Locke's thinking on the subject since he regards silver as fixed in quantity in the way that the size of the piece of leather is also fixed. Yet the unit of account was not subject to the same limitation. Silver in this form could be expanded, in a manner of speaking, to cover the contingency, provided that it was simply accepted at the higher rate.

After reviewing the historical evidence compiled by Lowndes, which showed a pattern over the centuries in England of devaluations and debasements of varying degrees, Locke softened the tenor of his argument without shifting his position. He remarked that setting the precise quantity of silver in the coin was relatively unimportant – it might be a fifth higher or a fifth lower than the present amount without making much difference – but it did matter how long the standard had been in place. 'The Harm comes by the change, which unreasonably and unjustly gives away and transfers Mens properties, disorders Trade, Puzzels Accounts, and needs a new Arithmetick to cast up Reckonings, and keep Accounts in.'[65] At one level his approach is straightforwardly conservative to the extent that he wants to adhere to an existing standard come what may. Considered together with his defense of the rights of landlords, such a characterization of Locke seems warranted. But the case is not so simple since, as Lowndes's historical examples make clear, the argument from 'tradition' in fact favoured devaluation. One could actually consider Locke as committing himself, Patrick Kelly has argued, to a 'new, and in the circumstances revolutionary, doctrine of insisting on the sacrosanctity of the monetary standard'.[66]

III

Enough has been said to indicate that Locke's presentation of his case, for all of its argumentative power, is less decisive than he suggested; that he did not always represent the position of his opponent, Lowndes, correctly; and that his preferences for how to settle the coinage crisis, though far from arbitrary, entailed privileging one group's interests over another's, and advocating an economic strategy that had as many downsides as those he ascribed to the devaluationist position. The predicament was genuinely difficult, and fairness to all parties, as Locke realized, would be difficult to achieve.[67] Nor was it possible to run a controlled experiment to determine precisely which solution would have the least deleterious effects.[68]

While Locke has been lauded for his contribution, especially by Macaulay in the mid-nineteenth century, for articulating views that authorized sound-money principles and the eventual adoption of the gold standard, more recent criticism has taken Locke to task for his economic blind-spots and limited analysis. Perhaps the most hard-hitting account has been provided by Joyce Oldham Appleby in an essay on 'Locke, Liberalism, and the Natural Law of Money'.[69] She comments on the 'superior reasoning' of Locke's opponents, and the stifling by Locke of what she regards as a fruitful line of economic development, represented by the stimulation of consumption and expanded purchasing power through currency-inflation. By contrast, Lowndes's *Report* provided a 'model of monetary analysis', while Locke's errors were 'obvious' to his critics, which included the failure to realize that money's status as legal tender makes a difference in the public's acceptance of coin (lightweight or otherwise). When the recoinage proceeded on Locke's principles, 'The folly and disaster predicted by Locke's critics was realized in full.'[70] She integrates Locke's position on money with his political principles, and identifies him as a key exponent of liberalism in economic policy as much as politics, although this is not without paradox since Locke, as she sees him, is a largely backward looking economic theorist, unable to assimilate key developments in current practice. Her critique is worth looking at more closely as a way of clarifying Locke's position and setting it in a more nuanced historical and philosophical context. The provocative account she provides arguably rests on a number of mistaken judgements, a rather narrow description of the terms of the debate, and assumptions about the historical evidence which cannot be sustained.

Appleby situates Locke in a mercantilist paradigm in which 'the sterility of domestic trade, the inelasticity of demand, and the beggar-thy-neighbour approach to international commerce' prevailed.[71] The alternative economic view, which Locke denigrated, identified the function of money as principally facilitating exchange at home, in which the 'extrinsic' or stamped value of the coin potentially carried a vital influence beyond the actual silver content. The circulation of coin depleted of silver demonstrated this possibility. But it is simply wrong for Appleby to assert that 'It was central to Locke's argument to deny that clipped coin ever passed at face value.'[72] In fact he was well aware that it did, as he indicates on several occasions.[73] His objection, as he makes especially apparent in *Some Considerations*, was that acceptance of lightweight money by tale instead of by intrinsic value invited foreign traders to exploit an arbitrage opportunity: they could pay for goods with lightweight coin but insist on heavy money when selling their own.[74] Locke concluded that the English should learn from this example because it showed that 'every one will see, (*when Men will no longer take Five clip'd Shillings for a Mill'd or weighty Crown*) that it is the quantity of Silver that buys Commodities and Pays Debts, and not the Stamp and Denomination that is put upon it'.[75] Locke regarded the current state of affairs as merely living on borrowed time, and he was right in the sense that a premium became payable when exchanging clipped coins for heavy by 1695.[76]

Although Appleby's critique includes the reasonable assertion that Locke privileged foreign trade over domestic,[77] we should consider carefully his reasons for regarding the two spheres of commerce as in fact inseparable from one another. His position can be understood by considering his comments on the Quantity Theory. To illustrate that theory, Locke imagined the situation of an island country isolated from trade with the rest of the world. For such a country, gold and silver was not necessary as a measure of value. Anything would do, as long as it was durable and limited in quantity. The inhabitants could drive their commerce with this entity, whatever the volume of trade, and have 'Counters enough to reckon by' serving as pledges of value that would rise with the increase of commodities.[78] But this scenario was not available to England or any other trading nation in the modern world after the introduction of gold and silver as agreed sources of value. Once this was the case, the dependence of price levels on the amount of money in circulation became apparent, and the money supply relied, in turn, on maintaining a favourable balance of trade. Without it, prices would decline along with economic activity, weakening the country. Locke tended to see this arrangement in static terms and did not recognize the equilibrating effects of a price-specie-flow mechanism later identified by Hume.[79]

On Locke's account, the risks of ignoring the privileged place of international trade were therefore considerable.

Nor was Locke alone in this view. Charles Davenant, who also contributed a paper during the coinage crisis to the Lords Justices, observed that if England were somehow economically isolated from other countries, then 'Sovereign power' might indeed demand that an ounce of silver procure as much domestic produce as an ounce and a quarter did previously, but it was impossible to take this action now because England was a 'Tradeing Nation' embedded in international exchanges. It was absurd 'to imagine and Assert that any valuation the Government here can put upon our money can alter its course abroad or put another price upon it then what the Generall practice of the Commerciall World Seemes to have established'.[80]

Locke's other proof of the durability of silver as the standard by weight receives no attention from Appleby. He regards devaluation as inefficacious since it would merely lead to a corresponding rise in prices; in other words, devaluation is a form of inflation with no net benefit in terms of the purchasing power of the coin, a judgement consistent with Locke's adherence to the Quantity Theory. For his part, Lowndes felt he was intervening in a situation in which a devaluation had already occurred through clipping. His re-rated silver simply accepted that fact.[81] The real question was whether prices would in fact rise as Locke predicted, but Lowndes's plan was not implemented so Locke's claim could not be put to the test.[82] Appleby herself cites a figure of inflation at 25 per cent in 1695.[83] This data could be used to support either Locke's or Lowndes's case: for Locke it would count as proof that the loss of silver in the circulating medium drove up prices; for Lowndes, that the inflationary impact had already been felt before recoinage was complete.

Appleby's account of the Recoinage is problematic since Locke receives full blame for a plan that departed in several key respects from the one he wanted put in place. Certainly she is correct in stating that Locke intended to ensure, above all, that creditors were not 'defrauded' by devaluation. But the story is more complicated when it comes to inequitable arrangements that gave latitude to the wealthy. Those with enough resources to owe taxes received the full benefit of the government's allowance of such payments in clipped coin during a five-month grace period. Locke emphatically opposed such an arrangement. He argued that the acceptance of light money by government officials encouraged renewed clipping; instead, he wanted coin to pass by weight forthwith, which would have placed the loss in the hands of holders of such coin.[84] Although debtors and the poor would not have received a net benefit, there would have been no bonus to speculators who traded in light coin or to the wealthy who had been able to hoard full-weight money. Thus Locke was far from responsible for this feature of the 'net transfer of income' made possible by the Recoinage.[85] On the issue of deflation caused by the Recoinage, it is important to point out that Locke identified as one of the advantages of his scheme that it would immediately encourage dishoarding of full weight coin (especially milled money), which would have bolstered the level of circulation.[86] No one knew exactly how much had been hoarded and how much melted down, but the expectation of sizable sums re-entering the economy was not unreasonable.[87] It is also possible that Locke would not have foreseen these deflationary effects. Apparently Lowndes did not grasp them either, since he commented that his plan had the advantage of allowing for a revaluation of coin at the old standard once economic affairs had settled, presumably after the war.[88]

The real purpose of Appleby's essay is to describe Locke's position as an attack on sovereign power in economic matters, and thus as a key source of liberal thinking on the freedom of the market from external control. As she puts it, 'Locke could have maintained that sovereigns ought not to tamper with the coinage . . . but his system was only truly coherent if the natural value of money prevailed whatever the government did.'[89] There are a number of assumptions packed in here that require some elucidation and comment. Appleby's thesis is correct insofar as it asserts that Locke wanted to identify a standard resilient to manipulation, but his argument was not so much with the sovereign as it was with figures in Parliament who threatened to undermine existing contracts by depreciating the silver in English coin. In fact, King William opposed devaluation and backed the plan put forward by Locke's supporters,[90] which complicates the political dynamics of the dispute. There are a couple of ways of constructing Locke's position on this matter. It is true that Locke integrates his monetary theory with his account of natural rights, in the sense that for Locke contracts are agreed in terms of silver by weight, which makes any alteration of the standard a violation of property. On his account, the role of government in protecting property makes a move against the rating of the coin (or for that matter its weight and fineness) an abuse of power. Yet Appleby goes too far when she attributes to Locke the strange position of 'turning the mint standard into an immutable fact of nature'.[91] Locke recognized, as we have seen, that the standard was arbitrary rather than conferred by nature, but once it was adopted the state had a responsibility to maintain it, as it had done for nearly 100 years.[92]

The difficulty with placing Locke in the bold relief of transitions from one set of economic principles to another, as Appleby does, is that this does not take enough account of the nuance of historical situation. Thus she gives little attention to the fact that the discussion over recoinage occurred in the context of a protracted war with France. Eliding this consideration serves to highlight differences of economic policy between Locke and his opponents, but it eliminates from view the necessity Locke was under of achieving a solution that would defend national interests during a highly precarious period. There are reasons for thinking that Locke would have regarded a country with a weakened currency as seriously under threat of military defeat, therefore necessitating a revaluation of the kind he proposed. In *Some Considerations*, he alludes to the then very recent history of emergency measures adopted in Ireland by James II following the Glorious Revolution. In the absence of precious metals, James authorized the coinage of base money in copper, brass and other forms, but the attempt ultimately failed. Locke observed that the currency had 'no more worth, than . . . its weight in Copper', and represented a loss to the country by the margin it passed above its weight. He concluded that 'no one suffered so much by it as he, by whose Authority it was made current'.[93] For similar reasons, England could ill afford to experiment with a deficient currency when the absolutist government of France jeopardized its future. Furthermore, the devaluation of the currency would have left those holding government debt with a loss. Such a mistaken course of action threatened English credit at a time when borrowing to fund the war was absolutely essential. To ignore these considerations does an injustice to Locke, it seems to me, and simplifies the difficult choices faced by the country in a time of crisis. Appleby's lack of engagement with texts directly supportive of Locke or broadly agreeing with his position also conveys the false impression that he was somehow isolated in maintaining his perspective on the Recoinage.

IV

Locke's caution in economic matters is nowhere more apparent than in his attitude to credit. The period of the 1690s has been widely recognized as a moment of innovation, even revolution, in which new financial instruments transformed government funding, creating a national debt, partly through the provision of loans by the Bank of England, established by Parliament in 1694. Loans were nothing new, of course, but the circulation of paper money and the convertibility of different kinds of debt expanded the money supply in unfamiliar ways. Thus, credit arrangements were a crucial part of this trend of innovation and experiment. The economic pressure of the Nine Years' War was especially important in effecting these transformations. Although Locke was an early investor in the Bank of England – he retained a keen sense of financial opportunities – he had reservations about the institutional role and potential monopoly it would enjoy. Credit more generally has a limited place in Locke's understanding of economic transactions. We have already seen his discomfort with what could be regarded as a semi-fiduciary coinage system, where values of money remained far higher than the silver content 'vouched' by their stamp. In a number of key areas of more formal credit arrangements he seems to have regarded credit as a modest player with little overall potential.

In *Some Considerations*, Locke stresses the privileged status of silver as a pledge. By contrast, bills, bonds or notes of debt agreed between two parties (presumably known to each other) could not be made acceptable to a third party, 'he not knowing that the Bill or Bond is true or legal, or that the Man bound to me is honest or responsible',[94] and such instruments therefore failed as 'current' pledges. If trust was the only issue for Locke, then it would seem possible to bolster these transactions with public backing of some kind, but here he became more emphatic. Public authority had no power to make bills assignable precisely because the law could not give them an intrinsic value equivalent to that of gold and silver, which were subject to 'universal Consent'. Foreign merchants could not be 'brought' to accept them, so such bills could play no significant role in trade. As for internal circulation, somewhat greater scope existed for these credit notes, yet Locke remained doubtful. Disputes over the legitimacy of these documents would be endemic, requiring some proof beyond mere appearance of their genuineness. The real risk was that these forms of credit would create an illusion of wealth, masking actual poverty which would manifest itself in moments of crisis, and thus cause greater damage.[95]

Locke did make a potentially important concession when he acknowledged that resorting to arrangements of this kind in the absence of sufficient currency was better than curtailing trade, especially if the alternative was to borrow money from neighbouring countries. But implementing such a scheme of credit required finding a way to assign bills so as to make them 'easie, safe and universal at home'. On the whole, however, Locke's view remains consistent with his restrictive definition of credit as 'nothing else but an Assurance of Money in some short time'.[96] Nor should we assume that Lowndes was somehow way ahead in his thinking on this subject. He described paper credit as 'at best hazardous' and something that 'may be carried too far'.[97] As the risky practice of using it had arisen in the context of missing silver in the English coin, Lowndes advertised as one of the advantages of his proposal that it would eliminate the need for paper credit.

Locke's contemporary, the economic theorist Charles Davenant, was much more open to the role of credit. His proposals during the currency crisis suggest the range of thinking possible during this period. Davenant composed two manuscripts of particular interest during the controversy, 'A Memorial Concerning the Coyn of England', dated November 1695,[98] written just prior to the decision to recoin, and 'A memoriall concerning Creditt', dated 15 July 1696, when the process was underway. In Davenant's judgement, recoinage at the existing standard was preferable to a devaluation, but unlike Locke he was not in favour of undertaking it during the war.[99] He shared the view that a devaluation would have no effect on the way foreign merchants assessed English coin, which would remain according to its intrinsic value; those who imported foreign goods would also have to respect this standard in their pricing. The influence of foreign commerce was so much a part of economic life that these values would prevail, 'and not such as Wee fancy to establish among our selves'.[100] Yet in general he took a much less dogmatic approach than Locke. For example, while he shared Locke's view that coining four million in money and calling it five million amounted to assigning it a 'fictitious value', Davenant was still capable of seeing this as potentially beneficial if the valuation gained acceptance. He reckoned that such a plan would fail if 'men should square all their dealings as probably they will, by the intrinsick value of the money',[101] but he avoided making a categorical statement on the subject or assumption about what would actually happen.

Davenant's innovative suggestion was that credit should take the place of the missing coin, at least during the period of the war. The process was in fact already going on, with 'fictitious wealth' in the form of credit having virtually the same 'power & effect' as money.[102] In order for the system to work, some good money was needed to give reputation to the rest.[103] But otherwise it was possible, in domestic exchange, to deal in tallies, bank bills, and goldsmiths' notes. The effect was to support specie transactions at the legal rate (by tale), because – though Davenant does not spell this out – the credit instruments were presumably transacted in terms of the unit of account. He did not guarantee that the public would continue to respond positively to such an innovation,[104] but it had the potential, as adoption of it advanced, to create an unexpected scenario in which credit rose in estimation. By analogy, money in this 'credit' form would become like heavy coin compared to base money (because credit kept to the 'full weight' measure of the legal unit of account).[105] Davenant shared many of Locke's basic assumptions, but his willingness to experiment stemmed from the belief that trade at home had to be sustained and repaired before any move could be made to address the adverse imbalance internationally.

In his 'Memoriall concerning Creditt', Davenant expanded on these points while again making it clear that a versatile approach was necessary in wartime conditions. English inability to sustain the wearying financial effects of the long conflict with France made it essential to find new resources. He gave more play to the role of banks in issuing paper but he also suggested an excise tax to raise £800,000, on the basis of which £6m in tallies could be struck and become in time like cash. Placement of a 'false or more than Intrinsick Value' on this sum would enable it to achieve the urgent goal of circulating.[106]

We might well ask how someone who started off with convictions that coincided in many ways with Locke could end up making proposals he would have emphatically rejected. The answer seems to lie in Davenant's greater sense of economic peril which a restoration of the old standard would only partly remedy. As a result, he was prepared to make innovative proposals that dealt in probabilities, with likelihoods rather than certainty.[107] Given the probabilism of Locke's theory of knowledge it is rather striking that this should be a point of contrast between them. But perhaps the largest difference comes in Davenant's willingness to live with a fictional or artificial economy. As he boldly remarked, 'nothing is more ffantasticall, and Nice than Credit', yet this was not a prelude to condemning it, even though it 'hangs upon opinion' and 'depends on passions of hope and fear'.[108]

The real faultline between them, then, may lie somewhere else – in opposing attitudes toward the imagination. Davenant was obviously open to the possibility of an 'imaginary' economy and fictitious value. By contrast, one of the consistent themes of Locke's *Essay* is its hostility towards the imagination. In a work of over 700 pages in its modern edition, it is striking that Locke has nothing positive to say about this mental faculty. When he added new chapters to the *Essay* in the fourth edition (1700) he consolidated the point, contributing discussions of the 'Association of Ideas' and 'Enthusiasm' that were both antagonistic toward unregulated flights of imagination. Thus he was never likely to embrace the concept of credit. The social bond that it represented, according to Davenant,[109] might have had some appeal to him, but opinion was certainly no guarantee of correctness and it was capable of leading a people astray and obscuring truth.[110]

It is no surprise, equally, to find Locke weighing in against a plan for devaluation that set no limits on the operation of imagination, where the value of money was controlled by whim rather than an external force with intersubjective validity.[111] Exponents of 'raising' the coin treated value as a creature to some extent of fancy: so long as clipped money was accepted, no real economic difficulty arose.[112] The value of money in such a case was extrinsic rather than intrinsic, detached from the anchor of silver. There is a paradox, of course, since Locke recognized that the decision to place a value on silver was itself 'imaginary'.[113] But the point is that once an agreement was made it became essential to respect it. In that sense it is like the agreement to leave the state of nature and to assign one's executive power to enforce the law of nature to the magistrate. The precise moment at which this decision occurred historically might be arbitrary, but once it happened, a series of vital consequences followed inexorably.

CODA

Resituating Locke in his historical moment produces, inevitably, a more complicated picture from which it is difficult to derive conclusions that support undifferentiated lines of argument. The orientation of his position on money might, as we have seen, be characterized as conservative and radical at the same time – as defending the interests of landlords and other creditors, on the one hand, or, on the other, as maintaining a sacrosanct standard that governments and sovereigns could not manipulate. He could be identified as a patriot defending his country at a moment of peril or as a self-interested investor with tenants of his own in his debt.

Similar problems arise in placing Locke in relation to the Financial Revolution. The bold lines sketched by Steve Pincus in *1688: The First Modern Revolution* contrast the land-based ideology of Tories, in which property and wealth remain finite, with a Whig position in which population, labour and manufacturing matter, above all, and riches are potentially infinite. Some plausible support at a philosophical level can be drawn from the discussion of property in the 'Second Treatise', yet there are difficulties in smoothing over major differences that indicate a lack of Whig consensus over these issues. The Whig establishment of the Bank of England is stressed by Pincus against the Tory alternative of a land bank, with Locke identified as 'one of the earliest supporters of and investors in the Bank of England'.[114] True, he did invest and receive his dividends, but Locke, as I have noted, also drafted an unpublished critique of the bank, questioning the incorruptibility of its managers, the risks of it becoming the plaything of government and king, and its status as a monopoly.[115]

A brief consideration of Locke's connections with Nicholas Barbon are instructive here. Barbon's endorsement of banking is remarked by Pincus, and he is ranged accordingly with a Whig position because he explained the reluctance to found such an institution – despite available wealth in the City of London – on the basis of fears over a despotic government (referring to James II), which not only ignored trade but raised the prospect of princely seizure of such a lucrative resource. These fears had of course been overcome with the Glorious Revolution.[116] This would ostensibly place Barbon in close company with Locke (if Locke had in fact been an unalloyed supporter of the bank). But even if we overlook Locke's opposing position on the bank and turn to the Recoinage, some telling differences between the two figures are immediately apparent. Barbon was in fact one of the most acute critics of Locke's position on money, arguing in favour of a devaluation and the extension of credit.[117] For Barbon, the nation's stock could be expanded indefinitely (a position that Pincus contrasts in general terms with the Tory zero-sum attitude to commercial competition),[118] but Locke was an adherent to a more traditional notion that insisted on the importance of a favourable balance of trade and that no silver would come to the Mint unless this account was in surplus. Thus the landscape looks very different if we place the Recoinage at the centre of it rather than the Bank of England, but either point of focus becomes problematic if it assumes a consensual Whig position in these matters.

Locke's decided reticence about credit – that cornerstone of the Financial Revolution – draws attention to what constituted his major legacy to the eighteenth century, of course, which was a 'hard money' position on currency questions. Here his influence was very substantial, not just in British arguments, but also elsewhere. In a Boston periodical of 1734, for example, Samuel Mather commended 'the judicious Mr. Locke' for holding that '*Silver is the Measure of Commerce by its Quantity*, by which its intrinsic Value is to be measured.'[119] Others, however – while acknowledging Locke's standing – maintained that he provided too restrictive a model for conducting trade in a colonial setting. In a 1740 *Inquiry into the Nature and Uses of Money*, Hugh Vance saluted 'the great Mr. *Lock*' before noting his discussion in *Some Considerations* of the currency options available to an island nation out of contact with the rest of the world (discussed above). For such a people, Locke had affirmed, any durable material could be used to measure and drive trade, but such an avenue was no longer available to England because it engaged in international commerce where gold and silver prevailed, whose standard could not be altered. Vance remarked that he too would have preferred this arrangement if 'we were on the same Footing', but colonial economies faced different conditions. 'For, what Mr. *Lock* says of Silver, that it is the Measure of the Quantity or the Extent of Trade in the World, the same may be truly said of *Bills* in this Province [Massachusetts].'[120]

When Macaulay came in the mid-nineteenth century to recount the events of the Recoinage in his *History of England*, he was famously celebratory of Locke's role. If the arguments put forward by Lowndes had prevailed, Macaulay believed, 'public credit, still in its tender and sickly infancy, would have been destroyed'. 'Happily', he continued, 'Lowndes was completely refuted by Locke' in a work which, he proclaimed, 'may still be read with pleasure and profit'.[121]

NOTES

1. P.H. Kelly, 'General Introduction: Locke on Money', in Kelly (ed.) *Locke on Money*, 2 vols. (Oxford, 1991), Table 4 (i, 116).
2. W. Lowndes, *A Report Containing an Essay for the Amendment of the Silver Coins* (London, 1695).
3. See for example J.O. Appleby, 'Locke, Liberalism, and the Natural Law of Money', *Past & Present*, 71 (1976), pp. 43–69; C.E. Challis, 'Lord Hastings to the Great Silver Recoinage, 1464–1699', in C.E. Challis (ed.), *A New History of the Royal Mint* (Cambridge: Cambridge University Press, 1992), pp. 381–2, 397.

4. E.g., T.J. Sargent and F.R. Velde, *The Big Problem of Small Change* (Princeton: Princeton University Press, 2002), ch. 16; A. Finkelstein, *Harmony and the Balance: An Intellectual History of Seventeenth-Century English Economic Thought* (Ann Arbor: University of Michigan Press, 2000), ch. 9; Appleby, 'Locke, Liberalism, and the Natural Law of Money'; Kelly, 'General Introduction', in *Locke on Money*, gives a more sympathetic account while noting the lack of a dynamic economic analysis in Locke.
5. W.A. Shaw, *Select Tracts and Documents Illustrative of English Monetary History 1626–1730* (1896; London: George Hardin, 1935), pp. 103–9.
6. Locke's most famous exponent was Thomas Macaulay in his *History of England*. For a recent defense, see W. Eltis, 'John Locke, the Quantity Theory of Money and the Establishment of a Sound Currency', in M. Blaug et al., *The Quantity Theory of Money: From Locke to Keynes and Friedman* (Cheltenham: Edward Elgar, 1995), pp. 4–26; and R.A. Kleer, '"The ruine of Diana": Lowndes, Locke, and the Bankers', *History of Political Economy*, 36/3 (2004), pp. 533–56.
7. Appleby is aware of the paradox in 'Locke, Liberalism, and the Natural Law of Money'.
8. The edges were inscribed to make any attempt to clip them obvious. Of course coins were still reduced in silver content over time by wear.
9. J.K. Horsefield, *British Monetary Experiments 1650–1710* (Cambridge, MA: Harvard University Press, 1960), pp. 77, 73 (the price in 1690 was 21s. 6d.).
10. See Kelly, 'General Introduction', i, 46; and Horsefield, p. 26.
11. See P. Kelly, '"Monkey" Business: Locke's "College" Correspondence and the Adoption of the Plan for the Great Recoinage of 1696', *Locke Studies*, 9 (2009), pp. 139–65.
12. J. Locke, *Further Considerations Concerning Raising the Value of Money*, in *Locke on Money*, ii, 472.
13. E.g., Sargent and Velde, p. 263; Appleby, 'Locke, Liberalism, and the Natural Law of Money', pp. 61, 68–9.
14. *Further Considerations*, in *Locke on Money*, ii, 403. For further discussion, see D. Carey, 'Locke's Philosophy of Money', forthcoming, and C.G. Caffentzis, *Clipped Coins, Abused Words, and Civil Government: John Locke's Philosophy of Money* (New York: Automedia, 1989).
15. *Further Considerations*, in *Locke on Money*, ii, 410.
16. *Further Considerations*, in *Locke on Money*, ii, 412.
17. *Further Considerations*, in *Locke on Money*, ii, 413.
18. *Further Considerations*, in *Locke on Money*, ii, 415.
19. *Further Considerations*, in *Locke on Money*, ii, 415.
20. *Further Considerations*, in *Locke on Money*, ii, 403.
21. *Further Considerations*, in *Locke on Money*, ii, 416.
22. Of course the crown would have benefited, conversely, from a devaluation when paying out annuities, while government debt would have been repaid at the raised rating of coin. The king was also debtor and would have escaped part of his burden. See Sir A. Feavearyear, *The Pound Sterling: A History of English Money*, 2nd ed., rev. E.V. Morgan (Oxford: Clarendon Press, 1963), p. 147.
23. *Further Considerations*, in *Locke on Money*, ii, 417. Locke does not spell out the source of income (rent) but it is clear by implication.
24. *Further Considerations*, in *Locke on Money*, ii, 417.
25. On Locke's finances, see Kelly, 'General Introduction', in *Locke on Money*, i, 100–5. For Locke's ongoing requests for payment of his annuity in the later 1690s, see letters to the third Earl of Shaftesbury printed in E.S. de Beer (ed.), *The Correspondence of John Locke*, 8 vols. (Oxford, 1976–89), iv, 424; vi, 665, 670; vii, 617–18.
26. *Further Considerations*, in *Locke on Money*, ii, 416–17.
27. This point is not considered by C.R. Fay, 'Locke versus Lowndes', *Cambridge Historical Journal*, 4/2 (1933), who remarks that Locke 'is strangely blind to the hardship which this deflation would impose' (p. 150).
28. It is worth noting that he shared this shortcoming with Lowndes, the author of the alternative plan proposing a devaluation.
29. On this point, see Kelly, 'General Introduction', i, 91. For a discussion of the economic issues, see A. Redish, *Bimetallism: An Economic and Historical Analysis* (Cambridge: Cambridge University Press, 2000).
30. *Further Considerations*, in *Locke on Money*, ii, 423.

31. See Feavearyear, p. 135. For a defense, see Kleer, '"The ruine of Diana"'.
32. *Further Considerations*, in *Locke on Money*, ii, 425.
33. In the *Essay* Locke often uses gold as a ready instance of a substance known only in terms of its nominal rather than its real essence. We cannot say with certainty that two parcels of gold are in fact the same substance; all we can do is closely attend to the qualities that they exhibit (through observation and experiment) and therefore improve the descriptions that we provide of them. By contrast, Locke refers in the context of *Further Considerations* to silver as 'being all of the same nature and goodness, having all the same qualities', which enables him to conclude that equal quantities retain the same value (*Locke on Money*, ii, 411).
34. On Locke's ignoring of the unit of account, see Kelly, 'General Introduction', in *Locke on Money*, ii, 455n.
35. Lowndes, pp. 68, 82–3.
36. M.-H. Li, *The Great Recoinage of 1696 to 1699* (London: Weidenfeld and Nicolson, 1963), argues that Lowndes's proposed devaluation was too great in view of the fact that the market rate of silver at 6s. 5d. was of very recent vintage (two or three months). Li suggests that a devaluation of 5 per cent would have been sufficient to accomplish Lowndes's goals, although he concedes that 'no one would know precisely what the market price of silver or gold would have been if there had been a devaluation' (p. 100).
37. Charles Davenant's position agrees with Locke on this point: 'when we talk of giving 6s 2d per ounce for Silver Bullion the only meaning is because of our Bad money, that we give Something which we call 6s and 2d but which is not in its intrinsick value, near worth that Ounce of silver we purchase'. 'A Memorial concerning the Coyn of England. November, 1695', in A.P. Usher (ed.), *Two Manuscripts by Charles Davenant* (Baltimore: Johns Hopkins Press, 1942), p. 14.
38. There is a lot of play given to this notion in *Further Considerations*, in *Locke on Money*, ii, 425–8.
39. *Further Considerations*, in *Locke on Money*, ii, 425. For a sharp reply to Locke on this issue, see Fay, 'Locke versus Lowndes', pp. 149–50.
40. Interestingly Locke misquotes Lowndes, substituting 'intrinsick value' for Lowndes's 'extrinsick value' in Lowndes's axiom. He quotes Lowndes as saying: 'whensoever the intrinsick value [*recte*: extrinsick] of Silver in the coin, hath been, or shall be less than the price of Silver in Bullion, the Coin hath and will be melted down' (*Further Considerations*, in *Locke on Money*, ii, 428; Lowndes, p. 68). This misquotation enabled Locke to answer that 'when the Coin, is as it should be, according to the standard (let the Standard be what it will) weighty and unclip'd, it is impossible that the value of Coin'd Silver should be less than the value or price of Uncoin'd [i.e., in bullion form]; Because, as I have shewn, the value and quantity of Silver are the same' (*Further Considerations*, in *Locke on Money*, ii, 428–9).
41. Davenant thought it was a mistake to attempt a recoinage during the war, in part because reminted money would still be carried off under adverse trade conditions. See 'A Memorial'.
42. *Further Considerations*, in *Locke on Money*, ii, 430.
43. See Kelly, 'General Introduction', i, 24–5, 62, and ii, 429n; Appleby, 'Locke, Liberalism, and the Natural Law of Money', p. 58.
44. *Further Considerations*, in *Locke on Money*, ii, 429.
45. Davenant agreed about the unfairness to landlords if a devaluation were undertaken, in part because it would transfer wealth to those who had 'born little in the Charge of this present Warr'. He opposed devaluation, but if it were implemented he called for enactment of a law to 'break all past Contracts, that relate to Letting land' so that landlords could recoup their losses. 'A Memorial', p. 24.
46. See the figures in D.W. Jones, *War and Economy in the Age of William III and Marlborough* (Oxford: Basil Blackwell, 1988), pp. 232–3, Table 7.5. Similar figures are given in S. Quinn, 'Gold, Silver, and the Glorious Revolution: Arbitrage between Bills of Exchange and Bullion', *Economic History Review*, 44/3 (1996), p. 481, Table 4. A higher level of depreciation is reported in sources quoted by Feavearyear, p. 120.
47. For an estimate that milled money amounted to 0.5 per cent of the total circulation in March 1696 (including new and old milled money), see Kelly, 'General Introduction', Table 1 (i, 112).

48. Horsefield points out that 'In the almost complete absence from circulation of full-weight coins, no one without special privileges could in practice insist on payment in them' (pp. 59–60). Lowndes had remarked in his *Report*, 'And it is freely submitted to Impartial Judgments, whether the propos'd Advance of Silver in the Coins can infer a Real Loss upon any Persons, other than such as can propose to themselves particularly the Receipt of Moneys in Weighty or Unclipt Pieces only, and the Conversion thereof to an Advantage, which Law or Reason would not allow them' (pp. 81–2).
49. *Further Considerations*, in *Locke on Money*, ii, 469.
50. Locke added goldsmiths and bankers to the list of those taking light coin which increased its wider acceptability. *Further Considerations*, in *Locke on Money*, ii, 470. One of Locke's contemporary critics, Henry Layton, confirmed that 'Men for this four or five years last past, have borrow'd many Thousand Pounds in Clipt Money, but he [Locke] notes no unreasonableness or injustice in compelling them to pay such Debts again in heavy Money, perhaps of twice the weight'. *Observations concerning Money and Coin* (London, 1697), p. 13. Quoted in Appleby, 'Locke, Liberalism, and the Natural Law of Money', p. 58.
51. *Further Considerations*, in *Locke on Money*, ii, 430.
52. N. Barbon, *A Discourse Concerning Coining the New Money lighter. In Answer to Mr. Lock's Considerations about raising the Value of Money* (London, 1696), p. 30.
53. As Kelly points out, *Further Considerations*, in *Locke on Money*, ii, 444n.
54. J. Locke, *Some Considerations of the Consequences of the Lowering of Interest, and Raising the Value of Money*, in *Locke on Money*, i, 266.
55. Davenant's analysis confirmed the negative impact on rents of falling prices in his 'Memoriall concerning Creditt' (1696), pp. 70–72.
56. *Further Considerations*, in *Locke on Money*, ii, 448.
57. Lowndes, p. 83.
58. *Further Considerations*, in *Locke on Money*, ii, 449–50.
59. In fact Locke's friend Benjamin Furly, a Quaker merchant based in Rotterdam, informed him in 1691 that France's economic decisions had driven up bullion prices with the effect of withdrawing good coin from Holland as much as from England. Furly concluded that the Dutch needed to raise the value of silver and gold to keep it in the country, a policy Locke of course resisted in England's case. See *Correspondence*, iv, 319–20.
60. *Further Considerations*, in *Locke on Money*, ii, 453. For the same argument, see *Some Considerations*, in *Locke on Money*, i, 311.
61. Lowndes, pp. 83–4.
62. It should be pointed out that Lowndes's scheme was also deflationary, though less drastically, reducing the total circulation by c. 16 per cent compared to c. 30 per cent under Locke's plan. For these calculations, see Horsefield, pp. 30–31.
63. See also *Further Considerations*, in *Locke on Money*, i, 456–7.
64. *Further Considerations*, in *Locke on Money*, ii, 450.
65. *Further Considerations*, in *Locke on Money*, ii, 463.
66. Kelly, 'General Introduction', in *Locke on Money*, i, 29. See Feavearyear: 'The sanctity which Locke attached to the Mint weights was something new' (p. 148).
67. In the prefatory letter to Lord Somers in *Further Considerations*, Locke expressed the hope that 'the Cure of this Evil be not ordered so as to lay a great Part of the burden unequally on those, who have had no particular Hand in it' (*Further Considerations*, in *Locke on Money*, ii, 403).
68. For the most careful attempt to assess the relative economic impact of the different contemporary proposals, see Horsefield, ch. 3.
69. This essay was incorporated into her influential book *Economic Thought and Ideology in Seventeenth-Century England* (Princeton: Princeton University Press, 1978), ch. 8.
70. Appleby, 'Locke, Liberalism, and the Natural Law of Money', pp. 45, 68, 47, 49, 60.
71. Appleby, 'Locke, Liberalism, and the Natural Law of Money', p. 67.
72. Appleby, 'Locke, Liberalism, and the Natural Law of Money', p. 66; see also p. 49.
73. See especially the passage quoted above from *Further Considerations*: 'our clip'd Money retains amongst the People (who know not how to count but by Current Money) a part of its legal value' (*Locke on Money*, ii, 469). In *Some Considerations*, he remarked that '*Clip'd* and *unclip'd Money* will always buy an equal quantity of any thing else, as long as they will without scruple change one for another' (*Locke on Money*, i, 319). See also

'Answer to My Lord Keepers Queries' (in *Locke on Money*, ii, 387).

74. See Carey, 'Locke's Philosophy of Money'.
75. Locke, *Some Considerations*, in *Locke on Money*, i, 322.
76. Kelly, 'General Introduction', i, 20.
77. Lowndes was also critical of those whose concerns about coin focused only on its value in foreign exchange and remittances, ignoring its principal role in facilitating 'Inland Commerce'. Lowndes, p. 74.
78. *Some Considerations*, in *Locke on Money*, i, 264.
79. For a helpful discussion, see Kelly, 'General Introduction', in *Locke on Money*, i, 78–9, 84–6. The applicability of the price-specie-flow mechanism to the economy in Locke's time is not certain.
80. Davenant, 'A Memorial', p. 17. If England had more trading muscle, he pointed out, things might be different.
81. *For Encouraging the Coining...* makes this point as well. See *Locke on Money*, ii, 613–16.
82. Davenant argued a different line. Recent price rises resulted from a 'complication of Causes' but mainly the adverse trade balance, affecting foreign exchange. War also increased the cost of foreign materials which was then felt throughout the economy; the poor condition of the coin was not the main culprit, though its 'badnesse... does all the while operate a little, Tho by wayes hard to be judged of, and by degrees very uncertaine'. 'A Memorial', p. 25.
83. Appleby, 'Locke, Liberalism, and the Natural Law of Money', 60. See also Horsefield, p. 78.
84. For objections raised against having coin circulate by weight, see Li, p. 69. Apart from the deflationary effect of reducing the money supply severely, the scheme did not incentivize the exchange of lightweight coin for newly minted money and would have removed the ability to raise funds for government loans by offering to accept clipped coins at face value. Nor had Locke offered a practical plan for how to determine the weight of coin in everyday transactions.
85. Appleby, 'Locke, Liberalism, and the Natural Law of Money', p. 61. On Locke's plan and his anticipation of problems caused by the scheme that was adopted, see *Further Considerations*, in *Locke on Money*, ii, 418–19. See also Kelly, 'General Introduction', i, 26–7.
86. See *Further Considerations*, in *Locke on Money*, ii, 369, 377, 419; and Kelly, 'General Introduction', i, 33, 90, and Table 1 (i, 112–13).
87. By contrast, Davenant had concluded that there was 'little heavy money Left among us' in hoard, based on the adverse rate of exchange and the savings to be made by paying in specie rather than by drawing bills of exchange. 'A Memorial', p. 11.
88. Lowndes, pp. 87–8.
89. Appleby, 'Locke, Liberalism, and the Natural Law of Money', p. 65.
90. See Kelly, 'General Introduction', i, 27. The reasons for this are complex and may have had much to do with his wish to retain his prerogative with respect to coinage. The king's position as a creditor (to whom taxes were owed) was offset by his need to borrow funds to support the war effort. It was only after the restrictions on government credit became apparent in the summer of 1696, when the Recoinage was underway, that he came to regard the revaluation as a mistake (Kelly, 'General Introduction', i, 37, 64–5).
91. Appleby, 'Locke, Liberalism, and the Natural Law of Money', p. 61.
92. *Further Considerations*, in *Locke on Money*, ii, 463.
93. *Some Considerations*, in *Locke on Money*, i, 311. For some discussion of James's experiment, which foundered when his French allies paid their soldiers in silver, see R. Heslip, 'Brass Money', in W.A. Maguire (ed.), *Kings in Conflict: The Revolutionary War in Ireland and its Aftermath 1689–1750* (Belfast: The Blackstaff Press, 1990), pp. 122–35.
94. *Some Considerations*, in *Locke on Money*, i, 234.
95. *Some Considerations*, in *Locke on Money*, i, 234, 235.
96. *Some Considerations*, in *Locke on Money*, i, 235.
97. Lowndes, p. 84.
98. Davenant's contribution was made at the solicitation of the Lords Justices (the Council of Regency that acted in the king's absence in Flanders).

99. Davenant, 'A Memorial Concerning the Coyn of England', pp. 39–40. Once the recoinage was underway in 1696, he questioned this approach, suggesting that a 'raising' of the crown and guinea would give a 'ffictitious Value' that would 'disperse it more among the people' and encourage dishoarding ('A memoriall concerning Creditt', pp. 102–3).
100. Davenant, 'A Memorial Concerning the Coyn of England', pp. 18, 21.
101. Davenant, 'A Memorial Concerning the Coyn of England', p. 22.
102. Davenant, 'A Memorial Concerning the Coyn of England', p. 25.
103. Davenant, 'A Memorial Concerning the Coyn of England', p. 27.
104. Davenant, 'A Memorial Concerning the Coyn of England', pp. 28–9.
105. Davenant, 'A Memorial Concerning the Coyn of England', p. 45.
106. Davenant, 'A memoriall concerning Creditt', p. 102.
107. E.g., Davenant, 'A Memorial Concerning the Coyn of England', p. 45.
108. Davenant, 'A memoriall concerning Creditt', p. 75.
109. Davenant, 'A memoriall concerning Creditt', p. 76.
110. See Locke's assessment of the so-called 'law of opinion' in the *Essay concerning Human Understanding*, corr. ed., ed. P.H. Nidditch (Oxford: Clarendon Press, 1979), II.xxviii.10.
111. For Locke's views on the imaginary value assigned to guineas at 30s., see *Locke on Money*, ii, 363–4.
112. For quotations from contemporary sources, see Appleby, 'Locke, Liberalism, and the Natural Law of Money', pp. 51, 52, 55.
113. *Some Considerations*, in *Locke on Money*, i, 233.
114. Steve Pincus, *1688: The First Modern Revolution* (New Haven: Yale University Press, 2009), p. 371. See also p. 392.
115. Bodleian Library MS Locke b. 3. Richard Kleer's essay, '"Fictitious Cash": English Public Finance and Paper Money, 1689–97', in C.I. McGrath and C. Fauske (eds), *Money, Power, and Print: Interdisciplinary Studies on the Financial Revolution in the British Isles* (Newark: University of Delaware Press, 2008), pp. 70–103, also indicates a considerable division within proponents of the bank about its merits.
116. Pincus, p. 390, quoting Barbon, *A Discourse of Trade* (London, 1690), pp. 29–31.
117. Barbon, *A Discourse Concerning Coining the New Money lighter*. For Barbon, 'Money is the Instrument and Measure of Commerce, and not Silver.' Intrinsic value was not a meaningful notion; rather, money serves as 'the instrument of Commerce from the Authority of that Government where it is Coined;... by the Stamp and Size of each piece the value is known' (sig. A7v).
118. Barbon, *A Discourse Concerning Coining the New Money lighter*, pp. 47–8.
119. A. McFarland Davis (ed.), *Colonial Currency Reprints 1682–1751*, 4 vols. (Boston: Prince Society, 1910–11), iii, 22. For the context of this discussion, see J.L. Brooke, *The Heart of the Commonwealth: Society and Political Culture in Worcester County, Massachusetts, 1713–1861* (Cambridge: Cambridge University Press, 1989), pp. 61–5.
120. H. Vance, *An Inquiry into the Nature and Uses of Money* (Boston, 1740), in *Colonial Currency Reprints*, iii, 402, 390. For parallel discussions of the merits of Locke's position in pamphlet exchanges in 1720s and 30s Ireland, see P. Kelly, 'The Politics of Political Economy in Mid-Eighteenth-Century Ireland', in S.J. Connolly (ed.), *Political Ideas in Eighteenth-Century Ireland* (Dublin: Four Courts Press, 2000), pp. 105–29; and E. Magennis, 'Whither the Irish Financial Revolution?: Money, Banks and Politics in Ireland in the 1730s', in McGrath and Fauske (eds), *Money, Power, and Print*, pp. 189–207.
121. T.B. Macaulay, *The History of England from the Accession of James II* [1848], 2 vols. (London: Longmans, Green, 1903), ii, 548.

CHAPTER THREE

Commerce and the Law of Nations in Hume's Theory of Money

CHRISTOPHER J. FINLAY

> [T]hat Coyne, which is not considerable for the Matter, but for the Stamp of the place, being unable to endure change of ayr, hath its effect at home only; where also it is subject to the change of Laws, and thereby to have the value diminished, to the prejudice many times of those that have it.
>
> (Hobbes, *Leviathan,* II.XXIV)

It has become almost a truism in Scottish historiography that the Act of Union in 1707 marked the sacrifice of 'sovereignty for empire', a formula virtually synonymous with the exchange of 'sovereignty for commercial success'. Leaving aside the question of personal venality, support by members of the Scottish parliament and the social elites, whose opinions counted in their deliberations in the early years of the eighteenth century, was motivated in large part by the need for access to colonial markets and international trade. Scotland's economic development lagged far behind that of England, and the vast potential for trading opportunities within British imperial jurisdiction offered, it seemed, a real chance at affluence in the wake Scotland's own disappointing imperial adventure, the Darien scheme.[1] But considered in the terms of contemporary political discourse, commercial success was not merely a matter of avarice for Scotland. Andrew Fletcher of Saltoun, the leading opponent of the kind of incorporating union realised in 1707, was impressive not merely for the strength of his polemics against an ignoble sacrifice of political independence, but for the subtlety with which he perceived the real weakness of any independence that was not also settled on a strong economic and fiscal base. Fletcher's neo-Machiavellianism recognized that independence is a fleeting good even for the strong in a world where international rivals compound the difficulties of internal corruption to threaten continually the existence of the independent commonwealth.[2] In this view, to become dependent on another power through conquest and incorporation meant the sudden death of the polity. But for Scotland to be left stranded without means of defence, or better still expansion, meant that the commonwealth would remain economically dependent even while politically independent, and its political strength would thus be continually undermined. Fletcher's ultimately unresolved dilemma is thus usually regarded as having helped define the problems addressed in the 'commercial humanism' of David Hume and Adam Smith.[3] In general terms, the questions for the Enlightenment Scots concerned how liberty in a meaningful sense could be realized alongside the ties of political dependence with which they were bound to the British composite monarchy.[4] Exploration of the issue prompted careful reconsideration of the relationship between sociability, liberty, commerce and sovereign independence.

In this context, Hume followed Thomas Hobbes in criticizing the idealization of what Quentin Skinner calls 'neo-Roman' ideas of liberty in early modern republican thought.[5] In place of the close association between individual liberty and the sovereign independence of the state, his account of liberty shifts attention away from political action as such and into the forms of sociability and commerce available in (and between) modern mixed polities.[6] In this essay, I examine these themes through the lens of David Hume's theory of money. Hume's theory of money forms a useful starting point because, as I argue, his ambivalence about innovations such as paper currency can be traced back to tensions within his more general social and political theory, particularly tensions between the forms of sociability made possible domestically within societies by government and those that were possible between individuals in different sovereign states. Looking at Hume's theory of money in this way permits an exploration of the nexus between a number of different elements in his thought – in particular, his account of the conventional origins of society and government; the theory of the 'law of nations'; and Hume's analysis of trade in contemporary Europe, in terms of economic theory and political history. In looking at the connections between these fields in Hume's thought, I hope to shed some light reflexively both on his conception of money and on his understanding of nationality and sovereignty in the context of eighteenth-century Europe. Examining some of the difficulties of his understanding of money – in particular his seemingly jarring views on international and national currencies – illuminates the importance of Hume's thinking about the theory of international justice for his understanding of international commerce and the society of nations. Money, as Hume wrote, is the 'oil' that lubricates the wheels of both domestic and international commerce.[7] The theory of money is therefore a key plank in Hume's contribution to the ideology of commercial modernity and political liberty in modern Europe, a central intellectual legacy of the Scottish Enlightenment. By focusing on some of the conceptual and practical difficulties in Hume's theory of money, it is possible to elucidate more clearly his views on the interconnections between the emergence of particular nations, the relations between nations, and the development of commerce.

I

The issue to be addressed at the centre of Hume's ideas about money is his ambivalence about paper currency and the importance he gives to specie. Hume made his most important pronouncements on money, about its definition, its uses and the forms it could take in *A Treatise of Human Nature* (1739 and 1740) and the *Political Discourses* (1752). Broadly speaking, the different discussions about money in the *Treatise* are all generally hospitable to the idea of paper currencies whereas those of the *Political Discourses* are considerably more ambivalent. The difference may be explained in part by the differing perspective between the two works: in the early work, Hume focused on money as a phenomenon and instrument first in the experience of the individual and secondly in the internal constitution of particular societies. In the *Political Discourses,* discussed below in section II, Hume's perspective widened to comprehend the use of monetary instruments between as well as within different societies. For the moment, Hume's discussions of money in the *Treatise* may usefully be divided into his treatment in the first published instalment of that work, in Books I and II 'Of the Understanding' and 'Of the Passions' respectively, and in Book III, 'Of Morals'. Hume analysed experience in the first two books of the *Treatise* in terms of the cognitive faculties of the individual whereas in the third book, particularly in part 2, his focus shifts to the foundations of social institutions, the rules of justice and basis of government, but also, in passing, the origins of money and language.

Throughout the *Treatise,* Hume's references to money are either incidental to the main subjects he is addressing or used to elucidate more general conceptual problems. The first case of this kind to be considered occurs in his discussion of 'Riches and Power' in Book II. Here Hume highlights possible misunderstandings about the nature and value of money by using the imaginary example of a miser hoarding his cash as an illustration. The miser, Hume states, believes himself to be all the richer because he never spends his money; the more money that accumulates as a result of his parsimony, the more rich he believes himself to be.[8] Hume argues, however, that the miser is in fact entirely wrong about his riches, and his self-delusion occurs as the result of a failure to appreciate the real nature of money. For, as Hume points out, money as such is not valuable in and of itself; neither should it be considered as possessing some inner potential that makes it valuable. The actual value of money arises from the extent to which the individuals who make use of it believe that it will be effective in facilitating exchange, and thus in acquiring certain goods. This belief refers to the supposed *power* of money; and, as Hume explained in the first two books of the *Treatise*, the word *power* basically designates a perceived probability that a given object, action or event will give rise to another successive event by way of causation. Thus, the value of money lies in the perceived probability that it will be used and accepted for the purposes of exchange and will be effective in causing the relevant events. The miser is, of all people, the least likely to make use of the money he has heaped up. Since he will never actually spend the sum, it does not actually constitute riches at all.[9]

In the same section of the *Treatise*, Hume observes that 'paper will, on many occasions, be consider'd as riches, and that because it may convey the power of acquiring money: And money', he adds, 'is not riches, as it is a metal endow'd with certain qualities of solidity, weight and fusibility; but only as it has a relation to the pleasures and conveniences of life'.[10] Thus, although he avoids referring to paper notes as 'money' per se, Hume recognizes that they can serve the purposes of money, provided that they are convertible into specie;[11] secondly, specie, i.e. what Hume refers to using the word 'money', is not 'riches' by virtue of its substance, but by virtue of what Hume calls its 'relation to the pleasures and conveniences of life'. There seems to be a *prima facie* case, therefore, for regarding paper currency as a viable substitute for hard cash and possibly even as viable a form of money itself based on this argument.

Hume does not deal with money at this point as a matter of economic theory, but as a way of explaining and clarifying the epistemological and psychological principles underlying one aspect of human experience (the causal relationship between possession of riches and feelings of pride). But he makes a number of important comments relevant to monetary theory nevertheless: from the miser we learn that the value of coins as bullion is insufficient to define them as 'money' in cases where they are inactive; they only really become money to the extent that beliefs can be invested in them, beliefs reflecting the probability that they will prove effective for certain purposes. Later in the *Treatise* (in Book III, part 2) Hume will explain the conditions required before a particular society can establish the use of money as a social practice. But from the reflections in Book II on using paper in exchange, it is clear that the investment of belief can be made in relation to non-bullion instruments provided they are used and likely to be effective in the same way as money. To extrapolate slightly, therefore, and describe Hume's comments in terms of monetary theory, it can be said that he regarded money in this context as principally significant as an instrument of exchange, rather than as a commodity in and of itself. He presented an explanation of the nature and purposes of money implying that it was defined fundamentally by its instrumental, token value in exchange (its 'power') and, as such, the notion of intrinsic or commodity value in money stays at least in the background if it does not remain wholly irrelevant.

In Book III of the *Treatise,* there are two issues of relevance to Hume's conception of money. To begin with, the treatment of promises in III.2.v has been interpreted persuasively by Carl Wennerlind as 'prefigur[ing] a monetary theory'. On this basis, he argues that Hume was, on the whole, 'a fiduciary theorist and practical metallist, rather than the theoretical metallist he is often thought to be'.[12] Hume presents promise-keeping as the third 'fundamental law of nature', i.e., as one of the originally artificial but nonetheless necessary rules by which societies are initially formed, the other two being 'stability of possession' (property) and the 'transference of property by consent'. In Wennerlind's view, the third rule – like the first two – provides a basis not just for sociability in general but for economic cooperation and exchange in particular. In his interpretation, the establishment of a convention of promise-making and promise-keeping constitutes a 'commitment mechanism in contractual relationships among strangers' (i.e., people who are not friends or members of the same family) and the form this typically will take is to use money. Only money can overcome the problems that barter poses as a basis for exchange. Since barter is plagued by various shortcomings that severely limit the extent of trade between strangers, a conventional 'mechanism' is needed. This will have an internal dimension in the commitment of an individual to their promise and also an external one in the form of a conventional symbol: the token used solves 'the credibility problem by functioning as a symbol and guarantor of the promise of resolution'.[13] To begin with, when the convention has just been established, Wennerlind writes, 'the symbol would only be valid between specific individuals as a promissory note. However, as more people realized the societal benefits of such an artifice, the symbol would become anonymous and function as money – a universal equivalent for all tradable property.' Since Hume is concerned primarily with the 'authenticity and solemnity of the promise' as what is essential to its effectiveness, the 'material or substance of money becomes irrelevant, which means that in some important sense Hume's monetary theory is based on a fiduciary understanding of money'.[14]

In the section dealing with the 'Obligation of Promises' (III.2.v), Hume states that the use of money was first established through an artificial convention in a similar way to the establishment of justice itself and the formation of languages. For this reason, it is necessary to place the discussion of money and promises analysed by Wennerlind in the wider context of Hume's account 'Of the Origin of Justice and Property' (III.2.ii). The key issue connecting conventions generally with the emergence of money in particular is raised in a passage where Hume argues that the rule concerning the stability of possession is derived from 'human conventions, [and] that it arises gradually, and acquires force by a slow progression, and by our repeated experience of the inconveniences of transgressing it'. This experience, he continues, 'assures us still more, that the sense of interest has become common to all our fellows, and gives us a confidence of the future regularity of their conduct'. It is 'only on the expectation of this, that our moderation and abstinence are founded. In like manner,' Hume writes, 'are languages gradually establish'd by human conventions without any promise. In like manner do gold and silver become the common measures of exchange, and are esteem'd sufficient payment for what is of a hundred times their value.'[15]

The use of money is presented by Hume as having emerged in the same way as the artificial principles of justice, *viz.* through the establishment of the conventions by which a society is constituted among a particular extended group of individuals. The meaning of money and thus the possibility of using it in transactions is artificially set within a society, having no original natural basis outside that society. It is worth noting too that while Hume imagines the first emergence of money as involving gold and silver specie, the token value of money is underlined by the fact that a piece of metal will exchange for 'what is of a hundred times [its] value'.[16] The important conclusion to be drawn from this passage is that the money used in a society is created by a convention particular to that society; thus its usefulness beyond the society in which it originated remains to be discussed and is in fact ignored in the *Treatise*.

To summarize what may be said about the concept of money and the theory of its origins articulated in the *Treatise*, we may make the following three observations: first of all, money is established as an instrument for the measure of value and for carrying out exchange by virtue of 'artificial' conventions similar to those which give rise to the rules concerning property, trade, and contracts, and participation in those same conventions. For this reason, money may be said to emerge at first as a convention within a given society and is, to that extent, one of the constitutive events in the history of a society's emergence. Secondly, the functions of money are performed by virtue of its conventional symbolism both of value and of the anticipated fulfilment of contracts. In the latter sense, as Wennerlind argues, Hume understands money theoretically as a fiduciary currency. Thirdly, because money's function is symbolic – representing value rather than embodying it intrinsically – its material substance may be *theoretically* unimportant.

However, as an examination of Hume's concerns in the essays dealing with money in the *Political Discourses* shows, there were wider theoretical as well as practical issues that made paper money highly problematic in contemporary Europe, and part of Hume's problem had to do with the asymmetry between domestic and international society seen in the political thought of Hobbes and echoed (as part III of this essay shows) in Hume's treatment of the law of nations in the *Treatise*.[17] This theoretical issue was closely tied to Hume's perception of the immediate and historical realities of European international relations.

II

At various points in the *Political Discourses* (particularly in essays 'Of Money', 'Of Interest', 'Of the Balance of Trade', and 'Of Public Credit'), Hume entertains the idea of paper credit taking on the role of money in civil societies. But for the most part he does so only hypothetically in order to warn against the dangers of allowing paper credit to play any significant role in an economy open to foreign trade. It is necessary to say 'open' economy because, in fact, Hume's conception of money would allow him to acknowledge paper money as a more efficient form of currency were a particular political society somehow insulated from trade with other nations. In his essay 'Of Money', Hume cites the views of some that where paper credit has already been allowed to expand through the hands of private bankers, it would serve the interests of the public if the state were to take over the production of paper currency, and thus 'enjoy the benefit of that paper-credit, which always will have place in every opulent kingdom'.[18] Furthermore, 'There are,' he writes, '... many people in every rich state, who, having large sums of money, would prefer paper, with good security; as being of more easy transport and more safe custody [than specie].'[19] In the context of a critical discussion, Hume admits further benefits arising from the development of paper currencies in 'Of the Balance of Trade'.[20]

Whatever conveniences this may afford to individuals using the currency, however, the public would derive no benefit and the society as a whole would lose a great deal by the over-expansion of paper credit. As Hume acknowledges in 'Of the Balance of Trade', adding paper money to the circulating specie in a society may provide the kind of short-term stimulus to industry that he observed with specie,[21] but the long-term effects were likely to be damaging for two principal reasons: paper credit, as he declares in 'Of Money', is, first of all, 'a counterfeit money, which foreigners will not accept of in any payment, and [secondly] which any great disorder in the state will reduce to nothing'.[22]

It is to the former reason – that 'foreigners will not accept of [it] in any payment' – that I want to give particular attention. The problem which arises for the society using large quantities of paper currency is twofold: first, it artificially inflates the cost of labour within the state and, hence, the price of exports, needlessly reducing their competitiveness; secondly, while currency in precious metals offers advantages to governments by giving them 'weight... in all foreign wars and negociations', paper money does not do so. Hume attributes efforts to increase money in a society artificially by means of paper currency to the fallacy of believing that 'because an individual would be much richer, were his stock of money doubled, . . . the same good effect would follow, were the money of every one increased . . . '[23]

Thus, while for Hume the idea of a paper currency made theoretical sense in the more purely philosophical terms of the *Treatise of Human Nature* (we might say in epistemological, metaphysical, and psychological terms), it made little practical sense in the international scene of European commerce. From the perspective of the *Treatise,* paper could be used as money since it needed only to be accepted as a conventional and symbolic measure of value and a fiduciary instrument of exchange, and principles explaining the natural history of civil societies showed how such conventions had been the defining and constitutive events in the emergence of particular societies. In the *Political Discourses*, Hume principally addresses the practical issues surrounding the management of money from the point of view of commercial societies in general as well as Britain in particular. An important part of his concern relates to the management of money as a currency operating between as well as within political societies. An area of tension in Hume's understanding of the nature, feasibility and value of paper money arises between the two perspectives.

It is my aim in the remaining sections of this essay to try and explain the tension between Hume's two perspectives by looking at them in the context of his views on international relations both in general, and in the contemporary European context. I turn in section III, therefore, to his account of the law of nations. Hume followed a broadly Hobbesian view of international relations in postulating only a thin layer of ethical and legal obligation beyond borders. For this reason, I argue, Hume was bound to regard conventional values such as money as having a much more limited influence over relations between people across the borders of different states than they had over transactions conducted within the same society.

III

To understand the relationship between Hume's ideas about money and commerce on the one hand and the laws of nations on the other, it is necessary to return briefly to his account of the 'artificial virtues' in III.2 of *A Treatise of Human Nature* (sections ii-vi). 'Artificial virtues' refer to the rules of justice which Hume sometimes paradoxically called the 'laws of nature'. These are the conventional rules which he regarded as the minimum regulatory prerequisites of human society. They must be discussed first because Hume maintains that the same rules hold between sovereign nations in global society as between individuals in particular societies, and for similar reasons.

Individuals need the collaborative efforts of others in order to extract from nature the food, clothing and shelter necessary for survival. Since they could barely survive a solitary existence, therefore, the conventions allowing them to live together in society must have occurred at the earliest point in the history of humanity; the survival of the species is barely conceivable without them. The three rules necessary for establishing a society are, respectively, the stability of possession (property), the transference of property by consent, and the making and keeping of promises. For individuals to be able to achieve a 'partition of employments'[24] and a basis for exchange sufficient to overcome the deficiencies of the species in the face of nature, they needed to be able to trust one another not to violate their possessions. While possession might be conceivable without the first convention, 'property' was defined by its stability and the respect accorded it by other persons. Hume regarded this rule as the most fundamental since it removed the primary obstacle to human cooperation, the fear felt by individuals whose possessions could be taken by force at any time. The second rule established a principle by which added convenience in possession might be achieved through exchange: no one ought to be forced to part with his property, but if he consented, then beneficial commerce might begin. Finally, to follow Wennerlind's interpretation once again, more abstract and complicated forms of exchange could be achieved if parties to a contract were in a position to refer to future goods (including labour) and to place trust in an engagement to deliver abstract quantities of goods, or goods not immediately present. If any of these three rules were absent, Hume believed, the basis for beneficial cooperation and exchange would collapse and individuals would effectively confront non-human nature with nothing but the inadequacies of the human body. All the rules were therefore necessary to human survival.

Once established, however, the three basic conventions could sustain social living up to a point but could not do so indefinitely. With the increase in wealth that cooperation brought, the peace of society would eventually come under threat from forces generated by its success (III.2.vii–x). The three fundamental rules allowed individuals to cooperate in industrious endeavours and commerce; where they were successful, or where one society acquired wealth by victory over another, the natural 'avidity' for goods was likely to provoke breaches of the rules. Human beings are selfish first and generous second, and then only to those close to them by way of friendship or blood relations. They are also imaginative creatures, prone to become more animated by proximate advantages than by the greater long-term or abstract benefits at whose expense they may be bought. For these reasons, the rules of justice would probably collapse were it not for the emergence of permanent government to enforce the rules, punish violations, and adjudicate in cases of dispute.[25]

Hume argued that human beings established the rules of justice through convention-forming behaviour and without superior direction from government or leadership. But the more successful the rules and the society built upon them, the greater the threat of self-destruction, as increased productivity and commerce created ever-growing incentives for rules violations. Sovereign government was therefore necessary for any society exceeding even a fairly low level of economic development.

Following in the footsteps of seventeenth-century natural rights theorists, Hume analyses international relations in analogous terms to his account of the relations between individuals. But whereas both Hobbes and Locke assumed that states remain in a state of nature with respect to each other much like that which prevailed between individuals prior to the establishment of government, Hume argues that nations are governed by the same rules as apply to individuals within societies. In section xi of III.2, Hume briefly outlines 'the Laws of Nations', following a line of argument partly analogous to that concerning the origins of justice and society. Out of the invention of justice and property and the establishment of justice is created 'a body politic', an entity which, as Hume notes, presumably in reference to Hobbes, some writers consider 'as one person': 'this assertion is so far just', he writes, 'that different nations, as well as private persons, require mutual assistance; at the same time that their selfishness and ambition are perpetual sources of war and discord'.[26] States are driven by interests similar to those motivating human beings in the formation of society which give rise *ipso facto* to a series of rights and duties whose content is the same as the laws of nature.

Hume states that 'the three fundamental rules of justice, the stability of possession, its transference by consent, and the performance of promises, are duties of princes, as well as of subjects'. The same interest, he writes,

> produces the same effect in both cases. Where possession has no stability, there must be perpetual war. Where property is not transferr'd by consent, there can be no commerce. Where promises are not observ'd, there can be no leagues nor alliances. The advantages, therefore, of peace, commerce, and mutual succour, make us extend to different kingdoms the same notions of justice, which take place among individuals.[27]

In addition to the laws of justice per se there are specific *laws of nations* applying only to international relations and not to the relations between persons. These include 'the sacredness of the persons of ambassadors, the declaration of war, the abstaining from poison'd arms, with other duties of that kind, which are evidently calculated for the commerce, that is peculiar to different societies'.[28] Although they are 'super-added to the laws of nature', however, they do not 'entirely abolish the latter'.[29]

But Hume's account reflects a similar background of empirical reality as the one which characterized the work of Grotius and Hobbes in international relations: no universal government existed to prevent violations of the laws of justice between nations parallel to the power over individuals exercised by particular states. In the case of civil society, permanent government was needed as soon as productivity and commercial development reached anything above a very basic level of success, otherwise it would collapse into a state of war. Hume clearly took it for granted at this stage that commerce between nations was a significant fact of contemporary international relations and, of course, his later writings were notable for their analysis of the dynamics of international trade as a mechanism for increasing affluence and power in contemporary European states. Surely such increased affluence would give rise among nations to the same danger as it did among individuals: it would increase the incentive to attempt unilateral hostilities in order to rob others of their wealth. The more successful the modern European economies were, in fact, the more likely it would seem that war would break out among them. It must be asked to what extent Hume is able to support the theory that a meaningful society of nations can exist internationally.[30]

Hume's solution to this problem so far as the abstract theory was concerned was to argue that the laws of nature had the same content internationally as they did when operating within societies, but that they were less strongly obligatory on nations than on individuals due to the lower levels of mutual reliance internationally. For this reason, the natural and consequently the moral obligations of justice are weaker between states than between individuals.[31] It is this aspect of international relations that gave spurious credence, Hume suggests, to the Machiavellian maxim that 'there is a system of morals calculated for princes, much more free than that which ought to govern private persons'.[32] Hume disputes the idea that the content of princely morals is any different from what would apply to subjects; if princes neglected morality altogether there would be 'perpetual war',[33] but he accepts that the same laws apply with less force:

> The same *natural* obligation of interest takes place among independent kingdoms [as within them], and gives rise to the same *morality*; so that no one of ever so corrupt morals will approve of a prince, who voluntarily, and of his own accord, breaks his word, or violates any treaty. But here we may observe, that tho' the intercourse of different states be advantageous, and even sometimes necessary, yet it is not so necessary nor advantageous as that among individuals, without which 'tis utterly impossible for human nature ever to subsist. Since, therefore, the *natural* obligation to justice, among different states, is not so strong as among individuals, the *moral* obligation, which arises from it, must partake of its weakness; and we must necessarily give a greater indulgence to a prince or minister, who deceives another; than to a private gentleman, who breaks his word of honour.[34]

Thus, the difference between the two levels at which the laws operate is not one of principle but of degree. The proportion, Hume states, is not one that can be fixed by philosophy but must be learnt from observation and experience in the 'practice of the world'.[35]

V

In 'Of the Rise and Progress of the Arts and Sciences,' published not long after the *Treatise* in the second volume of the *Essays, Moral and Political* (1742), Hume analyses the probable historical causes of growing commercial, intellectual, and artistic refinement in Europe.

In doing so, he adds an important further dimension to the more abstract theory of the *Treatise*.

On the account of Hume's theory offered so far, it might seem as if the needs of commerce could have militated in favour of political integration between the European nations or even incorporation within a single political unit. But for Hume, the independence of nations in Europe was not just a brute fact of early modern politics, but also a key element in explaining the success of commerce and the cultural and intellectual improvements of the Enlightenment era. The separation of peoples into distinct territories and under their own governments and laws was essential to European progress in part, Hume thought, because of the connection between the external independence of states and the maintenance of free government within states, a vital precondition for commerce.

Hume argues that there are two general conditions most conducive to the emergence of an era of significant cultural achievement of the kind seen in eighteenth-century Europe. The first, a necessary prerequisite, is 'the blessing of a free government'. Without a government limited by laws the arts and sciences will have no chance of emerging to any significant degree within particular states.[36] The second condition is that a cluster of neighbouring, independent states exists, interacting through commerce in things and ideas, and avoiding all-out war with each other.[37] This was the case in ancient Greece, and modern Europe is presented as a larger version of the ancient city-states of the Greek archipelago:

> Greece was a cluster of little principalities, which soon became republics; and being united both by their near neighbourhood, and by the ties of the same language and interest, they entered into the closest intercourse of commerce and learning. There concurred a happy climate, a soil not unfertile, and a most harmonious and comprehensive language; so that every circumstance among that people seemed to favour the rise of the arts and sciences. Each city produced its several artists and philosophers, who refused to yield the preference to those of the neighbouring republics: Their contention and debates sharpened the wits of men: A variety of objects was presented to the judgment, while each challenged the preference to the rest: and the sciences, not being dwarfed by the restraint of authority, were enabled to make such considerable shoots, as are, even at this time, the objects of our admiration.[38]

In the eighteenth century, after the Catholic monopoly of power and culture in the medieval era, 'affairs are now returned nearly to the same situation as before, and Europe is at present a copy at large, of what Greece was formerly a pattern in miniature'.[39] Geography assists politics in creating a new cluster of independent, neighbouring states: 'If we consider the face of the globe,' Hume writes, 'Europe, of all the four parts of the world, is the most broken by seas, rivers, and mountains; and Greece of all countries of Europe. Hence these regions were naturally divided into several distinct governments.' For this reason, 'the sciences arose in Greece; and Europe has been hitherto the most constant habitation of them'.[40]

The reason for the success of 'free governments' in first cultivating the arts and sciences is that they create a predictable environment for their citizens, one in which individuals can regulate their lives according to general rules. Whereas under despotism, the randomness of tyrannical whim is the force determining the vagaries of life in society, under government by law, property and punishment are regulated in a consistent manner. Under free governments eloquence more naturally springs up, 'emulation' is more 'animated and enlivened' in every accomplishment, and 'genius and capacity have a fuller scope and career'.[41]

Neighbouring, independent states have the further advantage of keeping power and authority within a limited compass. In extensive governments, tyranny is exercised easily because violence can be carried out on one part of the territory without observation elsewhere. Furthermore, the necessary distance between a people and the monarch adds to his mystique through lack of familiarity, and helps to increase his authority. Limiting the geographic extent of states – as eighteenth-century European states limited each other – therefore reduces the capacity of rulers to puff themselves up as tyrants.[42] Emulation occurs between smaller neighbouring states where there is 'a great intercourse of arts and commerce'. As between individuals within free societies, 'a mutual jealousy' occurs between the states themselves and 'keeps them from receiving too lightly the law from each other, in matters of taste and reasoning, and makes them examine every work of art with the greatest care and accuracy'. Borders and the peculiar prejudices of different nations reduce the capacity of popular opinion to communicate itself, a phenomenon which Hume believed would diminish the capacity of societies to discern good from bad art or science. After such a process of criticism and communication, 'nothing but nature and reason, or, at least, what bears them a strong resemblance', prevails over prejudice and more limited perspectives.[43]

Vital to the success of contemporary European commerce was the variation seen between different political cultures in the different states, arising from the interactions of republican and monarchical governments. The discovery of laws that limit government – one of the most difficult discoveries, Hume thought, in the emergence of human society in general – occurs first in republics. Hume argues that barbarous despotisms are unable to do so, whereas republics ultimately find it necessary with the passing of time to limit their magistrates in order to preserve liberty. 'Civilized monarchies' are those like contemporary France that have learned the arts of government and the importance of restraining all but the chief magistrate – i.e., the monarch himself – by laws. Modern monarchies, Hume argues, are not to be confused with the real tyrannies of more ancient times. The perfection which the modern variants have achieved they owe to republican governments: to become civilized it was necessary that monarchy 'borrow its laws, and methods, and institutions, and consequently its stability and order, from free governments'. In monarchies that have learned the rules of republics, a 'species of government arises, to which, in a high political rant, we may give the name of Tyranny, but which, by a just and prudent administration, may afford tolerable security to the people, and may answer most of the ends of political society'.[44]

The 'rise and progress of the arts and sciences' was a European phenomenon requiring a cluster of different states with different kinds of constitution and political culture as its preconditions. Different circumstances between nations helped increase the variety of cultural products that emerged as well as creating conditions in which the critical process of discernment between competing theories and products of artifice could be enacted. In contrast to the history of recent centuries in Europe that saw the near universal hegemony of medieval Catholicism and the near war of all against all of the centuries of Reformation, the contemporary condition of commerce, combined with the careful policy based on principles of the balance of power, appeared as an auspicious geopolitical environment. To reiterate, nothing, Hume observed, '*is more favourable to the rise of politeness and learning, than a number of neighbouring and independent states, connected together by commerce and policy*'.[45] In the *Political Discourses*, this picture of European inter-state relations was enriched by a closer analysis of the effects of commerce and refinement on the strength and technical expertise and in generating an interest in peace. War occurred, but was rendered less frequent, Hume thought, by the wisdom of the balance of power and the interests of commerce. Analysis of justice on two levels – within states and between them – shows how affluence was a polyvalent force creating a conflict of interest between cooperation and obedience on the one hand, and violation through disobedience on the other.

VI

I want to return, in conclusion, to the issue with which this essay commenced, the question of why it was that Hume appears to have affirmed the possibility of using non-specie financial instruments in everyday exchanges between individuals in civil society (i.e., in the *Treatise*, particularly in Book II) but rejected them as lacking practicability in the *Political Discourses*. An explanation is, of course, available based on direct readings from that volume: one part of the explanation would be that if a nation were to supplement its hard currency with paper currency it would leave itself open to the risk of losing all of the former and being left only with the latter as the price of its domestic product rose relative to its neighbours in times of economic prosperity. What I propose is that Hume's view can in turn be explained partly by reference to underlying assumptions derived from a background theory of the foundations of civil society, international justice, and the society of nations.

As I have argued in section I of this essay, in the *Treatise* Hume explains the original use of money in the context of his account of artificial conventions. Carl Wennerlind's work has shown this idea to be intimately linked to the foundational convention of promise-keeping, and Hume significantly points out that the use even of gold and silver in exchange is based on a convention similar to those in operation with justice and the creation of languages. The value of the metal is secondary, in this respect, to its symbolic value in exchange, indicated by the fact that the pieces of gold and silver are exchanged for things of 'a hundred times their value', as we have seen. Furthermore, in his analysis of human passions and the esteem for monetary wealth, Hume attributes the effectiveness of money and its meaningfulness to the ability of individuals to judge it probable that it will be offered and accepted in exchange in a given social context (based, as Book III shows, on the institutional frameworks established by prior social conventions). Thus, to summarize, Hume sees the value of money, its practical effectiveness, and its meaning in common life as an artificial construct arising through conventions originating *within* civil societies. Its meaning, usefulness, and value, are not reducible to a primordial, substantive value in the materials used; hence the possibility entertained in the *Treatise* of using substantially valueless materials like paper.

Between nations too, in Hume's view, there is, in a sense, a form of society, to the extent that nations behave like individual persons, depending on one another to an extent, and forming conventions by which they make a rule of avoiding mutual depredation, lying, etc. This is established in Hume's discussion of the laws of nations. The conventions are less binding, however, on nations due to their lesser degree of interdependency in general; consequently, while there is a propensity sometimes for nations to go to war, there is no need to establish a government to enforce international justice or adjudicate between nations. War is simply an unfortunate but occasional fact of life that is generally accepted as such. Hume appears to have believed that the interests of commerce and the wisdom of modern 'policy' were reducing the incidence of interstate conflict in eighteenth-century Europe by, on the one hand, increasing interdependency (based on the need to trade) and, on the other, establishing the prevalence of a set of conventional rules ('the balance of power'). Thus a precarious equilibrium was achieved in the relations between states, less strong than between individuals in particular societies, but strong enough to avoid a war of all against all.

Modern European states therefore had an interest in maintaining relations of exchange between their subjects but were less bound to honour promises (as well as to honour property rights and the right to part with property only voluntarily). This, I would suggest, provides a framework for international commerce in which individuals from one state would feel more confident trading within their own state and would have less reason to trust those operating from within other states. In the former case, a government exists with a duty to enforce conventional rules (formulated explicitly as laws), including the fulfilment of contracts and the honouring of monetary debts. Paper currencies have therefore, in theory, a higher probability of being redeemed when circulating only within a given civil society than when passing beyond its borders.

Thus, in international trade, a greater tendency to seek recourse to substances of primordial value would appear to be the logical result of Hume's theory of international justice. Conventions are less strong between nations than within; since these include the use of money, the probability of currencies being redeemed at face value is lower in international society than within the nation from which it originated. Where hard cash is available, a foreigner will more strongly prefer it to a paper currency used to supplement the national currency. Rather than arguing that Hume was essentially a metallist or a fiduciary theorist per se, I would suggest that he was simply ambivalent about different forms of currency and that this reflected features of the background theory through which international relations were understood in his moral and political thought. Money, I would conclude, is therefore an important indicator of the relative weakness of international law in Hume's political theory, something through which it can be measured and interpreted; by the same token, Hume's 'international thought' provides an important context for interpreting his concerns about money and international commerce.

NOTES

1. D. Armitage, 'The Scottish Vision of Empire: Intellectual Origins of the Darien Venture', in J. Robertson (ed.), *A Union for Empire: Political Thought and the British Union of 1707* (Cambridge: Cambridge University Press, 1995), pp. 97–118.
2. J. Robertson, 'Introduction', in Andrew Fletcher, *Political Works,* ed. J. Robertson (Cambridge: Cambridge University Press, 1997), pp. xix, xxii–xxv.
3. J.G.A. Pocock, *Political Thought and History: Essays on Theory and Method* (Cambridge: Cambridge University Press, 2009), p. 208.
4. On Fletcher's importance for the Scottish Enlightenment, see N.T. Phillipson, 'The Scottish Enlightenment', in R. Porter and M. Teich (eds), *The Enlightenment in National Context* (Cambridge: Cambridge University Press, 1981), passim, and J. Robertson, 'The Scottish Enlightenment at the Limits of the Civic Tradition', in I. Hont and M. Ignatieff (eds), *Wealth and Virtue: The Shaping of Political Economy in the Scottish Enlightenment* (Cambridge: Cambridge University Press, 1983), especially pp. 140–51. On Machiavellian ideas about Empire in Britain, see D. Armitage, *The Ideological Origins of the British Empire* (Cambridge: Cambridge University Press, 2000), ch. 5.
5. Q. Skinner, *Liberty before Liberalism* (Cambridge: Cambridge University Press, 1997) and 'Hobbes on the Proper Signification of Liberty', in Skinner, *Visions of Politics III: Hobbes and Civil Science* (Cambridge: Cambridge University Press, 2002), pp. 209–37.
6. E.g., in 'Of the Liberty of the Press' and 'Of Civil Liberty' in D. Hume, *Essays, Moral, Political and Literary,* ed. E.F. Miller (Indianapolis: Liberty Fund, 1985). See also C.J. Finlay, *Hume's Social Philosophy: Human Nature and Commercial Sociability in A Treatise of Human Nature* (London: Continuum, 2007).
7. Hume, *Essays*, p. 281.
8. D. Hume, *A Treatise of Human Nature*, 2nd ed., ed. L.A. Selby-Bigge and P.H. Nidditch (Oxford: Clarendon Press, 1978), II.1.x ¶9. References are to Book, Part, Section and Paragraph number.
9. Hume, *Treatise*, II.1.x ¶9. See also Finlay, *Hume's Social Philosophy*, pp. 100–4.
10. Hume, *Treatise*, II.1.x ¶3.
11. Hume, *Treatise*, II.1.x ¶3: 'Paper will, on many occasions, be consider'd as riches, and that because it may convey the power of acquiring money…'

12. C. Wennerlind, 'The Link between David Hume's *Treatise of Human Nature* and His Fiduciary Theory of Money', *History of Political Economy*, 33/1 (2001), pp. 139–60 (p. 140). See also C.G. Caffentzis, 'Fiction or Counterfeit? David Hume's Interpretations of Paper and Metallic Money', in C. Wennerlind and M. Schabas (eds), *David Hume's Political Economy* (London: Routledge, 2008), p. 149. For instances of the theoretical metallist interpretations, see J.A. Schumpeter, *A History of Economic Analysis* (1954; New York: Oxford University Press, 1986), and D.W. Vickers, *Studies in the Theory of Money, 1690–1776* (1959; New York: Augustus M. Kelley, 1968).
13. Wennerlind, 'The Link', p. 140.
14. Wennerlind, 'The Link', pp. 140–41.
15. Hume, *Treatise*, III.2.ii ¶14.
16. Hume, *Treatise*, III.2.ii ¶14.
17. On the significance of this tension between norms governing domestic and international society in seventeenth and eighteenth-century political thought, see R. Tuck, *The Rights of War and Peace: Political Thought and the International Order from Grotius to Kant* (Oxford: Oxford University Press, 1999).
18. Hume, *Essays*, p. 284.
19. Hume, *Essays*, p. 284.
20. Hume, *Essays*, pp. 318–19.
21. Hume, *Essays*, p. 317n13.
22. Hume, *Essays*, p. 284. Caffentzis distinguishes between the 'natural fiction' of money based on bullion which is 'arrived at unconsciously and universally through conventions' and paper currency as an 'artificial fiction' arising 'consciously and particularly and expressed in promises'. Caffentzis, 'Fiction or Counterfeit?', p. 150.
23. Hume, *Essays*, p. 316.
24. Hume, *Treatise*, III.2.ii ¶3.
25. See C.J. Finlay, 'Hume's Theory of Civil Society', *The European Journal of Political Theory*, 3/4 (2004), pp. 369–91.
26. Hume, *Treatise*, III.2.xi ¶1.
27. Hume, *Treatise*, III.2.xi ¶2.
28. Hume, *Treatise*, III.2.xi ¶1.
29. Hume, *Treatise*, III.2.xi ¶2.
30. Hume does not actually use this term, but following the analogy he makes between the behaviour of individuals and states it is appropriate.
31. Hume, *Treatise*, III.2.xi ¶3–4.
32. Hume, *Treatise*, III.2.xi ¶3.
33. Hume, *Treatise*, III.2.xi ¶2. Hume mentions perpetual war in connection with the need for stability of possession.
34. Hume, *Treatise*, III.2.xi ¶4.
35. Hume, *Treatise*, III.2.xi ¶5.
36. Hume observes, '*That it is impossible for the arts and sciences to arise, at first, among any people unless that people enjoy the blessing of a free government.*' *Essays*, p. 115.
37. Hume, *Essays*, p. 119.
38. Hume, *Essays*, pp. 120–21.
39. Hume, *Essays*, pp. 120–21.
40. Hume, *Essays*, p. 123.
41. Hume, *Essays*, p. 119.
42. Hume, *Essays*, pp. 119–20.
43. Hume, *Essays*, p. 120.
44. Hume, *Essays*, p. 125.
45. Hume, *Essays*, p. 120.

CHAPTER FOUR

Leviathan's Defenders: Scottish Historical Discourse and the Political Economy of Progress

PAUL TONKS

Metropolitan British governance in the long eighteenth century, and thus the security of Britain's evolving empire, has been viewed increasingly by modern historians as having rested on a complex matrix of administrative and fiscal institutions that developed most notably during the Glorious Revolution and its aftermath and evolved subsequently over the long period of strategic rivalry and military conflict with Britain's rivals in Europe and around the globe.[1] Historians have labelled this model of government – an increasingly centralized and efficient one, at least in comparative terms with Britain's major rival, France – the 'fiscal-military state'. The so-called 'sinews of power' of the British fiscal-military state were at the heart of ideological conflict in the late eighteenth and early nineteenth centuries, in all parts of the British Atlantic World and beyond. Both defenders and critics of the British governmental system in this era of revolutions in the Atlantic world stressed the crucial importance of the fiscal-military state in deciding the fate of both Britain and its rivals. Competing historical interpretations of the growth, impact and durability of the fiscal-military state, shaped by the context of the challenges of the American and French Revolutions, were central to this key political battle.

What was ultimately at stake in this argument? Quite simply, the very future of the political, social, and economic structures that constituted British governance, and thus, in turn, the future shape of the broader international order. Radicals such as the leading transatlantic campaigner Tom Paine were certain that British global power was doomed to imminent collapse due to its reliance on an oppressive and ultimately unsustainable fiscal-military regime that produced increasingly costly wars. Writing at a time of acute fiscal pressure on the British state, which led eventually to the Bank Restriction Act the following year, Paine made this point explicitly and succinctly in his influential 1796 pamphlet, *The Decline and Fall of the English System of Finance*:

> It is worthy of observation, that every case of failure of finances, since the system of paper [money] began, has produced a revolution in governments, either total or partial. A failure in the finances of France produced the French Revolution. A failure in the finances of the assignats broke up the revolutionary government, and produced the present French Constitution. A failure in the finances of the Old Congress of America, and the embarrassments it brought upon commerce, broke up the system of the old confederation, and produced the federal Constitution. If, then, we admit of reasoning by comparison of causes and events, the failure of the English finances will produce some change in the government of that country.[2]

This essay examines the articulation by a cadre of Scottish writers of a historically framed political discourse that defended the established order in Britain against the determined, and potentially extremely damaging, radical challenge mounted by figures such as Paine. Administrations in the eighteenth-century Atlantic world, including those in power in the era of the American and French Revolutions, were well aware of the long tradition of resolute and politically harmful opposition to the evolution of the mechanisms of government finance embodied in the British fiscal-military state. The commentators discussed in this essay, in a fashion that paralleled and indeed built explicitly upon the arguments of earlier 'Court' defenders of the British system of government against the 'Country' or 'Real Whig' opposition to the growth in governmental power that has been termed the 'financial revolution', sought to outline an historical account of British state formation that expounded the nature and impact of the Financial Revolution and the ideological debates that had taken place in its wake in the late seventeenth and eighteenth centuries in order to counter the radical challenge head on.

These authors' method was characteristically Scottish, in Hume's celebrated sense of the eighteenth century as the historical age and

Scots as the historical nation, in that they deployed an historical account of state-formation that vindicated what Colin Kidd has usefully called the 'Anglo-British' constitutional settlement of the Hanoverian regime.[3] Historians of British anti-radicalism in this epoch have focused principally on counter-revolutionary arguments in the intellectual mode of Edmund Burke, interpreted chiefly in terms of the role of prescriptive tradition, and, at a more popular level, the militant Church-and-King loyalism mobilized in England by figures such as John Reeves (the founder of the 'Association for Preserving Liberty and Property against Republicans and Levellers').[4] In contrast, this essay highlights the approach of four influential Scottish commentators who sought boldly to claim the mantle of progress and commercial modernity as central to the defence of British governance: Patrick Colquhoun, Sir John Sinclair, William Playfair, and George Chalmers.

What did these four figures understand by progress or, in one of the most resonant terms of the eighteenth century, improvement? Ironically – although perhaps in a sense unsurprisingly, given the terrain that they were contesting with their radical opponents – their chief conception of liberty in the modern Enlightenment age of commerce and reason appears to have been almost Jeffersonian. That is, its central focus was, in essence, the 'pursuit of happiness' by individuals and families. In a view that may be called Hamiltonian, as we shall explore in due course, the freedom to pursue happiness in the eighteenth-century Atlantic world could only exist securely, however, if the state was capable of protecting the basic security of its subjects. Along with a Lockean view of human progress, then, focused on the growth of individual and public welfare through commerce and the acquisition of property, went an essentially Hobbesian understanding of international relations. The relationship between polities in a world of clashing empires and, in the Revolutionary Atlantic, ideologies, was inherently unstable and threatening. Only a state that possessed the capacity to defend itself and its subjects could provide freedom in the most fundamental sense of security from external threat. These figures were convinced that the British fiscal-military state could provide that security and stability in a world of danger, and so could ensure the best protective or defensive shield for its subjects to pursue the socio-economic progress upon which personal freedom rested.

These four authors all adapted and employed the insights of eighteenth-century Scottish political economy to defend the existing institutions of government, including the highly controversial structures of the fiscal-military state, as vital to the best interests of all British subjects. They depicted the hostile critique of the British fiscal-military state, one of the most prominent tropes of radical thought from the very origins of the fiscal-military state in the late seventeenth century and then similarly to the fore in 'Country' or opposition polemics throughout the long eighteenth century, as a dangerous and destructive project that was actually naively anti-modern in its rejection of the post-1688 state apparatus on which British security depended. As we have noted, this quartet's method was thus characteristically Scottish in the crucial intellectual sense that they built upon the central Scottish Enlightenment preoccupation with commercial modernity and deployed historical exposition to achieve their goals. Moreover, they were self-conscious and explicit about the kind of historical exegesis that was necessary in their view. They shared Burke's sceptical disdain for abstract principles and responded to the challenges of revolutionary radicalism with a detailed empirical account of historical processes. Emphasizing their use of official data, they catalogued the historical progress of socio-economic improvement in Britain across the eighteenth century through statistical analysis of national wealth and power. They engaged with central concerns of major figures such as David Hume and Adam Smith in their historical political economy of state-formation, particularly the functioning and prospects of public credit, in order to develop a compelling case for the 'practical liberty' that historians have come to conceive of as crucial to the conservative rejection of political and socio-economic radicalism.

Concern with the political economy of the modern state was especially intense in the era of the American and French Revolutions, although, as we have noted, the transatlantic radical assaults on the fiscal-military state built upon the earlier critique that was central to 'Country' political discourse. In turn, conservative defenders of the established order in this period self-consciously and explicitly viewed themselves as taking on the challenge of both past and present criticism. This key facet of political debate in fact engendered a more confident and stridently asserted defence of the British governmental system in response to, and rejection of, the much better-known radical assault on the British funding system, which we shall seek to highlight in the writings of these four commentators. My contention is that detailed consideration of these authors' arguments helps us to understand more fully the success of the British government in fending off the powerful ideological challenge mounted by its radical critics in this age of international revolutions.

I

The quartet of Scottish thinkers discussed in this essay requires some introduction. Patrick Colquhoun (1745–1820) was a prominent figure in Scottish, and wider British, public life.[5] He was three times Lord Provost of Glasgow, eighteenth-century Scotland's chief commercial city, and was the guiding force behind the foundation of the Glasgow Chamber of Commerce in the early 1780s. He had spent five years in Virginia as a young man as an agent in the Chesapeake-Glasgow tobacco trade, a formative experience that no doubt shaped his firm personal and public support for metropolitan authority during the American Revolution, when he was a principal contributor to a fund to raise a regiment in Glasgow for service in suppressing the colonial rebellion. Colquhoun was a Commissioner from Glasgow to the Convention of Royal Burghs of Scotland in 1781, and in 1782 was chosen as a Commissioner from the Convention to lobby Parliament on the linen trade. He published a number of important pamphlets on commercial matters in the 1780s and was diligent in support of those who had suffered losses as a result of the American Revolutionary War. He moved to London in 1789 and was actively involved in the struggle against the radicals in the 1790s crisis, particularly in his role as a London magistrate from 1792. His early biographer, G.D. Yeats (writing in 1818), stressed that Colquhoun did not simply advocate coercion to defeat the radical challenge: 'Mr. Colquhoun, with the wisdom and benevolence of a true political-economist, clearly saw that the mere action of coercive law, without attention to the removal of the discontents, would be insufficient in restraining those who are urged on to violence by deprivation of food.'[6]

Colquhoun was self-consciously a product of the Scottish Enlightenment intellectual, cultural, and indeed social milieu. His biographer emphasized that 'He had the honour to be known by the late Dr. [William] Robertson, Mr. [Edward] Gibbon, Mr. [Edmund] Burke, and Dr. Adam Smith, the two last have partaken of his hospitality.'[7] Colquhoun's expansive vision of improvement, the great touchstone of the Scottish Enlightenment, which he described as covering a 'great variety of subjects, political, moral, statistical, and historical',[8] shared the same concern with the practical application of political economy as Playfair, Chalmers, and Sinclair. The culmination of Colquhoun's outlook was his *Treatise on the Wealth, Power and Resources of the British Empire, in every Quarter of the World*. This was published in 1814, and a corrected and expanded edition appeared the following year. As Colquhoun declared:

> The great and primary object in this has been to render it useful in improving the state and condition of society; to convey to the mind a general and more correct idea of the structure of the body politic in all its component parts; with a view to the accomplishment of those progressive improvements which may arise from the suggestions and disclosures which are now offered to the consideration of those assigned to execute the powers of Government, and also to the public at large whose co-operation is always of importance in every free government, in whatever regards the national prosperity, and the comfort and happiness of the people.[9]

Colquhoun was explicit about his methodology and stressed his rigorously empirical approach based upon the 'medium of public documents' and the 'rules of political arithmetic'.[10] He sought chiefly to promote optimism about the economic and political health of Britain. Colquhoun expressed the confident hope that 'an investigation, no less curious than useful, systematically arranged and brought within the narrowest compass, supported and elucidated by every existing accessible official fact, might afford some assistance to the national credit at this important crisis'.[11] 'It is therefore humbly presumed,' Colquhoun went on, 'that a Work embracing the whole range of political economy may prove useful and interesting, not only to the statesman, but also to the land-holder, the agriculturist, the merchant, the trader, the manufacturer, and the stock-holder.'[12]

Sir John Sinclair was well known to contemporaries as the promoter of the *Statistical Account of Scotland*, one of the great and lasting achievements of the eighteenth-century Scottish Enlightenment concern for practical knowledge and improvement. A public servant, most notably through his role as a Member of Parliament and President of the Board of Agriculture, he was also author of *The History of the Public Revenue of the British Empire* (published originally in 1785, with a second edition in 1790, and an expanded third edition in three volumes in 1803–1804). It is important to stress, moreover, that Sinclair viewed his various administrative and literary efforts as a uniform whole dedicated to the improvement of his nation;[13] his ambitious vision of improvement was worked out from his estates in the Northern Highlands to the rest of Scotland, and indeed the whole of the British Empire.

William Playfair was one of the most strident Pittite commentators of the French Revolutionary era and the younger brother of John Playfair, Professor of Natural Philosophy at Edinburgh University. Playfair settled in Paris in the late 1780s. Having been an early enthusiast for the French Revolution, as a member of the Anglophone community in Paris who had witnessed the storming of the Bastille, Playfair became one of the Revolution's most determined opponents. He wrote a number of anti-revolutionary pieces in the 1790s, following his disenchantment with political radicalism. These influenced other British opponents of the French Revolution, such as Sir John Sinclair's colleague at the Board of Agriculture, Arthur Young, who cited Playfair's negative appraisal of French public finances in his own influential 1793 tract *The Example of France a Warning to Britain*. Playfair was, in fact, the first editor of Adam Smith's *Wealth of Nations* in 1805, to which he added supplementary chapters that engaged with Smith's account of the evolution and future prospects of public credit in particular.[14]

The Edinburgh Annual Register for 1823, in its obituary of Playfair, noted that 'Politics and political economy were his favourite topics, and there has scarcely been a subject of political interest, connected with either, during the last forty years, that has not elicited a pamphlet from his prolific pen.'[15] Probably Playfair's most popular effort, however, was his *History of Jacobinism, Its Crimes, Cruelties and Perfidies: Comprising An Inquiry into the Manner of Disseminating, under the Appearance of Philosophy and Virtue, Principles which are Originally Subversive of Order, Virtue, Religion, Liberty and Happiness*, first published in London in 1795, which has been called 'one of the most influential counterrevolutionary works of the decade'.[16] This was published initially by subscription, and subscribers included leading Members of Parliament. It was widely read in Great Britain and in the United States, where the English radical-turned-ultra-Federalist William Cobbett republished it in Philadelphia in 1796.[17]

George Chalmers was one of the most prolific eighteenth-century Scottish analysts of British colonial and commercial relationships. Chalmers essayed a defence of the British imperial state in the turbulent period following the American Revolution by laying out what he considered to be its underlying strength and fundamental utility for its subjects. He came to particular prominence in the 1780s as one of a triumvirate of administration writers, along with his mentor Charles Jenkinson and Lord Sheffield, who articulated and defended a revamped commercial policy towards the newly independent United States.[18] He had emigrated to Maryland in the early 1760s and fled to London in 1775, where he became Secretary to the Loyalist Association of American refugees. He became Chief Clerk at the British Privy Council's Committee for Trade and Plantations in the reorganization of the Board of Trade after the War of American Independence, where he was right-hand man to Jenkinson (Lord Hawkesbury, later first Earl of Liverpool).

II

We have noted that Colquhoun, Sinclair, Playfair, and Chalmers all shared and built upon the deep preoccupation with commercial modernity that characterized the eighteenth-century Scottish Enlightenment. Their approach, in common with the leading Scottish thinkers, was profoundly historical. Colquhoun's analysis of the growth of the modern state emphasized that 'The revenues raised for the support and defence of all empires, kingdoms, and states are of such vital importance, as they relate to the prosperity and the general happiness of every country, that in considering this branch of the subject a short historical account of its rise and progress in Great Britain and Ireland, from the earliest periods to the present time, cannot fail to prove interesting.'[19] William Playfair likewise explained in his 1805 *Inquiry into the Permanent Causes of the Decline and Fall of Powerful and Wealthy Nations*: 'One of the most solid foundations on which an inquirer can proceed in matters of political economy, as connected with the fate of nations, seems to be by an appeal to history, a view of the effects that have been produced, and an investigation of the causes that have operated in producing them.'[20] Their historical exegesis propounded *genuine* liberty as a progressive process rather than a virtue to be revived or recovered. All four placed a fundamental stress on the recent historical record of enormous economic progress, concentrating on the period after the Glorious Revolution, which required the emergence of the powerful British fiscal-military state, and what they considered to be its ameliorating effects. In their view, the complex system of debt finance, properly managed, was central to British government, and indeed was the only reliable basis of secure liberty for citizens in a *modern* commercial state such as that of Great Britain.

For Colquhoun, Chalmers, Playfair, and Sinclair, the best interests of Britons depended ultimately on their relationship to a uniquely strong and stable state. This argument was clearest in their analysis of fiscal regimes, in particular those of late eighteenth/early nineteenth-century Great Britain, France, and the United States. Playfair, for example, stressed that 'the power of nations may now almost be estimated by their disposable revenues'.[21] Playfair highlighted how the nature and structure of government had been transformed since the establishment of the modern funding system. 'In no circumstances does the British empire differ so widely from all nations recorded in history, or from any now in existence, as with regard to national debt', Playfair commented. 'Not only the invention of contracting debt to carry on war is but of recent origin, but no nation has ever carried it to near the extent it has arrived in England.'[22] Colquhoun stressed the direct link between the evolution of private and public credit, which historians have come to term the Financial Revolution, and defined succinctly its particular importance for Britain: 'It is a species of confidence in the resources of the state and the stability of individuals engaged in commerce and manufactures, which is to be found in no other country.' Public credit, 'stimulated by the confidence in the solidity of the circulating medium of the national banks', ensured British prosperity and security according to Colquhoun. 'This confidence gives energy to commercial enterprise,' he argued. 'It is the peculiar character of Great Britain; and distinguishes this country from all the nations of the earth, and from France in particular.'[23]

Playfair sought to draw attention to his personal knowledge of French circumstances during the early Revolutionary period as proof of his qualification to address the nature of the conflict between the British and French states and its likely outcome. The engine of the French revolutionary currency, the *assignats*, in his view was one of destruction and anarchy. The French, due to their violent overthrow of the political and socio-economic order, were simply unable to achieve the necessary success in managing public finances that was the most crucial requirement of modern government.[24] In fact, in the mid-1780s Sinclair had pointed out the very grave political and economic problems that faced France, particularly due to its unwise support for the rebellious Americans. Sinclair told his readers in

1804 that his analysis had been vindicated by the course of events in the 1790s, in which France's disastrous fiscal experiments had been built upon, and deepened, a profound socio-economic crisis.[25] Colquhoun too warned of the dangers of revolutionary projects, and the tragic unexpected outcomes that were produced. He drew on the history of mid-seventeenth century conflicts in the British Isles and the depredations of the Cromwellian regime as a historical lesson for Britons in the era of the French Revolution. 'Thus we see the ravages on public and private property, and the shocking tyranny, barbarity and oppression, which revolutions produce,' Colquhoun wrote at the end of the Napoleonic Wars. 'It has been the lot of the present generation to know, that scenes of equal or even greater atrocity have taken place in a neighbouring country, from the contagion of which this nation has been happily sheltered.'[26]

Strikingly, a key ground for British conservative rejection of radical arguments on the dangers posed by the funding system was in fact the nature and impact of the American Revolution. George Chalmers, for example, argued, in essence, that Americans in the aftermath of their Revolution had remembered once again the central blessings of British liberty, as secured by the structures of strong and stable central government. Chalmers contended that the framers of the 1787 United States Constitution had abandoned Tom Paine's dangerously destabilizing radicalism for the same fundamental principles as those that underpinned the Anglo-British Constitution. Chalmers's unsurprisingly hostile account of Paine's activities during the American Revolution in his notorious *Life of Pain* (first published in 1791 and republished subsequently in many editions on both sides of the Atlantic) constituted a continuation of his earlier historical analyses of the development of the American Colonies within the British imperial system in his *Political Annals* (1780) and *Introduction to the History of the Revolt of the American Colonies* (1782). Chalmers was forced to admit that Paine's thought, though pernicious, was deeply influential on the course of the American Revolution. He lamented in a mocking pun, 'Yet it cannot be denied, that *common sense* was universally perused, and loudly praised.'[27] Crucially, though, Chalmers made a very important claim about the character and impact of the American Revolution by insisting that the newly independent Americans had rejected Paine's radicalism, so influential during the course of the Revolutionary War, after that war's end. The adoption of the Federal Constitution of 1787 revealed Americans' renewed recognition of the need for liberty to be balanced properly with order and authority, as exemplified in the crucial sphere of government finance, something that Paine's political philosophy ignored, or rather wholly failed to comprehend, in Chalmers's view.[28]

A conservative reading of the new US Federal Constitution was, then, very important for British critics of the French Revolution, who were anxious to confront their radical opponents' claims that French revolutionary radicalism was analogous to American political values, which had drawn a good deal of support and sympathy in the broader British Atlantic World. 'In the former revolutions of the modern world,' the well known English commentator Arthur Young explained, 'the people soon settled into a form of government nearly resembling that which they had enjoyed before the troubles, they never dreamed of making new experiments *on principle*. Even in the case of America the fact holds true in almost every instance; for there is not now in the world a constitution so near the British as that of the United States.'[29] A good deal of attention has been paid by historians to British radicals' enthusiasm for perceived American constitutional principles,[30] but it is important to remind ourselves that this conservative interpretation of American political development post-Independence was fairly common amongst Britons in the 1790s, whose views of America were coloured by their response to events in Europe.

George Chalmers's description of American government in this epoch, like that of so many of his contemporaries in Britain, America itself, and indeed France, reflected his opinion of developments in Revolutionary France. Chalmers and Playfair shared Edmund Burke's abhorrence of Paine's abstract revolutionary principles of liberty, that is, natural rights, as the cause of ultimate tyranny – something that they believed Americans had wisely retreated from. Their central theme, shared by Colquhoun and Sinclair, was that liberty is tangible and measurable in terms of economic improvement; it is a quality that is attained and preserved primarily through the stability and security of strong government, as embodied in Britain's fiscal-military state.

Evaluation of the American Revolution and its aftermath in the terms of Scottish political economy was indeed crucial to Chalmers's refutation of Paine's radicalism. Chalmers, who was echoed in this regard by William Playfair and later by Sir John Sinclair, emphasized the disastrous currency problems that had faced Americans following the Revolutionary War, which he contrasted sharply with the British system of state finance (whereas Paine viewed them as essentially equivalent, at least in the inevitable long-term outcome of depreciation and eventual bankruptcy, as indicated above in my quotation from Paine's tract *The Decline and Fall of the English System of Finance*). Chalmers noted mockingly in his pseudonymous 'biography' of Paine that Paine had sought to 'teach America and Europe the nature of paper money'.[31] The American mode of finance during the War of Independence was likewise an important issue for Playfair in his supplementary chapters in his 1805 edition of Smith's *Wealth of Nations*: 'When the American States had secured their independence, there were no funds, no revenues from which this paper, that had ruined many individuals, but had answered the purpose for which it was created, could be paid,' Playfair argued. 'It remained long thus, in an unarranged state, till at last some order was established in the revenue department, and it was funded, in the European mode, in stock, bearing interest.'[32] In other words, the Americans had been fortunately rescued post-Revolution by Treasury Secretary Alexander Hamilton's adoption of British-style institutions and practices.

Sir John Sinclair put forward a similar argument in his 1811 *Speech... on the Subject of the Bullion Report*. Sinclair wished to demonstrate to his audience that the British use of paper money was in fact quite different from the system that had been employed by the Revolutionary governments in America and France, which had destroyed the stability of property and thus led to its own demise because it was based on compulsion and ultimately confiscation of property. 'The paper currency of America, and the assignats of France, were issued by these Revolutionary Governments without any controul whatsoever, as the only means by which they could be enabled to carry on the contests in which they were respectively engaged,' Sinclair argued. 'The paper currencies of America and of France were issued to such excess, that it became necessary to compel the people to take them in payment of those articles which these Governments required. Hence their depreciation originated, and their ultimate annihilation.' Sinclair contended that, in starkly different fashion, the British employment of paper currency 'increases only in proportion to the growing prosperity of the country'.[33]

Colquhoun, Chalmers, Playfair, and Sinclair all recognized the radical political economy of public revenue enunciated by Paine and his British, American, and French supporters as self-consciously central to their ideological appeal. It was thus vital that defenders of

British governance debunk it determinedly. Chalmers, for instance, highlighted this key thread of Paine's radicalism, which was crucial to the radical critique of unreformed British government: 'All that he had retailed in his *Prospects on the Rubicon*, with regard to money, and credit, and commerce, he interweaves into his *Rights of Man*.'[34] Chalmers sought to portray Paine's bullionist views, which he regarded as fundamental to Paine's account of government finances, as ridiculously ignorant. Paine's obsession with specie, shared with other critics of British governance such as Richard Price, led to a declensionist narrative of British prosperity. 'By thus asserting money [i.e., coined precious metals] alone to be wealth, and shewing how much coin had been brought into this island, and how little remained in it,' Chalmers explained, 'he endeavours to prove, that Great Britain has, at present, less commerce and opulence, than this island had, in former times.' Chalmers referred to David Hume's *History of England* to argue that this was patent nonsense because the expansion of British commerce had improved the fundamental quality of life for all Britons. He claimed that the great majority of British subjects astutely rejected the radicals' pessimism, realizing that they had security and success as a result of the British mode of government: 'The nation exulted in her prosperity, while he sat calculating, with arithmetical precision, the depth of her distresses, and the benefits, but not the miseries, of anarchy.'[35]

Chalmers launched a full-frontal assault on Paine and his admirers' economic diagnosis of British constitutional failure in his 1794 reworking of his *Estimate of the Comparative Strength of Great Britain* (an optimistic account of British economic and political health first published in 1782). The ostensible target for Chalmers was a fellow Scot, and indeed also a former resident of the American colonies, James Currie. Currie is best known to posterity as the editor and early biographer of Scotland's national bard, Robert Burns,[36] but he was prominent in the early 1790s as a radical Dissenting opponent of the slave trade and advocate of political reform.[37] Currie produced a pamphlet in 1793 entitled *A Letter, Commercial and Political, Addressed to the Rt. Honble. William Pitt, in which the Real Interests of Britain, in the Present Crisis, Are Considered, and Some Observations are Offered on the General State of Europe* (published under the pseudonym 'Jasper Wilson').

Currie's radicalism was manifested most clearly in his hostility to the mechanisms of public credit employed by the British government. It was on this crucial ground of the relationship between economic strength and the stability of the British system of government that Chalmers determined to undermine Currie, who had presented, in essence, an analysis and critique of the British fiscal-military state. Chalmers sought to rebut Currie and the radicals by giving an historical account of Britain's economic and governmental development in order to demonstrate conclusively that the nation was more successful and stable than ever, and that this gave her inhabitants the greatest measure of genuine liberty that they had ever experienced. The arguments of critics of the British state during the crisis of the French Revolution, like those of the earlier misguided American opponents of the authority of Westminster, were, in Chalmers's view, illusory and dangerous because they sacrificed a real present liberty on the basis of chimerical fears of disaster and oppression. Chalmers's argument was echoed by Patrick Colquhoun, who contended that the 'progress of the British revenue during the last century and up to the present period, furnishes the most incontestable proofs of the rapid increase of the wealth of the country since the union [of 1707 between the Scottish and English Parliaments]'.[38]

Chalmers, like Sinclair, Colquhoun, and Playfair, thus evinced the 'sceptical' or 'scientific' Whiggism associated with leading Scottish Enlightenment thinkers such as David Hume.[39] He combined this intellectual sympathy with an admiration for the seventeenth-century English theoreticians and historians of statecraft. Indeed, he was well versed in the key writings of the English thinkers who had shaped the nascent discipline of political economy, figures such as William Petty, Charles Davenant, and Gregory King (having republished some of their most important texts). Ultimately, his was a contention that the modern – by which he meant post-Glorious Revolution – Anglo-British state embodied the most secure mechanism of personal and familial progress for its subjects and that its stability was a crucial bulwark against the dangerous innovations of revolutionary radicalism in the late eighteenth century.

III

This period of the Atlantic Revolutions was an era in which faith in human progress infused many spheres of thought and action. Indeed, I have sought to highlight the self-conscious embrace of progress by supporters of the British system of governance; for the commentators that I have drawn attention to, it was revolutionary radicalism that represented the greatest threat to progress, rather than the maintenance of the institutions of the British state. A deep faith in the possibility of progress, however, was certainly central to those radical enthusiasts for the American and French Revolutions who wished to put an end to the international conflicts that had been exacerbated by the rivalries associated with European colonialism, and out of which had grown the fiscal-military state or the 'funding system'. These competing views of progress, and evaluations of its achievability, were very different, though.

Conservatives hostile to the radicals' enthusiasm for revolutionary change were sceptical about the prospects for an end to the competitive international state system. Playfair, for example, was convinced that 'While the causes from which wealth and power rise in superior degree, are liable to change from one nation to another, wealth and power must be liable to the same alterations and changes of place; so long any equal balance amongst nations must be artificial.'[40] Playfair reasoned that 'In whatever the superiority consists, emulation and envy prompt to rivalship in peace, and to frequent trials of strength in war. The contempt and pride which accompany wealth and power, and the envy and jealousy they excite amongst other nations, are continual causes of change, and form the great basis of the revolutions amongst the human race.'[41] Conflict between nations was, unfortunately, inevitable and the upshot was that states must ensure that their system of government, particularly their mode of finance, was capable of preserving the basic security of their subjects from direct external threats.

This sceptical view of international relations in the period, and the resultant stress on the need for a governmental system that could secure the resources necessary for national defence, was in fact expressed perhaps most famously by Alexander Hamilton in an America deeply divided by these very fundamental questions over its constitutional direction and future place in the world.[42] Hamilton's vision was of a nation shaped by international commerce, and this would involve necessarily the requirement to evolve a fiscal-military state capable of acting in the fashion of Britain.[43] He gave clear expression to his views in Federalist Number 34: 'To judge from the history of mankind,' Hamilton observed:

> we shall be compelled to conclude that the fiery and destructive passions of war reign in the human breast with much more powerful sway than the mild and beneficent sentiments of peace; and that to model our political systems upon

> speculations of lasting tranquility is to calculate on the weaker springs of the human character. What are the chief sources of expense in every government? What has occasioned that enormous accumulation of debts with which several of the European nations are oppressed? The answer plainly is, wars and rebellions . . . The expenses arising from those institutions which are relative to the mere domestic police of a State . . . are insignificant in comparison with those which relate to the national defense.[44]

I have noted that Chalmers engaged with a radical pamphlet by Dr James Currie that allowed him to attack the perceived pessimism of leading radical critics of the British governmental system. In many ways, however, Chalmers's principal target was David Hume, and through him the radical Painites who had come to enunciate a vision of universal peace through international revolution and the establishment of pacific commerce (which lay at the heart of Paine's arguments in *Rights of Man, Part II*, for example). This is readily intelligible, however, when we recall how Hume's anxiety about the British government's apparently ever-increasing reliance on public credit, due to its entanglement in overseas colonial expansion, had been seized upon by critics of British governance such as the Welsh Dissenter Richard Price in his widely read *Observations on the Nature of Civil Liberty, the Principles of Government, and the Justice and Policy of the War with America* (1776). Chalmers's admiration for Hume's central intellectual achievement and political insight as the foremost historian of British state-formation and modern commercial liberty was thus tempered by Hume's dire view of the British funding system, which was in fact an explicit theme of Currie's attack on the Pittite system of war finance.

We can see fairly close points of contact between Hume's profound worries about the British fiscal-military state, the product of his Enlightenment cosmopolitanism and a sincere wish that wars between European states could be ended (hence his evolving scepticism towards the traditional Whig doctrine of 'Balance of Power'[45] and British commercial imperialism), and the universalistic faith in pacific commercial republicanism articulated by Paine in *Rights of Man, Part II* and elsewhere. It is not surprising, then, that radical critics of British governmental institutions in the late eighteenth century deployed Hume's political economy of the international state system, or at least a gloss on it.[46]

Chalmers believed that he could confront the radicals in this crucial area. He published two expanded editions of the *Estimate* in 1794, providing a lengthy and systematic attempt to record the mutual growth of commerce, public credit and liberty in Britain that had developed over the preceding century – in the crucial sense of the improved quality of life of the British populace through socio-economic development. Chalmers ridiculed Currie's misguided application of Hume in his mock 'Dedication'. Chalmers depicted Hume's analytical method in evaluating public credit as profoundly misconceived, and noted that late eighteenth-century radicals had fallen into precisely the same trap. Hume had failed to appreciate how a vibrant economy like that of Britain could bear an increased national debt through its commercial growth: 'Hume, in considering his subject, regarded England, as a youth of *fifteen*, who was never to grow up to be a man of *fifty*, with all the knowledge and experience, the strength and activity, of fifty, who can move easily under burdens, which would crush a stripling.'[47] Colquhoun emphasized too how history had disproved the expressed fears about the prospects for the British funding system of Hume and Smith, amongst many others: 'Nothing can so strongly demonstrate the imperfection of human nature, even when applied to individuals who have ranked highest in the scale of society as men of foresight, wisdom and talents,' Colquhoun noted, 'as the discoveries which time and experience have made of the fallacy of the various predictions of the ablest writers of the last century, respecting the dangerous tendency of the national debt, and the ruin which it must bring upon the country, if suffered to increase.'[48]

Colquhoun, Chalmers, Sinclair, and Playfair sought to demonstrate that the underlying strength of the British economy, which was the bedrock of British political stability and the very essence of meaningful freedom because it was the means of improving the people's lives, had proved capable of supporting the increases in the national debt that extensive modern warfare required. They wished to refute what they considered to be the speculative arguments of radical opponents by communicating the empirical record of rapid progress in trade, which had brought enormous material benefits to the British populace and allowed successive governments to fight a series of increasingly costly wars to defend the nation and its political system. 'Nothing can be adduced as a stronger proof of the rapid advance of the country, in the accumulation of wealth, than the financial operations during the greater part of the two wars of the French revolution, from 1793 to

1813,' Colquhoun argued. 'During this period, chiefly under the guidance of a most enlightened and able minister [William Pitt] the science of finance appears to have advanced nearly to a height almost approaching perfection.'[49]

Sinclair echoed Colquhoun, Playfair and Chalmers in his exposition of the long tradition of pessimism about the prospects of British fiscal strength that dated back to the late seventeenth-century beginnings of the modern fiscal-military state and the simultaneous evolution of the shrill critique of this mode of governance that was such a prominent strand of 'Country' or opposition discourse from that period forward. He also believed that it was necessary to contradict these potentially demoralizing assertions of British vulnerability. 'As any ideas of that nature are, in a particular manner, contrary to the interests of a state that depends upon credit for supplying the means of defending itself, or of annoying its enemies, it is thought that a greater benefit cannot be conferred upon the public, than by proving how groundless such opinions are,' Sinclair stressed, 'from its appearing to be an indisputable fact, that similar desponding apprehensions have been publicly avowed by persons of respectable authority for above a century past, during which period it is well known that the nation has enjoyed no inconsiderable degree of happiness and prosperity.'[50] Sinclair thus affixed to his *History of the Public Revenue* a long list of extracts from British authors, such as the radical Scottish Whig co-author of *Cato's Letters*, Thomas Gordon; the Country Tory, Lord Bolingbroke; David Hume; Adam Smith; and Richard Price, who had all, in Sinclair's view, asserted that the British system of government finances inevitably would collapse, with disastrous consequences. Sinclair, in fundamental agreement with Colquhoun, Chalmers, and Playfair, noted the 'progressive assertions of the miserable state of the nation for above a century past, though the event has proved that it has continued to prosper, notwithstanding the melancholy apprehensions which many able and intelligent individuals entertained'.[51]

These authors' arguments were thus in one sense fundamentally positive, in that they offered an essentially optimistic historical reading of the growth of the British Leviathan and couched their assessment of its legitimacy in utilitarian terms. Their key criterion for defending the British governmental system was that it had facilitated the growth of unparalleled individual and national prosperity for its subjects. It was this measurable 'improvement' that constituted true freedom for the average person in their view. Their mode of argument was also negative, however, in the sense that they expressed a sceptical rejection of the cosmopolitan vision of republican revolutionary internationalism. The international state-system of competitive rivalry leading to conflict, although in many senses regrettable, was sadly inevitable. To seek to construct a polity on the basis of its overthrow, which was how they characterized the project of the radicals, was an absurd utopian delusion. The fiscal-military state was necessary because repeated conflicts were bound to take place in the essentially Hobbesian state of nature in which nations related to each other. Great Britain was thus fortunate to possess her peculiarly stable matrix of institutions, although she had to be careful to guard and employ them properly. Playfair commented in 1805 that Britain 'has better credit than any nation ever had, so, likewise, it is the only one whose efforts have never been in any way, or at any time, either restricted or suspended, for want of money to carry them into effect'.[52]

These writers thus came to enunciate a self-consciously modified Smithian political economy that sought to balance freedom of trade with the primary concern of strategic security as the fundamental goal of responsible government. Chalmers referred in a 1785 pamphlet on the economic relationship between Britain and Ireland to Adam Smith's famous view of the navigation acts: 'The truth then is, that the vast augmentation of the riches of Britain, during the effluxion of the last hundred years, did not arise from the act of navigation, but, in spite of this law, which was enacted for a quite different and more valuable purpose, namely, the naval defence of the country.'[53] There was a strong parallel between the stance that they evolved in the 1790s and 1800s and Alexander Hamilton's project in the post-Revolutionary United States, as we have seen.

Colquhoun, Playfair, Sinclair, and Chalmers laid out how the American and the French Revolutions had grown out of, and in turn produced, fiscal crises – echoing, in fact, Paine and the radicals in their key focus upon the profound impact of systems of public credit on modern political societies, as I have emphasized. These four, however, contrasted the revolutionary American and revolutionary French use of paper money, which was disastrous, with the greater security of British public credit. 'The consequence of a paper like the French assignats or the American paper, between which there is a great similarity in many points,' Playfair argued, 'is, that it enables the government using it to swindle, (for this is the only applicable term) all those who have consumable property.'[54] Crucially, these

Scottish commentators contended that in the years after the War of Independence Americans such as Alexander Hamilton had learnt the key lessons of their new nation's radical experiment in revolutionary governance and wisely drew back from it in the very period when the French Revolutionaries had launched upon an even more dangerous political, social, and economic path predicated on the complete destruction of all established order and thus the security of property, upon which genuine practical liberty depended. In fact, then, these Scottish defenders of the British system of governance enunciated a crucial differentiation of British institutions and practices from those of the revolutionaries in France and, earlier, the United States. It was, in the opinion of these authors, the very fundamental differences between the nature of the British fiscal-military state and the revolutionary governments in France and America that ensured that Britain could, with prudent management and the preservation of her present order by the defeat of revolutionary radicalism, continue to thrive.[55]

NOTES

1. For historical background see in particular J. Brewer, *The Sinews of Power: War, Money and the English State, 1688–1783* (London: Routledge, 1989) and the seminal work of P.G.M. Dickson, *The Financial Revolution in England: A Study in the Development of Public Credit, 1688–1756* (1967; Aldershot: Ashgate, 1993). A very influential discussion of British state finances in the era of the French Revolutionary and Napoleonic Wars is given in P.K. O'Brien, 'Public Finance in the Wars with France, 1793–1815', in H.T. Dickinson (ed.), *Britain and the French Revolution, 1789–1815* (Basingstoke: Macmillan, 1989), pp. 164–87. The historical impact of the Anglo-British fiscal-military state in the late seventeenth and eighteenth centuries is laid out in N. Ferguson, *The Cash Nexus: Money and Power in the Modern World, 1700–2000* (London: Allen Lane, 2001).
2. P.S. Foner (ed.), *The Complete Writings of Thomas Paine*, 2nd ed., 2 vols. (New York: Citadel Press, 1969), ii, 664. Foner highlights the significance of this pamphlet in his introductory remarks: 'This pamphlet was written in Paris, and completed 8 April 1796. It was published simultaneously in France, England and America, and soon circulated all over Europe. So important did the English government regard the pamphlet, that it commissioned two pamphleteers, Ralph Broome and George Chalmers, to write a reply. The French government ordered 1,000 copies of the pamphlet nineteen days after it was first published', p. 651. Chalmers, whose writings are discussed explicitly in Paine's pamphlet, is a key figure for my discussion in this essay.
3. C. Kidd, *Subverting Scotland's Past: Scottish Whig Historians and the Creation of an Anglo-British Identity, 1689–c.1830* (Cambridge: Cambridge University Press, 1993). An excellent introduction to the intellectual contours of eighteenth-century Scotland, and particularly the major interest in history in the Scottish Enlightenment, is A. Broadie, *The Scottish Enlightenment: The Historical Age of the Historical Nation* (Edinburgh: Birlinn Press, 2001). Also valuable for its discussion of Scottish historiographical traditions is D. Allan, *Virtue, Learning and the Scottish Enlightenment: Ideas of Scholarship in Early Modern Scotland* (Edinburgh: Edinburgh University Press, 1993).
4. See J.C.D. Clark, *English Society, 1660–1832: Religion, Ideology and Politics during the Ancien Regime* (Cambridge: Cambridge University Press, 2000).
5. See 'Iatros' [G.D. Yeats], *A Biographical Sketch of the Life and Writings of Patrick Colquhoun, Esq., LL.D.* (London, 1818).
6. Yeats, *Biographical Sketch*, p. 19.

7. Yeats, *Biographical Sketch*, p. 51.
8. P. Colquhoun, *A Treatise on the Wealth, Power and Resources of the British Empire, in every Quarter of the World, including the East Indies: The Rise and Progress of the Funding System Explained; With Observations on the National Resources for the beneficial Employment of a redundant Population, and for rewarding the Military and Naval Officers, Soldiers, and Seamen for their Services to their Country during the late War. Illustrated by Copious Statistical Tables, constituted on a New Plan, and Exhibiting a collected View of the different subjects discussed in this Work*, 2nd ed. (London, 1815), p. viii.
9. Colquhoun, *Treatise*, p. ix.
10. Colquhoun, *Treatise*, p. vi.
11. Colquhoun, *Treatise*, p. vi.
12. Colquhoun, *Treatise*, p. vii.
13. See Sir John Sinclair, *History of the Public Revenue of the British Empire*, 3rd ed., 3 vols. (1803–4; New York: Augustus M. Kelley, 1966), iii, pp. iv–v.
14. For a modern reprint, see Adam Smith, *An Inquiry into the Nature and Causes of the Wealth of Nations*, 3 vols., ed. W. Playfair (London: Pickering & Chatto, 1995). Smith's original publishers, Cadell and Davies, commissioned Playfair's edition of the *Wealth of Nations*.
15. *The Edinburgh Annual Register for 1823* (Edinburgh and London, 1824), Part iii, p. 332.
16. William Cobbett, *Peter Porcupine in America: Pamphlets on Republicanism and the Revolution*, ed. D.A. Wilson (Ithaca: Cornell University Press, 1994), p. 182.
17. Cobbett appended his own similarly vituperative and strident *History of the American Jacobins, Commonly Denominated Democrats*. He was moved to express his approbation of Playfair's denunciation of French revolutionary radicalism, and his interrelated defence of British governance, in a particularly fulsome 'Dedication': 'I have seldom known a greater pleasure than I now feel, in rendering you my thanks, in this public manner, for your spirited efforts in the cause of order and *true* liberty.' Cobbett, *Peter Porcupine*, p. 184.
18. See J.E. Crowley, *The Privileges of Independence: Neomercantilism and the American Revolution* (Baltimore: Johns Hopkins University Press, 1993), ch. 4.
19. Colquhoun, *Treatise*, p. 129.
20. W. Playfair, *An Inquiry into the Permanent Causes of the Decline and Fall of Powerful and Wealthy Nations, Illustrated by Four Engraved Charts. Designed to Shew how the Prosperity of the British Empire may be Prolonged* (London, 1805), p. 1.
21. Playfair, *Inquiry*, p. 19.
22. Playfair, *Inquiry*, p. 234.
23. Colquhoun, *Treatise*, p. 79.
24. Playfair, *A General View of the Actual Force and Resources of France, in January, MDCCXCIII* (London, 1793), pp. 23–4.
25. Sinclair, *History of the Public Revenue*, iii, 316.
26. Colquhoun, *Treatise*, p. 165.
27. [G. Chalmers], *The Life of Thomas Pain, with a Review of his Writings; Particularly of Rights of Man, Parts First and Second. By Francis Oldys, A.M. of the University of Philadelphia*, 5th ed. (London, 1792), p. 32.
28. Chalmers, *Life of Thomas Pain*, pp. 33–4.
29. A. Young, *The Example of France a Warning to Britain* (London, 1793), pp. 112–13. Young continued: 'I think, *since the events in France*, that it [the US Federal Constitution of 1787] is inferior, for the plain reason of not providing so well against the danger now most to be apprehended, *popular power*.'
30. A very valuable example would be M. Durey, *Transatlantic Radicals and the Early American Republic* (Lawrence, KS: University Press of Kansas, 1997).
31. Chalmers, *Life of Thomas Pain*, p. 49.
32. Playfair, supplementary chapter, in Smith, *Wealth of Nations*, ed. Playfair, iii, 492.
33. Sinclair, *The Speech of the Rt. Hon. Sir John Sinclair, Bart. on the Subject of the Bullion Report, in the House of Commons* (London, 1811), pp. 11–12.
34. Chalmers, *Life of Thomas Pain*, p. 84.
35. Chalmers, *Life of Thomas Pain*, p. 159.
36. See A. Noble and P.S. Hogg (eds), *The Canongate Burns* (Edinburgh: Canongate, 2001),

pp. lviii–lxiv.

37. See M.S. Phillips, *Society and Sentiment: Genres of Historical Writing in Britain, 1740–1820* (Princeton: Princeton University Press, 2000), p. 240n.
38. Colquhoun, *Treatise*, pp. 197–8.
39. See D. Forbes, *Hume's Philosophical Politics* (Cambridge: Cambridge University Press, 1975).
40. Playfair, *Inquiry*, p. 11.
41. Playfair, *Inquiry*, p. 14.
42. For a very interesting discussion of the important debate in the post-revolutionary United States over the evolution of the fiscal-military state, and its desirability or otherwise in early national America, see M.M. Edling, *A Revolution in Favor of Government: Origins of the U.S. Constitution and the Making of the American State* (New York: Oxford University Press, 2003).
43. See I. Kramnick, 'The "Great National Discussion": The Discourse of Politics in 1787', *The William and Mary Quarterly*, 3rd ser., 45/1 (1988), pp. 25–6.
44. W.R. Brock (ed.), *The Federalist* (London: Dent, 2000), p. 162.
45. See J. Robertson, 'Universal Monarchy and the Liberties of Europe: David Hume's Critique of an English Whig Doctrine', in N. Phillipson and Q. Skinner (eds), *Political Discourse in Early Modern Britain* (Cambridge: Cambridge University Press, 1993), esp. pp. 371–3.
46. A point highlighted with characteristic perspicuity by J.G.A. Pocock. See 'Hume and the American Revolution: The Dying Thoughts of a North Briton', in Pocock, *Virtue, Commerce, and History: Essays on Political Thought and History, Chiefly in the Eighteenth Century* (Cambridge: Cambridge University Press, 1985), pp. 139–40: 'It is therefore the more piquant to discover, as a warm admirer of Hume's diagnosis of the American crisis, none other than Dr. Richard Price – dissenting minister, radical Whig, torchbearer of the natural rights of Americans, Englishmen, and Frenchmen, Unitarian millennialist, and future object of the passionate denunciations of Josiah Tucker and Edmund Burke. And what Price most applauded in Hume was the support he could give to the reduction of the whole crisis to the single issue of the National Debt.'
47. G. Chalmers, *An Estimate of the Comparative Strength of Great-Britain, during the Present and Four Preceding Reigns; and of the Losses of her Trade from every War since the Revolution. A New Edition, Corrected, and Improved; with a Dedication to Dr. James Currie, the Reputed Author of 'Jasper Wilson's Letter.'* (1794; New York: Augustus M. Kelley, 1969), p. x (this facsimile reproduces the second and longer of the two editions of the *Estimate* published in 1794).
48. Colquhoun, *Treatise*, p. 287.
49. Colquhoun, *Treatise*, p. 193.
50. Sinclair, *History of the Public Revenue*, ii, Appendix IV, p. 51.
51. Sinclair, *History of the Public Revenue*, ii, Appendix IV, p. 51.
52. Playfair, *Inquiry*, p. 189.
53. [G. Chalmers], *Arrangements with Ireland Considered* (London, 1785), p. 45.
54. Playfair, supplementary chapter, in Smith, *Wealth of Nations*, ed. Playfair, iii, 508.
55. I owe a large debt of gratitude to the Office of Research Affairs at Yonsei University for financial support that has allowed me to participate in several conferences that have helped me to refine my ideas. Additionally, I would like to thank the United Board for Christian Higher Education in Asia for a research grant that allowed me to travel from Korea to Britain. I would like to thank especially Prof. Jack P. Greene and the Seminar in Early American History at Johns Hopkins University for comments on an early version of this chapter. I would like to thank also the Centre for Irish-Scottish Studies at Trinity College Dublin, and Dr Michael Brown in particular, for the opportunity to present on this topic at a colloquium on the 1790s. I am grateful also to Dr Andrew Noble for inviting me to develop my ideas in a lecture at the Institute for Advanced Studies in the Humanities at Edinburgh University and a seminar paper at Strathclyde University and to Dr Max Edling for inviting me to speak on this subject at a Swedish Historical Association meeting at the University of Uppsala. I would like to thank also Prof. John Marshall, Prof. John Pocock, and Prof. Colin Kidd for their helpful comments. Thanks also to Dr Matt Lauzon and Dr Craig Yirush for their generous support and enlightening conversations.

II: Change & Exchange in the British Empire

CHAPTER FIVE

Money and Empire: The Failure of the Royal African Company

ROBIN HERMANN

In September 1682, Andrew Crosbie, one of the factors (or local agents) of the Royal African Company of England, wrote from West Africa to his employers in London to explain why a predecessor of his would not be returning home as they had requested. 'Mr John Winder, your honours chiefe factor for this coast,' he explained, was 'panyard by the Blacks',[1] that is, held as security by a local African authority due to his failure to pay for 15 slaves.[2] In the long history of the slave trade, the fate of John Winder – and others like him who were similarly taken[3] – represents a profound reversal of the usual direction of the trade itself. Instead of Europeans buying Africans from other Africans, here we have Africans taking possession of one European and treating his body as a literal security for the debt that he owed and had accrued in the course of conducting business for the Company.

Winder's desperate straits are an emblem of the aspirations and ultimate failure of the Royal African Company itself. On the one hand, the Company for a time provided the frame for the triangular trade joining together London, the West African coast, and the plantations of colonial America and the Caribbean. The Company helped to create the early modern Atlantic world. On the other, the relationship within that world between the Company's economic need and the English Crown's political desires destroyed the Company. Chartered as a royal monopoly in 1672 to supply slaves to colonial planters, enrich the Crown and the mother country through the importation of African gold, and to maintain England's strategic interests on the West African coast, the Company for eighty years was caught between the hammer of a chronic shortage of currency and the anvil of the Crown's imperial vision. In pursuit of those objectives, the Company's factors were forced to offer up not only the essentials of that business but eventually themselves as media of exchange. The Company's need to serve the two masters of money and empire within the Atlantic world it had helped to create gave birth to a fatal contradiction that it could not resolve.

While my two chief sources for this analysis – the correspondence of the Company and *The Trans-Atlantic Slave Trade: A Database on CD-Rom*[4] – have been most obviously and most importantly used to chart the extent of human suffering and greed, they also throw light on questions of economic history largely unasked by historians of the slave trade. Most particularly, they illuminate for economic historians the complex trade flows of England's newly demarcated Atlantic world, and how the expanding economy of that world imposed terminal constraints on British merchants. The same records simultaneously illustrate the limited reach of the British Empire in the early modern period, and suggest – for the Company at least – that the two questions of money and empire are inextricable.

Although economic historians have often seen early modern Europe as a specially advantaged unit on the cusp of global economic domination, recent scholarship insists that domination was a modern event.[5] An examination of the spectacular failure of the Company reinforces that claim, for it suggests that late seventeenth and early eighteenth-century West Africans dealt with all Europeans with whom they did business from a position of strength, and not simply because they had military parity with Europeans or that the Europeans were prevented by hostile terrain and the threat of disease from conducting slave raids of their own. The Company began operating in West Africa with the deck stacked against it. Its factors' status as aliens in the West African cultures they traded with often forced them to use economic and social middlemen and interlocutors such as the Afro-Portuguese as cross-cultural brokers – although the rates their benefactors charged steadily eroded the Company's profits.[6] Its predecessors had fortified positions off of the Slave Coast[7] and in the Gambia River, which gave somewhat easier access to slaving states, but not to the gold of the Gold Coast[8] the Portuguese had already monopolized. Disease and destitution among the English in Africa lent employment in West Africa a grave reputation, and limited the Company to hiring men of poor quality and bad faith.[9] And although the Company's factors and servants in Africa did the directors and stockholders in London no favours – by embezzling

Company goods, trading outside the monopoly with interlopers, and generally neglecting the corporate interest – its goals created a fatal contradiction within the North Atlantic world system. As a trading firm, the Company had dispatched its ships and servants to West Africa for two reasons: to secure gold for the Company's use in the mother country, and to buy slaves for the American and Caribbean colonists. Both transactions, however – even when they could be undertaken, which was not always the case – carried inherent costs that steadily worsened the Company's situation each time its factors bought gold or slaves.

The high cost of gold on the African coast made buying it often prohibitively expensive for the cash-strapped Company, but to use it as a currency only made matters worse – not to mention that doing so was explicitly prohibited by the terms of its charter. West African rulers sought gold for slaves and used that gold to represent their authority through display, but also to cement it by paying mercenaries and for other military costs.[10] And what the African rulers and states gained in economic and political strength, the Company lost in access to gold and slaves. Even the Company's factors disobeyed orders and used gold to meet their slave quota; in turn, that gold gave Africans who did business with these factors capital to further dominate the area and the trade. The increased power of such states then allowed them to shut the Company out of the trade – or at the very least to set the terms to their best advantage – by insisting on gold for tribute costs or by using their new military strength. European demand for slaves encouraged restructuring of African states, requiring that they become more efficient and powerful slavers to stay in business.[11] But this position was a double-edged sword for the Royal African Company, as it decreased its strength relative to these newly powerful states and made its employees more vulnerable – for example, to the kind of imprisonment John Winder endured. Thus, to achieve its economic goals, the Company weakened itself as a political agent. And although it was that weakness that determined the failure of the firm in all of its goals, it is in the matter of money that the consequences of its failure become most clear. By examining the Company's monetary problems, we can appreciate how early modern Britain's imperial vision foundered. It was not the weakness of the Company that caused the failure of this imperial dream. Instead it was that dream that caused the Company itself to fail.

I

Chartered as a royal monopoly in 1672 to supply slaves to the colonial planters, enrich the mother country through regular importation of bullion, and maintain England's strategic interests on the West African coast, the Company earned consistent profits in its first decade of operation. But it found itself after the Revolution of 1688 unable to meet the costs of the various demands placed upon it.[12] After a bitter debate in 1709 over the worth of the Company's monopoly, the Crown reconstituted the Company as an overseer of the African trade, while allowing private traders into the markets in return for an *ad valorem* duty of 10 per cent. The Company struggled on in this curious limbo between pure monopoly and perfect competition, but in vain, as even sustained government loans failed to arrest its decline. Exactly eighty years after its incorporation, the Crown dissolved the Company and paid its shareholders about £25,000 in reparation.[13]

This limp record appears particularly dismal when compared with that of the East India Company during this period. Both companies functioned as imperial agents under Charles II and successive governments. Authorized to export munitions and erect fortifications, both companies were further empowered to make war or peace with 'non-Christian princes or people' in order to facilitate trade.[14] But where the Royal African Company had to solicit costly loans from the government near the end of its life, at roughly the same time the government found itself having to borrow from the East India Company.[15] Both chartered companies laboured under costs that had little to do with business and everything to do with the Crown's imperial vision and the pressing need to maintain political capital in the metropolis. To understand why the Royal African Company failed where the EIC succeeded is to comprehend the intricate relationships of money, politics, and commerce in London and on the West African coast.

For all the advances made in late seventeenth-century England during the 'financial revolution', English merchants overseas remained consistently dependent on specie. Bank-notes and stock certificates only work as currency instruments if the society in which they are used has developed the institutions necessary to accept them. The absence of such institutions forced English merchants in India and West Africa to traffic in gold instead of the credit instruments that their counterparts trading in Europe found so convenient. For the EIC, securing the specie necessary to conduct business proved relatively easy. Investor confidence in their profitable cargoes ran high, and this in turn influenced both Cromwell and Charles II to sanction the Company's export of fantastic quantities of bullion. The 1661 charter, for example, set the limit at £50 million.[16] To the Restoration elite and its economists, the luxury goods the EIC brought home more than outweighed this violation of mercantilist principles. But the directors of the Royal African Company found it difficult if not hopeless to compete for access to English specie. Where the permission to export bullion had been embedded in the charter of the EIC, the Crown instead assigned the Royal African Company the task of *importing* gold and silver from the fabled African mines as part of their commerce in slaves on the coast.[17] Moreover, the structure of the Atlantic trade itself meant that the directors could not drum up or attract anywhere near the same level of investor confidence that the EIC enjoyed. The Atlantic trade appeared far too complex and too risky. The Indian trade, by contrast, was relatively simple: EIC ships sailed around the Cape of Good Hope to the Indian Ocean, bought goods from the Company factories there, and returned home laden with diversified, exotic cargoes. The Atlantic trade, however, entailed not only a higher risk, since with three legs of ocean crossings the potential for disaster remained higher, but offered a lower return as well. The political and economic constraints of the trade thus left the Company with a chronic shortage of operating cash. That deficiency caused the monopoly to fail.

While it is easy enough to show the Company's difficulties in making its enterprise turn a profit,[18] few scholars have considered the Company's economics in the context of a world system and asked whether there were difficulties inherent in the Company's approach to the Atlantic world.[19] The Royal African Company's monopoly arose from political maneuvers rather than market dominance. The theory of monopoly holds that such an artificial monopoly will quickly fall prey to outside competition, because it achieved its status through political control rather than control of the market. As we will see, in the case of the Company this theory obtained, as the Company's political costs proved fatal to its economic health. For the Company, money and empire worked at cross-purposes within the Atlantic world: to pursue one was actively to deny the possibility of maximizing the other. By examining the Company's problems in the context of the Atlantic world, we can better understand how that world operated and the failure of the Company.

II

Modern economists find it easy to define money. They make ready distinctions between commodity and fiat money, and assume that all economies progress naturally from the first system to the second.[20] In that shift, the general welfare rises while the efficiency improves. What this theory fails to represent, however, is the moment of transition between the two monetary systems and that living through such a moment could be stressful. The period of English history in which the Royal African Company began its operations is one such moment. The career of the firm during the late seventeenth and early eighteenth centuries coincided with the long cultural and economic process in which the English, through innovations in borrowing and the use of paper money, overcame the limitations of commodity money without completely abandoning it.[21] In that transition, participants in the fledgling economy of paper still operated on the mercantilist principle that large reserves of gold and silver were required to ensure economic security and prosperity, both at home and abroad.

Moreover, the emerging credit economy helped to encourage dependence on the commodity currency the new world of money was supposedly leaving behind. Expansions in any credit supply had to be matched by proportional expansion in the *specie* supply in order to support credit. And while the Financial Revolution made war and trade possible on a scale never before ventured, fluid credit left the English nostalgic for the old world of fixed values embodied by coin.[22] That nostalgia increased the export price of gold still further, which helped to create a fatal contradiction for the Company, whose directors were able to fund the firm with paper credit, but were unable to provide their factors and servants with the necessary specie to do business in the North Atlantic world.

On the one hand, then, the new systems of lending and financing made it easier for the Company to begin and continue its operations at home and in America, where its debts and bills of exchange were honoured.[23] On the other, it provided them with little in the way of ready currency with which to deal on the West African coast. Throughout the latter half of the seventeenth century gold and silver were, despite the advances of the so-called 'financial revolution', still valuable – and sometimes value-added – commodities at home, and thus their export price was prohibitively high. As such, the Company's imports of African gold were welcome to the Crown and

English money market, and had that been the extent of the firm's trading it would have had little difficulty in turning a profit. But their political obligations to the American planters required the Company to take part in the slave trade, in which the gold it imported to London would have served it far better on the African coast. Because its slaves went to the Caribbean, and the American sugar it imported could not compete with the fantastic range of goods the East India Company brought home, the RAC remained a weak player in London politics. As such, it could only look helplessly on as the EIC exported bullion to India with the government's blessing to bring back the exotic commodities so prized by London consumers. Bullion was crucial to the lubrication of the trade in the Indian Ocean, and ready supplies of it helped the East India Company to compete in, and eventually dominate, those markets.[24] The RAC's commodities were not so prized, leaving it exposed to a balance-of-payments dilemma. In England, currency was moving away from commodity money and towards a fiat system, while in America, slaves were paid for in kind, in various European coinages, or in paper, none of which was unfamiliar to the Company.[25] But in West Africa a bewildering array of competing local currencies confronted the Company.[26] The 'financial revolution' may have made King William's War possible, but it did very little for Royal African Company agents on the Gambia where bills of exchange and notes from the Bank of England had no meaning.

Instead, the commodities that had value on the West African coast became both a medium of exchange and a measure of value for European and African traders alike. Gold may have been the most prized commodity on the coast, but it was far from the only one. Any commodity that had value – from cloth to iron bars to cowrie shells – could become currency, a fact that gave Company factors hope until they realized that their suppliers of goods from England and other points in the trading network could not keep up with the fluctuations in local African markets. As months elapsed between a factor's letter explaining what he required and the arrival of those goods, the factor was often left with goods that had little value and could not be used as money. And the chimera of gold mines to match those of South America turned out to be one of the great lies of early modern European ventures into Africa. Though Europeans hunted for one, no African Potosi existed.[27] This is not to say that no gold existed on the West Africa coast, but that for a number of reasons the Company could not use it to pay for slaves. This deficiency did not do mortal damage to the RAC in the late seventeenth century, when its textiles and other trade goods could compete as currencies with gold, but when local sources of gold began drying up in the early eighteenth century, its scarcity drove up the price it could command.[28] And by the time the English came to West Africa with the intent to trade, the Portuguese had already been there for over a century, having built a trade castle on the Gold Coast in 1480 and had also begun to intermarry into the existing Akan community.[29] In the late seventeenth century, then, the Afro-Portuguese of the Gold Coast were well placed to act as cross-cultural brokers, giving the European Portuguese a natural advantage over the English in the gold trade. Moreover, the Portuguese trading for gold were not prohibited, as the RAC was, from using that gold again to pay for slaves; the Company's charter, by contrast, bound the firm to import that gold home to London to alleviate England's chronic currency shortage. From 1672 to 1713 the Royal Mint coined 548,327 guineas from the Company's gold,[30] which, depending on the guinea's current value, amounted to at least £575,743 and at most £603,159 – not an inconsiderable sum if the total circulating medium in England has been estimated at between £14.5 and £20 million in 1700.[31] While that total does not account for all of the gold bought by the Company in West Africa – as some of its factors disobeyed orders and paid for slaves and corn with gold when they lacked valuable trade goods[32] – it does account for *most* of it, since if the Company had been free to spend the gold it bought, as the Portuguese and the English interlopers were, its business in Africa would have been much easier. As it was, however, the monetary needs of the home country trumped the firm's commercial desires, as the political nature of the firm's monopoly allowed the English government to dictate the nature of its economic goals.

III

In the correspondence of the Royal African Company in Africa, the want of goods – most notably cowries and gold – for use as a medium of exchange is one of the chief problems cited by the agents of the Company.[33] Their problem lay not so much in the lack of capital to buy trade goods, but rather in their inability to provide an attractive range of valuable goods – particularly since they had difficulty, given the West African climate, finding a market for English woollens, one of their chief exports.[34] European and African traders on the coast practised what Philip Curtin refers to as 'assortment bargaining', in which each trader brought a different assortment of goods to be traded, and attempted to maximize the number of cheap goods in the mix while keeping the number of truly valuable goods as low as possible.[35] On the ground in Africa this meant that the Company's agent had to keep track of a dizzying array of 'vendable' commodities and those 'that will not readyly vend'.[36] The former were not always, and indeed, very rarely, in ready supply from the Company's factories or the canoes sent down the coast. The sole exception to these rules of supply and demand was, of course, money. In all of the correspondence of the Company there is never any hint that cowries or gold are in danger of falling from favour in the market.[37]

Unable to use their specie on the African coast, and – particularly in the eighteenth century – faced with mounting difficulties of vending their trade goods as they steadily lost value in local markets, Company factors had two options to pay for slaves and their several operating costs: use the local currency of cowries, or resort to unreliable media of exchange. As we will see below, the second choice carried with it several disastrous consequences, but even to acquire enough cowries to do business and maintain the forts was no simple matter. John Thorne, the Company's factor at Offra[38] in the early 1680s, pointed to the difficulties the currency-poor English faced on the African coast. On 19 August 1681 Thorne made clear the importance of money as he requested his superiors to 'send some Booges [i.e., cowries] by your next Shipping and they will put off any goods you shall send downe besides, [since] without them you must expect little to be done, for tis all one their money here, as silver and gold is with us'.[39] A second letter, in December, reiterated the near-constant clamouring of the factors on the coast for 'booges', but also reminded his superiors of the consequences of that shortage:

> I would desire your worship to send booges down by the first opportunity for I have none for my present use but am forct to borrow of the blacks, and they will not lend above 50 lbs of booges for a slave and att the arrival of a ship will have 78 lbs for them, for I have not any goods that I can put off for booges but to great loss.[40]

Here we see part of the complexity of the economy of the slave trade in West Africa, as well as the interaction of the different value systems of Europeans and Africans on the coast. Thorne does not tell his superiors what goods he then had, but they must have been worth more to him – if not to the Africans – than the cowries, if he could not part with them. Moreover, Thorne's principal dilemma – that the Africans will only lend him fifty pounds of cowries for slaves but demand seventy-eight pounds when ships arrive to purchase them – illustrates a sophisticated and robust money market. Slaves, like gold and cowries, are not only commodities, but also currency, and a money of account, that can command fifty pounds of cowries when business was slow but worth a great deal more when competition became fierce, requiring the African slavers to respond in kind by dramatically marking up the price. As difficult as Thorne's situation appeared in December, by March it had worsened still further. Ordered by the Company to depart for England,[41] he wrote back to say

> I would most willingly have compplied therewith could those persons you have sent down discharged the debts I have bin forc't to contract with the blacks, for want of booges or other goods to maintaine the factory, but till that is complied with they will not lett me goe.[42]

Thorne then goes on to detail what he had been obliged to borrow money from the Africans for. Among the expected necessities such as cowries and slaves there are some surprises, such as a 'flag and staff' for the fort, which Thorne eventually paid for with two slaves. He promised to obey the order to leave the country 'as soone as possible . . . [but it] cannot be until the ballance of my account is sent downe which I owe to the Blacks of this towne, having borrowed it out of necessity'.[43] Andrew Crosbie's letter detailing the circumstances of John Winder's being 'panyard', cited above, dramatized the very real and sometimes catastrophic dangers of trying to escape African credit networks. But flags and factors were not the only risks facing the Company when taking loans from the Africans. John Carter, who was usually more vocal and melodramatic about his difficulties than the other factors recorded in the correspondence, wrote a terse, four-sentence letter to his superiors from Whydah[44] on 9 January 1686, which ended with his 'Hopes not to [have to] Pawn the Factory' in order to obtain goods on credit.[45] Under the pressures of the currency shortage, the RAC factors were forced to offer up not only their factories but also themselves as a medium of exchange in the place of cowries and gold.

The myth of African gold mines was, of course, the bait that drew the English into Africa in the first place, but once there the RAC factors had a rude awakening. Much of the gold in the West African slave trade was imported by the Portuguese rather than produced locally. In the early eighteenth century, after the decline of the gold trade on the Gold Coast, the Portuguese imported gold from newly discovered deposits in South America to the slave-trading areas of West Africa where its scarcity and appeal made it more valuable than the Company's textiles or imported cowries. This steady access of the Portuguese to Brazilian gold and their consequent trading advantage in Africa is a consistent feature of the RAC factors' correspondence. The complaints surged in the 1720s, after the Company had lost its legal monopoly and was annually failing to make a profit.[46]

The basis for these complaints of Portuguese superiority in the slave trade is made clear by a series of letters from Whydah in 1727 and 1728. Abraham Duport, the factor of William's Fort, reported the price of slaves in December 1727 in gold, instead of in cowries as his seventeenth-century predecessor John Thorne had. And, as he wrote, he expected 'severall more Portugueeze Vessells . . . so [that] in all probability [the price of] slaves may rise and Gold be more plenty, for the ships that are here brought very little with them'.[47] Here we see how much the lack of the current medium of exchange paralyzed the Company's factors. Duport can only have been looking forward to the arrival of the Portuguese and their gold if he had a way to buy some of it for himself, and on the African coast the primary currency that interested the Portuguese was slaves.[48] Whether that gold was then taken back to England or used in Africa to lubricate trade there is unknown, but the paradox of the RAC's situation is clear enough: lacking a viable currency in the African markets, they were forced to sell their primary commodity simply to stay in business. Portuguese gold undercut English attempts to secure their own slaves for the American market, as is evident in the new taxonomy of slaves the gold created: because of the demand for their gold in West Africa, the Portuguese could set prices, and insist on the highest quality slaves, usually young males.[49] The English then referred to these slaves as 'Portugeeze' or 'gold' slaves, as their quality and method of purchase set them apart from the lower-quality slaves that other traders bought through assortment bargaining at higher prices.[50] What makes this new practice all the more interesting is the fact, as David Eltis notes, that while the market had accepted this new taxonomy, slave buyers had discontinued the older method of using ethnically-based 'guardians' to maintain order on slave ships.[51] Instead of ethnicity, then, what appears to have determined rank among slaves following the 1720s was the medium with which they were bought – and what quality that medium connoted.

The ability of the Portuguese to import prodigious amounts of gold to West Africa did more than restrict and limit the purchasing power of the cash-strapped English. It heightened African demand for gold while proportionally reducing the inclination of Africans to accept any other currency commodity besides gold. The increasing availability of gold reshaped the money market in West Africa, as indigenous rulers hoarded gold for display and military might. These rulers thus drove up the market price for gold by effectively removing the opportunities for consumption of the gold that they hoarded for themselves. Since they needed it for non-market purposes they refused to sell it, which created the seemingly paradoxical situation in which the greater supply of gold increased its price. Moreover, the primacy of gold as a medium was increased by political change. The RAC factors wrote home to lament the Dahomian conquest[52] of Whydah in 1727 since

> while they [the Dahomians] have the trade of this Country the Gold Trade is Ruin'd, for whereas the Whydahs delighted in nothing but fine Cloaths and Warehouses full of Cowries and other goods, these cun[n]ing people delights [*sic*] in nothing but gold . . . .[53]

The Dahomians then brought the RAC's commerce to a grinding halt by refusing to do business in any other medium of exchange but gold. The English interlopers – inspired to enter the market in the eighteenth century by Philip V's concession of the *asiento* to the English in the Treaty of Utrecht[54] – were able to respond to this demand due to their piracy of the gold markets on the Gold Coast and their freedom to use it as a currency in Africa.[55] The king of Dahomey also spoiled English chances of getting their hands on any gold by

> pick[ing] the best [slaves] out and send[ing] them to Ardah, which is within less than a Days journie of this Place [i.e., William's Fort, Whydah], and there sends for the Portugeeze Captains and sells all the fine slaves for Gold to them himself and what they won't buy for Gold those he sends down here to dispose of for Goods, by which means he engrosses all the Gold

> into his own hands, so that for as fine Cargoes Captains Hill and Hurst has here they both declare, not to have taken 40 oz. Gold since they have been here, tho' there is perhaps as much Gold in Whydah Road now as there has been for these Severall Years past and the French are so covetous of it that they sell Six Grand Cabess Cowries for 1 oz. Gold and can't Purchase it....[56]

Once the Portuguese and the Dahomians had monopolized the gold trade, control over much of the slave trade naturally shifted to them as well:

> its almost Incredible to Believe the same time they [the Dahomians] traded here what vast Quantitys of gold the[y] picked up amongst the portugueeze for their [*sic*] was neither English nor french could purchase a gold Slave whilst they [the Dahomians] were here for they always picked out those Choice Slaves for them [the Portuguese] and sold the rest to the English & French....[57]

Lack of gold and cowries blighted the Company's factors' attempts to trade. Portuguese competition, and the enforced reliance of the Company on commodity money, pushed factors into desperate measures, all of which revolved around their need to acquire a medium of exchange. Economic historians can appreciate the irony of John Thorne's having to sell slaves for gold. Yet what remains the most pathetic consequence of the Company's chronic and terminal lack of currency on the African coast is the instruction sent to a new agent to find some way to cancel a deceased predecessor's debts, since 'what small matter of Wearing Apparel found on his Death will not sell'.[58]

Before we leave this stage of the RAC's Atlantic trade there remains the problem of their monopoly to consider. The requirements placed by the English Crown on the Company in Africa in return for its monopoly in America effectively worked, because of their endemic lack of currency, to negate any benefits the Company might have expected to enjoy from that monopoly. Charles II granted the Company the right to exclusive trade in gold and slaves in Africa and the West Indies, but in return required it to establish a military as well as an economic presence there.[59] In practice this meant the Company had to establish forts, arm their trading vessels, and in general act as a political as well as a commercial agent. The inherent volatility and danger of the slave trade – a tendency the gold trade did not share – made this appear somewhat reasonable, and indeed, guns and gunpowder were twice as important for slaving ships to have as they were for their counterparts trading in gold.[60] The pirating interlopers may have similarly had to arm their ships but as they did not operate on the scale of the Company their costs were proportionally smaller. While various agents did maintain the forts established by the Company well into the nineteenth century, the economic consequences of these investments were drastic. For the Company, the forts, the gunpowder, and the corn and other foodstuffs required to feed the factors and their servants, were all fixed costs that counted against profits. The forts failed to dissuade Portuguese competition, and the guns of the Company did not prevent English 'interlopers' from breaking the Company's monopoly.[61] The interlopers operated as individual firms who bore little or none of the fixed costs of the Company, and were therefore free to enter the market, buy freely with gold, and exit before incurring any of the costs the Company paid to remain on the coast.

The correspondence of the factors provides ample evidence of the burdens for the Company of the Crown's imperial vision on the African coast. In the largest volume of extant Company correspondence there are over a hundred letters concerning the trade for corn alone. Moreover, the dearth of gunpowder and coin in the Company's factories illustrates how the dual problems of money and empire converged. On 23 October 1728, Duport complained to the Company that

> I am in prodigious want of Gun Powder and Provisions and desire you'l please supply me if possible you can for I'm fully resolved to Blow up the Fort before I'll go prisoner a Second Time to Ardah.[62]

'Powder and Provisions' to supply the fort were one of the requirements of the Company's charter, and the need to maintain these lessened Duport's effectiveness as a commercial agent on the coast. His claim that 'Powder [and] Cowries . . . will be a Commodity' illuminates the constraints that the demands of empire and the problems of money imposed, since gunpowder was indeed at times a vendible commodity on the African coast. Yet, as Duport's letter explains, without ammunition for their forts the Company could not fulfill its political requirements to the Crown. But lacking a viable currency the Company's factors could neither pay for his basic operational expenses, nor do business effectively with the Africans. Duport was thus left with the choice of using the gunpowder as a currency commodity to stay in business, or of maintaining the forts of the Company – he does not seem to have been able to do both. John Winder's situation was still worse: one of John Thorne's replacements, he reported that the 'condition of the Royall Companys affaires are at present upon this Coast... for want of goods... soe bad, that I know not how to maintain myselfe, and the *Rest of the Royall Company's Servants*, finding noe goods in the possession of Mr Wendover....'[63] But for Winder, this was only the beginning: although we have no records that John Thorne was 'panyard' – as John Winder would later be – Thorne had, of necessity, become enmeshed in African credit, and

> Express'd much willingness to be discharged and told me he would goe off... provided I could pay those Blacks those booges he [Thorne] had been forct to borrow off them *for maintenance of the ffactory, and himselfe his sallary*, otherwise he could not gett away, the blacks being resolved to be satisfied before his departure....[64]

Here, the price of the Company's monopoly becomes clear: forced to pay for forts, guns, ammunition, and servants to maintain it all,[65] the Company's factors lacked the cash to meet the rising costs of the Company's operation, let alone to conduct trade. Josiah Pearson's 24 November 1694 letter illustrates this untenable dynamic: commenting on the state of the slave trade he claimed that 'although Slaves are very plenty in these parts... I purchase onely some four Slaves to dispose to ships that come hear [*sic*] for Bugees to defray Factory Charges for without Bouges in these parts there is noe Liveing for a whiteman'.[66] Like Duport, Pearson was forced to sell the Company's primary commodity to acquire a medium of exchange. But Pearson's transaction was still more desperate, since cowries, much like wampum outside of North America, had no value outside Africa, while gold at least could be imported back to the mother country. The duties assigned by the Crown and the need to face down 'interlopers' made what little money the Company did have work much harder than the money of other English traders or the Portuguese.

To acquire even a small number of slaves for export to the Americas on the African coast required of the Company a remarkable expenditure of time and resources, and such efforts left them helpless against competitors. The Portuguese maintained a military presence on the Slave and Gold coasts akin to that of the English, but their ability to pay with both African and American gold ameliorated the burden of those costs. Similarly, what currency the English interlopers did have could be freely spent on slaves; unlike the Portuguese, their investment in the infrastructure of the trade was lower as well, since they operated fewer ships, and for fear of capture and prosecution they did not linger on the African coast, incurring none of the costs of maintenance that so bedevilled the Company. The Company could do nothing to lower its fixed costs, mandated as these were by their charter, but it could lower its variable costs by buying and shipping fewer slaves. Such reduction fits the standard definition of a monopolist's behaviour. The Company steadily reduced deliveries of slaves from 1673 to 1711.[67] For each rough decennial period, while the aggregate number of slaves imported to the West Indies fell, the prices of slaves in Barbados and Jamaica rose. This was the only way for the Company monopoly to turn a profit.[68] If the Company had operated only in the domain of economic theory, all would have been well. It could have reduced the input costs of its production while artificially increasing demand for its products. But its charter, which granted exclusive rights to sell its slaves in America, proved to be the Company's undoing.

IV

Although the Company's directors hoped that the constant demand for slaves in the Caribbean would help them recoup the many and varied losses the Company suffered in West Africa, monetary problems plagued them in this stage of the Atlantic world as well. Once the African coast had dropped off the horizon, the masters of the Company's slave ships understood that, for them, the most dangerous third of their voyage was now behind them.[69] Potential danger still lay ahead in the journey to America and return to Britain, but they had survived the inhospitable and disease-ridden 'white man's grave',[70] and were assured of high demand for the goods in their holds, a welcome reversal from the struggles they had had to endure to gain some purchase in the West African trade. But the West Indies proved far less generous than traders sometimes dreamed. Here, too, the Company felt the bite of the chronic absence of money in their corner of the Atlantic world. While slaves *could* be paid for in credit, kind, or in coin, the colonies, as relatively new enterprises, had little in the way of minted currency to use in these exchanges.[71] Sugar planters had the choice to pay in kind, but as the Company's ships usually arrived either before or too long after the harvesting of the crop, traders could not easily exercise that option. That left credit as the ubiquitous medium of exchange for this leg of the trade, and the bane of the Company. Throughout the Company's eighty-year existence, planters in the Caribbean and Virginia remained in debt to the Company's American factors. Since the legal machinery of debt recovery in the late seventeenth and early eighteenth centuries was never on the side of the creditor,[72] the Company could not extract payment for its slaves but, legally bound by its charter to sell its cargo to the Crown's American subjects, had few other options than to continue selling them.[73]

But if the Company could not secure payment for the slaves it had already sold, it could, as a true monopoly, reduce the number of slaves it sold to the planters and by so doing reduce its debt. In 1689, the directors wrote to the agents at Jamaica to inform them that the number of slaves coming in would soon fall:

> The patiance we must exercise must exceed our reason to followe such a trade; & it seemes we have not yett given soe much creditt as your island requires, notwithstanding our capitall stock is nere all amongst you, & we cannot see a likelyhood of saveing our stocke from ruine *better than by slackeing our future supplyes*.[74]

Here we begin to see how the problems of money and monopoly converged to ruin the Company in America, just as they had in Africa. The difficulty of purchasing slaves in Africa led the Company eventually to use its legal monopoly to act as an economic monopolist in the American leg of the slave trade. The difficulty of securing payment for those slaves it did carry only served to strengthen that inclination. And yet because the Company's monopoly was political in origin and did not derive from its control of the market, the planters, unsatisfied with the low number of imported slaves, had several non-economic means to challenge and eventually dissolve the charter.[75] Money, or more accurately, the lack of it, created a set of problems for the Company both in Africa and America that it attempted to solve through a manipulation of its power as a monopoly. The tension that process created between the Company's legal and economic monopolies brought it down.

V

A Company ship began any voyage in London, where domestic agents used the credit and capital of the Company to stock the ship with English and Indian textiles as well as assorted other trade goods they thought would buy slaves on the West African coast. Because of the limitations of Britain's own money economy during the late seventeenth and early eighteenth centuries, the Crown's charter for the Company prohibited the exportation of gold for use in Africa, and as a result, the RAC found itself by the end of the seventeenth century unable to compete effectively with the Portuguese, or even with English interlopers. The Company's African factors found themselves crippled by the lack of an effective medium of exchange. Without gold or cowries it was close to impossible to pay the various operating costs, much less purchase enough slaves to stay in business. Once the Company's slaves finally made it to America, further complications awaited. With no shared currency to pay for the slaves, and the sugar crop still waiting to be harvested, planters had little choice but to go in debt to the Company's American factors. When the Company's ship returned to London, with little to show for its journey but a record of steadily increasing debt, the Company had nothing with which to purchase its next round of trade goods for Africa but its remaining capital stock. As this pattern repeated itself, the Company lost money rapidly.

The absence of money in the Company's transactions at one point in this system created almost insurmountable problems for it down the line. The inability of the Company's factors to use gold to buy slaves on the African coast, particularly in the early eighteenth century, prevented them from delivering the number of slaves the American and Caribbean planters – with their crucial political connections in London – required. Moreover the return of the Company's ships from America with debt and sugar – quickly declining in value in a glutted market[76] – rather than cash meant that the Company's directors could not then appeal to a government already displeased with the firm for its failure to satisfy the planters to allow the Company to export bullion to, rather than import it from, Africa on the strength of goods it was bringing in from the West Indies. The burdens of this triangular trade left the firm with nothing attractive to take on to West Africa. And the debt which the planters contracted for the slaves did the Company little good in London. The American factors might one day extract payment for the loan, but without hard cash, the Company had no choice but to undertake the voyage again and to become further enmeshed in a trans-oceanic cycle of credit and mortal debt.

The Company's specie shortage arose at least in part from the political burdens of its economic monopoly. The Company's charter, which had on paper granted it absolute dominance among English merchants in the trade of the emergent Atlantic world, proved a millstone for its factors and captains. Had the Crown either understood the currency contours of the African coast and allowed the Company to import specie, or freed the firm from the costs of its imperial vision, the Company's situation would have improved. It is that fact which is most instructive about the Company's ultimate failure. Every student knows that imperialism began when trade followed the flag into Asia and Africa, but the history of the Company forces us to rethink that formulation. In the government's imperial vision, the Company was primarily a political actor with economic functions, whereas the Company saw itself as an economic unit created through political ends. The refusal of the government to allow the Company to act in its economic interests, which ran counter to the imperial goals of the government, caused the company to collapse. By following the money, we learn that in this case, the schoolboys got it wrong: it was instead the *failure* of trade that followed the flag.

NOTES

1. 'Panyar' is an Anglicization of the Portuguese 'penhorar' (lit. 'distrain') and refers throughout the correspondence of the Royal African Company to the seizure, either of goods or persons, for security to enforce payment. See Robin Law (ed.), *The English in West Africa, 1681–1683: The Local Correspondence of the Royal African Company of England, 1681–1699, Part 1* (Oxford: Oxford University Press, 1997), p. xvii. Wilder's creditor, 'Captain Beebe', was a 'local authority'. Law's edition of *Further Correspondence* contains a note stating that 'From his prominence in dealings with the Europeans, this man [Captain Bibe or Prince Bibe or Captain Biby] may have been the Yevogan, or "Captain of the White Men"' (p. 77n102). There is some account of this indigenous title and office in Law, *The Slave Coast of West Africa, 1550–1750* (Oxford, 1991), pp. 206–7.
2. *The English in West Africa, 1681–1683*, p. 237. Crosbie's litany of Winder's offenses against the Africans which resulted in his being 'panyard' begins with Winder's 'not well considering the interest of your Honors in studying and consulting the humours and dispositions of these people, whoe will neither be slighted by a high and lofty carriage or abused by bad language. . . . ' (p. 238).
3. D. Eltis, *The Rise of African Slavery in the Americas* (Cambridge: Cambridge University Press, 2000), pp. 155, 188.
4. D. Eltis, S.D. Behrendt, D. Richardson, and H.S. Klein (eds), *The Trans-Atlantic Slave Trade: A Database on CD-Rom* (Cambridge: Cambridge University Press, 1999).

5. K. Pomeranz, 'Political Economy and Ecology on the Eve of Industrialization: Europe, China, and the Global Conjuncture', *The American Historical Review*, 107/2 (2002), pp. 425–46; and R. Bin Wong, 'The Search for European Differences and Domination in the Early Modern World: A View from Asia', *The American Historical Review*, 107/2 (2002), pp. 447–69.
6. K.G. Davies, *The North Atlantic World in the Seventeenth Century* (Minneapolis: University of Minnesota Press, 1974), p. 252; P.D. Curtin, *Economic Change in Precolonial Africa: Senegambia in the Era of the Slave Trade* (Madison: University of Wisconsin Press, 1975), pp. 92–100. On the need for and function of cross-cultural brokers generally see P.D. Curtin, *Cross-Cultural Trade in World History* (Cambridge: Cambridge University Press, 1984), pp. 1–14.
7. In the seventeenth century the Slave Coast referred to the section of the Gulf of Guinea coast of West Africa lying between the mouth of the Niger River on the east and the mouth of the Volta River on the West. The correspondence of the Company analyzed here comes from its employees situated on the Slave Coast.
8. The Gold Coast lay just to the west of the Slave Coast; the coastal areas of present-day Ghana make up much of the historical Gold Coast area.
9. Davies, *North Atlantic World*, p. 117.
10. R. Law, 'The Gold Trade of Whydah in the Seventeenth and Eighteenth Centuries', in D. Henige and T.C. McCaskie (eds), *West African Economic and Social History: Studies in Memory of Marion Johnson* (Madison: African Studies Program, University of Wisconsin-Madison, 1990), pp. 105–18.
11. M.A. Klein, 'The Impact of the Atlantic Slave Trade on the Societies of the Western Sudan', *Social Science History*, 14/2 (1990), pp. 231–53 (pp. 233–6).
12. K.G. Davies, *The Royal African Company* (London: Longman, 1957), pp. 348–9.
13. Davies, *Royal African Company*, pp. 344–5.
14. Sir P. Griffiths, *A Licence to Trade: The History of English Chartered Companies* (London: E. Benn, 1974), p. 85.
15. Griffiths, *Licence to Trade*, p. 96.
16. Griffiths, *Licence to Trade*, p. 86.
17. Griffiths, *Licence to Trade*, pp. 67–8. In fact, no such gold mines existed.
18. Griffiths, *Licence to Trade*, pp. 185–212.
19. Other than Davies, D. Galenson in *Traders, Planters, and Slaves: Market Behavior in Early English America* (Cambridge: Cambridge University Press, 1986), pp. 1–28, is one of the few scholars to consider this problem. Galenson demonstrates that the constraints of the North Atlantic world and the Company's lack of any means of properly enforcing its charter-given monopoly prevented it from doing effective business and turning a profit over the long term.
20. By fiat money I am here referring to a currency system in which the medium of exchange has no inherent value as a commodity and is only given value by those who exchange it.
21. L. Neal, *The Rise of Financial Capitalism: International Capital Markets in the Age of Reason* (Cambridge: Cambridge University Press, 1990); D.W. Jones, *War and Economy in the Age of William III and Marlborough* (Oxford: Blackwell, 1988), chs. 1–5; P.G.M. Dickson, *The Financial Revolution in England: A Study in the Development of Public Credit, 1688–1756* (London: Macmillan, 1967), chs. 16 and 20; P.J. Cain and A.G. Hopkins, *British Imperialism: Innovation and Expansion* (London: Longman, 1993), pp. 58–84.
22. J. Lamb, *Preserving the Self in the South Seas, 1680–1840* (Chicago: University of Chicago Press, 2001), p. 146.
23. Galenson, *Traders, Planters, and Slaves*, pp. 81–5; Davies, *Royal African Company*, pp. 316–26; C.L. Killinger III, 'The Royal African Slave Trade to Virginia, 1689–1713' (MA thesis, College of William and Mary, 1969), pp. 70–72.
24. For the Company's export of silver, see Jo)nes, *War and Economy*, p. 17; for the role of silver in the Indian Ocean, see K.N. Chaudhuri, *Trade and Civilization in the Indian Ocean: An Economic History from the Rise of Islam to 1750* (Cambridge: Cambridge University Press, 1985), pp. 215–18.
25. Davies, *Royal African Company*, p. 316.
26. Curtin, *Economic Change*, ch. 6.
27. Curtin, *Economic Change*, pp. 205–6. For the inability of Company agents to find, or

purchase, gold in West Africa, see R. Law (ed.), *Correspondence of the Royal African Company's Chief Merchants at Cabo Corso Castle with William's Fort, Whydah, and the Little Popo Factory, 1727–1728* (Madison: African Studies Program, University of Wisconsin-Madison, 1991), letter 5 from Abraham Duport, in which he describes the 'Trade... [as] but indifferent, and very little Gold circulates (as for my Part I see non haveing not wherewithall to Purchase it) the Natives not careing to lay it out any more than just for their bare Subsistance' (p. 12).

28. Eltis, *Rise of African Slavery*, p. 178.
29. P.D. Curtin, *The Rise and Fall of the Plantation Complex: Essays in Atlantic History* (Cambridge: Cambridge University Press, 1990), p. 43.
30. Davies, *Royal African Company*, p. 225.
31. J.R. Wordie, 'Deflationary Factors in the Tudor Price Rise', *Past & Present*, 154/1 (1997), pp. 32–70 (p. 64).
32. Davies, *Royal African Company*, p. 226.
33. I cite the references to a want of money, cowries, gold, or commodity-*cum*-currency in the rough chronological order of the volumes of RAC correspondence. Also included in this inventory are all letters which mention the extending of credit from English to African traders – or vice versa – since any such process implies the lack of a circulating medium of exchange. The first volume, R. Law (ed.), *Correspondence from the Royal African Company's Factories at Offra and Whydah on the Slave Coast of West Africa in the Public Record Office, London 1678–1693* (Edinburgh: Centre of African Studies, Edinburgh University, 1989): letters 1, 2, 3, 4, 5, 6, 7, 16, 20, 23, 24, 28. The second volume, *The English in West Africa, 1681–1683*: letters 3, 4, 5, 6, 7, 8, 10, 11, 16, 24, 25, 27, 28, 30, 31, 79, 99, 100, 101, 112, 122, 198, 200, 202, 211, 227, 242, 267, 369, 376, 377, 397, 439, 458, 465, 477, 479, 480, 481, 482, 483, 484, 485, 486, 487, 488, 490, 496, 530, 544, 561, 570, 575, 584, 586, 597, 603, 617, 633. The third volume, R. Law (ed.), *Further Correspondence of the Royal African Company of England Relating to the 'Slave Coast', 1681–1699* (Madison: African Studies Program, University of Wisconsin-Madison, 1992): letters 3, 5, 6, 7, 9, 11, 12, 15, 16, 20, 21, 23, 29, 30, 38, 41, 45, 46, 49, 50, 61, 63, 66, 67, 71, 79, 80, 88. The fourth volume, *Correspondence of the Royal African Company's Chief Merchants*: letters 5, 6, 8, 11, 15, 16, 18, 19, 22, 26. 'Booges' and 'Bouges' are Anglicized versions of either the Portuguese *buzio* or the Dutch *boesjies* – it is unclear which from the sources – which both mean, of course, cowrie; see *Correspondence of the Royal African Company's Chief Merchants*, p. 51n68.
34. Davies, *Royal African Company*, pp. 342–3.
35. Curtin, *Economic Change*, pp. 247–53.
36. *Correspondence of the Royal African Company's Chief Merchants*, pp. 22–3.
37. See Abraham Duport's letter of 23 December 1727: 'I'd make no Contract for Slaves till this Fort is well stockt with merchandize, and more particularly cowries... which are always a staple Commodity'. *Correspondence of the Royal African Company's Chief Merchants*, p. 17.
38. A port city on the Slave Coast just west of Badagri in what is now Nigeria. Also known as Ardra and Jakin.
39. *Further Correspondence of the Royal African Company*, p. 5. The 'putting off' of goods here refers to assortment bargaining described above (i.e., as Law notes, 'the practice of selling different goods in combinations (or "assortments"), whereby Africans would accept cheaper or less desired goods only together with those in higher demand'. *Further Correspondence of the Royal African Company*, p. 72n16. See also Thomas Clark and Hugh Elliot's letter from Offra, 17 September 1678: 'If your Honours send good store of Bouges to stay in Factory by us it is their money and if any goods should lye by us the bouges would help put them off'; *Correspondence from the Royal African Company's Factories*, p 8. It is interesting to note here that while the Portuguese had not come to surpass the efforts of the RAC in the West African slave trade in the 1680s as they would in the 1720s, the strength of the competition had increased regardless. From 1672–80, the RAC exported approximately 4,239 slaves on average each year, while the Portuguese exported an average of 175, and English interlopers failed to export any. From 1681–90, in contrast, the RAC's average was approximately 6,624, the interlopers' was approximately 513, and the Portuguese traders' average was approximately 825. Totals derived from *The Trans-Atlantic Slave Trade*.

40. *The English in West Africa, 1681–1683*, p. 226. In his enclosure with this letter, Thorne lists a series of goods and their expected value in slaves. The 691 pounds of cowries are expected to buy 12 slaves at 58 lbs of cowries per slave.
41. In essence, Thorne had been fired and a 'Mr Arthur Wendover' had been sent to replace him. As his correspondence from the Offra factory is a steady litany of complaints, insufficiencies, bad debts, and failure, it is not difficult to see why. See *The English in West Africa, 1681–1683*, letters 476–82. See also p. 228n35.
42. *The English in West Africa, 1681–1683*, p. 228.
43. *The English in West Africa, 1681–1683*, p. 228. See also William Cross's February 1681 letter, in which he reports that his lack of goods for slaves was supplied – on credit – by African traders. *Correspondence from the Royal African Company's Factories*, p. 25.
44. Major slaving port on the Slave Coast in what is now Benin. Also known as Ouidah and Glehoue.
45. *Correspondence from the Royal African Company's Factories*, p. 51 and n3. Law interprets this as 'another typically melodramatic posture by Carter', but in the context of the other letters we have examined, this conclusion appears too easy.
46. The total number of slaves embarked by the three groups – RAC, Portuguese, and English interlopers – tells much of the story for the 1720s. From 1720–30, the RAC embarked an approximate average of 1,317 slaves per annum, while the Portuguese and the interlopers embarked approximate averages of 7,747 and 18,706 respectively. Totals derived from *The Trans-Atlantic Slave Trade*. These figures do not include the trade conducted by the Dutch and French for these years.
47. *Correspondence of the Royal African Company's Chief Merchants*, pp. 12–13.
48. *Correspondence of the Royal African Company's Chief Merchants*, p. 13n27.
49. *Correspondence of the Royal African Company's Chief Merchants*, p. 15n35; see also Galenson, *Traders, Planters, and Slaves*, pp. 71–114, for factors of demand in the American markets.
50. *Correspondence of the Royal African Company's Chief Merchants*, pp. 14–15.
51. Eltis, *Rise of African Slavery*, pp. 228–31.
52. In the 1720s, Agaja, the oba of Dahomey – a kingdom just north of Whydah (Ouidah) in what is now the southern part of Benin – led a successful drive of conquest toward the coast, conquering Allada and Whydah, in order to monopolize control of the slave trade for the benefit and profit of the state. See P. Curtin, 'The West African Coast in the Era of the Slave Trade', in P. Curtin, S. Feierman, L. Thompson, and J. Vansina, *African History: From Earliest Times to Independence*, 2nd ed. (London: Longman, 1995), pp. 203–8.
53. *Correspondence of the Royal African Company's Chief Merchants*, p. 34.
54. M.A. Burkholder and L.L. Johnson, *Colonial Latin America*, 2nd ed. (New York: Oxford University Press, 1994), p. 235.
55. Eltis, *Rise of African Slavery*, p. 175.
56. *Correspondence of the Royal African Company's Chief Merchants*, p. 20. For some idea of the scale of the problem referred to here, it is important to remember that the average price of a slave in gold in the 1720s was a little over 6 ounces. Therefore, if Captains Hill and Hurst had failed to take over 40 ounces of gold in trade, they did not have enough gold to purchase seven slaves. Also, before the Dahomian conquest, the price of gold in cowries had been only four grand cabess, or 16,000 cowries, per ounce. See *Correspondence of the Royal African Company's Chief Merchants*, p. 20n44.
57. *Correspondence of the Royal African Company's Chief Merchants*, p. 34.
58. Francklin, Reed & Peake, Cabo Corso Castle, to Thomas Wilson, William's Fort, Whydah, 7 June 1728, in *Correspondence of the Royal African Company's Chief Merchants*, p. 30.
59. For the 'Fourth Charter' of the RAC, see *Collections of the Virginia Historical Society*, new series, 6 (1887), pp. 37–53; see also Davies, *Royal African Company*, pp. 97–100.
60. Eltis, *Rise of African Slavery*, p. 176.
61. For example, see *The English in West Africa, 1681–1683*, letters 6–8, 23, 36, 49, 53–4, 56, 58–9, 62, 65–6, 68, 72, 75, 78, 80, 84, 86, 93–4, 98, 103, 107, 109, 117–18, 162, 209, 212, 219, 223, 228–9, 254, 257, 259, 261, 271, 315, 318–19, 326, 334, 340–3, 371, 373–4, 379, 383–4, 387, 391, 398–9, 409–10, 420–21, 434, 446, 456, 459, 462, 465–6, 474, 476, 479, 485, 490, 494, 498, 503–4, 518–19, 526–7, 530, 543, 549–50,

553, 571, 575, 577, 579, 582, 586, 590, 604, 613, 633, 636, 639.

62. *Correspondence of the Royal African Company's Chief Merchants*, p. 15. Duport had been taken captive in the Dahomian conquest of Whydah.
63. *Further Correspondence of the Royal African Company*, p. 10; my emphasis.
64. *Further Correspondence of the Royal African Company*, p. 10; my emphasis.
65. On the matter of servants, see Duport's 12 November 1727 letter, in which he complains that 'The Company has been Pleased to reduce their Castle Working Slaves to the Number of Ten' which would not suffice to maintain William's Fort which stood 'on 3/4 of a Mile of Ground within some few Feet of Circumference, and the Buildings all of Mudd Walls covered with thatch, which [I] am continually obliged to Repaire'. He therefore asked the Company to hire 'free People to do it' since the slaves were apparently failing at the task. *Correspondence of the Royal African Company's Chief Merchants*, p. 12.
66. *Further Correspondence of the Royal African Company*, p. 58.
67. Davies, *Royal African Company*, pp. 363–4.
68. Galenson, *Traders, Planters, and Slaves*, p. 18.
69. Davies, *Royal African Company*, p. 291.
70. J. Thornton, *Africa and Africans in the Making of the Atlantic World, 1400–1800*, 2nd ed. (Cambridge: Cambridge University Press, 1998), pp. 142–3; D.R. Wright, *The World and a Very Small Place in Africa* (London: M.E. Sharpe, 1997), pp. 44–5.
71. Davies, *Royal African Company*, p. 316.
72. Davies, *Royal African Company*, pp. 324–5; Galenson, *Traders, Planters, and Slaves*, pp. 16, 22; Killinger, 'The Royal African Slave Trade to Virginia', p. 111.
73. The directors in England tried various schemes to secure ready payment for their slaves, but nothing they proposed could supply the planters with the coin the Company so desperately needed. In 1692 the Company ordered its American factors to accept nothing but cash or payment in kind for slaves; this policy failed so dramatically that only a month later it criticized the agents for *not* extending credit to the planters. See Galenson, *Traders, Planters, and Slaves*, p. 84.
74. Quoted in Davies, *Royal African Company*, p. 324, my emphasis; note also that the total number of slaves imported by the RAC did indeed fall from 2,695 in 1689 to 879 in 1690.
75. Galenson, *Traders, Planters, and Slaves*, p. 18. For example, from 1675–79 the Company delivered an average of 1,000 slaves to Jamaica annually. In 1680 Jamaica's planters complained to the British Lords of Trade and Plantations that the Company was not bringing in adequate supplies of slaves. The Lords of Trade stepped in with a settlement the Company could not hope to fulfill, which then prolonged the argument for several years.
76. D. Egerton, A. Games, J.G. Landers, K. Lane, D.R. Wright, *The Atlantic World: A History, 1400–1888* (Wheeling, IL: Harlan Davison, 2007), p. 229; B.W. Higman, 'The Sugar Revolution', *The Economic History Review*, n.s. 53/2 (2000), pp. 213–36 (p. 226).

CHAPTER SIX

Britain's Political and Economic Response to Emerging Colonial Economic Independence

HERMANN WELLENREUTHER

Eighteenth-century British commentators widely recognized the economic importance of the American colonies, yet modern historians have been reluctant to identify economic causes as triggering the American Revolution, even as they view the colonies through the lenses of the Acts of Trade and Navigation and note the colonial annoyance with British efforts in reinforcing these legislative acts. The contradictions are obvious. They hinge on what definition of the 'political' and 'economic' we follow. Today the two terms are carefully kept apart; yet the eighteenth century insisted on their connectedness. While contemporary historians stress that the colonists saw Britain as corrupt, tyrannical, and in decline, the revolutionary colonists extended that argument by insisting that the consequence of British corruption was a policy to destroy the colonial right to property by imposing trade restrictions and taxes, and thereby violating the right to internal sovereignty. To the colonists this was one whole: they reacted to British policies by adopting economic measures designed to bring the mother country back to a sensible view of their rights and resorted to political tactics designed to frustrate British politics. Smuggling, boycotts of British trade, ostracizing British custom officials, petitioning Parliament and the crown, voting for violent resolutions, and frustrating the efforts of royal governors all served but one end: to force the mother country to change her political course. Colonial writers in their many pamphlets subjected British politics to political as well as economic analyses. Most historians, on the other hand, in recent decades have tended to ignore the economic side of the colonists' arguments.[1] Their account of colonial interpretations of English policy has resulted in a highly refined view of the political causes of the American Revolution alongside a rather crude analysis of revolutionary economic arguments.

Some will claim that this critique diminishes the excellent work of historians like Thomas M. Doerflinger, John J. McCusker, Gary B. Nash and other economic historians.[2] They have indeed enriched our understanding of eighteenth-century colonial trade and of the Atlantic economic world. Yet by carefully restricting their argument to the world of trade and, in the case of Nash, to living and working conditions, they too ignore the interconnectedness of political and economic issues. The importance of these connections was demonstrated in the 1970s by Joseph Ernst in his fine study of the Currency Acts and colonial reactions to these laws.[3] At the same time these studies, again with the exception of Ernst's work, have fragmented our understanding of the colonial economy by concentrating on the economies of the large colonial ports. In this respect, economic historians have mirrored, in some ways, the approach of those concerned with the political history of the colonies. Both groups have offered increasingly sophisticated analyses of ever smaller segments of the North American world. And both have left it to the imagination of the reader to fit these perceptions into one whole. The result is a bewildering array of sophisticated analyses of individual colonies, individual ports and isolated economic regions, and an almost total lack of a sophisticated analysis of the function, role, and importance of the colonial economies in the larger British Empire. This essay represents a modest effort to reconstruct the contours, function, and significance of the macro-economic structure of the Atlantic British Empire.

The starting point of this reconstruction is an investigation of the relationship between legislation affecting colonial trade, and the changing economic relations between the colonies and the mother country. Economic trade and implications of changes in the seventeenth and eighteenth centuries in Britain seemed to be satisfied throughout the eighteenth century with the imperial trade regulations passed in 1696.[4] Although the list of enumerated goods changed as a reflection of different needs of British industry, the trade system as such was left untouched – even in the decades after the Seven Years' War. Thus if there were changes in the macro-economic structure of the relations between Britain and North American colonies, they were not reflected by the Acts of Trade. The focus of this essay will be on precisely those changes. My thesis is simple: from an economic point of view the colonists achieved independence well before 1775. Earlier economic dependence on Britain had by that time turned in fact into economic dependence of the mother country on the colonies.

I

In 1763, one British author expressed a view widely taken for granted: 'The British Colonies are to be regarded in no other light, but as subservient to the commerce of their mother country; the colonists are merely factors for the purpose of trade, and in all considerations concerning the Colonies, this must be always the leading idea.'[5] From the time of the publication of the first Navigation Ordinances in 1650/51, England pursued a policy to ensure the colonies' subservience to its commercial interests. These initiatives and the Acts of Trade and Navigation decreed that all *imports* to British colonies from countries outside the British Empire were first to be landed in Britain and then shipped in British bottoms to the colonies; certain colonial products could only be exported to Britain. These regulations reflected the conviction of seventeenth-century England that colonies were but providers of raw materials.

Over the years, the British concept of colonies, British economic interests, and the economies of the colonies changed.[6] Trade regulations established between 1650 and 1696 survived these changes: particular products – tobacco, furs, sugar, and naval stores were the most important ones – remained 'enumerated goods'; they could only be exported to the mother country. Given the importance of such products in the seventeenth century, these regulations made sense. Both in terms of bulk as well as value they represented the largest part of colonial exports. Other colonial products were allowed to be shipped directly to ports outside the British Empire, notably the major products of the middle and the northern colonies. These were welcome in non-British colonies as well as in the British sugar islands and thus, too, of some use to parts of the British Empire.[7]

By the middle of the eighteenth century, the economic needs of Britain and the economic structure and agricultural production of the colonies in the Atlantic world had changed. In this essay I will first describe these changes from the colonial perspective and then discuss some of the economic and political implications of these changes and their impact after the Seven Years' War on the increasingly difficult relationship between the colonies and the mother country.[8]

II

Most products exported from the North American colonies around 1700 were sent to England; those goods not consumed by the mother country were re-exported to the European continent. As colonial trade increased in complexity, colonial exports found new markets. This is especially true for Charleston whose chief export product was rice. This staple product was taken off the list of enumerated goods by Parliament in 1730 (3 Geo II, c. 28).[9] While in 1738 most rice was still exported to Britain and part of it from thence re-shipped to the Mediterranean, thirty years later less than half of Charleston's rice exports reached the British consumer; instead 30 per cent was directly shipped to the Mediterranean, while over 20 per cent ended up either in other American colonies (4.15 per cent), or the West Indies (16.4 per cent).[10] Similar shifts away from the British market occurred in the export trade of the other major ports.[11]

The message is clear: in the early part of the eighteenth century *most* colonial exports went to Britain, by the late 1760s, however, the *smallest* percentage of exports of rice, grain products, and other colonial goods (except for tobacco and naval stores) ended up in Britain and Ireland. Although these figures do not reflect the value of the goods exported from Philadelphia, New York, and Boston, a brief reflection on the colonial exports confirms these tonnage statistics. First, furs, a product of considerable importance in the seventeenth century and, compared with bulk material of considerable value, represented in 1739 only less than 3 per cent of colonial exports, as Table 6.1 makes clear.[12]

The second important product was tobacco. In the eighteenth century it continued to be exported in considerable, yet not increasing quantities to Britain. But most of it was almost immediately re-shipped to France as soon as it cleared customs.[13] Of the three seventeenth-century classical colonial export products, only sugar retained its importance for the direct trade between Britain and her colonies. Yet sugar was a product of the West Indies and, therefore, of little importance to *direct* trade relations between the North American colonies and Britain. Even from the point of view of *indirect* earnings, sugar played only a limited role in American-British trade.[14]

Nevertheless, the pattern of destinations of ships leaving major colonial ports confirms the impression gained from the Charleston figures. Only a fairly small part of colonial exports ended up in the mother country, while the bulk was either transported to other British or non-British colonies in the New World or to continental Europe. In short, the classical colonial products that had prompted to some extent the passage of the Acts of Trade had lost their attraction to the mother country.[15] From the point of view of Britain's economic needs the *American* colonies produced, with the exception of naval stores, *nothing* that was of any significance to the mid-eighteenth-century British economy.[16] From the perspective of colonial exports, retaining the Acts of Trade made no economic sense.[17]

Table 6.1: Percentage of export of furs from North American Colonies' total exports to Britain in 1700 and 1739 (in Pounds Sterling)

	1700			1739		
	total export	furs	%	total export	furs	%
All Colonies	410,821	16,935	4.12	612,472	18,299	2.99
New England	43,145	2,532	5.87	37,842	2,014	5.32
New York	18,269	5,160	28.25	14,988	4,119	27.48
Pennsylvania	4,792	752	15.69	6,605	267	4.04
Virginia/ Maryland	329,994	2,530	0.77	361,059	626	0.14
Carolina	14,620	599	4.19	191,787	7	0.004

Sources: US Bureau of the Census, *Historical Statistics of the United States: Colonial Times to 1970*, 2 vols. (Washington, DC: USGPO, 1975), ii, 1176–7, S.1188; J.J. McCusker, 'The Current Value of English Exports, 1697–1800', *William and Mary Quarterly*, 3rd ser., 28 (1971), pp. 607–28. The data from the *Historical Statistics* were multiplied with McCusker's data on the consumption price index for the relevant years.

In the eighteenth century the continental colonies' economies changed in two ways. First, wheat and rice production expanded while tobacco production after 1740 either slightly declined or stagnated. Second, in the late seventeenth and early eighteenth century, colonial wheat was exported mainly from Philadelphia and New York, reflecting the agricultural produce of the regions that supplied goods for the trade of these two leading colonial trading centres. The major recipients of colonial grains were the West Indies and the Iberian countries. In the early eighteenth century, wheat exports from the colonies were of importance only within the *American* Atlantic market. This was to change by the middle of the century.

Table 6.2: Exports of Wheat and Wheat Products in the year 1770 to various regions (in bushels and tons)

	Great Britain	Ireland	Southern Europe	West Indies	Total
Wheat in bushels	1.56%	19.96%	78.35%	0.12%	751,240
Bread and Flour in tons	0.57%	7.81%	40.34%	51.12%	45,868

Source: US Bureau of the Census, *Historical Statistics of the United States: Colonial Times to 1970*, ii, 1184.

In 1770 most wheat was shipped to the Mediterranean; about half of the grain products (bread and flour) was transported to the West Indies, with most of the rest going to Ireland and Southern Europe. In the early part of the century wheat had been a *minor* item in the colonial export trade to Europe. After the Seven Years' War this changed largely because the colonies increasingly turned from tobacco as a traditional staple product to the cultivation of wheat. Large quantities of wheat were exported from Norfolk, Virginia, the rising star among colonial ports in those days. Most significantly, almost 80 per cent of this wheat was exported not to Britain or parts of the Empire, but to the European continent, especially to the Mediterranean region.[18]

III

These figures suggest that something had gone wrong. By the middle of the eighteenth century the major part of colonial produce from North America reached not Britain but either other parts of the Empire or, more significantly, parts of continental Europe or colonies of other European nations. These changes, however, did not result, as I have already pointed out, in alterations of the legal framework for the colonial export trade. It is at least worth considering whether modifications of the Acts of Trade would have made any difference to the colonial perception of the mother country. The problem was the British grain lobby. Any attempt to include wheat on the list of enumerated goods would have evoked the determined resistance of that all-powerful British agricultural interest. And since it most likely would have also increased the price of colonial wheat, such a measure would have seriously hurt colonial exports without benefiting Britain. The latter argument saved the colonies.[19]

Britain and colonial contemporaries argued that the Acts of Trade and Navigation were sensible instruments in securing the colonies as export markets for British manufactures. Such an argument, however, shifted the perspective from the colonies as suppliers of raw materials within the Empire to Britain as the supplier of finished products. From Britain's standpoint, around 1700 the export of manufactures to the American world represented a small percentage of all exported British manufactured goods. By 1720, exports to the American colonies had climbed to 22.5 per cent and by the early 1770s to 43 per cent of all exports of British manufactures.[20] The downside of this impressive importance of the colonies as markets for British products was that dependencies changed too: the seventeenth-century *colonial* dependency on England's willingness to buy colonial raw materials changed by the 1770s to *Britain*'s dependency on the colonial markets to purchase British manufactures. Earlier the colonies were in trouble if the English market absorbed fewer colonial products; by 1770 British manufacturers had to lay off workers if colonial markets for British goods shrank or – worse yet – even closed.[21]

In the light of these dramatic changes it is again important to recall that the legal framework of imperial trade established in the 1690s was not suited to these new economic realities – nor is it easy to imagine meaningful adaptations of the Navigation Acts to these new circumstances short of adopting Adam Smith's free-trade package. Benjamin Franklin, for one, thought such changes unnecessary. In his pamphlet *The Interest of Great Britain Considered, with Regard to her Colonies, and the Acquisitions of Canada and Guadeloupe* (1760), he argued that the economic relationship between Britain and her colonies was characterized by a neat division of labour: Britain supplied North America with manufactures while the colonies continued to supply Britain with agricultural products.[22] Franklin's thesis reflected seventeenth-century English views of the colonies; the shrewd author was probably aware that while British economics had changed, perceptions of the colonies had remained the same. Yet it is equally possible that Franklin's views mirrored colonial self-perception as a virtuous rural society untainted by the corruptions of manufacture, money, and what contemporaries referred to as the 'moneyed interest'. Such views we usually associate today with Thomas Jefferson's eulogies of the virtuous yeoman.

What Franklin avoided discussing in his contribution to the lively debate on what position Britain should retain in a future peace treaty (following the end of the Seven Years' War) was the colonies' willingness to embellish their balance of trade with Britain by illegally importing manufactures from non-British sources. Yet he was aware of the problem. Two years earlier on 19 March 1759, he had confided to Isaac Norris, his political ally in Philadelphia, that

> many Members in both Houses [of Parliament] . . . are Friends to Liberty and of noble Spirits, yet a good deal of Prejudice still prevails against the Colonies, the Courtiers think us not sufficiently obedient; the illicit Trade from Holland etc greatly offends the Trading and Manufactoring Interest; and the Landed Interest begin to be jealous of us as a Corn Country, that may interfere with them in the Markets to which they export that Commodity.[23]

Franklin's remarks suggest that manufactured goods were not only imported legally from Britain but also illegally from the Netherlands – a trade that, according to Claudia Schnurmann, stretched back to the early seventeenth century.[24] And we might add that there were also direct trade relations between some French and North American ports.[25] That Franklin was not worried about the colonial ability to pay for the imports from England is understandable: first, the illegal imports could be paid by bills of exchange drawn on merchants in Southern Europe who had received colonial shipments of wheat or other non-enumerated products; and second, due to the presence of the British Army in North America in 1759, large amounts of English currency circulated in the colonies.

That situation soon changed. With the disbanding of most of the British Army after 1762, the flow of sterling into the colonies slowed down to a trickle. At the same time, stricter control of imports into the colonies probably cut into the amount of illegal imports from the Netherlands.[26] Both developments drained sterling currency from the colonies.

By 1764 colonial ability to pay for the large imports from Britain began to diminish – although few recognized this problem. When in the same year the Houses of Parliament passed the Currency Act, few colonial protests reached London; most colonial agents were instructed to focus their attention on the evil effects of the Sugar Act (4 Geo III, c. 15), passed a few weeks earlier.[27] This was to change in the coming years. In the early 1770s, the colonies claimed that the effects of the Currency Act were destroying the colonial ability to pay for British imports as well as ruining colonial economies. In 1770,

New York petitioned for permission to emit paper money nominally worth £120,000 that was *only* to be legal tender in payments to the colonial treasury and to the colonial loan office. This petition was granted; in 1773 the privilege was extended to all other colonies.[28]

IV

Since the passing of the first Navigation Ordinance in 1650/51, the colonies' external trade had been one of the major controversial issues in the otherwise reasonably peaceable relationship with the mother country. Throughout the colonial period the prohibition on exporting colonial products to European countries outside the British Empire provoked colonial protests as well as large-scale evasion. Yet, after the first emissions of paper money this paper money issue overshadowed older charges of evading customs regulations and smuggling. Since the 1720s British pronouncements branded colonial efforts to solve perennial colonial currency shortages as efforts to cheat British merchants out of their just claims. Despite colonial protests of innocence and claims that paper money with legal tender was necessary fuel for the colonial economies and was freeing scarce colonial sterling reserves for payment of British imports, in 1751 and 1764 these largely unjustified charges of British merchants prompted Parliament to pass the two Currency Acts.

This debate was about more than just the interest of British merchants.[29] At issue was the problem of who had the right to decide the structure of colonial economies. For the British this was clear – the anonymous author I cited at the start of section I represented the voice of Britain. Before the 1770s the colonists were by-and-large happy with the mother country's regulation of the colonies' external trade. But as the repeated defiance of royal instructions on paper money bills makes amply clear, they rejected the British notion that these emissions were subject to British regulations.[30] For colonists, paper bills were indeed colonial matters. They represented the colonies' answer to Britain's monopoly of the mint. Denying the colonies the right to emit paper bills denied them an essential part of their colonial economies. As some colonial authors argued, the mother country's rejection of paper bills prevented them from exercising the right to provide for themselves as well as the ability to absorb large quantities of British manufacture. For the colonists the implication was clear: if they could not legally pay for British imports they either had to secure them illegally or accept the implication of British monetary policies and opt for independence.

Before 1775 few colonial authors went so far. But that does not imply that the currency issue and the structure of colonial trade were areas outside colonial political concerns. A number of problems, most of them not yet explored in this essay, were at issue. First and most importantly, colonial economies clearly emancipated themselves from their seventeenth-century dependency on the English market. After the Seven Years' War this colonial reliance on Britain was restricted to two products: tobacco and sugar; of these, only West Indian sugar depended on the purchasing power of the British market, for most colonial tobacco was absorbed by France, with Britain enjoying the custom duties.[31]

Second, West Indian and Southern colonial plantation elites adopted fundamentally different strategies in protecting and integrating sugar and tobacco into the larger framework of relations with the mother country. Already in the seventeenth century, the West Indian elites responded to these challenges by moving to England and becoming part of the English political nation. The Molasses Act of 1733, the Sugar Act of 1764, and further successful efforts to secure their product a most favoured position on the British market underline the success of this strategy. The tobacco elites of Maryland and Virginia chose a drastically different path. They created their own colonial worlds around the needs of the tobacco crop and increasingly cut their once equally close ties to the mother country.[32] No Byrd of the third generation lived for any extended period in England, and after 1740 only one member of the Virginia elite, the irascible and virtuous Arthur Lee, enjoyed for years the pleasures of English gentility. In the Seven Years' War, Virginia tried to solve its monetary problems with the emission of so-called 'tobacco notes' as their own colonial currency, rejected British critique of these emissions and stressed the virtues of Virginia's internal sovereignty.[33] When external market concerns threatened Virginia's planters' economic well-being, they did not pressure the English Parliament into providing a privileged shelter for their crop, but responded by cutting tobacco production and developing new agricultural products – wheat mostly. Put differently, West Indian planters defined their staple product sugar as the key element of their relationship with the mother country. This economic and political bilateralism helped reduce to insignificance the kinds of problems that on the American continent plagued Virginia's and Maryland's relations with Britain. In peace time, both Barbados and Jamaica did not need a special currency for their internal economies – because internal economies outside the sugar economy scarcely existed.

Third, the 'locality' of tobacco (which was grown only in Virginia and Maryland) meant that elites there gradually re-joined the course of the middle and northern colonies. Since the seventeenth century these colonies had developed home markets; at first they did so out of necessity because their products – wheat and meat for the most part – had commanded no British market. In time these colonies developed increasingly sophisticated economies whose market mechanisms demanded the creation of a locally acceptable, omnipresent and adaptable currency. It is not accidental that credit features were attached to almost all these colonial currencies. Imperial interference with these colonial currencies thus not only threatened emerging colonial economies but more specifically endangered the fragile colonial credit systems that had evolved since the 1720s. Economic expansion in the colonies was largely funded by credit, since very few immigrants brought enough money to North America to purchase their lands with cash and most planters financed the acquisition of new lands, slaves or agricultural implements with credit. Tampering with the colonial currency systems directly affected the basis on which economic expansion of most colonies rested.[34]

Fourth, with the rising importance of exports, colonies developed an economic duality that was governed by three different currency systems: by colonial paper bills and non-English hard currency for export markets linked to other colonial economies;[35] by the pound sterling for imports and exports focused on Britain; and by bills of exchange and again non-British currencies for colonial products marketed to non-British regions. The development of the colonial export markets outside the British Empire suggests that of the three currencies, the pound sterling by 1770 probably was of the least significance as a means of fueling colonial exports. This observation applies not only to the middle and northern colonies. With the rising importance of wheat as an export product it also pertains to Virginia and Maryland. And the emergence of the European continent as the principal market for rice as well as the continuing importance of the non-British West Indies finally suggests that non-British currencies were more important for Charleston's export trade than sterling.

My analysis of the colonial economies and their function within the British Empire rests, one could argue, largely on hypothetical assumptions that bear no close resemblance to the thinking of the colonists themselves. For if it is true that colonists considered their paper currencies of such importance, why did they not politicize paper bills the same way they elevated tea, for example, to the status of a political statement within the imperial struggle? Or why, if the size and importance of external markets were of such importance for the relationships between colonies and Britain, do they play such a minor role in the many pamphlets published after 1763? True, the ability to pay for British imports with earnings gained in non-British markets is a subject that received considerable colonial attention, but by and large the issue is far less prominent in colonial thought than for example the problem of taxation, representation, or colonial rights. And finally, why did the colonists, if paper bills and the related credit facilities were so vital to colonial economic well-being, not stand up as one and resort to desperate measures when Parliament and Crown in 1764 passed the currency bill into law?

I think that these objections rest on an assumption that is problematic in itself. Colonists did not separate economic from political concerns in the way these remarks suggest. The question of colonial rights included the right to structure and shape their own internal economic worlds – as the colonists made amply clear in their reasoning against the parliamentary claim to tax the colonies.[36] Yet there is a more important reason why the key features of this macro-economic development remained outside the war of words between the colonies and England: most of these large-scale economic developments – the emergence of markets for colonial products outside the empire, for example, and the use of bills of exchange to finance this export – met with wholehearted approval from the British economic and political nation. Dumping rice that could not be sold in Britain on the Iberian countries was a good thing. And selling colonial wheat and fish, unwanted in Britain, to starving Catholics in southern European climes was again better than dumping them into the sea, particularly if the resulting bills of exchange paid for British manufactures.

Important features of the development of non-British markets for colonial goods were non-controversial, acceptable to all, and not subject to complaint or comment. This Atlantic agreement seems to have extended to the circulation of non-British currency in North America, whose existence the Crown had repeatedly approved.[37] More importantly, there is ample evidence that the Board of Trade did not object in principle to the existence of a paper currency in the colonies. Once a solution had been found that satisfied the fears of British merchants, Parliament sanctioned these colonial currencies without impairing their functions for the internal colonial economies. On the contrary, the law of 1773 strengthened the internal monetary nature of these colonial currencies by making the bills legal tender for official payments only to colonial institutions.

These arguments suggest a final and crucial objection. Why did the colonies not raise the issue of the outdated regulations of the Acts of Trade and Navigation? My answer is simple: because the Acts of Trade and Navigation had *partially* become irrelevant to the colonies.[38] The British had a slightly different point of view. At least in 1762–3, they toyed with the idea of tightening some of the features of the Navigation system – especially those relating to imports of European goods to the colonies.[39] But these measures, irritating as they were for colonial merchants, were at best half-hearted. All reforming attempts were soon subordinated to the need to raise money as efficiently and in as cost-effective a way as possible from the colonies' external trade. But these measures were not designed to reverse developments that had essentially freed the colonial economies from imperial domination.

Indeed, Britain had no option but to sanction the colonies' search for markets outside the Empire. It was in Britain's best interests to accept the colonies' path towards external economic independence. In granting the colonies the right in the early 1770s to an internal colonial currency the English Parliament in essence gave this development its stamp of approval. Economically in the early 1770s the colonies already enjoyed their independence. The irony is that they achieved this with Britain's approval. Any other policy would have damaged British exports. And that of course would have violated the governing idea, which I quoted above, that 'British Colonies are to be regarded in no other light, but as subservient to the commerce of their mother country; the colonists are merely factors for the purpose of trade, and in all considerations concerning the Colonies, this must be always the leading idea.'[40]

V

In this essay I have suggested that changes in the macro-economic structure of the export trade of Britain's North American colonies are important for our understanding of the events associated with the American Revolution. First, these changes meant that after 1700 a sharply increasing amount of colonial agricultural products was exported to non-British markets in the West Indies and the European continent; the colonists were aware that even significant amounts of tobacco, the chief North American 'enumerated' staple product, were re-exported to France. These macro-economic changes were seldom discussed by colonists and remain largely ignored by modern research. The silence of the colonists is of course explained by a very simple fact: since the 1730s they were aware that colonial exports to non-British markets could easily be misconstrued as trading with potential enemies, a charge very effectively levelled at the colonists during the controversy over the Molasses Act of 1733. Yet indirectly, these macro-economic changes loomed large in colonial discourse about trade. For they held centre-place in the argument that the unfavourable colonial balance of trade with Britain forced colonists outside the British market to earn money to pay off debts accumulated by the heavy imports of British manufacturing goods.[41]

The importance of these non-British export markets, too, explains the nature of the currency problem and why it was viewed differently by colonial and by British merchants. As these non-British markets emerged, bills of exchange and non-British currency became increasingly significant for colonial merchants while on the other hand British merchants who had little part in this trade but dominated large parts of the bilateral trade with the colonies were almost exclusively concerned with the soundness of the currency they were dealing with – sterling. I am aware that I am broaching arguments that have not yet been adequately explored. But if my assumptions are correct they would explain why the Currency Act of 1764 caused comparably little stir in North America and why the British government in the early 1770s acceded to the colonial demand for a paper currency with legal tender only within the colonies, thus at least theoretically freeing the internal money market from the concerns associated with colonial-British monetary and trading relations.

Finally, the importance of the macro-economic changes might well go some way toward explaining why the American export trade did not collapse after 1775 despite British efforts to block American ports and inflict maximum damage on American export trade. By and large, I am impressed by the ease with which American merchants intensified trading relations with the Netherlands and France, continued trading to the Mediterranean, and pushed trade in the West Indies with the Dutch, French, Danish, and Spanish. We lack systematic studies of the Revolutionary export trade. But what we know of the activities of the firm of Willing & Morris and of William Bingham; of the importance of trade with St Eustasius, St Martinique and other islands; and of trade with Amsterdam, Nantes, and Bordeaux, suggests continuity as well as flexibility, but not dramatic decline.[42] These export markets can only be explained by their existence and familiarity during the colonial period.[43]

NOTES

1. Two welcome exceptions from earlier scholarship are O.M. Dickerson, *The Navigation Acts and the American Revolution* (Philadelphia: University of Pennsylvania Press, 1951); and J. Ernst, *Money and Politics in America, 1755–1775* (Chapel Hill: University of North Carolina Press, 1973).
2. T.M. Doerflinger, *A Vigorous Spirit of Enterprise: Merchants and Economic Development in Revolutionary Philadelphia* (Chapel Hill: University of North Carolina Press, 1986); J.J. McCusker, and R.R. Menard, *The Economy of British America, 1607–1789. With Supplementary Bibliography* (Chapel Hill: University of North Carolina Press, 1991); G.B. Nash, *The Urban Crucible: Social Change, Political Consciousness, and the Origins of the American Revolution* (Cambridge, MA: Harvard University Press, 1979). My argument differs significantly from that advanced by M. Egnal, *A Mighty Empire: The Origins of the American Revolution* (Ithaca: Cornell University Press, 1988).
3. Ernst, *Money and Politics.*
4. The *locus classicus* for discussion of the Acts of Trade and Navigation is still L.A. Harper, *The English Navigation Laws: A Seventeenth-Century Experiment in Social Engineering* (New York: Columbia University Press, 1939).
5. Cited in P.N. Miller, *Defining the Common Good: Empire, Religion and Philosophy in Eighteenth-Century England* (Cambridge: Cambridge University Press, 1994), pp. 164–5.
6. See K.E. Knorr, *British Colonial Theories 1570–1850* (1944; London: Frank Cass, 1963). I have followed the convention of referring to 'Britain' only post-1707.
7. The standard accounts are G.L. Beer, *The Origins of the British Colonial System, 1578–1660* (1908; repr. Gloucester, MA: P. Smith, 1959); Harper, *The English Navigation Laws*; T.C. Barrow, *Trade and Empire: The British Customs Service in Colonial America 1660–1775* (Cambridge, MA: Harvard University Press, 1967).
8. For further discussion of evidence cited in this essay see H. Wellenreuther, *Ausbildung und Neubildung: Die Geschichte Nordamerikas vom Ausgang des 17. Jahrhunderts bis zum Ausbruch der Amerikanischen Revolution 1775* (Münster and Hamburg: Lit Verlag, 2001).
9. For the negative effects of declaring rice an enumerated good on its price and on the recovery of the price of rice after it had been taken off the list see G. Rogers Taylor, 'Wholesale Commodity Prices at Charleston, 1732–1791', *Journal of Economic and Business History*, 4 (1932), pp. 356–77.
10. See Wellenreuther, *Ausbildung und Neubildung*, p. 399.
11. See Wellenreuther, *Ausbildung und Neubildung*, p. 407.
12. In interpreting this table it should be kept in mind that the figures for exports in the 'total' column refer *only* to the total exports to Britain. In addition, the major ports of the middle and northern colonies had been exporting large amounts of goods to the West Indies and by the early eighteenth century they had begun to ship wheat and some other goods to Southern Europe. Had these exports been included in the figures in the column 'total', then the percentage for 'furs' exported would have been even smaller.
13. The standard account is J.M. Price, *France and the Chesapeake: A History of the French Tobacco Monopoly, 1674–1791, and of its Relationship to the British and American Tobacco Trades*, 2 vols. (Ann Arbor: University of Michigan Press, 1973).
14. The standard account of the sugar trade to Britain is F.W. Pitman, *The Development of the British West Indies, 1700–1763* (New Haven: Yale University Press, 1917). I am aware of the indirect importance of West Indian sugar for the export trade, but that trade focused on the non-British sugar islands at least until 1766, when the reform of the customs administration forced colonial merchants to give up the illegal importation of French molasses to North America.

15. Passage of these acts was also prompted by the general conviction among colonial empires that trade within a colonial empire had to be controlled by the mother country in the interest of the mother country.
16. The production of indigo in North America and copper never reached levels significant for the export trade although both were declared 'enumerated goods'; on indigo see S. Fairlie, 'Dyestuffs in the Eighteenth Century', *Economic History Review*, 17 (1964–65), pp. 488–510, who, however, erroneously believes that indigo was only in the 1740s inserted into the list of enumerated goods. Prior to 1691, indigo had been exported in significant quantities from the British West Indies to England. It became a minor export item from the Carolinas after about 1740. See R. Davis, 'English Foreign Trade, 1660–1700', *Economic History Review*, 7 (1954–55), pp. 150–66, esp. p. 159. Copper was declared an 'enumerated good' because of rising British demand as a result of rapid growth of the bronze industry between 1710 and 1750. See H. Hamilton, *The English Brass and Copper Industries to 1800* (London: Longman, 1926), pp. 112–16, 284–92.
17. It only makes sense if one takes the considerable customs receipts on tobacco as the prime justification for the Acts of Trade and Navigation. But even these amounted to a less than respectable sum because most customs payments were remitted upon the re-export of tobacco.
18. On the shift from tobacco to wheat production in Virginia and Maryland, see P.G.E. Clemens, *The Atlantic Economy and Colonial Maryland's Eastern Shore: From Tobacco to Grain* (Ithaca: Cornell University Press, 1980); and D. Klingman, 'The Significance of Grain in the Development of the Tobacco Colonies', *Journal of Economic History*, 29 (1969), pp. 268–78.
19. I base my argument that putting wheat on the list of enumerated goods would have increased its price on the experience with Carolina rice (see note 9, page 135). On the agricultural interests' fears about colonial wheat production see below note 23 for Benjamin Franklin's remarks.
20. McCusker and Menard, *The Economy of British America,* p. 40. The figures include re-exports of colonial goods from Britain to European continental countries.
21. In the revolutionary period colonists began to realize that Britain was dependent economically on the colonies; hence they considered British merchants their best friends and relied mainly on them to present the economic side of their grievances to Parliament; this worked during the three crises triggered by the Stamp Act, the Townshend duties and the Tea Act albeit with diminishing effects on British political and public opinion. In the 1770s I see a slight shift. Colonists broadened their argument in accordance with general contemporary theory and suggested that Britain's economic wealth and thus political power depended on Britain's commanding colonial produce; thus the Secret Correspondence Committee of the Continental Congress suggested in its instructions for Silas Deane as congressional agent in France 'That the commercial advantages Britain had enjoyed with the Colonies had contributed greatly to her late wealth and importance. That it is likely great part of our commerce will naturally fall to the share of France; especially if she favours us with this application... and that as our trade was rapidly increasing with our increase of people, and in a greater proportion, her part of it will be extremely valuable.' Reprinted in *The Papers of Benjamin Franklin*, ed. L.W. Labaree et al. (New Haven: Yale University Press, 1959–), xxii, 372.
22. Reprinted in *The Papers of Benjamin Franklin*, ix, 59–100, esp. pp. 78–87.
23. *The Papers of Benjamin Franklin*, viii, 295. I know of no study of Dutch-American illicit trade for the period after the 1720s.
24. C. Schnurmann, *Atlantische Welten: Engländer und Niederländer im amerikanisch-atlantischen Raum 1648–1713* (Cologne: Böhlau Verlag, 1998).
25. On trade between France and the North American colonies see A.-M. Arnould, *De la balance du commerce et des relations commerciales extérieures de la France dans toutes les parties du globe, particulièrement à la fin du règne de Louis XIV*, 2 vols. (Paris, 1791); E. Buron, 'Statistics on Franco-American Trade', *Journal of Economic and Business History*, 4 (1931–32), pp. 571–80; G. Martin, 'Commercial Relations between Nantes and the American Colonies during the War of Independence', *Journal of Economic and Business History*, 4 (1931–32), pp. 812–29; J. Meyer, 'Les difficultés du commerce Franco-Americain vues de Nantes (1776–1790)', *French Historical Studies*, 11/2 (1979), pp. 159–83.

26. The legal basis for these stricter controls by the Navy was an Act passed on 19 April 1763. Section 9 of the Act (3 Geo III, c. 22) extended the 'Hovering Act' of 1718 to the colonies. See Barrow, *Trade and Empire*, pp. 176–7. The intention of this act is clearly expressed in its title: 'An Act for the further Improvement of his Majesty's Revenue of Customs, and for the Encouragement of Officers making seizures; and for the Prevention of the clandestine Running of Goods into any Part of his Majesty's Dominions', in O. Ruffhead (ed.), *The Statutes at Large, from Magna Charta, to the End of the Last Parliament, 1761* [*and continued to the 20th Year of the Reign of George III, inclusive*], 13 vols. (London, 1763–80), ix, 54–7.
27. The Sugar Act received the royal assent on 5 April 1764; the Currency Act, not a governmental measure but a private initiative by the merchant Anthony Bacon, received the royal assent on 19 April 1764; the colonial agents had agreed to a compromise version of the act that forbade only new emissions of paper bills while letting the old ones continue in circulation, although they were to be recalled as stipulated in the laws. P.D.G. Thomas, *British Politics and the Stamp Act Crisis: The First Phase of the American Revolution 1763–1767* (Oxford: Oxford University Press, 1975), pp. 64–5; Ernst, *Money and Politics in America*, pp. 43–88; the law is printed in *Statutes at Large*, ix, 199.
28. J.M. Sosin, *Agents and Merchants: British Colonial Policy and the Origins of the American Revolution, 1763–1775* (Lincoln, NE: University of Nebraska Press, 1965), pp. 137–40; Ernst, *Money and Politics in America*, pp. 280–1, 308–11; R.C. Simmons and P.D.G. Thomas (eds), *Proceedings and Debates of the British Parliaments Respecting North America, 1754–1783*, 6 vols. (Millwood, NY: Kraus International, 1982–87), iii, 253–5, 493, 495, and 503. The law 13 Geo III, c. 57, is printed in *Statutes at Large*, xi, 793–4. The law conceded the colonies the right to decide themselves about future emissions of paper money.
29. Scottish merchants trading to Virginia and Maryland were less affected by these issues although they too complained that being forced to accept paper money for goods paid for in sterling currency posed serious problems.
30. The Board of Trade had tried to enforce first position with a circular instruction that forbade governors acceding to laws emitting paper bills without a suspending clause, L.W. Labaree (ed.), *Royal Instructions to British Colonial Governors, 1670–1776*, 2 vols. (New York: D. Appleton & Co, 1935), i, 214–19; this led to large-scale evasions in all the colonies. The most comprehensive study of this issue is L. Van Brock, *The Currency of the American Colonies, 1700–1764: A Study in Colonial Finance and Imperial Relations* (New York: Arno Press, 1975).
31. R. Price, *Observations on the Nature of Civil Liberty* (London, 1776; repr. Charlestown, SC, 1776), pp. 68–9, suggests on the basis of customs receipts that these may have brought in as much as £300,000 per year.
32. See T.H. Breen, *Tobacco Culture: The Mentality of the Great Tidewater Planters on the Eve of the Revolution* (Princeton: Princeton University Press, 1985).
33. For the critique of the Board of Trade and the House of Burgesses' justification of the emission see G. Reese (ed.), *The Official Papers of Francis Fauquier, Lieutenant Governor of Virginia, 1758–1768*, 3 vols. (= *Virginia Historical Society. Documents*, vols. 14–16) (Charlottesville: University Press of Virginia, 1980–83), ii, 909–14; H.R. McIlwaine (ed.), *Journals of the House of Burgesses of Virginia* [1619–93, 1695–1706, 1710–15, 1718, 1727–34, 1736–40, 1742–9, 1752–8, 1762–76], 13 vols. (Richmond, VA: The Colonial Press, 1905–15), x, 174–5.
34. I am aware that this is seemingly contradicted by the considerable indebtedness of Southern planters to British merchants. Without ignoring this I accept J.M. Price's argument in *Capital and Credit in British Overseas Trade: The View from the Chesapeake, 1700–1776* (Cambridge, MA: Harvard University Press, 1980), pp. 18–19, that these loans should not be viewed as forms of indebtedness but rather as investments by British companies which took advantage of the fact that investments in North America yielded markedly higher returns than investments in Britain. See similarly J.F. Shepherd and G.M. Walton, *Shipping, Maritime Trade and the Economic Development of Colonial North America* (Cambridge: Cambridge University Press, 1972), pp. 165–6: 'Nevertheless, these balances do suggest that the tobacco-growing regions together with the lower South did not face a growing indebtedness to Great Britain, as is so frequently

asserted. We suggest that the growing indebtedness of the colonies with Great Britain was due to other areas. If long-term investments had been made by the British investors, it seems that the investment opportunities in the southern colonies would have been the more favoured ones from their viewpoint, and it seems less likely that long-term British capital would have gone to the middle colonies and to New England.'

35. We still know very little about how much non-English hard currency circulated in the colonies prior to 1785, when the new currency system was adopted. Thomas Jefferson, *Notes on the State of Virginia*, ed. F. Shuffelton (Harmondsworth: Penguin, 1999), pp. 176–7, suggests in Query XXI, that non-English currencies were used in Virginia as early as 1645, when the English Privy Council supposedly 'established [the value of] the Spanish piece of eight at six shillings'. Jefferson lists the major non-English currencies circulating in Virginia in the eighteenth century and provides the dates on which their values were fixed in relation to sterling.
36. These arguments are summarized by E.S. Morgan, 'Colonial Ideas of Parliamentary Power', *William and Mary Quarterly*, 3rd ser., 5 (1948), pp. 311–41, repr. in J.P. Greene (ed.), *The Reinterpretation of the American Revolution* (New York: Harper & Row, 1968), pp. 151–81.
37. Foreign currencies in the British colonies were regulated by the Act for ascertaining the Rates of Foreign Coins in her Majesty's Plantations of 1707, 6 Anne, c. 30.
38. 'Partially' of course refers to the Act's stipulation that all goods imported from non-British countries had to be shipped via Britain, which was the cause of the smuggling that Franklin reported.
39. I am aware that Dickerson, *The Navigation Acts and the American Revolution*, does not share my point of view.
40. See note 5.
41. Shepherd and Walton, *Shipping, Maritime Trade, and the Economic Development of Colonial America*, ch. 8; see *Considerations upon the Act of Parliament, whereby a Duty is laid of six Pence Sterling per Gallon on Molasses, and five Shillings per Hundred on Sugar of Foreign Growth, imported into any of the British Colonies* (Boston, 1764), repr. in B. Bailyn (ed.), *Pamphlets of the American Revolution, 1750 –1776* (Cambridge, MA: Harvard University Press, 1965), pp. 361–77, esp. 363–7; S. Hopkins, *The Rights of Colonies Examined* (Providence, RI, 1765), repr. in *Pamphlets of the American Revolution*, pp. 507–22, esp. 513–15.
42. Some material on this trade can be gleaned from E.M. Nuxoll, *Congress and the Munitions Merchants: The Secret Committee of Trade during the American Revolution, 1775–1777* (New York: Garland, 1985); O.W. Stephenson, 'The Supply of Gunpowder in 1776', *American Historical Review*, 30/2 (1924–25), pp. 271–81; on trade with St Eustasius see R.L. Scribner (ed.), *Revolutionary Virginia: The Road to Independence*, 7 vols. in 8 (Charlottesville: University of Virginia Press, 1973–83), iii, 206–7; v, 118–23, 274, 398–9; vi, 239–40; vii, 96, 120, 215, 254, 304, 373, 484, and 499. For Virginia's purchases of arms in foreign markets see D.E.F. Reynolds, 'Ammunition Supply in Revolutionary Virginia', *Virginia Magazine of History and Biography*, 70 (1965), pp. 56–77; on New England's trading relations with the French West Indies prior to 1774, see D.B. Goebel, 'The "New England Trade" and the French West Indies, 1763–1774: A Study in Trade Policies', *William and Mary Quarterly*, 3rd ser., 20 (1963), pp. 331–72; A.J. O'Shaughnessy, *An Empire Divided: The American Revolution and the British Caribbean* (Philadelphia: University of Pennsylvania Press, 2000); on Bingham, see R.C. Alberts, *The Golden Voyage: The Life and Times of William Bingham, 1752–1804* (Boston: Houghton-Mifflin, 1969); and M.L. Brown, 'William Bingham, Agent of the Continental Congress, in Martinique', *Pennsylvania Magazine of History and Biography*, 61 (1937), pp. 54–87; and on Robert Morris see C.L. Ver Steeg, *Robert Morris: Revolutionary Financier. With an Analysis of his Earlier Career* (Philadelphia: University of Pennsylvania Press, 1954), pp. 13–22 and 29–37; and C.L. Ver Steeg, 'Stacey Hepburn and Company: Enterprisers in the American Revolution', *South Carolina Historical Magazine*, 55 (1954), pp. 1–5; on trade with Cuba, J.A. Lewis, 'Anglo-American Entrepreneurs in Havana: The Background and Significance of the Expulsion of 1784–1785', in J.A. Barbier and A.J. Kuethe (eds), *The North American Role in the Spanish Imperial Economy, 1760–1819* (Manchester: Manchester University Press, 1984), pp. 112–26, esp. 116–19; and N. Böttcher, 'Cuba and the Thirteen

Colonies during the North American War of Independence', in H. Pietschmann (ed.), *Atlantic History: History of the Atlantic System, 1580–1830* (Göttingen: Vandenhoeck & Ruprecht, 2002), pp. 481–95; on Maryland's trade with France during the Revolutionary period, see E.C. Papenfuse, 'An Uncertain Connection: Maryland's Trade with France during the American Revolution, 1778–1783', in C. Fohlen and J. Godechot (eds), *La révolution américaine et l'Europe* (Paris: CNRS, 1979), pp. 243–64, and K. Sullivan, *Maryland and France, 1774–1789* (Philadelphia: University of Pennsylvania Press, 1936).

43. For a detailed discussion of American trade patterns between 1775 and 1783, see H. Wellenreuther, *Von Chaos und Krieg zu Ordnung und Frieden: Der Amerikanischen Revolution erster Teil, 1775–1783* (Münster and Hamburg: Lit Verlag, 2006), pp. 397–440.

CHAPTER SEVEN

'The Sacredness of Public Credit': The American Revolution, Paper Currency, and John Witherspoon's Essay on Money (1786)

ROGER J. FECHNER

Of the multitude of crises Americans faced during the revolutionary period – economic, military, political, social – the fiscal crisis was of utmost importance to the success of their emergence as an independent nation. As the newly formed state and the national governments struggled to solve this problem in the 1770s and 1780s, their leaders debated the advantages and disadvantages of hard money versus paper currency for commercial, governmental, and personal transactions. In the process American political economists wrote numerous essays and pamphlets on the currency controversy relative to funding the Revolution and the war, and the resulting public debt. Their writings also contributed to understanding the fundamental role of currency in creating public credit in the ongoing financial revolution in the eighteenth-century British Atlantic world.[1]

John Witherspoon, the ardent nationalist President of the College of New Jersey at Princeton, published his *Essay on Money* with the Scottish-American firm of Young, Stewart, and McCulloch of Philadelphia in 1786 during the fiscal crisis of the Articles of Confederation government. It was one of the most cogent works on the relationship between currency, commerce, and public credit written at the time. Witherspoon usually opposed paper currency unless backed by specie and championed the hard money cause throughout his academic and political careers in America from his arrival from Scotland in 1768 until his death in 1794. He reasoned that the new United States of America could not emerge as a strong, stable nation, like his native Great Britain, without public credit based on the solid standard of gold and silver, and supported by a national bank. The only exception to his hard money position was that he did allow for limited use of paper money in the form of commercial paper to facilitate trade. The 60-page essay, published under the full title *Essay on Money, as a Medium of Commerce; with Remarks on the Advantages and Disadvantages of Paper admitted into general Circulation*, appeared anonymously as the work of 'A Citizen of the United States', and best expressed Witherspoon's economic, financial, and monetary position the year before the Constitutional Convention of 1787.[2]

Dr John Witherspoon (1723–94), native of Scotland – cleric, ecclesiastical politician, theologian, and later moral philosopher and president of the College of New Jersey from 1768 until his death – rendered exceptional service to his adopted country as a revolutionary patriot in the Second Continental and Articles of Confederation Congresses from 1776 to 1782. One of its most dedicated and effective legislators, despite his numerous absences to attend to college affairs, he participated as a member of 120 committees.[3] A key committee on which Witherspoon took a leading role was the Committee on Finance, which he joined in May 1777.[4]

Witherspoon consistently took a 'hard money' or specie stance on the currency question, a minority position in Congress and with the general public which favoured a 'soft money' or paper currency solution to the new nation's financial problems during the 1770s and the 1780s. He allied himself with such leading hard money men as Robert Morris, the famous Philadelphia banker and merchant, who was Superintendent of Finance for the Confederation government, and Roger Sherman, the New Haven merchant and leader of the Connecticut delegation.[5] Witherspoon worked with Morris, Sherman, and others to oppose the use of paper money as legal tender on the grounds that it was not creditworthy unless its issue was severely limited and could be paid back in specie. A fiscal conservative throughout his entire congressional career, he fought to ensure that the national government was financially strong. He argued that all the debts it incurred had to be accompanied by legislation to extinguish those same debts to guarantee the nation's public credit. After his retirement from Congress in 1782, Witherspoon continued to speak and write in favor of specie and to limit the use of paper currency to commercial transactions.[6] The political context in which Witherspoon wrote on economic issues was marked by financial experiment, innovation, and crisis, the war of independence, and the difficulties of nation-building and the centralization of economic policy.

I MONEY AND THE TEACHING OF MORALS

When Varnum Lansing Collins briefly mentioned the *Essay* in his 1925 biography of Witherspoon, he concluded that its contents derived from his two surviving congressional speeches, 'Part of a Speech in Congress, on Finances' of 22 July 1782 and 'Speech in Congress, on a Motion for Paying the Interest of Loan-Office Certificates' of 9 September, 1982.[7] But Collins was only partially correct that the *Essay* was based on these two short speeches. In fact, the contents and contexts of the work, Scottish and American, are much more complex and extensive than Collins intimated.

Witherspoon had a life-long interest in economic issues. Indeed, his ideas and actions on political economy began during his Scottish ministry as pastor, church leader, and theologian (1745–68). During his pastoral ministry, first at Beith and then at Paisley, Witherspoon witnessed the remarkable growth in internal and international commerce, especially in the Glasgow region due to Great Britain's trade with its North American colonies. Since his congregation at Paisley contained a large number of handloom weavers' families, he was well aware of the critical role that commerce played in their lives.[8] He also took a particular interest in the relationship between banking, commerce, and money in 1767, which would later become a major focus of his American writings on financial matters, notably his *Essay*. This interest is best revealed in his 26 October 1789 response to Alexander Hamilton's letter asking advice on banks, money, and trade:

> It is true that from the very earliest part of Life It has been a favourite Object with me to attend to the Sate of Society & the Operation and Influence of political Causes & among the rest Money as a Medium of Commerce & things connected with it. It happened also that about 32 years ago we had several accurate Discussions in Scotland & England respectg the banking Companies on which subject I read much & wrote some but my Knowledge of theses Matters is all general & theoretical. It is always My desire if possible to read the first & radical principles of any thing & when those are well

> understood You may look through as it were the whole Effects with great Celerity as well as certainty.[9]

Witherspoon's concerns continued through his American career as college president, moral philosopher, revolutionary essayist, and statesman. The evolution of his ideas and actions on the intimate relationship between economics and politics can be traced in his Princeton *Lectures on Moral Philosophy* c. 1770–72, through his revolutionary writings – letters, essays, and sermons – 1774–76, to his congressional committee reports and speeches, 1776–82, all of which shaped his argument for specie currency, commercial paper, and public credit in the *Essay*.

When Witherspoon arrived in America in August of 1768 to take up his duties as the President of the College of New Jersey (now Princeton), two new responsibilities – one educational, the other political – required him to focus on economic ideas and policies much more deeply and seriously than he had in Scotland. During his 26-year tenure in office, he molded Presbyterian Princeton into one of the leading American colleges of the era. As president, he was also the chief faculty member and, typical of college leaders during the revolutionary era, Witherspoon taught a wide variety of subjects, the most important of which was moral philosophy, the capstone course of the curriculum.[10] His *Lectures on Moral Philosophy*,[11] composed soon after his arrival, drew eclectically on the works of a variety of ancient as well as seventeenth- and eighteenth-century moral philosophers. Most important in shaping Witherspoon's ideas on moral philosophy, of which political economy was a sub-topic, was the leading Glasgow moralist Francis Hutcheson (1694–1746). Indeed, Witherspoon borrowed heavily from Hutcheson's ideas in the posthumously-published *System of Moral Philosophy* (1755), although he frequently took issue with Hutcheson's arguments and language, as he would do later in the *Essay*.[12]

Witherspoon's most serious theoretical analysis came in his final lecture, Lecture XVI, to which he would later return in detail in his *Essay*. In the lecture he examined the nature of money in a discussion 'Of the Value of Property', a subject that political economists considered to be an essential part of all contracts. Witherspoon adopted the standard view of Enlightenment thinkers that the actual utility, or at least the perceived utility, of anything was what defined its use value and thereby 'becomes the object of human desire'. Still, he argued, just because utility normally gives objects their worth, it does not always do so. The worth of any object is ultimately based on two factors, its scarcity and its desirability.[13]

Witherspoon concluded that money in and of itself had no actual worth: 'It is not wealth properly, but the sign of it, and in a fixed state of society the certain means of procuring it.'[14] Citing evidence from ancient history, he noted that the commercial exchange of goods was first carried on by barter, a difficult, if not impossible method of trade, because most goods were too large to be portable and too difficult to divide into smaller quantities. Hence, as human societies progressed in size and complexity, mankind realized that it was essential to designate a substance that represented wealth and which also provided a quantitative means of measuring the worth of all goods.

Witherspoon argued that any substance that qualified as a generally accepted sign and standard of wealth must have four essential characteristics or qualities; it must be 'valuable . . . durable . . . divisible . . . and portable'. Historical use and contemporary commercial practice both showed that the precious metals, gold and silver, had all the requisite qualities. Thus, they had been adopted as money because they were both a sign and a standard of wealth. Furthermore, he argued that they were also objects of trade like any other commodity and, as such, they were subject to the same laws of supply and demand. Witherspoon also accepted the standard argument of political economists of his time that the governing class in any nation established the worth of gold and silver, and signs and standards of value of commercial goods. He warned that rulers had to pay close attention to the relative abundance or scarcity of precious metals as articles of trade, however, because if they neglected this their laws would only have limited results since other countries would not recognize their standard of worth. Furthermore, even in a nation's internal trade the worth of money was a function of the available quantity of gold and silver. It followed, therefore, that the governing class should never capriciously alter the worth of money, as it would hurt internal as well as international commerce.[15]

II ECONOMIC NATIONALISM

Witherspoon's American economic nationalism from the early to mid-1770s grew logically out of the ideas on political economy he had first developed in his *Lectures* and his increasing participation in the American Revolution. Witherspoon's evolution from steadfast North Briton to revolutionary American is best illustrated in his essays, letters, pamphlets, and sermons from 1771 to 1776. The overriding theme of his revolutionary writings was that the major cause of American independence was economic in nature.[16]

As early as 1771 and 1772, Witherspoon wrote two letters to the *Scots Magazine* in which he decried the ignorance of British citizens (of all economic and social classes) regarding their American colonies. He also developed an argument, which he was to repeat again and again in his subsequent revolutionary writings, that the immigration of British citizens to America was economically positive to the home country itself as well as to its colonies across the Atlantic. Witherspoon's major contention was that Britain's settlement of the rich lands on the North American continent brought wealth to the entire empire through trade. In response to British criticism that his own assistance to British emigrants was draining the homeland's economy of valuable labour, he was singularly unapologetic, especially in enabling those from Scotland to lead a successful life in America.[17]

Commerce and manufactures were central themes in Witherspoon's first specifically revolutionary pamphlet, *Thoughts on American Liberty* (1774). He urged the First Continental Congress to institute all-colonial agreements for the non-importation and non-consumption of British goods immediately. Witherspoon also recommended that it should direct Americans to encourage native industry, especially manufactured goods, by instituting several important innovations to foster internal economic self-sufficiency such as granting subsidies for manufacturing; creating public markets for selling native manufactured goods; attracting important manufacturing men in all fields to emigrate from Britain to America; and the founding of organizations in major urban centers, especially port cities, to raise monies to encourage manufacturers and working men to come to America and to print such schemes in British newspapers.[18] Soon after independence was declared in July 1776, Witherspoon, citing Hume as his authority, justified the separation from Great Britain partly on the grounds that an independent America would benefit both nations through increased trade, repeating an argument he had first made in 1771–2.[19]

III POLITICAL SERVICE

The second major responsibility John Witherspoon undertook in his adopted land was his active participation in local, provincial, state, and national politics from 1774 to 1791, especially in the Second Continental and Articles of Confederation Congresses. His political service to Somerset County and the Province of New Jersey from 1774 to 1776 did not involve him directly in financial matters. But in the Second Continental and Articles of Confederation Congresses he had ample opportunity to put his 'hard money' currency position into practice. Although his major focus as a Congressman was on foreign policy and war, he became increasingly involved in financial issues throughout his long and distinguished congressional career. The knowledge of monetary problems he had gained in Scotland from his observations and studies and from reading, researching and writing his *Lectures* and his revolutionary works served him well during his congressional service as he sought to deal with a wide range of fiscal questions – raising money to fight the war; reforming the Board of Treasury; regulating trade; maintaining the value of national currency; advising the states on their fiscal responsibility to the national government; and, most importantly, strengthening national public credit in conjunction with attacking paper money as legal tender while advocating specie currency as the only sensible solution to the new nation's monetary crisis. Complex financial issues were fundamental to the new nation's struggle to achieve a national identity during the revolutionary era, and Witherspoon was at the very heart of that struggle.[20]

Witherspoon's first significant encounter with monetary issues in Congress occurred on 14 February 1777, when he voted against a motion proposed by the New England states requiring that Congress should also engage in price fixing on imported goods, worker pay, native manufactured items, and food. His reasoning clearly reflected the view that economic authority must be centralized in the national government, not the states:

> I believe the regulations would be just, if the quantity of money and the scarcity of goods bore an exact proportion to each Other. But the price of goods is by no means proportioned to the quantity of money in every thing... Remember laws are not almighty. It is beyond the power of despotic princes to regulate the price of goods... I fear if we fail in this measure we shall weaken the Authority of Congress. We shall do mischief by teaching the continent to *rest* upon it. If we limit *one* article, we must limit *every* thing, and this is impossible.[21]

A major turning point in Witherspoon's congressional career relative to financial and monetary issues was his appointment to a committee on finance charged with fashioning plans and methods for paying the yearly costs of the national government in May 1777. His major ally and friend on the committee was Robert Morris, the most knowledgeable member of Congress on financial and monetary matters, who also agreed with Witherspoon that paper currency would depreciate rapidly if its emission was not limited and if its value could not be recovered in specie.[22]

In a letter of 20 March 1780, 'On the Affairs of the United States', written to a friend in Scotland, Witherspoon considered the new nation's fiscal crisis. The last paragraph of the letter is especially revealing of his concern that the ongoing emission of paper currency had caused the rapid decline in the value of money. 'The distress of this country by the depreciation of the money, has been very great. Many have suffered great losses; not a few have been utterly ruined.' Still, he was pleased to report that the monetary crisis had not altered the American people's support for the Revolution and the war.[23]

Soon after he returned to Congress in December 1780, Witherspoon wrote to Governor William Livingston of New Jersey regarding congressional business. Once again, he emphasized that the fiscal crisis was the greatest problem the country faced:

> The Distress of our Finances is the most important & alarming Circumstance in our Situation. A committee has it under Consideration but whether their Measures will be radical & effectual it is impossible to say. My Opinion is that Relief must come from the particular States & they must do it by giving up Attachment to Paper Money & by Loans & Contracts being in the Credit of individuals to assist the Public.[24]

Witherspoon's desire to create and maintain a strong central government marked all of his activities in Congress in 1781, but no more so than his work on financial and monetary issues. In the middle of May Witherspoon chaired a committee tasked with developing stratagems and methods for raising monies to support the military effort and to exercise better control over national finances. Not surprisingly, heading Witherspoon's 14 May list was his proposal that state governments revoke all statutes granting paper currency legal tender status. Another key monetary recommendation was that Superintendent Morris acquire an amount of specie 'for the most pressing exigencies of the pubic affairs'.[25] Neither proposal was accepted.

Late in the month, under Witherspoon's leadership, the committee adopted Morris's far-reaching plan for a United States national bank, a plan which Congress approved. Congress also suggested to the states that they prohibit any other banks as long as the war was on; that the national bank's currency be accepted for every financial transaction; and that counterfeiting its money be made a major criminal act.[26] After experiencing numerous defeats to strengthen the national government's finances, the successful creation of a national bank was a major victory for hard-money men such as Morris, Sherman, and Witherspoon.

During his final term in Congress in 1782, Witherspoon continued to emphasize the necessity of public credit and a monetary system based on specie for the national government. On 22 July he addressed the issue of public credit in a speech criticizing his friend Morris's proposal that the United States postpone taking out bills of credit on European nations to meet interest obligations on government loan-office certificates, a late seventeenth-century English invention which had been in use in the American colonies since the early eighteenth century and which were issued by loan offices (synonymous with land banks as 'A means used by several colonies [one of which was New Jersey] to circulate paper money in the form of currency issued on loan and secured, or backed, by a mortgage.'[27] They were 'domestic loans' and served as 'government bonds' sold at state offices to affluent citizens bearing an interest rate of 4 per cent to 6 per cent to support the national government.[28] Witherspoon claimed they would do great harm to public credit and the American public's confidence in its national government as well its reputation among European creditors. His solution to the problem was, not surprisingly, specie currency: 'A disposition to pay and visible probable means of payment are absolutely necessary to credit; where that is once established it is not difficult to borrow. If Congress would but lay down a foundation of credit, enough money could be borrowed in this country.'[29]

Once more he attacked paper money as the cause of the continental dollar's rapid depreciation: 'The old continental money was disgraced and sunk, first by the act of March 18th, 1780 ... telling you would pay no more of your debt than six pence in the pound. This was afterwards further improved by new estimates of depreciation, of seventy-five and one hundred and fifty, for new state paper, which itself was sunk to two or three for one ... '[30]

Witherspoon returned to the problems of paper currency one last time in his final speech on 9 September 1782. Congress had continued to issue paper currency without any means to support its redemption, thereby creating a crisis in the American public's view of the national government's credit. It simply could not pay the interest on loan office certificates it had issued, damaging American holders of these certificates as well as the country's ability to borrow money from continental European nations. Both would lower further the new nation's public credit standing and cause even more depreciation in its currency. Again, Witherspoon lashed out against such financial measures:

> Public credit is of the utmost moment to a state at any time, but it is all in all in a time of war. The want of it defeats the wisest measures, and renders every department torpid and motionless. It cannot be denied, that by many unhappy, if not unwise measures, public credit among us has been reduced to its lowest ebb, first by a monstrous and unheard of emission of paper money; next by an act of bankruptcy, reducing it to six pence on the pound; then by a table of depreciation.[31]

Clearly, John Witherspoon's practical political experience in dealing with financial and, especially, monetary issues in Congress between 1776 and 1782 confirmed his strong support for specie currency as the solution to the American fiscal crisis that he had earlier expressed in theory in his *Lectures* and his revolutionary writings. Still, in the blush of victory after the war was over, Witherspoon, like many ministers of the time, foresaw a glorious future for the new nation. In his famous sermon, 'Delivered at a Public Thanksgiving after Peace', of 19 April 1783, even he had to admit, despite his consistent opposition to paper money during the Revolution and war, that depreciated paper currency had funded the war:

> Another difficulty we had to encounter, was the want of money and resources for carrying on the war. To remedy this evil an expedient was fallen upon which I do not look upon myself as obliged either to justify or approve. It was, however, embraced by the plurality as necessary, and upon the whole less hazardous than any other, which in our situation was practicable. The difficulty of raising, clothing, paying and supporting an army with a depreciated currency, which its own nature, the arts of interested persons, and the unwearied attempts of our enemies were pushing on to annihilation, may be easily perceived. Yet

> the war has not only been supported, but we have seen the fall and ruin of the money itself with the least injury to the public cause.[32]

Although Witherspoon remained a staunch advocate of specie, the exigencies of funding the war had taught him that paper money had a practical role to play in extraordinary circumstances in what economic historians have called the 'mixed character of the colonial currency system, a system of currency finance'.[33] He would reconsider the proper role of paper money in the new nation's economy at greater length in his *Essay on Money* three years later.

IV THE *ESSAY*

The culmination of Witherspoon's ideas on and practical experience with paper currency and public credit was his *Essay on Money* of 1786, certainly his fullest and most original contribution to economic thought and practice. The timing was propitious as it appeared in the year of Shays' Rebellion, when the new nation found itself in a deep financial crisis as it struggled to recover from debts incurred during the Revolution and war. The impetus for the *Essay* came about when various congressional colleagues – even those who had been strong paper money supporters – realized the merit of his hard money position and urged him to publish on the fiscal crisis.[34] The rigorous debate in articles and pamphlets was sparked by the fact that several state governments issued bills of credit, some of which, at least to a degree, they made legal tender.[35] He described the paper money issue as 'a matter of great delicacy and danger'.[36]

Although he continued to borrow ideas from Hutcheson (as he had done in his *Lectures*) and based his position on theoretical principles not original to himself, the *Essay* was marked by a logical structure and forceful argument in its practical applications. For example, he took great care throughout carefully to distinguish bank, commercial, and monetary paper. A scholarly contribution replete with footnotes to a wide variety of sources, it was nonetheless a practical work in keeping with Witherspoon's general philosophy of life. Finally, what makes the *Essay* significant and sets it apart from the large majority of works on money that poured forth from American printing presses during the late eighteenth century is that he analyzed the paper money controversy in his adopted nation in the context of his European, especially his

Scottish, intellectual background as well as his American political experience.

Witherspoon anticipated those critics who questioned his credentials because he was not a professional merchant and therefore lacked first-hand knowledge of business. Witherspoon responded that although he was not a man of commerce, he was an academician who took his ideas from history and the best thinkers of his own time as well as from his own experiences in politics and his observations of daily life. In fact, he argued that merchants were ill-equipped to discuss the general theoretical principles of money and commerce because they focused their attention narrowly on activities of buying and selling. They did not possess any special advantage over philosophers, especially one like himself who not only knew and understood the general theory of political economy but who also had considerable experience in the practical politics of banking, commerce, finance, and money.[37] There is a double irony in Witherspoon's position because his congressional hard money allies such as Robert Morris and Roger Sherman were themselves bankers and merchants. Nor did Witherspoon manage his own personal finances or the college's very well, finding himself and the College of New Jersey frequently in debt.[38]

Witherspoon organized the *Essay* in a logical manner, as he had his college lectures. In response to the absence of theoretical principles typical of other essays on money during the period, he devoted more than the first third to monetary theory. The second third drew five major inferences, 'to deduce the practical consequences' of his theory.[39] In the final third, he developed a proposal on the proper use of commercial paper issued by banks, not as currency issued by governments, especially state governments, but as a circulating medium. He ended the *Essay* with a twelve-point summary and brief conclusion.

A. MONETARY THEORY

In answering the fundamental questions 'what gave rise to money, and what is its nature and use',[40] Witherspoon, once again, drew on arguments Hutcheson had made in his *System*.[41] Still, Witherspoon did more than just paraphrase Hutcheson, for he added his own theoretical insights and specific examples based on history, personal experience, and practical politics, making much of his analysis fuller and richer than Hutcheson's.

Witherspoon constructed his theory on three 'first principles' of commerce. The first was that the evolution of mankind from savagery to a commercial society required the creation of a common standard of calculation that would determine the relative value of different kinds of goods. Such a standard had to be an object familiar to both buyer and seller and be of universal utility. The second was that the agreed standard of value would consist of a symbol or sign representative of the missing goods, and the basis of calculation in all its multiplying and dividing. Such symbols or signs also had to be readily portable to facilitate commerce. The third necessary requirement for an effective means of exchange was that a comprehensive sign or means of universal trade must be '*a pledge* or standard of value that may be a security or equivalent for the thing given for it, and at all times be sufficient to purchase a like value of any thing that may be needed by him that holds it'.[42]

Witherspoon asserted that there must be some instrument of trade that possessed all three qualities – 'barter... signs... signs possessed of real value'.[43] History and everyday usage showed that precious metals, specifically gold and silver, met the three major attributes of his 'first principles' and were, therefore, ideal instruments for commercial exchange, far better than any other alternatives. The medium of exchange must have five fundamental characteristics: value, rarity, portability, divisibility, and durability. He argued that if the means of exchange lacked any of these essential qualities or was deficient in them that the monetary system would work poorly or not at all.[44] To support his theoretical argument that gold and silver were the most perfect substances for money, Witherspoon delved into the history of Western civilization during ancient times to provide evidence to show how they emerged as the preferred medium of exchange over baser metals such as brass, copper, lead, iron, and tin. He concluded that no other substances combined the five fundamental qualities except gold and silver, for 'such is the true reason why these metals have been applied as instruments of commerce, since the beginning of the world, or as far back as history enables us to penetrate'.[45]

Witherspoon paid considerable attention to his analysis of gold and silver as valuable, because he considered this as their most important attribute. By valuable Witherspoon meant that the means of exchange 'must possess inherent value in reality separate from its form'. If the medium did not have intrinsic value, it would be a mere symbol. According to Witherspoon, the medium of exchange 'must be not only a standard of computation, but a standard of value; and therefore capable of being a pledge and security to the holder, for the property that he has exchanged for it'.[46] Gold and silver possessed the necessary qualities to play this role.

In a footnote Witherspoon cited an anonymous author who had written a pamphlet in which he denied that gold and silver had any intrinsic value except as money, but rather argued that their real value was extrinsic. Witherspoon rejected such a notion and reiterated his argument that gold and silver were valuable both as money and as commodities.[47] He pointed out that the anonymous author attempted to support his position by citing one American and two Scottish eminent authorities on money. The American he cited was none other than Benjamin Franklin, who, he summarised, had claimed that 'Gold and silver are not intrinsically of equal value with iron; a metal of itself capable of many more beneficial uses to mankind. Their value rests chiefly on the estimation they *happen* to be in among the generality of nations and the credit given to the opinion that estimation will continue; otherwise a pound of gold would not be a real equivalent for a bushel of wheat.'[48]

The second author he cited was the Scottish political economist James Anderson, who had argued that money had no intrinsic worth but rather that numerous countries had simply found it helpful in making business transactions run smoothly. In fact, its worth was not natural but a man-made fiction, 'so that although useless in itself, it has come to be accepted among all civilized nations, as a token proving that a person possessed of it had given something of real value in exchange for it, and is on that account accepted of by another in exchange for something that is of real utility and intrinsic worth'.[49]

Although Witherspoon agreed with many of Franklin's and Anderson's other ideas on political economy, especially the idea that labour creates wealth, he rejected their notion that money had no intrinsic worth and that it did not have economic utility. Indeed, their argument was mistaken if they defined money as gold and silver, 'because they are both of material use for the purposes of social life'. Witherspoon thought that what led both Franklin and Anderson to the wrong conclusion was their 'abstracting the idea of taking money in the single light of a sign, without considering it as a standard'. To be sure, he argued, the use of gold as gold, just like any other article of trade, is limited to that of a 'sign of property'. Witherspoon used the example of a gold coin to explain his point. As a gold coin, it had no other value than as a medium of exchange. On the other hand, however, if the gold coin was melted down and shaped into a ring or some other useful item it 'is what is called, with perfect propriety, its intrinsic value'.[50]

In the same footnote Witherspoon firmly rejected the Scottish economist Sir James Steuart's definition of money: 'By money, I understand any commodity which purely in itself is of no material use to man, but which acquires an estimation from his opinion of it, as to become the universal measure of what is called value, and an adequate equivalent of any thing alienable.' He thought that Steuart dismissed the idea that gold and silver had intrinsic value and rather argued that their usefulness as money was based on 'accidental opinion'.[51]

B. THEORETICAL INFERENCES AND PRACTICAL APPLICATIONS

Witherspoon drew out the logical implications of his theoretical position and used his inferences to examine contemporary American public opinion as well as legislation that had been passed or was projected regarding commerce, money, and public credit. This undoubtedly constituted the most original and important sections of the *Essay*.

In his first inference Witherspoon argued that his monetary theory was so clear that all educated people could or should be able to understand a circulating medium. Still, he found that most Americans did not really recognize the true meaning of the term as expressed in their oral and written discourse. For example, one author in a recent newspaper article had claimed that it was a universally accepted conclusion that money was in very short supply. Witherspoon branded such an assertion nonsense, because it was based on a complete misunderstanding of the true definition of money. According to Witherspoon: 'The circulating medium is not yours nor mine.' Rather, 'It is that indefinite quantity of the precious metals that is made use of among the nations connected in commerce. Whether any particular person, city, or nation is rich or poor, has more or less comparatively of it, is nothing to the purpose. Everyone will receive of the circulating medium that quantity which he is entitled to by his property or industry.'[52]

Witherspoon was also informed by his theory that money itself was an article of trade as well as a sign and standard of the means of trade. This was so because 'its value as a standard does and must always follow and accommodate itself to its value as a commodity'. Therefore, the value of money was governed by the same law, the law of supply and demand.[53] Here Witherspoon was clearly arguing for the first time in his analysis the paradox that gold and silver were not in short supply but that they were really in too great a supply.

On this basis Witherspoon resumed his attack on paper money. He reminded his readers of how the extreme discharge of it during the late War of Independence revealed that the increase in the amount of currency led to its irregular depreciation and consequent price inflation. Although some authors blamed the wartime monetary depreciation on forgery and unfavorable public opinion, Witherspoon attributed the currency's decline in value to one thing and one thing only, its increasing quantity. It was obvious to him, therefore, that paper money, which he defined as 'bills bearing that the person holding them is entitled to receive a certain sum specified in them', was not real currency: 'It is barely a sign without being a pledge of standard of value, and therefore is effectually defective as a medium of universal commerce.' Once again, he decried the emission of paper money by the states for use as legal tender to pay all debts as 'an absurdity so great that it is not easy to speak with propriety upon it'.[54] Furthermore, Witherspoon noted that the fault was unique to American state governments, because it had never been practised by European nations. Since it was absolutely necessary that all currency must have a criterion of worth, it was impossible for paper money to succeed because it lacked this key component and was, therefore, worthless.

Witherspoon's second inference dealt with commercial contracts and why paper money was in direct opposition to the fundamental rules of trade. He asserted that all trade was based on contract and supported his claim with a syllogism that was a logical extension of his previous argument: 'Money is the medium of commercial transactions. Money is itself a commodity. Therefore every transaction in which money is concerned, by being given or promised, is strictly and properly speaking a bargain, or as it is well called in some language, an agreement', in other words a contract. When the states issued paper currency as legal tender during the war, they intervened in trade in a manner that was grossly unfair. Accordingly, he argued that the price-fixing laws and the emission of paper currency that states had instituted during the Revolution and war distorted the fundamental character of lawful commercial contracts.[55] Witherspoon's position was that 'one of the essential conditions of a lawful contract, and indeed the first of them, is, that it be *free* and *mutual*. Without this it may be something else, and have some other binding force, but it is not a contract. To make laws therefore, regulating the prices of commodities, or giving nominal value before the law was made, is altering the nature of the transaction altogether.'[56]

As to laws that made paper currency legal tender, Witherspoon concluded that since such money had no intrinsic value and therefore no power, it was in direct opposition to the fundamental rules of trade. Always the teacher, he attempted to educate his readers by emphasizing a fundamental distinction between European countries and American states. Established European nations did not issue paper currency because they had long had a monetary system based on specie. On the other hand, the new American states, following their colonial experience, never had a hard money system because of the lack of sufficient specie caused by an unfavorable balance of trade. The result was that they resorted to experimenting with a wide variety of paper currencies.[57]

Witherspoon's third major inference was that commercial paper was really a promissory note, not money. He held that it was not money because by its very character it was a sign of financial obligation but not a standard of value. Rather, it was 'a promise of some person or body of men to pay money either on demand or at a particular time'.[58] Witherspoon was careful to enumerate and distinguish among several different kinds of commercial paper. Unlike in Europe, in America the purpose of bank notes and state paper currency was to function as money and to have all the attributes of money in commercial transactions. Witherspoon pointed out that the worth of both was ultimately dependent on the public's estimation of their value in any commercial transaction between creditor and debtor. He reasoned that bank notes were much more preferable to paper currency as financial instruments, because they could easily be exchanged for specie and because there were laws governing their use. Witherspoon recognized that exceptional cases existed in the American past in which state paper currency was completely accepted by public opinion and was used freely as legal tender to deal with the financial exigencies caused by the war.[59]

Witherspoon thought the major issue with gold and, especially, silver as money was that the public perceived that they were becoming less and less portable because of their size and heaviness. Hence, whereas the public's demand for paper currency was largely based on the belief that specie was in short supply, Witherspoon countered that 'gold and silver used as a circulating medium are so cheap, and the quantity of a moderate sum is such an incumbrance [*sic*] that we want paper, which can be much more easily carried, and much more effectually concealed'.[60]

Although Witherspoon adamantly opposed the use of paper money as a 'circulating medium', he did think that commercial paper as an alternative for specie was useful in two ways – to facilitate commerce and 'for anticipating or extending credit'.[61] Bills of exchange possessed great utility because they could be transported much more easily and swiftly than goods themselves or precious metals. Witherspoon also thought that commercial paper had great utility in enabling credit arrangements between buyers and sellers in a variety of situations, by far its most important function. He rightly noted that the founding of banks, which used commercial paper in extending credit, had been especially valuable in fostering great improvements in the English and Scottish economies in the eighteenth century. Thus, Witherspoon favoured commercial paper issued by banks as possessing three positive attributes as a method of extending credit: it was backed by specie; it was easy to transport; and it was the major role of banks to grant commercial credit which was eventually helpful to all economic classes.[62]

In his fifth and final inference Witherspoon considered the disadvantages or vices of commercial paper. He demanded that his readers pay special attention to this issue, because it involved inflation, a problem he had stressed throughout the *Essay* and one the citizenry appeared least to understand. 'The evil is this: All paper introduced into circulation, and obtaining credit as gold and silver, adds to the quantity of the medium, and thereby, as has been shown above, increases the price of industry and its fruits. This consequence is unavoidable, and follows as certainly from good paper as bad, or rather more Certainly, for the medium is increased only by that which obtains credit.'[63] He argued that historical experience showed that if paper was used in large quantities for business transactions, specie would automatically disappear. He also criticized those contemporary authors who said that because foreign trade was causing a specie drain that more paper money should be introduced into the American economy. On the contrary, Witherspoon responded that when America had an unfavourable international trade balance, the emission of large quantities of paper money had especially malevolent results because it siphoned off specie much more rapidly. He stressed the signal importance of the relationship between currency inflation and the payment of debts, because the time delay in paying off debts was affected adversely by fluctuations in the value of currency.[64]

Witherspoon concluded that every kind of paper introduced into the economy caused specie drain. But the worst kind of paper was of an uncertain kind, backed up merely by compulsory statutes. Such statutes by their very nature created public doubt based on distrust, which led to sluggish trade. Uncertain paper also destroyed credit and caused wary citizens to keep their specie out of circulation for fear of losing it in business transactions by receiving payment in paper money.[65]

Witherspoon also raised the issue of the wisdom of using paper in commercial transactions. Here, he struck a middle course. He was not entirely opposed to the circulation of paper, which would solve the problems of expanding credit in trade. Still, he wanted such paper supported by specie. He argued that the solution 'depends entirely upon another [problem] whether the evil that is done by augmenting the circulating medium, is or is not overbalanced by the facility given to commerce, and the credit given to particular persons, by which their industry and exertions are added to the common stock'.[66] Witherspoon reasoned that a country's choice to employ paper money or not depended ultimately on changing states of affairs relative to the strength or weakness of its economy. Countries with strong, stable internal economies but which also had a very limited international commerce would not require paper currency. Those with a large and complex trade could possibly profit from its introduction.[67]

He admitted that he did not have a detailed understanding of the American economy to judge whether or not paper money would be advantageous, but he guessed that some attractive quality in it created the need for it when contrasted with its absence in Europe. He recalled that in the economic history of the American colonies their legislatures saw benefits to issuing paper currency and that several knowledgeable writers such as Franklin had argued that its introduction stimulated economic expansion and progress.[68]

Witherspoon argued that if such arrangements had merit it was in the form of paper money issued as loan-office certificates. As a strong supporter of agrarian expansion in the new nation, he favoured such certificates because they extended credit to farmers, and thereby increased the settlement of the public domain and enhanced the fertility of the land. In a similar vein, Witherspoon thought that a major flaw in the use of bank notes as currency was that banks discriminated against farmers by not granting them credit to clear and develop America's vast land resources. He shared with other political economists of the time the view that agriculture was the principal source of wealth in America, even more so than in other nations. Loans in the form of national loan-office paper to farmers to develop their lands would therefore be most advantageous to national wealth.[69]

Witherspoon did not take a rigid position on these matters. He was willing to entertain paper money on certain conditions:

> The plan should be so conceived, as that the increase of the circulating medium should be as little as possible, consistently with these ends. It should be perfectly secure, so as to create an absolute confidence. And as it is of the nature of an obligation, no force whatever should be used, but the reception of it left entirely to the inclination and interest of the receiver.[70]

He warned his readers that any departure from these three requirements would create a defect in the scheme. The finest kind of paper money that satisfied these requirements were European national and private bank notes, because they were always backed by specie.[71]

C. BANKS AND COMMERCIAL PAPER

As to the advantages of bank company notes, Witherspoon reiterated the three key qualities that made them superior to the worthless paper-currency state legislatures issued. First, they were secure in that they could be always be redeemed for gold and silver. Second, they were easily sent from one location to another, which was a general quality of all commercial paper. And third, the main function of banks was to extend credit for businessmen, which was universally beneficial to all economic strata of society. He argued that the value of bank notes should be as large as possible in light of the commercial needs of society and the bank's required income. A major problem that Witherspoon detected with bank notes as a circulating medium in Scotland was that 'very small denominations of paper do the greatest injury by entering into general circulation, and chiefly affecting the industrious part of the community'.[72]

Many Americans had criticized banks on the grounds that they ruined credit rather than expanding it and that they practised usury. Witherspoon disagreed and made the ingenious point that banks actually prevent (or at least limit) usury by extending credit. Based upon his prior knowledge and experiences with Scottish banks,[73] it is not surprising that Witherspoon would reach the following conclusion. 'One would rather think that the regular credit which is or ought to be given by banks should prevent usury. Agreeably to this it is found in fact, that the institution of banks in Scotland lowered the interest of money, which indeed seems to be the natural effect of every such institution, from the increased circulation.'[74]

Witherspoon was well aware of the universal demand for paper money in America from his general observations and participation in Congress. Since the demand was so strong and so widespread, he concluded that there must be some serious cause for it. In his view, advocates of paper money were wrong in seeking a 'circulating medium'. Rather, what they really wanted was '*credit*', just as they had in an earlier era with the loan-offices certificates emitted in the form of 'bills of credit'. To remedy the powerful public demand for paper money in the form of bills of credit, Witherspoon made a proposal based on his monetary theory for a way in which a loan-office might be created with such limited parameters that it would meet the public need in a manner that would outweigh the inherent defects it would possess.[75] His proposal, while impractical, was nevertheless ingenious and deserves to be quoted in full:

> any state that thinks it necessary, should emit a sum of suppose one hundred thousand pounds, and that the following rules should be laid down in law, and invariably adhered to. (1.) That not a shilling of that money should issue from the loan-office treasury, but upon mortgage of land to the amount of double the sum in value. (2.) That it should not be legal tender for any debts contracted or to be contracted, but receivable in all taxes within the state, and payable for the wages of Council [Senate] and Assembly, and the fees and perquisites of all public officers, after it has been received. (3.) That at the end of twelve calendar months, a sum precisely equal to the interest that had accrued or become due in that time, should be consumed by fire, and public intimation given of its being done. The same thing should be done every subsequent year. (4.) That at no time any part of this money should be made use of in the payment of public debts, but that which had been first levied in taxes. It would not be proper even to borrow from the stock for this purpose by anticipation.[76]

Paper notes would create the intended result by promoting trade and extending credit. Furthermore, his scheme would produce few problems, because the amount of the emission would be small and strictly limited to begin with and would be constantly reduced over time until it disappeared. He concluded that if the first emission worked, then it could well be tried again.[77]

Witherspoon anticipated various objections to his plan, including the criticism that his proposed paper bills would not be considered money; that they would not be used by debtors to settle their obligations; and that they would not circulate. His response was that such bills of credit would not serve those debtors who only wanted to reimburse their creditors half of what they owed. 'But I affirm, that it would get better into circulation than by a tender law, which creates general and just suspicion. Tender laws, as had already been proved, may be made use of by deceitful persons to do particular acts of injustice, but are not sufficient to procure general circulation, not excite and reward industry, without opinion and approbation of the public.'[78]

At the conclusion of his proposal for loan-office certificates as bills of credit, Witherspoon turned philosophical. He hoped that state government leaders would not pass any laws, including his proposal, 'but what are founded upon justice, supported by reason, and warranted to be safe by the experience of former ages, and of other countries'.[79] He thought the action of political and natural principles were comparable in their regularity and their reliability. Any law that was flawed, even if its errors might not be ascertained immediately or even over time, would eventually reveal its weakness. He also reasoned that a real hazard was that its weakness would come to light just at the time when a solution was not possible. This danger was inherent in all political acts, but it was especially true with regard to trade.[80]

V CONCLUSION

When Witherspoon published his *Essay* in 1786, he must have felt a strong satisfaction in knowing that many of his former paper currency opponents in Congress had adopted the 'hard money' position he had so long advocated. Even though he had been heavily criticized for backing specie as the only legitimate legal tender while in Congress, his steadfast support of that position throughout the years that culminated in the *Essay* now placed him in the majority. He would certainly have experienced a sense of vindication when Connecticut delegate Roger Sherman, his old ally in Congress, successfully persuaded his fellow founders to adopt what became known as the 'hard money clause' of the United States Constitution, Article 1, Section 10: 'No state shall . . . coin money, emit bills of credit; make anything but gold and silver coin a tender in payment of debts . . .' This development came on 28 August 1787, as reported by James Madison, his most brilliant former student and unquestioned leader of the nationalists at the Convention, in his celebrated journal of the debates.[81] Although there is no direct evidence that Witherspoon's *Essay* played a role in the adoption of the 'hard money clause', it is highly likely that Morris, Sherman, Madison, Hamilton, James Wilson, and other nationalists had read it and approved of Witherspoon's argument for specie currency to replace paper money in the states. In December 1787, as a Somerset County delegate to the New Jersey Ratification Convention, Witherspoon capped his campaign for hard money by voting in favour of the new Federal Constitution.[82]

There is direct evidence, however, that Witherspoon's positions on public credit and banking in the *Essay* helped to shape the ideas and policy proposals of Alexander Hamilton, the nation's first Secretary of the Treasury, on those critical issues in 1789 and 1790. On 20 October 1789, as Hamilton was preparing his 'Report Relative to a Provision for the Support of Public Credit' for Congress of 9 January 1790, he wrote to Witherspoon seeking his counsel on a delicate matter. Should the government differentiate between its reimbursements to the initial owners of public bills of credit (largely soldiers who had been paid for their military service with such government securities) and their present owners (largely businessmen who speculated in the depreciated securities) as it sought to extinguish the public debt caused by the Revolution and war and build a sound foundation of credit? The Princeton president's reply to Hamilton of 26 October was a resounding no. He confessed that the troublesome problem of the 'proper provision for public debt' was still very much on his mind. Reiterating his consistent position on public credit that began in his *Lectures* and continued through his revolutionary writings, his congressional service and his *Essay*, Witherspoon responded to Hamilton as follows: 'The Evil that has pervaded our whole Affairs in America has been the want of a just sense of the sacredness of public Credit.' He warned the Secretary of the Treasury in no uncertain terms that differential payments to various classes of owners of public promissory notes would seriously damage the citizenry's trust in its new government and that it would destroy the nation's credit.[83]

Furthermore, in the same letter Witherspoon informed Hamilton that he had 'read much and wrote some' on the principles and practices of banks. It is fairly certain, therefore, that when Hamilton was preparing his 14 December 1791 'Report on a National Bank' for Congress that one of the key authorities who shaped his thinking on banking was Witherspoon.[84] Hamilton's third report to Congress, his 5 December 1791 'Report on the Subject of Manufactures', also fulfilled Witherspoon's proposal for encouraging manufacturing in his revolutionary writings and his *Essay*. Finally, he was undoubtedly pleased to learn that Congress had approved Madison's 1789 tariff of 5 per cent on all imported goods, a measure that gave the new government a much-needed source of steady income.[85]

By uniting Scottish economic theory with his practical experience in American politics, Witherspoon's *Essay* provided a powerful analysis of the relationship between currency, public credit, and trade at the precise time that Americans were creating their fundamental laws in the Constitution of 1787, including those on monetary policy and public credit. When Witherspoon died on 15 November 1794, the new nation's political leaders had already laid a firm fiscal foundation for its future economic growth. A cornerstone of that arrangement consisted of laws that guaranteed a hard money or specie standard in banking, commerce, national and international finance, and public credit, a standard which Witherspoon had championed throughout his political career in the American Revolution and the Early Republic.

NOTES

1. Still the best overview of eighteenth-century American hard money and paper currency works is J. Dorfman, *The Economic Mind in American Civilization*, 2 vols. (New York, 1946), i, 111–499. Unfortunately, Dorfman did not consider Witherspoon's *Essay*, except for two brief passages, pp. 216, 266.
2. John Witherspoon, *Essay on Money, as a Medium of Commerce; with Remarks on the Advantages and Disadvantages of Paper admitted into general Circulation* (Philadelphia, 1786). References are to this edition, hereafter cited as *Essay*. The *Essay* was later reprinted in *The Works of the Rev. John Witherspoon*, 4 vols. (Philadelphia, 1800–1802), iv, 203–44. On other editions see V. Lansing Collins, *President Witherspoon: A Biography*, 2 vols. (Princeton: Princeton University Press, 1925), ii, 256–61.
3. Collins, ii, 4.
4. Collins, ii, 26.
5. On Morris see C.L. Ver Steeg, *Robert Morris: Revolutionary Financier* (Philadelphia: University of Pennsylvania Press, 1954), pp. 42–186; and on Sherman see R. Sherman Boardman, *Roger Sherman: Signer and Statesman* (Philadelphia: University of Pennsylvania Press, 1938), pp. 78–313, 345–60.
6. Collins, ii, 137–8, 166–7.
7. Collins, ii, 26–7.
8. For an overview of Scotland's rapid economic growth and its role in the Anglo-American commercial empire in the second half of the eighteenth century, see T.M. Devine, *The*

Scottish Nation, 1700–2000 (London: Allen Lane, 1999), pp. 105–69. On Paisley cotton and linen textile manufacturing and its weavers in the eighteenth century see S. Clark, *Paisley: A History* (Edinburgh: Mainstream, 1988), pp. 25–31.

9. John Witherspoon to Alexander Hamilton, 26 October 1789. H.C. Syrett et al. (eds), *The Papers of Alexander Hamilton*, 27 vols. (New York: Columbia University Press, 1961–87), v, 464. Hereafter cited as *Papers*.
10. Collins, i, 102–56.
11. J. Scott (ed.), *An Annotated Edition of Lectures on Moral Philosophy by John Witherspoon* (Newark, DE: University of Delaware Press, 1982). References are to this edition (cited as *Lectures*). The text is also printed in *Works*, iii, 269–374.
12. Francis Hutcheson, *A System of Moral Philosophy*, 2 vols. [1755]. Rpt. with an introduction by Daniel Carey (Bristol: Thoemmes Press, 2000). Hereafter cited as *System*. For Witherspoon's appropriation of Hutcheson's moral philosophy see R.J. Fechner, 'The Moral Philosophy of John Witherspoon and the Scottish-American Enlightenment' (PhD thesis, University of Iowa, 1974), pp. 172–277, and 'The Godly and Virtuous Republic of John Witherspoon', in *Ideas in America's Cultures: From Republic to Mass Society*, ed. H. Cravens (Ames, IA: Iowa State University Press, 1982), pp. 7–25. See also Scott, 'Introduction', pp. 5, 6, 26–8, 35–7, 42–3 and 'Notes', 71–2, 75, 77–8, 82–5, 88–90, 107, 112–13, 120, 122, 128–32, 134–5, 137–9, 142, 147–9, 156–8, 165–7, 173–5, 177, 182–4, 187, 189.
13. Witherspoon, *Lectures*, 178 and 183n15. See Hutcheson, *System*, ii, 55–6.
14. Witherspoon, *Lectures*, 178.
15. Witherspoon, *Lectures*, p. 179. See Hutcheson, *System*, ii, 58–64.
16. Collins, i, 102–237, and ii, 3–80, 186–90.
17. Witherspoon, 'Ignorance of the British with Respect to America' (1771) and 'Letter Sent to Scotland for the *Scots Magazine*' (1772), in *Works*, iv, 281–91.
18. Witherspoon, *Works*, iv, 297–300.
19. Witherspoon, 'Address to the Natives of Scotland Residing in America', in *Works*, iii, 54–5. See D. Hume, 'Of the Jealousy of Trade', in *Essays Moral, Political and Literary*, ed. E.F. Miller (Indianapolis: Liberty Fund, 1987), pp. 327–31.
20. For an extensive discussion of Witherspoon's congressional service, see Collins, ii, 3–81. The historical literature on financial issues during the American Revolution is vast. The classic modern studies are E.J. Ferguson, *The Power of the Purse: A History of American Public Finance, 1776–1790* (Chapel Hill: University of North Carolina Press, 1961) and J.A. Ernst, *Money and Politics in America, 1755–1775* (Chapel Hill: University of North Carolina Press, 1973). A stimulating study of the financial and political history of money in America is J. Goodwin, *Greenback: The Almighty Dollar and the Invention of America* (New York: Henry Holt and Company, 2003), esp. pp. 42–168, which covers the Revolution and Early Republic.
21. 'Benjamin Rush's Notes of Debates', in P.H. Smith (ed.), *Letters of Delegates to Congress, 1774–1789*, 25 vols. (Washington, DC: Library of Congress, 1976–98), vi, 276. Hereafter cited as *Letters of Delegates*.
22. Collins, ii, 26–7.
23. Witherspoon, *Works*, iv, 380, 384.
24. John Witherspoon to William Livingston, 16 December 1780, *Letters of Delegates*, xvi, 452–3.
25. Collins, ii, 50–1.
26. Collins, ii, 51.
27. Ernst, p. xvii; see also pp. 3–42, 245–90, 312–18.
28. Ver Steeg, pp. 43–4, 99, 120.
29. Witherspoon, 'Part of a Speech in Congress on the Finances', in *Works*, iv, 345.
30. Witherspoon, 'Part of a Speech in Congress on the Finances', in *Works*, iv, 340.
31. Witherspoon, 'Speech in Congress on a Motion for Paying the Interest of Loan-Office Certificates', *Works*, iv, 333–4. See Dorfman, pp. 205–79. On bankruptcy and its relationship to paper currency see B.H. Mann, *Republic of Debtors: Bankruptcy in the Age of American Independence* (Cambridge, MA: Harvard University Press, 2002), pp. 166–220.
32. Witherspoon, *Works*, iii, 70–71.
33. Ernst, p. 354. Ferguson summarized the system of currency finance succinctly: 'Congress

stuffed the maw of the Revolution with paper money', p. 29.

34. Collins, ii, 26–7.
35. Witherspoon, *Essay*, pp. 1–2.
36. Witherspoon, *Essay*, p. 1.
37. Witherspoon, *Essay*, p. 60.
38. On this latter point, see Collins, ii, 119–20, 163–74, and 179–80.
39. Witherspoon, *Essay*, p. 2.
40. Witherspoon, *Essay*, p. 2.
41. Hutcheson, 'The Value of Goods in Commerce and the Nature of Coin', in *System*, ii, 53–64.
42. Witherspoon, *Essay*, p. 8.
43. Witherspoon, *Essay*, 9.
44. Witherspoon, *Essay*, pp. 8–10.
45. Witherspoon, *Essay*, pp. 10–12. See Hutcheson, *System*, ii, 56.
46. Witherspoon, *Essay*, pp. 10–12. See Hutcheson, *System*, ii, 56.
47. Witherspoon, *Essay*, p. 12.
48. Witherspoon, *Essay*, p. 13. Franklin's argument appears in his pamphlet, *A Modest Enquiry into the Nature and Necessity of a Paper-Currency* (Philadelphia, 1729), pp. 18–23.
49. Witherspoon, *Essay*, p. 13. Anderson's position is set out in his *Observations on the Means of Exciting a Spirit of National Industry Chiefly Intended to Promote Agriculture, Commerce, Manufactures and Fisheries of Scotland* (Edinburgh, 1777), p. 278.
50. Witherspoon, *Essay*, pp. 14–15.
51. Witherspoon, *Essay*, pp. 14–15. On Steuart's position see his *Inquiry into the Principles of Political Economy* [1767], 2 vols., ed. A.S. Skinner (Chicago: University of Chicago Press, 1966), i, 44.
52. Witherspoon, *Essay*, pp. 22–3.
53. Witherspoon, *Essay*, pp. 24–5.
54. Witherspoon, *Essay*, pp. 29.
55. Witherspoon, *Essay*, pp. 29–33.
56. Witherspoon, *Essay*, p. 31.
57. Witherspoon, *Essay*, pp. 33–6.
58. Witherspoon, *Essay*, p. 37.
59. Witherspoon, *Essay*, pp. 36–7.
60. Witherspoon, *Essay*, pp. 38–9.
61. Witherspoon, *Essay*, p. 40.
62. Witherspoon, *Essay*, pp. 40–42.
63. Witherspoon, *Essay*, pp. 43–4.
64. Witherspoon, *Essay*, p. 45.
65. Witherspoon, *Essay*, p. 45.
66. Witherspoon, *Essay*, p. 45.
67. Witherspoon, *Essay*, p. 45.
68. Witherspoon, *Essay*, pp. 46–7.
69. Witherspoon, *Essay*, pp. 50–52.
70. Witherspoon, *Essay*, p. 47.
71. Witherspoon, *Essay*, pp. 46–7.
72. Witherspoon, *Essay*, p. 49.
73. Witherspoon, *Essay*, p. 50.
74. Witherspoon, *Essay*, pp. 49–50.
75. Witherspoon, *Essay*, pp. 52–3.
76. Witherspoon, *Essay*, p. 53.
77. Witherspoon, *Essay*, pp. 54–5.
78. Witherspoon, *Essay*, p. 55.
79. Witherspoon, *Essay*, p. 56.
80. Witherspoon, *Essay*, pp. 55–6.
81. See Madison's personal journal of the Convention's proceedings, *Notes of Debates in the Federal Convention of 1787 Reported by James Madison*. Bicentennial Edition (New York: Norton, 1987), pp. 541–2.

82. Collins, ii, 164–5.
83. Alexander Hamilton to John Witherspoon, 20 October 1789 and John Witherspoon to Alexander Hamilton, 26 October 1789, in *Papers*, v, 457 and 464–5. Cited in W. Sterne Randall, *Alexander Hamilton: A Life* (New York: HarperCollins, 2003), pp. 378–79 and 400n17.
84. See Randall's argument for this point, p. 397.
85. S. Elkins and E. McKitrick, *The Age of Federalism: The Early American Republic, 1788–1800* (New York: Oxford University Press, 1993), pp. 65–75.

III: Credit and the Matter of the Irish Public

CHAPTER EIGHT

'The Public Wealth is the Sinew, the Life, of Every Public Measure': The Creation and Maintenance of a National Debt in Ireland, 1716–45[1]

CHARLES IVAR McGRATH

The phrase quoted in my title comes from a pamphlet, first published in 1754, in support of the Irish House of Commons' stance in the 'money bill dispute' of 1753.[2] The sentiments expressed there are reminiscent of arguments employed by John Brewer in *The Sinews of Power* (1989) or P.G.M. Dickson's use in *The Financial Revolution* (1967) of Joseph Addison's personification of public credit as a beautiful virgin surrounded by those acts of parliament which were believed to sustain the existing order. The same literary device is repeated by Linda Colley in *Britons* (1992) and examined in greater detail by J.G.A. Pocock in *The Machiavellian Moment* (1975). These and other historians have argued that the English financial revolution of the late seventeenth century was, depending on the emphasis, instrumental in forging a nation, a fiscal-military state, or an empire. A central aspect of all of these arguments is the importance of the concept of public credit, in relation both to the British government's ability to finance war in the eighteenth century through the creation of a national debt, and to the large numbers of British people, from lords to labourers, who, by means of credit systems, developed a greater vested interest in the survival of the nation, state or empire. Confidence, trust, mutual dependence, and obligation are just some of the words utilized to explain this phenomenon.[3] While the Irish experience does not fit snugly into the work of such historians, the views stated in the 1754 pamphlet demonstrate that some of these considerations are valid in an Irish context.[4]

The advent of a national debt in 1716 was a significant event in Irish history, yet it remains an under-explored subject. This essay traces the origins of that debt and its growth during the period 1716–45. A number of constitutional and political issues surrounding the debt are also examined, including the extent to which the existence of the debt in itself represented an expression of a new-found confidence within the Protestant community in their own sense of identity as the 'Irish Protestant nation' in the aftermath of the Glorious Revolution.[5]

I

One of the most visible signs of change in Ireland after 1691 was the advent of regular parliamentary sessions, and the placement of parliament at the centre of a constitutional framework that was peculiar to the eighteenth century. Since 1692 the Irish House of Commons had won a series of constitutional concessions from government in relation to Poynings' Law and the crown prerogative in initiating legislation in the Irish parliament. The Commons' main weapon had been its control of the amount and duration of the additional supplies required to meet the government's increased expenditure following the war of 1689–91, costs which arose in particular from the maintenance of a large standing army.[6] The post-Revolution army on the Irish Establishment was made up from reduced regiments, with a higher than normal ratio of officers to enlisted men, so that in time of emergency active regiments could be transported quickly to England or elsewhere, brought up to strength either with draughts from other Irish regiments or new recruits raised in Britain, and put in the field without delay. The remaining regiments in Ireland could then be brought up to war-time strength with new recruits and additional companies, or new regiments could be raised.[7] As such, Ireland paid for and maintained a substantial part of the British standing army, and therein actively contributed to Britain's eighteenth-century wars and the emergence of the first British empire.[8]

By 1714 this new constitutional framework had evolved to a point where a number of principles – based upon a significant relaxation in the application and interpretation of Poynings' Law and a real diminution of the crown prerogative in initiating legislation – had been accepted by the executive and legislature. These new principles included biennial parliamentary sessions; the reduction of the government's legislative programme to a token supply bill and two or three other minor measures at the beginning of a newly-elected parliament; the use of a parliamentary procedure known as 'heads of bills' for drafting the vast majority of Irish legislation; and the control of the ways and means of raising supply by the Commons. The combination of these principles gave parliament control of the public purse-strings, a reality that was firmly established by the time the first Hanoverian parliament met in 1715. It was also evident that this new constitutional reality was predicated in part upon keeping the government money-hungry, a practice which was assisted by the slow increase in expenditure throughout the century. The introduction of parliament-sanctioned borrowing and a national debt in 1716 heralded a new phase in the evolution of this framework.[9]

The commencement of government borrowing conceded further power to parliament, as the sanctioning of borrowing and the servicing of the ensuing debt were dependent upon parliament. At the same time, the people who lent the money – the public creditors – were Protestant peers, judges, bishops, MPs, clergymen, merchants, and the like, who, as part of the Irish Protestant community, already depended for their survival upon the maintenance of the Revolution settlement in 'church and state'. Although the creation of a national debt increased the government's reliance upon parliament, it also ensured that parliament, and the wider Protestant community, developed an even greater vested interest in supplying the necessary funds for servicing the national debt and, in the wider context, for maintaining an army capable of defending Ireland and actively contributing to the British 'fiscal-military state'. As such, the history of the national debt is central to our understanding of the eighteenth-century Irish constitution, of the emergence of a self-aware and confident Irish Protestant nation, and of Ireland's role in the first British empire.

II

A key aspect of the English financial revolution was the creation and maintenance of a national debt. Similarly, the introduction of parliament-sanctioned government borrowing in Ireland in 1716 was a highly significant occurrence.[10] The first loan of that parliament-sanctioned national debt was raised on the basis of an unlimited vote of credit by the Commons in 1716, and the promise in the third money act of the 1715–16 session that provision for repayment of an unspecified principal sum, with interest, would be made in the next session. Therein, parliament acted as the security for the debt by promising to provide for the servicing of it 'out of the next aids to be granted by parliament'. In other words, parliament sanctioned the borrowing of money on the credit of the nation. The government borrowed £50,000, thereby bringing into existence the first national debt in Ireland.[11]

The immediate financial necessity for the vote of credit and loan legislation was the renewed Jacobite threat following the Hanoverian succession. Already in 1715 Ireland's military contribution to securing the new regime had involved sending four regiments to England and eight to Scotland, an action which had left the army in Ireland under-strength and the Protestant community worried about their own security.[12] Throughout January 1716 the Commons demonstrated their real concern over the threat from the Jacobite rebellion in Scotland and their continuing fear of the Catholic majority in Ireland, as evidenced by the passage of an act for attainting the Pretender and in a series of resolutions, addresses, and an association.[13]

The vote of credit occurred on 28 January. On that day, immediately after receipt of directions from England, the lords justices informed parliament of an imminent threat of invasion and of the king's orders for raising new forces. Given the general acceptance by this time that responsibility for raising supply lay with the Commons, the lords justices then made a direct appeal to the Lower House for money. The Commons readily complied by passing a vote of credit, which was signified in a resolution that whatever money should be paid into the treasury by any person for the defence of Ireland would 'be made good by this House, with legal interest . . . out of such aids as shall be granted . . . the next session'. On 29 January the Commons presented an address to the lords justices desiring them to bring the military Establishment up to strength and to raise such extra forces as they perceived to be necessary, and that in order 'to render this more effectual, [the Commons] have engaged to make good whatever sums of money shall be advanced by any person for that service'.[14] The resulting legislation specified that the loan was sanctioned due to the fact that 'the exigence of the public affairs' might require 'an expense and greater supplies, than the funds already granted'.[15] The loan was used to raise thirteen new regiments.[16]

The significance of these events was not lost on contemporaries. The joint chief secretary, Charles Delafaye, believed that 'never [a] parliament did greater things, especially the vote of credit the like to which was never known here before'.[17] The lords justices concurred: 'Their vote of credit is a resolution without precedent here... [and] will very much contribute to [his majesty's] service, which could not possibly have been carried on any other way at this time, in a country where we have no Bank nor East India Company to supply the emergencies of the government.'[18] This latter remark highlighted the different stage of development of fiscal structures in Ireland. England's financial revolution had not been repeated in Ireland for numerous reasons: lack of an overriding need or requisite economic climate; lack of public creditors; and the absence of a robust capital market, to name a few.[19] By 1716, however, a number of factors had changed: a boom in the Irish economy following the peace of 1713; twenty years of regular parliamentary supply (which had sustained an unprecedented higher level of income for the government) had created a sense of stability within Irish fiscal practice and of confidence in the security of future parliamentary duties; and the existence of an immediate need.[20]

Although what had occurred was unique for Ireland, there was no difficulty in raising the loan. In fact, it appeared that more money was made available than was required and that, as far as can be ascertained, the loan was made in ready specie.[21] Such developments would seem to be in part a reflection of the buoyant economic climate, but possibly even more so of the Protestant community's vested interest in the defence of the Hanoverian succession and their sense of confidence built up over the previous two decades in the apparatus of the state.

Examination of the subscribers to the loan bears testimony to the business-minded attitude of these new public creditors, but also reflects the extent to which a significant number of the Irish Protestant community felt confident enough to invest their capital in government. With interest at 8 per cent, payment of which, along with the principal, was secured by parliament, investment in the loan scheme certainly represented an attractive proposition to a person with disposable income. The largest subscription – £5,000 – came from William Conolly, Speaker of the Commons and a successful businessman. At the same time, seventeen more MPs, four past or future MPs, six peers, three bishops, three judges, four women, three clergymen, two aldermen, and twenty unidentified private people were included on the list of sixty-three individual subscribers.[22] Amongst the names were those of Conolly's main political rivals, the lord chancellor, Alan, Baron Brodrick, and his son St John Brodrick. Other significant individuals included James Hamilton, Earl of Abercorn, Bishops St George Ashe of Clogher and John Stearne of Dromore, the lord chief justices of the king's bench and common pleas (William Whitshed and John Forster respectively), Revenue Commissioner Thomas Medlycott, Attorney-General George Gore, Solicitor-General John Rogerson, the private bankers Benjamin Burton and Francis Harrison, the future deputy vice-treasurer Luke Gardiner, Charles Delafaye and his fellow chief secretary Martin Bladen, Under-Secretary Eustace Budgell, Postmaster-General Isaac Manley, and the infamous Colonel Henry Luttrell.[23]

The advent of a national debt necessitated a degree of innovation in supply legislation from 1716 onwards. The 1716 act is best described as an additional duties act which incorporated a clause that, in keeping with the vote of credit, sanctioned the loan and directed that the principal sum and the interest should be repaid out of the supplies to be granted in the next parliamentary session. A second clause stated that interest payments were in fact to be made every six months from the date of the initial loan, out of the supplies granted in the 1715–16 session. This apparent inconsistency arose because of the fact that the vote of credit had not taken account of the need to start paying interest from the commencement date of the loan. This second clause therefore rectified the omission, so that the interest payments were provided for on the security of the 1715–16 additional supplies in general, without appropriation of a specific fund. Thus, although there was a general undertaking to repay the principal, the only legislative provision for servicing the debt applied to the interest and was restricted in legal terms to the same two-year duration applicable to the main supply acts passed in 1715–16. In the absence of a specific appropriated fund, the onus for paying the interest rested with the government; thus the servicing of the debt was dependent upon the level of priority given to the debt within the broader scheme of annual payments to be made on the Establishment.[24]

The provisions for servicing the debt were clarified to some extent by parliament in 1717. In the second main supply act of the 1717 session it was acknowledged that the existing Establishment pay arrears and the further supplies required by government meant that the current debt of £50,000 'may not be fully... paid out of the aids granted this present session'. Therefore it was enacted that the public creditors would continue to receive interest payments every six months 'out of such his majesty's . . . revenue as shall come to the [vice-treasurer's] . . . hands, until they are respectively paid . . . [their] principal sums'. There was also a general undertaking that any part of the £50,000 not repaid by November 1719 would be paid 'to whom[ever] the same shall be then due', which implied (as in 1716, without foundation) that a substantial part of the principal would be cleared by the time the two main supply acts of 1717 expired in November 1719, and that the remainder of the debt would be cleared quickly thereafter.[25]

Thus, the 1717 act allowed for the debt to be serviced out of the public revenue in general, inclusive of the hereditary revenue, which was an even more generalized provision than that which had been made in 1716. As before, without a specific appropriated fund, the onus for servicing the debt rested with the government. The 1717 act also renewed the general undertaking to continue interest payments until such unspecified time as the principal would be repaid. In theory this undertaking allowed for interest payments to continue beyond the two-year duration of the 1717 supply act, though the stated intention of clearing the debt on or shortly after the expiry of that act implied a limit to the time in which such payments could be made. In practical and legal terms, however, the period within which interest would with any certainty be paid was once again restricted to the same two-year duration of the supply act. For all intents and purposes, the general undertaking regarding the continued payment of interest and eventual repayment of the principal could be construed as nothing more than a promise by parliament, or at least the acceptance of some degree of obligation upon the part of that assembly, to ensure that at some unspecified point in the future public creditors would be repaid their money, and that in the interim parliament would, at each biennial session, ensure that provision was made for the continuation of interest payments. In keeping with that general undertaking, in the following five parliamentary sessions to 1727–8, the same provisions for servicing the debt were included in the main two-year duration supply act passed in each session.[26]

III

In the context of the eighteenth-century constitutional framework, the significance of the ongoing legislative process relating to the national debt during the years 1716 to 1727–8 was that from the outset the Commons had ensured that all aspects of the national debt were comprehended within the parameters of the Lower House's post-Revolution understanding of the politics of supply. The central consideration was that the restriction of all of the main supply legislation to a two-year duration ensured the continuation of biennial parliamentary sessions and kept the government dependent upon parliament to meet its financial commitments, which now included the national debt.[27]

It was also evident from the legislation passed between 1716 and 1727–8 that during this time only the interest on the debt was paid to the public creditors, and even those payments were always in arrears.[28] A number of reasons can be put forward for the government's failure to meet the interest payments: a general negative impact upon fiscal affairs because of an economic downturn in the 1720s and an ensuing loss of confidence in Irish trade and manufactures; an increasing shortage of ready specie; the collapse of the South Sea Company; the failure of the national bank project in 1720–1; the Wood's halfpence affair in 1722–5; and the scandal in 1725 over the treasury losses incurred through the private investments of the deputy vice-treasurer, John Pratt. Yet the most significant reasons for the government's failure to meet payments were the continuing opposition of MPs to the imposition of new duties; increasing government expenditure; occasional security crisis expenses; and, most significant, parliament's failure to appropriate a specific fund for servicing the debt.[29]

The government's failure to meet its financial commitments in the 1720s led to another fiscal experiment during the 1725–6 parliamentary session. At the Christmas recess the government was despondent at the refusal of the Commons to countenance the imposition of any new duties. As was becoming common practice, the Lower House had chosen to overestimate the projected return from a renewal of the existing additional duties for the forthcoming two years and to underestimate the amount of the Establishment pay arrears.[30] Yet in early 1726, as a result of renewed fears of war, the Commons agreed to an address to assure the king that 'they will put his military Establishment . . . in a good condition; which supposes a deficiency in what they have already done. And my lord lieutenant [John, Lord Carteret] . . . is in hopes that at the next meeting a vote of credit may be obtained, to make the government perfectly easy here.'[31]

However, instead of pushing for a vote of credit, the government was happy to act upon an ensuing address from the Commons, that

£10,000 from the supplies already granted be set aside for payment of 7 per cent interest upon warrants for army pay that was in arrears, in order 'to make the warrants . . . have a currency among the people, till money came in to pay them off'.[32] The theory was that 'bankers and other monied men' would advance money upon the security of the warrants, for which they would receive interest payments for two years, after which time parliament would provide a fund to clear the principal.[33] Thus, the Commons undertook in principle for a percentage of the Establishment pay arrears to be transformed into part of the national debt, by agreeing to take that percentage of the pay arrears upon themselves as a debt secured on the credit of the nation.

The scheme proved successful and the warrants 'were immediately cleared by money advanced by several persons'. During the next two years £8,395 was paid in interest upon the principal of £59,967, which was due to be repaid to the creditors at the end of 1727. However, such repayment 'being liable to many difficulties', in particular the absence of a parliamentary fund, in December 1727 the Commons renewed their address of early 1726, requesting that £10,000 from the duties to be voted in 1727–8 be applied towards continuing the interest payments for a further two years. The executive accepted this method of extracting itself from the 'difficulties' of repaying the principal, with the justification that the continuation of interest payments put the government 'upon as good a footing for the next two years, as ever it was in this kingdom'.[34]

Such measures were only for the interim, however, and did not address the question of making a more comprehensive provision for servicing the national debt. The first step in that direction occurred in 1729. It was evident from the outset that the new arrangements were influenced by the experience of the 1726–7 experiment. In November 1729 the Commons' committee of public accounts reported that the 'debt of the nation' (an all-encompassing term to describe the national debt of £50,000, the arrears of interest of £2,504, the £59,967 advanced on the warrants for army pay in 1726 and a further percentage of the Establishment pay arrears), stood at £220,731. This represented a substantial increase from the £127,372 reported in 1727. The government had learnt long before that the Commons would not provide for the whole of the Establishment pay arrears, which stood at £317,170 in 1729.[35] Thus the executive's strategy was to press for some form of parliamentary provision 'to answer the interest of about £200,000 of our debts, till we are able to pay the principal'.[36] There was good hope of success, as the yield in the public income had been reduced, not by mismanagement, but by bad harvests, economic recession, and famine, a point which had prompted the lord lieutenant to ask the Commons to grant a supply which would 'answer the exigencies of the government in such manner as shall be most expedient, and may be least burdensome to the people'.[37]

The Commons complied by agreeing to a new loan of £150,000, and, unlike on previous occasions, also accepted the need to impose new duties in order to provide sufficient revenue for servicing the national debt. In a significant development, the Lower House decided to enact a specific appropriation of these new duties to pay the interest, 'and to apply the surplus, if any, to the discharge of the principal'. In so doing, the Commons transformed the national debt into a funded national debt. The government accepted the need for a specific appropriation, but a difficulty arose over the executive's wish to have one all-inclusive supply bill which would include clauses for renewing the existing additional duties and for imposing and appropriating the new duties. The Commons refused to comply and instead drafted the heads of two supply bills, because MPs apprehended that

> the appropriating clause . . . may be thrown out in England if [it is] in the grand money bill, and that we can not refuse passing it if such an alteration should be made, for then we must be undone by letting the funds run out, which the kingdom can not bear[.] [B]ut if in a separate bill these new duties with the appropriating clause should be altered, or any part of them be thrown out of the bill in England, we can refuse passing the bill, without much detriment to the country.[38]

The first heads of a supply bill – the 'grand money bill' – were the heads for the traditional main supply bill which re-imposed for two years the existing additional duties voted to provide extra income towards the government's revenue at large. The second heads of a supply bill allowed for the new loan of £150,000, and imposed several new duties which were appropriated for payment of the interest, at a new rate of 6 per cent per annum, on the loans of £50,000 and £150,000, and if money remained thereafter, for repayment of the principal. As such, these new duties were voted in order to provide a specific and secure fund for servicing the whole of the national debt, which would increase to £200,000.

The new loan of £150,000 was to be provided for clearing part of the pay arrears, 'which cannot at present be discharged... without [imposing] such supplies as would greatly burden your majesty's faithful subjects'. In taking subscriptions, priority was to be given to warrants for army pay that was in arrears, which warrants were to be treated as 'ready money' and preferred over specie, and would include those warrants upon which interest had been paid since 1726.[39] Thus, the loan would serve to transform £150,000 of the pay arrears into a funded debt.[40] Thereby, the Commons had drafted the heads of a bill which would put the principle established in 1726 into more substantive practice, by taking £150,000 of the Establishment pay arrears upon themselves as a debt secured on the credit of the nation.

Before the heads of the loan bill were finalized, a further difficulty arose over the executive's desire that the imposition of the appropriated duties should be open-ended, to cease only when the debt was cleared. Once again the Commons refused to comply, and the duration for the appropriated duties – and the legal requirement for interest payments – was restricted to the usual two-year time frame.[41] It was not surprising that many MPs, out of fear that in time such an act as the executive desired might assume permanency and become a source of supply to the government that was beyond the control of the Commons, opposed an open-ended duration for the new duties. Thus, as since 1716, the Commons made certain that the national debt was tied into the politics of supply, by which the Lower House ensured the continuation of biennial sessions and kept the government dependent upon parliament.[42]

The loan bill, having been sent to England for consideration in accordance with Poynings' Law, was returned to Ireland with a number of alterations made to it by the British privy council. The main justification given for the alterations was that the changes did not affect the duration or appropriation in the act, and were only intended to ensure 'that all those who had advanced their money to supply the exigencies of... government might have an equal security for their interest till the principal were repaid them'. The king and council hoped that the Irish parliament would pass the bill despite the alterations, as the bill in itself 'appears to be so necessary, not only for supporting the honour of the government, but for the satisfaction and security of those who have already lent their money or are willing to advance further sums for the public service, upon parliamentary credit'.[43]

The original heads of the bill sent from the Commons to the Irish privy council, and from there to England, had not included the usual general undertaking for the continued payment of interest until such unspecified time as the principal would be cleared, and instead had imposed a specific restriction on the payment of interest to two calendar years. The British privy council had therefore removed the two-year restriction on interest payments and restored the general undertaking to continue such payments 'until such time as ... [the public creditors] be respectively paid their principal at one entire payment'. While these alterations did not interfere with the duration of the act, they did reinstate a feature of all previous acts since 1716 which had imposed an obligation upon parliament to renew the legislation every two years until the principal was repaid.[44] As Charles Delafaye, now an under-secretary of state in England, pointed out, the 'gentlemen of Ireland would not have it imagined that they should intend to draw people in to lend their money, pay two years interest and then drop the creditors without so much as a promise of the payment of any further interest or of the principal'.[45]

The second substantive alteration was wholly concerned with clarifying an aspect of the appropriation clause. One of the innovations in the heads of the bill had been the introduction in the appropriation clause of the concept of a 'sinking fund', the purpose of which would be to apply any surplus arising from the appropriated duties, after payment of the interest, towards the clearance of the principal. However, this sinking fund had only been sketched in theoretical terms in the heads, without any details of how the surplus would be applied towards clearing the principal. It therefore fell to the British privy council to place the theoretical sinking fund on more solid ground, by including a clarifying phrase which stated that any such surplus would be applied 'in such order and manner, as by an act or acts of parliament hereafter to be made shall be directed and provided, and to no other use, intent, or purpose whatever'.[46] Thus the details for the implementation of a sinking fund were to be confirmed by an act of the Irish parliament at some point in the future.

The bill was endangered by the British privy council's alterations. On receipt of the altered bill from England, the lord lieutenant expressed his concern for its fate in the Commons, noting that 'above £50,000' had already been subscribed, 'more than can be received [towards the loan], supposing the bill should pass; so that the security was looked upon here to be sufficient, before the alterations were made'. He also pointed out that 'the substance of the more essential of those alterations' had already been proposed in the Commons before the heads of the bill had been completed, but that the Lower House had rejected the suggested changes at that time. There seemed little reason to think the House would have changed its opinion in the intervening period.[47]

The main threat to the bill, however, stemmed from the long-standing opposition in the Commons to any alterations, regardless of whether they were valid or not, being made to supply bills.[48] Thus the primary argument used against the altered bill in the Commons focused upon 'the ill consequences of passing any money bill that was altered, which might be drawn into a precedent, to prolong or increase our taxes as the crown is pleased'. This argument 'brought on' the favourite topics of the post-Revolution parliamentary opposition: 'Poynings' Law, . . . the power and prerogative of the king and council, and the precedents of money bills [being] altered'. The opponents of the bill also tried to imply that the appropriation clause had been made ineffectual by the addition of the British privy council's clarifying phrase, by arguing that 'if the king should [return] an act of parliament for the application of the [surplus] it could not be disposed of as was intended by the transmitted bill'. This argument, however, was considered by the majority to be 'so absurd, that no other answer was given to it, but that it might as well be expected that the king would send a regiment of dragoons to take the money out of the treasury as [return] such a bill, for as the bill was worded the vice-treasurer could not pay it upon any warrant or order of the king's, so that it must lie in his hands till dispersed of by parliament'.[49]

Ultimately, the underlying fear being played upon in the Commons by the opposition appeared to be (as it had been on many occasions since the Revolution) that the alterations made by the British privy council to the loan bill might by some uncertain means enable the executive to survive financially without recourse to parliament. It was understandable that such a fear should arise at a time when the Commons had finally agreed to introduce a whole new schedule of additional duties, and with it a new source of public income. Such a fear was unfounded, however, because the alterations did not affect the two-year duration of the duties or their appropriation for that same period towards servicing the national debt. Regardless of the alterations, parliament would still have to be reconvened biennially in order to re-impose all of the additional duties, including the appropriated ones.[50]

In the end, the strength of the arguments for the bill ensured its success, including that its loss would cause a great increase in the debt and 'put us in danger of a land tax, besides the injury done to [the public creditors] . . . who could have no interest for two years, which was the highest injustice to those who had advanced their money on the public credit'.[51] The altered bill passed in both Houses and received the royal assent on 22 December 1729.[52]

The resulting act was the first Irish act to be wholly concerned with legislating for a loan and providing a secure fund for servicing the national debt.[53] It was also the first act to incorporate the principle of a 'sinking fund'. As Hugh Boulter, Archbishop of Armagh, described it: 'the . . . [act] is made up of several little taxes, by which it is proposed' if more than £12,000 per annum is raised, '[then] to sink part of the principal'.[54] And, thanks to the British privy council's clarifying phrase in the appropriation clause, the Irish Commons would at some point have to make an explicit declaration in law of how their theoretical sinking fund would work in practice.

As in 1716, there was no shortage of people willing to subscribe to the 1729 loan.[55] As stipulated in the act, a large number of the subscriptions were taken in the form of warrants for army pay that was in arrears.[56] By March 1730, £51,600 had been subscribed in this form. The majority of the 84 subscribers were army officers, though there were also civilians, such as the private bankers Daniel Falkiner and David La Touche, and government officials, such as Under-Secretary Thomas Tickell and Lord Chancellor Thomas Wyndham. A further £90,000 had been subscribed in ready money at the same time by 86 individuals, including the new undertakers Sir Ralph Gore and Marmaduke Coghill, the future undertaker Henry Boyle, the leading opponent of the altered loan bill Richard Bettesworth, Solicitor-General Robert Jocelyn and Chief Secretary Thomas Clutterbuck. Seven people were creditors for both debentures and ready specie, so that the total number of individual subscribers was 163.[57]

The list of subscribers to the loan demonstrated, as in 1716, not only the business aptitude of people, but also the confidence of many individuals in the central apparatus of the state, and of their understanding of a public credit system. In fact, the competition amongst potential subscribers led to conflict in the Commons in March 1730. Although the act stipulated that army warrants were to be preferred over ready specie, the need to export £40,000 in hard cash for the pay arrears of the Irish troops stationed in Gibraltar had necessitated the acceptance of coin subscriptions before all of the warrants had been subscribed. The immediate need for the £40,000 had caused the lord lieutenant to take 'the subscription from about fifty parliament men, and several others whom he had a mind to gratify', an action which had caused other potential subscribers to object that 'the letter' of the act had been contravened.[58]

IV

The passing of the 1729 loan act was significant in relation to the wider contexts of the role of fiscal considerations as a part of the post-Revolution constitutional framework, and of the Protestant community's own sense of identity in the eighteenth century. Since the 1690s the Commons had demonstrated a clear understanding of the fact that control of income gave a new power to parliament, and ensured regular parliamentary sessions and a greater degree of government accountability. At the same time, parliament continued to provide for the government's immediate financial needs, primarily because of the Protestant community's identification of their own security in a Catholic-dominated country with the government's ability to pay for an enlarged military Establishment. That same security concern had served as the cause for the creation of a parliament-sanctioned national debt in 1716. But the creation and maintenance of that debt also served to reinforce and magnify the Protestant community's commitment to paying the government's bills, which from 1726 onwards led to further experiments in the utility of a public credit system for relieving the pressures of army pay arrears and the introduction of a comprehensive provision for servicing the national debt.

The Protestant community's commitment to paying the government's bills was placed in even starker relief by the fact that the government's creditors were for the most part members of that same community. Thus, a significant number of people in Protestant Ireland, including peers, bishops, judges, MPs, merchants, bankers, military officers, clergymen, and numerous others who remained anonymous, had a vested interest in ensuring the continued provision of sufficient supplies for servicing the debt. At the same time, the creation and maintenance of the debt was predicated upon an understanding of a public credit system in which money was borrowed on the credit of the nation.

The nation in question was that self-same Irish Protestant community. Ever since the national debt had come into existence in

1716, it had become accepted parlance in the Commons to talk of the 'debt of the nation' and the 'credit to the nation'.[59] By the early 1730s, even in pamphlet literature which expressed concern at the growing debt, the accepted terms of reference were to that debt being a matter for the public and the nation. In one instance, when a proposal for a new loan was opposed because it would lay 'the nation under the severest bonds', it was acknowledged that the money would be 'lent on the public faith' (though the writer's belief was that all the money would be provided by MPs, which thus obliged them to do the government's bidding).[60] These terms of reference were consistent with the prevailing sense of the debt (and the public credit facilities that went with it) being a concern of the public and the nation, which in governmental and institutional terms in Ireland in the first half of the eighteenth century meant a Protestant public and a Protestant nation.[61] By the 1750s these various considerations would be bound together in the argument that all public financial and revenue matters in Ireland were part of a broader concept or theoretical construct defined in general terms by the idea of the 'public wealth', which was 'the sinew, the life, of every public measure'.[62]

The extent to which a community of people existed in 1716–29 who were prepared to act as public creditors can be demonstrated by examination of the 226 subscribers to the 1716 and 1729 loans and the subscribers to the unsuccessful national bank projects in 1720–1. Given that seven of the 226 subscribers contributed to both the 1716 and 1729 loans, the total individual subscribers to the loans was 219. These 219 individuals were of course the ones whose subscriptions had been successful. Comparison with the bank lists from 1720–1 allows for a projection of how many more willing lenders might have existed. The number of individual subscribers to the two rival bank projects in 1720 totalled 371, while a further 117 individual subscribers were included in a later composite list. Thus, a total of 488 individuals were prepared to subscribe to a national bank in 1720–1. Of these, 46 subscribed to one loan and a bank, with a possible two more, while seven others, plus a possible one more, subscribed to both loans and a bank. That still left 432 individuals who had been prepared to subscribe to a bank (at least in theory), but were not on either of the loan lists. There are many reasons why this may be, but it suggests that many more potential public creditors existed within the Irish Protestant community in the period.[63]

Table 8.1: Public creditors and potential creditors, 1716–29[64]

Subscribers	1716	1720–1	1729
Peers	6	16	2
Bishops	3	4	2
Judges	3	1	2
MPs	18	117	50
Past or future MPs	4	30	3
Women	4	18	15
Clergy	3	11	4
Merchants	—	51	—
Bankers	—	2	1
Merchant/Bankers	—	3	—
Goldsmiths	—	1	—
Military Officers	—	23	44
Aldermen	2	4	—
Lord Mayor	—	1	—
Other	20	206	40
Totals	63	488	163

The rejection of the national bank project by parliament in late 1721 demonstrated that the bank lists did not reflect the majority view in parliament, and probably within the wider Protestant community. However, it was not necessary for a majority either within parliament or the wider community to be in favour of or actively involved in a public credit system for such a system to function successfully (as had been demonstrated by the ongoing debate in England on the issue since the 1690s).[65] Account must also be taken of the fact that the initial proposals for a bank were made in the summer of 1720 in completely different circumstances to those prevalent in late 1721. The first proposal occurred during the height of the mass speculation (including substantial amounts of Irish capital) in the South Sea Company, and at a time when public confidence in such schemes seemed to know no bounds. Thus, when initially proposed, the prospects for a national bank scheme in Ireland seemed very good. The collapse of the South Sea Company that autumn, however, had an extremely detrimental effect upon the Irish economy and public confidence in general, and the bank project in particular. The Irish economy had already been in decline prior to the summer of 1720, and continued to deteriorate thereafter. Trade restrictions due to quarantines to prevent the plague spreading from mainland Europe increased the hardship, as did the impact of bad weather on the harvest, which caused famine conditions in the winter of 1720–1. The combination of these factors, in conjunction with the innate conservatism of the landed country gentlemen in parliament and the ongoing constitutional and factional conflicts within Irish politics for which the bank project became a sacrificial lamb, made the task of the critics of the bank, and of a public credit system in general, a great deal easier, and ensured the defeat of the proposal.[66]

It is therefore not surprising to find that although 117 MPs appeared on the bank lists, a number of these subscribers actually voted against the proposal, as evidenced by the three divisions in parliament – two on 14 October and one on 9 December 1721 – which all went against the proposal, 103–95, 98–91, and 150–80 respectively.[67] Examination of the extant division lists, for the first and third votes, provides a degree of qualification to such bald figures.

Table 8.2: Voting pattern of MPs on the national bank lists, for and against the bank proposal, October and December 1721

For		Against	
Oct.	Dec.	Oct.	Dec.
59	51	27	37
[95]	[80]	[103]	[150]

(Totals for the two divisions are given in square brackets.)

Of the 117 MPs on the various bank lists, 45 voted for the bank on both occasions, while 25 voted against on both occasions; 10 who voted for and one who voted against in October did not vote in December; five who voted for and eight who voted against in December had not voted in October; four who voted for in October voted against in December; and one who voted against in October voted for in December. The total of MPs who voted for the bank at some point was 65, while the total against was 39. Of the 13 unaccounted for MPs from the lists, one died before the 1721 session commenced, another was elevated to the House of Lords, and the remainder were either absent or abstained from voting.[68]

A further qualification to these figures arises from the fact that while only 93 of the original subscribers to the two bank projects appeared on the later composite list, 117 new names appeared there for the first time, including the pro-bank pamphleteer Henry Maxwell. This composite list included 40 of the MPs who voted for the bank, 13 of whom, including Maxwell, made their first appearance as subscribers. It may have been that Maxwell and these 12 other pro-bank MPs felt the need in the autumn and winter of 1721 to put their money, at least theoretically, where their mouth (or in Maxwell's case, his pen) was. Three of the 'against' voters also appeared on the composite list, two of whom made their first appearance there and only voted against the proposal in the third division, in December 1721.[69]

Thus, while the aftermath of the South Sea Bubble, the worsening economic climate, the conservatism of the country gentlemen, and the vagaries of faction politics clearly had a negative impact upon the confidence of a significant number of the original subscribers to a bank project, the majority of MPs who subscribed at some point in 1720–21 to a national bank proposal remained in favour of the project. However, in terms of the wider Protestant community, the absence of 278 of the original subscribers from the later composite list, which totalled 210 names, would seem to suggest that much of the early enthusiasm outside parliament for the bank project had been dispelled by late 1721.

From a broader perspective, the extent to which a body of potential public creditors already existed and continued to exist thereafter, despite the defeat of the bank project, may be assessed to some degree by examination of those people who subscribed to both a loan and a bank. Of the 12 people who definitely subscribed to the 1716 loan and a bank, Benjamin Burton, Francis Harrison, and Jacob Peppard voted against the bank proposal, Benjamin Parry and Oliver St George voted for it, and St John Brodrick initially voted for and then against it. The decision to vote against the proposal by Burton and Harrison, who were partners in one of the most important and reputedly safe private banks at that time which had survived the South Sea crisis and had close links to the government, may well have convinced other MPs to vote the same way.[70] Similarly, Brodrick's decision to vote against the bank in December, despite being one of the original petitioners for a bank charter, may also have influenced a number of MPs.[71] The same might be said of Brabazon Ponsonby, who also voted against the bank in December despite having been one of the named petitioners in the second proposal of 1720.[72] Brodrick and Ponsonby had also been included among the 21 commissioners for the bank in the charter issued by the king in July 1721, though the extent to which this may have had an influence upon voting patterns is tempered by the fact that of the remaining 13 MPs named as commissioners, 12 voted for the bank and one either abstained or was absent.[73]

There still remained a further six people, none of whom were MPs in 1721, who had subscribed to the 1716 loan and a bank. Apart from Luke Gardiner, it is impossible to make any projections as to the attitude of these people in late 1721. As for Gardiner, his appointment as deputy vice-treasurer in 1725 may account for his absence from the list of public creditors in 1729 given that the deputy vice-treasurer was responsible for taking subscriptions, a situation which may have served to exclude him on ethical grounds from being a public creditor.[74] The fact that his predecessor, John Pratt, although a subscriber to a bank, did not subscribe to the loan in 1716, would seem to confirm such a view. The right of the deputy vice-treasurer to make use of public revenue in his hands for his own private use would also have served as grounds for excluding him from being a public creditor.[75]

More revealing are the subscribers to a bank and the 1729 loan. Of the 34 people who definitely subscribed to both, James Barry, Thomas Carter, Hugh Henry (another Dublin banker who acted for the government along with Benjamin Burton), the accountant-general Mathew Pennefather, Richard Tighe, Frederick Trench, and Richard Warburton voted against, Thomas Bligh, Francis Burton (a nephew of Benjamin Burton), David Chaigneau, the chancellor of the exchequer Sir Ralph Gore, Francis Lucas, Henry Singleton, and Sir Thomas Taylor voted for, and Arthur Hill (who in the 1730s was to become a partner in a private bank with Gardiner) initially voted for and then against the bank. The remaining 19 people who subscribed to both included three future MPs, Thomas Staunton, Thomas Napper, and Daniel Falkiner (who became a partner in Burton's bank in 1726 following the death of Harrison), the second baron of the exchequer Sir John St Leger, the Rev. Josiah Hort (who was a dean in 1720–21, but by 1729 had become bishop of Kilmore), and the private banker David La Touche. There remained the seven definite subscribers to both of the loans and to a bank, six of whom were MPs: Sir Gustavus Hume initially voted against and then for the bank, while Postmaster-General Isaac Manley, Revenue Commissioner Thomas Medlycott,

Henry Sandford, Anthony Sheppard, and Major-General Owen Wynne all voted for it. Nothing is known of the remaining multiple subscribers.[76]

It is not surprising that the multiple subscribers were wholly in favour of the bank proposal, and that seven of the MPs who voted for a bank also subscribed to the loan in 1729. It is more illuminating, however, to discover that seven of those who voted against the bank were prepared to lend money to the government in 1729, a fact that adds weight to the argument that a significant number of the MPs who opposed the bank did so not out of suspicion of the concept of a national bank or a public credit system, but from concern about specific economic difficulties at that point in time. Certainly the number of private bankers who voted against the bank, having originally subscribed to the proposals, and in 1716 and 1729 were prepared to lend money to the government, would seem to support such a view, and might suggest that those private bankers who were not MPs but had subscribed to a bank proposal and were at other times willing to lend money to the government, may have arrived at the same conclusion by late 1721.[77] Given the absence of 278 of the original bank subscribers from the 1721 composite list, a similar assessment to that suggested for the private bankers might be applied to the wider Protestant community in late 1721.

V

Regardless of the extent to which opposition to the national bank project had become widespread within the Protestant community by late 1721, by 1729 confidence had been sufficiently restored in the concept of a public credit system as to enable the government to take full advantage of the 1729 loan act. The innovations in the 1729 act, and the concomitant altered attitudes of the executive and legislature to the idea, and practicalities, of a national debt, marked the start of the second phase of the history of that debt. The following years demonstrated that a more practical arrangement had been attained in 1729, and that a more coherent understanding had emerged of the idea of a public credit system.

In the next parliamentary session in 1731–2, a new loan of £100,000 was legislated for, thereby increasing the principal of the funded debt to £300,000.[78] There had been little difficulty in securing this new loan. At the end of 1730, Robert Clayton, Bishop of Killala, had felt that if the government's affairs 'should require an additional loan of £50,000 it will be no difficult matter to obtain it next sessions'.[79] Closer to the convening of the session, the lord lieutenant, Lionel Cranfield Sackville, Duke of Dorset, was of the opinion that 'if I could satisfy myself with proposing nothing more, than continuing the funds on the foot they now stand, and the providing an interest for an additional loan, I should not apprehend any great difficulty'. His main concern, however, arose from the executive's belief that the new additional duty upon spirits in the 1729 loan act had encouraged smuggling, and consequently lessened the income from the older duties on spirits, both additional and hereditary, 'which in the end brings a further debt upon the Establishment'. Thus the executive hoped 'to find out some other tax which may be clear of these objections, and not only produce sufficient to pay the interest of the loan, but likewise supply for a sinking fund'.[80]

At the opening of the session Dorset did not overcomplicate his appeal to the Commons for supplies, choosing only to express his concern at 'so great a deficiency in the public revenues', and his confidence that the Lower House would 'make the necessary provision for the debt due to the Establishment, and for the support of his majesty's government'.[81] At the end of October the debt of the nation was reported by the committee of accounts as £335,466, though they also noted an estimated surplus of £10,811 on the appropriated loan duties, after the payment of interest, which was still in arrears by £3,463. On 4 November the committee of ways and means resolved to allow for the new loan of £100,000, while at the same time resolving that the surplus of £10,811 be applied towards discharging the principal.[82] The whole process was perceived to have been 'carried on with great ease and quietness'.[83]

The only difficulty to arise occurred when the government attempted to get the duration for the appropriated duties in the heads of the loan bill changed from two to 21 years. This desire on the part of the government was a compromise endeavour when compared with the attempt to get an open-ended duration in the 1729 act, and was more in keeping with the type of loan legislation enacted by the Westminster parliament. However, while long-term durations for appropriated duties were not uncommon in Britain,[84] the Irish parliament remained opposed to breaking with their established adherence to a two-year duration for all of the main additional duties. Thus, not surprisingly, the government's wishes were overridden by the Commons once again.[85]

With the duration of the appropriated duties settled at two years, the 1731 loan bill encountered no further difficulties. In drafting the heads of the bill, the Commons had taken full account of all of the alterations made in England to the 1729 bill, so that on this occasion the British privy council saw no reason to make any substantive changes, returning the bill with a small number of minor 'literal' amendments, which did not create any problems in the Irish parliament.[86] In the resulting act it was specified that the loan of £100,000 was provided in order once again to clear Establishment pay arrears, which otherwise could not be discharged without imposing such taxes 'as would greatly burden your majesty's faithful subjects'. Thus, as in 1729, the loan served as both a means of avoiding over-taxation at a time of economic hardship and of transforming £100,000 of the pay arrears into a funded debt.[87] The act also re-asserted the general undertaking to continue interest payments until the principal was cleared, reduced the rate of interest to 5 per cent, and, in keeping with the government's earlier wishes, dropped the duty on spirits and imposed several other duties instead. A number of innovations were also introduced. It was enacted that separate accounts were to be kept of the appropriated duties by both the treasury and the revenue commissioners, which introduced greater transparency in the loan accounts and made it easier for parliament to identify any misuse of the appropriated funds. Of greater significance was the enactment that any surplus from the appropriated duties was to be applied towards discharging the principal by means of a lottery. Whenever £5,000 of surplus was held in the treasury, the names of creditors would be drawn by lottery to decide which creditors were to be repaid their principal.[88] With this, the theoretical sinking fund of 1729 became a reality.

Thus in 1731, as since 1716, the Commons made certain that the national debt was tied into the politics of supply, by which parliament ensured the continuation of biennial sessions and kept the government dependent upon parliament. As Bishop Clayton noted in January 1732, 'as they now have experience that they can raise money on parliamentary security from two years to two years, I believe they will hardly be prevailed upon to grant it for a longer time'.[89]

As before, there was little difficulty in finding people to subscribe to the new loan, though by way of inducement an act was passed for reducing the legal interest rate on any loans in Ireland to 6 per cent. Given that parliamentary taxation offered the best security for any creditor's money, setting the interest rate on the government loan at 1 per cent below the national rate was deemed attractive enough to ensure the loan would be fully subscribed.[90] Thus, despite Chief Secretary Walter Cary's refusal to subscribe out of pique at the failure to secure a 21-year duration (having claimed that he would have struck debentures to himself for £40,000 if the act was for 21 years), the number of potential subscribers was such that 'many' MPs had their subscriptions refused.[91] Dorset expressed pleasure at the outcome of events, although he exaggerated when he claimed that the Commons had 'entirely discharged the Establishment' and had 'taken it upon themselves as a national debt'.[92] In truth, as they had done in principle in 1726–7 and in practice in 1729, the Commons had taken a percentage of the pay arrears upon themselves as a debt secured on the credit of the nation.

In each of the following four sessions to 1739–40, an act for servicing the debt was passed. All four acts adhered to the various stipulations laid out in the 1731 act regarding the imposition for two years of appropriated duties for servicing the debt, the separate accounting procedures, the sinking fund, and the general undertaking to continue interest payments until the principal was cleared.[93] The executive's adherence to these stipulations, and the extent to which they were both practical and successful, was demonstrated from 1733 onwards.

At the start of the 1733–4 session the Commons entered into exhaustive inquiries into the produce of the appropriated duties. It was quickly evident that during the previous two years a surplus had arisen from those duties, though at the time of the Commons' inquiries the government had still not commenced repayment of the principal.[94] It appeared, however, that the failure to start repayments had stemmed from a lack of communication between revenue departments rather than from any desire on the part of the executive to use the surplus for other purposes.[95] From his own account of events, Dorset had discovered on his arrival in Ireland prior to the start of the session that over £20,000 of surplus was held in the treasury. He had therefore ordered the deputy vice-treasurer 'to give public notice, that the said sum with the interest due upon it should be paid off and discharged, pursuant to the . . . [1731 loan] act'.[96] The deputy vice-treasurer accordingly published advertisements to notify the public creditors that £20,000 of the principal would be paid off on 24 December 'in such manner as the [1731] act directs'.[97] Public notice was given in the *Dublin Gazette*, while the executive deemed it necessary to publish another advertisement in London, 'there being, as it is said, many proprietors of the loan in England'.[98] Dorset took a personal pride in reporting to the English ministry that the people of Ireland 'are extremely pleased to see the national debt decreasing after the rate of' £10,000 a year, 'and promise themselves a still greater decrease of it for the time to come'.[99] Cary hoped that this 'sinking fund' would 'with good management pay the whole debt in a few years'.[100]

In keeping with the published advertisement, £20,000 of the principal was cleared at the end of 1733, and a further £4,700 in June 1734, so that by the time parliament re-assembled in 1735, the funded debt was reduced to £275,300. By March 1737 the principal had been reduced to £261,000, and two years later to £241,000. By March 1741 it was further reduced to £227,000. Throughout all of this time the interest continued to be paid as well.[101] As such, the reduction of the national debt between 1733 and 1741 demonstrated that the various provisions for servicing the national debt made since 1729 were having the required effect.

The pattern of repayments that developed between 1733 and 1741 suggested that in time the national debt would be cleared. However, despite the fact that the 1729 and 1731 loans had allowed for the substantial reduction of the pay arrears from £317,170 in 1729 to £182,695 in 1733, the continuing practice in the Commons of reducing the amount of the government's reported pay arrears to a lower figure upon which the ensuing vote of supplies would be based, resulted in a creeping increase in pay arrears throughout the 1730s, from £182,695 in 1733 to £210,180 in 1741.[102]

The renewed security crisis following the outbreak of war with Spain in 1739 provided the Commons with the motivation for dealing with the problem of the increasing Establishment pay arrears, because a significant part of government expenditure was diverted to more immediate military needs. The danger was that the pay arrears would escalate dramatically and get out of control at a time when the army took on greater importance, both in relation to the security of Ireland and in the wider context of making a contribution to the British war effort.[103]

The first war-related extraordinary financial provision did not, however, deal with the pay arrears. Towards the end of the 1739–40 session, the lord lieutenant, William Cavendish, Duke of Devonshire, notified the Commons about reported preparations in Spain for an invasion of Ireland. The government desired that the Commons, in taking the necessary steps for their own security and defence, would provide money for purchasing 20,000 arms for the Protestant militia in Ireland. After some debate and extensive inquiry into the public accounts, the Commons complied by passing a vote of credit for a sum not exceeding £35,263, with interest of 4 per cent, to be borrowed for the said purposes, the repayment of the principal and the interest to be provided for out of the supplies to be voted in the next session. As such, the loan was raised in the same manner and upon the same basis as the first loan in 1716: on the security of supplies to be voted in a later session; on foot of an immediate security crisis; and to pay for an extraordinary non-Establishment expense. However, unlike in 1716, the 1740 loan was not formalized in statute, the vote of credit having occurred long after the main supply acts had passed. The government borrowed £25,000 on the strength of the vote of credit.[104]

The problem arising from the continuing increase in the pay arrears was tackled in the 1741–42 session. During their usual inquiries into the public accounts, the accounts committee reported a projected rise of £16,500 in the pay arrears in the following three months. Theoretically, such a scenario could have led to an additional £132,000 in pay arrears, on top of the existing £210,180, by 1743. The threat of such a rapid escalation in pay arrears prompted the Commons to report the debt of the nation at £353,856, which was about £17,000 higher than the original figure reported by the accounts committee. Thereafter the Lower House resolved to sanction a new loan to the government of £125,000.[105] Devonshire reported that the court party had contrived 'to raise the money upon the credit of the old loan without laying any new burden which would not be seasonable for the distress in the country has been greater than can well be imagined. I believe Dublin was never known to be so empty in a parliament winter which is certainly owing to want of money.'[106] As in 1729 and 1731, the justification for further borrowing was tied in with economic hardship and a desire not to burden the population with new taxes. However, in 1741, the country was in the throes of the worst of several famines to occur in Ireland during the eighteenth century, a human calamity of such major proportions that the financial considerations of the executive seemed trivial by comparison.[107]

The new loan bill did not meet with any difficulties in Dublin or London.[108] In the resulting act it was stipulated that the loan was provided for the purpose of discharging a percentage of the

Establishment pay arrears, 'without [imposing] such supplies as would greatly burden your majesty's faithful subjects'. Thus, as in 1729 and 1731, the loan served to transform part of the pay arrears into a funded debt, as the Commons once again took a percentage of the pay arrears upon themselves as a debt secured on the credit of the nation. However, given that the £25,000 borrowed in 1740 for militia arms was to be computed as part of the new loan, only £100,000 of the existing pay arrears were to be transformed into a funded debt by the 1741 loan act. As usual, the act re-imposed for a further two years the appropriated duties for servicing the debt, and renewed the provisions for the sinking fund, the separate accounting procedures, and the general undertaking to continue interest payments until the principal was cleared.[109]

The new loan was soon subscribed in full, so that the principal of the national debt increased to £352,000 by early 1742. However, during the next two years the appropriated duties continued to produce a surplus, so that by the time parliament reconvened in late 1743, the principal debt had been reduced, by means of the sinking fund, to £340,700. At the same time, the Commons made no difficulty in the 1743–4 session in passing a supply act for continuing the various provisions, in the standard manner and form, for servicing the debt for a further two years.[110]

The ongoing war with Spain, the outbreak of hostilities with France, and in particular the Jacobite rebellion in Scotland, resulted in another loan in 1745. From early 1744 there were rumours of an intended French invasion somewhere in the British Isles in support of the Pretender, which rumours resulted in Irish regiments being put on standby for transportation to any relevant flash-point. At the same time, with war on the Continent, the army in Ireland continued to serve as a source of both ready-formed regiments and general draughts of soldiers for service in England and abroad, while the remaining regiments recruited new men in order to bring the Irish military Establishment back to full strength.[111]

Fears of an invasion and rebellion were realized in the summer of 1745, when the young Pretender landed in Scotland. The ensuing Jacobite military campaign represented, for a while, a significant threat to the Revolution settlement of 1688–9 and the Hanoverian succession of 1714. Although that threat was finally extinguished in April 1746 at Culloden, the original crisis necessitated a significant readjustment in the dispositions of the British army and an escalation in government expenditure, both of which requirements involved

Ireland directly. The military readjustments in Irish terms involved the transportation of two regiments to England in late 1745, the advent of the recruitment of Irish Protestants in Irish-based foot regiments (prior to 1745 it was official policy to recruit only in Britain for all foot regiments stationed in Ireland), and the calling out of the militia.[112]

The reaction of the Irish Protestant community to this latest Jacobite threat was in keeping with previous occasions, and was best exemplified by the proliferation of loyal addresses from around the country.[113] When parliament assembled in October 1745 both Houses responded in keeping with the general sentiment within the wider Protestant community, the Commons requesting that a proclamation (later enshrined in statute) be issued offering £50,000 for the capture of the young Pretender should he land in Ireland, and both Houses entering into loyal associations to George II.[114] On a more practical level, the Commons also addressed the lord lieutenant, Philip Dormer Stanhope, Earl of Chesterfield, to provide 30,000 firelocks and bayonets and 10,000 broadswords for the use of the militia. However, this extraordinary expenditure would require an extraordinary supply, the need for which was compounded by the Commons' resolutions that it was essential to erect an artillery battery at Cork harbour for security purposes and the protection of trade.[115]

In November the Commons agreed to raise the required sum by means of a loan of £70,000 at 4 per cent interest.[116] The ensuing bill did not encounter any problems in Dublin or London.[117] The resulting loan act stipulated that the loan had been sanctioned because the money could not otherwise be raised 'without such supplies, as would greatly burden your majesty's faithful subjects'. The act conformed to all previous loan legislation regarding the two-year imposition of the appropriated duties (including several new duties) for servicing the debt, the sinking fund, the separate accounting procedures, and the general undertaking to continue interest payments until the principal was cleared. The government borrowed £58,500 on the security of the act.[118]

Once again, there proved little difficulty in finding public creditors. The names of these public creditors, along with those who had subscribed since 1731, were recorded in a series of ledgers kept by the teller of the exchequer, Nathaniel Clements.[119] The total number of individual subscribers on the Clements lists for the period 1745 to 1759 was 700. When the lists from 1716 and 1729 are amalgamated with the lists from 1745 to 1759, the number of possible public creditors increases to 919. The total of individual public creditors can be reduced to 844 by discounting equivalent surnames from the Clements lists in cases where the surnames are the same or similar to those on the 1716 or 1729 lists. Such a process implies that 75 people from 1716 or 1729 were still included on the lists in 1745–59. If so, an extra 625 people had become public creditors since 1729. It is not possible, however, to identify the vast majority of the names on the Clements lists. On the basis of title, only 283 out of the maximum calculation of 700 public creditors for 1745–59 can be grouped in some form.[120]

Table 8.3: Public creditors, 1745–59

Identifier	Number of Subscribers
Women	98
Military Officers	78
Clergy	39
Doctors (Dr)	31
Aldermen/councillors	19
Banks	8
Judges	4
Hospitals	2
Trinity College Dublin	2
Peers	1
Charities	1
Total	283

The overall impression conveyed by the various lists of public creditors is of a complex and diverse community of people lending money to the government for a variety of reasons, including self-interest and financial profit, but also on the basis of a confidence and trust in the existing apparatus of the state, and of a government able to fulfil its commitments as a recipient of public credit. As such, it is representative of a community identified and set apart by its unique focus of interest, yet at the same time flexible in its membership because of the complex nature of that single interest.

VI

However, a subtle shift had occurred in relation to the national debt and the politics of supply in 1745. Although the justification for the new loan in that year – the desire not to overburden the people – was the same as that given in all previous loan acts since 1729, other aspects of the act, particularly the stated purpose of the loan, suggested that circumstances were not the same as before. Despite the ongoing war, and the rebellion in Britain, the Commons had not seen fit to deal with the Establishment pay arrears, which had been the *raison d'être* for the greatest part of previous loan legislation and other government borrowing.

The answer lay in the public accounts of the nation. The pay arrears reported by the government in 1745 stood at £118,879, which was £34,174 less than in 1743, and £91,301 less than in 1741. When these arrears of £118,879 were combined with the funded debt of £335,300 (£5,400 having been cleared since 1743) and some other non-Establishment arrears, the total arrears and funded debt came to £474,209. The accounts committee, however, computed the debt of the nation at the lower figure of £258,518, which had been reached by estimating the funded debt at £330,465, and then subtracting a new-found 'credit to the nation' of £71,947. While the government was still reporting substantial pay arrears, the Commons, after three decades of constantly including a percentage of those arrears as part of the composite 'debt of the nation', had finally arrived at the point where, according to their own calculations, the existing sources of public revenue were sufficient for the government's needs. Thus, there was no necessity to raise a loan for the purpose of transforming the pay arrears into a funded debt.[121] While this new-found 'credit to the nation' did not preclude the biennial renewal of the main parliamentary duties after 1745, nor the continued provision of appropriated duties for servicing the national debt in 1747, 1749, and 1751, it did preclude the imposition of any new duties, appropriated or otherwise, and represented the start of a new phase in the history of the national debt, in which the credit to the nation was used to reduce the funded debt to an all-time low.[122]

The reality was that Irish public finances were in a relatively healthy state by the mid-1740s. The main reasons for the alteration in financial affairs in the country were a significant improvement in the economy and some unexpected savings in government spending which had been facilitated, ironically, by the large number of Irish regiments transferred to the British military Establishment during the 1739–48 war. The peace of 1748 added to the new economic prosperity. The end result was a significant improvement in the income from the public revenue, facilitating an extraordinary acceleration in the repayment of the funded debt, which by 1759 stood at only £5,200.[123]

This new phase in the history of the national debt brought with it a whole new set of theories, ideas, fiscal criteria, and political problems, best exemplified by the 'money-bill dispute' of 1753. Although the dispute took place against the background of a power struggle among the leading Irish undertakers, the focus of the ensuing conflict between the executive and legislature was on the control of expenditure.[124] The central question was whether the government or the Commons had the right (depending on which side of the political divide it was viewed from) to dispose of the crown's surplus in the treasury, or the public wealth held in trust in the same place. The government argued that the surplus was at the disposal of the crown because it arose from the hereditary revenue and the non-appropriated parliamentary duties, an argument which was based on the view that the hereditary revenues in particular were the property of the crown. The majority of Irish MPs, however, saw the treasury surplus as a sinking fund for the national debt. For the most part, the funded debt had been raised in order to clear the government's Establishment pay arrears, and, given that the Establishment had always taken primacy when it came to government expenditure (including the disposal of money arising from the hereditary revenue), then it stood to reason that any surplus revenue should be applied in the first instance towards clearing a debt incurred for paying the Establishment, without the need for any previous consent from the crown. This viewpoint was validated to a degree by the fact that between 1717 and 1727–8 the government had consented to the stipulation, in each of the two-year supply acts passed for servicing the national debt, that both the interest and the principal of the debt should be paid out of the revenue at large, including the hereditary revenue, without appropriation of a specific fund.[125]

The truth was, however, that by the 1750s the Commons had arrived at a very different understanding from the government of all matters fiscal, which centred on a belief that all public income, whether it derived from the hereditary revenue, parliamentary taxation, or the loans that made up the national debt, was part of the public wealth, and therefore at the disposal of the nation, as represented by parliament. Thus, the treasury surplus was seen as a 'credit to the nation' to be used to clear the national debt, which had been raised on the credit of the nation as a debt of the nation. As such, the conflict in 1753–4 brought to the fore once again the burgeoning sense within the Protestant community of belonging to a nation.

Questions remain, in particular as to whether or not Irish Catholics acted as public creditors in this period. As yet, an answer remains elusive. However, what can be ascertained is that the period from 1716 to 1745 witnessed the emergence of a new-found confidence and sense of identity within the Irish Protestant community, which was expressed in part through the actions of that community's representatives in parliament in relation to implementing innovative financial practices for the benefit of the Irish government, and through the wider community's willingness to act as public creditors. For a time, an unprecedented period of economic prosperity and increased public income in the late 1740s created a circumstance in which it appeared that those various financial innovations and the flexible and complex community of public creditors would no longer be necessary. But, with the decline in the economy in the 1750s followed by the outbreak of the Seven Years War, it became only a matter of time before the government would need to call upon that community once more. In late 1759 the Irish parliament legislated for a new loan, which was to be the first in a rapidly increasing – both in regularity and amount – series of loans legislated for in the second half of the eighteenth century, as the Irish national debt escalated dramatically in order to keep pace with ever-increasing government expenditure within the wider context of the emergence of the British Empire.[126]

NOTES

1. I wish to thank Dr A.P.W. Malcomson for reading and commenting on this paper. I also wish to acknowledge the financial assistance provided by the Irish Research Council for the Humanities and Social Sciences.
2. *Common Sense: In a Letter to a Friend. To which is prefixed an Explanatory Preface. By the Author of Ireland in Tears* (London, 1755), p. 48. The pamphlet was first published in Dublin in 1754 and re-printed in London the following year with a new preface and altered pagination.
3. J. Brewer, *The Sinews of Power: War, Money and the English State, 1688–1783* (London: Routledge, 1989); P.G.M. Dickson, *The Financial Revolution in England: A Study in the Development of Public Credit 1688–1756* (London: Macmillan, 1967), p. xxi; L. Colley, *Britons: Forging the Nation 1707–1837* (New Haven: Yale University Press, 1992), pp. 56–71; J.G.A. Pocock, *The Machiavellian Moment: Florentine Political Thought and the Atlantic Republican Tradition* (Princeton: Princeton University Press, 1975), pp. 423–61; Pocock, *Virtue, Commerce, and History: Essays on Political Thought and History, Chiefly in the Eighteenth Century* (Cambridge: Cambridge University Press, 1985), pp. 98–102, 108–23; M.J. Braddick, *The Nerves of State: Taxation and the Financing of the English State, 1558–1714* (Manchester: Manchester

University Press, 1996); H. Roseveare, *The Financial Revolution 1660–1760* (London: Longman, 1991). See also D. Hume, 'Of Public Credit', in *Essays Moral, Political, and Literary*, rev. ed., ed. E.F. Miller (Indianapolis: Liberty Fund, 1985), pp. 349–65; A. Smith, 'Of Public Debts', in *An Inquiry into the Nature and Causes of the Wealth of Nations*, ed. R.H. Campbell and A.S. Skinner, 2 vols. (Oxford: Clarendon Press, 1976), ii, 907–47 (V.iii).

4. For earlier private credit systems in Ireland, see J. Ohlmeyer and É. Ó Ciardha (eds), *The Irish Statute Staple Books, 1596–1687* (Dublin: Dublin City Council, 1998).
5. On Irish Protestant identity, see D.W. Hayton, 'Anglo-Irish Attitudes: Changing Perceptions of National Identity among the Protestant Ascendancy in Ireland, ca. 1690–1750', *Studies in Eighteenth-Century Culture*, 17 (1987), pp. 145–57.
6. C.I. McGrath, *The Making of the Eighteenth-Century Irish Constitution: Government, Parliament and the Revenue, 1692–1714* (Dublin: Four Courts Press, 2000).
7. Nat. Arch., SP 63/373/88, 112, 144, 148–50, 193, 242–3; 63/374/26–7, 42–3, 59–60, 63–5; 63/375/49; 63/377/28–9, 59–60, 171–2; 63/378/35–6; 63/387/50–1, 197–8; 63/388/170, 196; 63/389/117; 63/390/234; 63/391/184–5; 63/397/88, 90–1, 97–9, 111, 115–18, 129, 143; 63/399/7, 9, 42, 46, 58; 63/403/63; 63/404/82; 63/406/1, 30–1, 37–8, 79, 113, 118–19, 121, 125, 139, 143; 63/407/146–8; 63/408/98–101, 106–8, 110–12, 130; A.J. Guy, 'The Irish Military Establishment, 1660–1776', in T. Bartlett and K. Jeffery (eds), *A Military History of Ireland* (Cambridge: Cambridge University Press, 1996), pp. 216–17, 228.
8. Brewer, *Sinews of Power*, p. 32.
9. McGrath, *Irish Constitution*, passim; C.I. McGrath, 'Central Aspects of the Eighteenth-Century Constitutional Framework in Ireland: The Government Supply Bill and Biennial Parliamentary Sessions, 1715–82', *Eighteenth-Century Ireland*, 16 (2001), pp. 9–34.
10. T.J. Kiernan, *History of the Financial Administration of Ireland to 1817* (London: P.S. King & Son, 1930), pp. 145–6.
11. *The Statutes at Large Passed in the Parliaments Held in Ireland*, 20 vols. (Dublin, 1763–1801), iv, 325–7; *The Journals of the House of Commons of the Kingdom of Ireland*, 21 vols., 3rd ed. (Dublin, 1796–1800), iii, 60, 73–6, 80, 86, 92–3, 98, 112; iii, pt. ii, p. xxxviii; Kiernan, *History of the Financial Administration*, pp. 145–6; McGrath, *Irish Constitution*, pp. 286–7.
12. Nat. Arch., SP 63/373/88, 112, 144, 150, 193, 242–3; SP 63/374/26–7, 42–3; NLI, MS 694, p. 68; *CJI*, iii, 9–10, 73–5, 92; iii, pt. ii, p. lxxvi.
13. *CJI*, iii, 60–4, 67–8, 72–3; Nat. Arch., SP 63/374/22, 26–7, 38, 42–3, 47, 49, 53–4, 57–8. On Jacobitism, see É. Ó Ciardha, *Ireland and the Jacobite Cause, 1685–1766: A Fatal Attachment* (Dublin: Four Courts Press, 2002).
14. *CJI*, iii, 73–5; Nat. Arch., SP 63/374/59–60; S.J. Connolly, 'The Defence of Protestant Ireland, 1660–1760', in Bartlett and Jeffery (eds), *Military History*, pp. 239–40.
15. *Stat. Ire.*, iv, 325–7.
16. Duke of Grafton and Earl of Galway to James Stanhope, 30 Jan. 1716 (Nat. Arch., SP 63/374/63–5).
17. Charles Delafaye to [?Robert Pringle], 30 Jan. 1716 (Nat. Arch., SP 63/374/59–60).
18. Lords Justices to Stanhope, 30 Jan. 1716 (Nat. Arch., SP 63/374/63–5).
19. Dickson, *Financial Revolution*; Brewer, *Sinews of Power*; Roseveare, *Financial Revolution*; C.I. McGrath, 'The Irish Revenue System: Government and Administration, 1689–1702' (PhD thesis, University of London, 1997), pp. 1–7.
20. *Accounts of Net Public Income and Expenditure of Great Britain and Ireland, 1688–1800* (London, 1869) [HC 1869–69 (366), xxxv.1, 483]; L.M. Cullen, *An Economic History of Ireland since 1660*, 2nd ed. (London: B.T. Batsford, 1987), pp. 43–4; McGrath, *Irish Constitution*, pp. 50, 54–5, 64, 70–72.
21. Charles King to ——— 15 Feb. 1716 (Nat. Arch., SP 63/374/101–2).
22. *CJI*, iii, pt. ii, pp. cxiii–cxiv.
23. *CJI*, iii, pt. ii, pp. cxiii–cxiv. On these individuals, see E.M. Johnston-Liik, *History of the Irish Parliament 1692–1800: Commons, Constituencies and Statutes*, 6 vols. (Belfast: Ulster Historical Foundation, 2002), iii, 194–5, 266–9, 270–72, 299–300, 316–18, 474–9; iv, 43–4, 208–9, 257–60, 279–80, 340–42, 371, 450–51; v, 190–91, 240–41; vi, 187–9, 538–40.
24. *Stat. Ire.*, iv, 325–7; *CJI*, iii, 92; McGrath, 'Constitutional Framework', pp. 15–16.

25. *Stat. Ire.*, iv, 433–8; McGrath, 'Constitutional Framework', p. 16.
26. *Stat. Ire.*, iv, 504–8; v, 1–5, 75–81, 137–42, 201–6; McGrath, 'Constitutional Framework', pp. 16–17.
27. McGrath, 'Constitutional Framework', pp. 9–34.
28. *CJI*, iii, pt. ii, pp. cvi, clvi, cxciv, ccxxxvi, ccxc, cccxxx, ccclxii.
29. Nat. Arch., PC 2/86, pp. 440, 453; 2/87, pp. 197, 211–14; 2/90, pp. 401, 409, 418, 458–9; 2/91, p. 22; SP 63/375/66–7, 152–3, 162–3, 188–9, 204–5, 208–9; 63/377/61–2, 103–4, 109–10, 121–2, 125, 131–2, 171–2, 228, 232–3, 240–41, 244–5, 269, 275; 63/378/135–6, 137, 141–2; 63/379/61–70, 87; 63/380/22, 81–2, 110; 63/381/1–4, 7–11, 13–20, 122–4, 135–6, 145–6, 165–6, 178–83, 194–5, 224–9; 63/382/1–2; 63/383/71–2, 180–81, 208–9, 229, 231–4; 63/384/18, 33–5, 64–6, 112–29, 139; 63/385/15–18; 63/386/214–16, 221, 225–8, 232–4, 250–51, 256, 292–4, 308, 312–13, 344, 346; 63/388/208; 63/389/17, 40; 63/390/113–14, 121, 173–7, 187; 63/391/33–4, 73, 75, 77–9, 81–2, 184–5; BL Add. MS 21122, ff. 7, 13, 15–16, 17–19, 24–6, 27–8, 35–6, 59–65, 88–9; Cullen, *Economic History*, pp. 46–9; M. Ryder, 'The Bank of Ireland, 1721: Land, Credit and Dependency', *Historical Journal*, 25 (1982), pp. 557–82; J. Kelly, 'Harvests and Hardship: Famine and Scarcity in Ireland in the Late 1720s', *Studia Hibernica*, 26 (1992), pp. 65–105.
30. Lord Chancellor Richard West to the Duke of Newcastle, 26 Oct., 16 Nov.; Carteret to same, 28 Oct., 16 Nov.; Hugh Boulter, Archbishop of Armagh, to same, 16 Nov. 1725 (Nat. Arch., SP 63/386/214–15, 221–5, 292–4, 308, 312–13); Marmaduke Coghill to Edward Southwell, 30 Oct. 1725 (BL Add. MS 21122, ff. 24–6).
31. West to Newcastle, 27 Jan. 1726; Carteret to same, 28 Jan. 1726 (Nat. Arch., SP 63/387/13–14, 17–19); *CJI*, iii, 442–3. See also Nat. Arch., SP 63/387/21.
32. Isaac Manley to [?], 25 Feb. 1726 (Nat. Arch., SP 63/387/73). See also Nat. Arch., SP 63/387/50–1, 55–6, 59–60, 75, 77, 79–82, 130; BL Add. MS 21122, f. 29; *CJI*, iii, 444–5.
33. Boulter to Newcastle, 22 March 1726 (Nat. Arch., SP 63/387/114–16).
34. Carteret to Newcastle, 23 Dec. 1727; 11 Jan. 1728 (Nat. Arch., SP 63/389/123–4; 63/390/1); *CJI*, iii, 490–1, 495.
35. *CJI*, iii, pt. ii, pp. ccclxii, ccclxxvii.
36. Boulter to [Newcastle], 23 Oct. 1729 (Nat. Arch., SP 63/391/184–5).
37. *CJI*, iii, 579–80; Cullen, *Economic History*, pp. 44–50; R.E. Burns, *Irish Parliamentary Politics in the Eighteenth Century*, 2 vols. (Washington, DC: Catholic University of America Press, 1989–90), i, 234–44.
38. Coghill to Southwell, 8 Nov. 1729 (BL Add. MS 21122, ff. 91–2).
39. *Stat. Ire.*, v, 337–40; McGrath, 'Constitutional Framework', pp. 16–19.
40. Boulter to [Newcastle], 23 Oct. 1729 (Nat. Arch., SP 63/391/184–5).
41. Boulter to Newcastle, 13 Nov. 1729 (Nat. Arch., SP 63/391/204); Coghill to Southwell, 13 Nov. 1729 (BL Add. MS 21122, ff. 95–6).
42. McGrath, 'Constitutional Framework', pp. 9–34.
43. [Newcastle] to Carteret, 25 Dec. 1729; Delafaye to Thomas Clutterbuck, 27 Dec. 1729 (Nat. Arch., SP 63/391/280, 286–7).
44. Minutes of the privy council committee on Irish bills, Whitehall, 1 Dec. 1729 (Nat. Arch., PC 2/91, pp. 92–3); *Stat. Ire.*, v, 337–40.
45. Delafaye to Clutterbuck, 27 Dec. 1729 (Nat. Arch., SP 63/391/286–7).
46. Minutes of the committee on Irish bills, 1 Dec. 1729 (Nat. Arch., PC 2/91, p. 93); *Stat. Ire.*, v, 337–40. On sinking funds, see Smith, 'Public Debts', pp. 731–2, 735–6.
47. Carteret to Viscount Townshend, 14 Dec. 1729; Clutterbuck to Delafaye, 14 Dec. 1729 (Nat. Arch., SP 63/391/254, 260–1). See also Nat. Arch., SP 63/389/111–12.
48. McGrath, *Irish Constitution*, chs. 3–7.
49. Coghill to Southwell, 20 Dec. 1729 (BL Add. MS 21122, ff. 97–100).
50. Delafaye to Clutterbuck, 27 Dec. 1729 (Nat. Arch., SP 63/391/286–7).
51. Coghill to Southwell, 20 Dec. 1729; 3 Jan. 1730 (BL Add. MS 21122, ff. 97–100, 103); Boulter to Newcastle, 16, 20 Dec. 1729 (Nat. Arch., SP 63/391/264–5, 268); P. McNally, *Parties, Patriots and Undertakers: Parliamentary Politics in Early Hanoverian Ireland* (Dublin: Four Courts Press, 1997), pp. 137–8.
52. *CJI*, iii, 624.
53. *Stat. Ire.*, v, 337–40; *CJI*, iii, 597–601, 620–5; Kiernan, *History of the Financial*

Administration, pp. 147–8.

54. Boulter to Newcastle, 22 Nov. 1729 (Nat. Arch., SP 63/391/238–9).
55. Carteret to Townshend, 14 Dec. 1729 (Nat. Arch., SP 63/391/254). See also Nat. Arch., SP 63/391/260–1.
56. *Stat. Ire.*, v, 337–40.
57. *CJI*, iii, pt. ii, pp. cccxcvi–cccxcviii. The final calculation for the loan was £59,758 in army warrants and £90,242 in ready money (*CJI*, iv, app. p. v). For individuals, see Johnston-Liik, *Irish Parliament*, iii, 179–80, 241–6, 437–8, 442–5; iv, 129–30, 284–6, 488–90.
58. Coghill to Southwell, 18 April 1730 (BL Add. MS 21123, ff. 1–4).
59. For examples, from 1715 to 1729, see *CJI*, iii, 45–6, 318, 405, 408–9; iii, pt. ii, pp. vii, xi, cv, cxvi–cxvii, clxv, cxcvi, ccxii, ccxliii, ccxcii, ccciv, cccxxxvi, ccclxxvii. The examples increase in prevalence in the ensuing volumes of the *CJI*.
60. *Reflections on the National Debt; with Reasons for Reducing the Legal Interest; and against a Public Loan. With Some Advice to the Electors of Members of Parliament* ([Dublin], 1731), pp. 11–13. Another pamphlet published around the same time, arguing for a reduction in interest rates, expressed the view that the national debt had been 'secured on the public faith' (*Reasons for Regulating the Coin, and Reducing the Interest; with a Scheme for paying part of the National Debt without burthening Ireland* ([Dublin], 1731), pp. 21–2).
61. For consideration of the Irish Catholic nation in this period, see T. Bartlett, *The Fall and Rise of the Irish Nation: The Catholic Question, 1690–1830* (Dublin: Gill & Macmillan, 1992).
62. *Common Sense*, p. 48.
63. For the bank lists, see NLI, MS 2256, pp. 27–8, 31–3, 39, 41, 63–5, 67–9; F.G. Hall, *The Bank of Ireland, 1783–1946* (Dublin: Hodges Figgis, 1949), pp. 23–4.
64. *CJI*, iii, pt. ii, pp. cxiii–cxiv, cccxcvi–cccxcviii; NLI, MS 2256, pp. 27–8, 31–3, 39, 41, 63–5, 67–9; Hall, *Bank of Ireland*, pp. 23–4.
65. Dickson, *Financial Revolution*, pp. 15–35; Hume, 'Public Credit'; Smith, 'Public Debts'; Pocock, *Machiavellian Moment*, pp. 423–61; Pocock, *Virtue, Commerce, and History*, pp. 103–23.
66. Roseveare, *Financial Revolution*, pp. 54–8; Ryder, 'Bank of Ireland', pp. 557–82; J. Griffin, 'Parliamentary Politics in Ireland during the Reign of George I' (MA thesis, UCD, 1977), pp. 100–12; J. Johnston, 'Berkeley and the Abortive Bank Project of 1720–21', in Johnston (ed.), *Bishop Berkeley's Querist in Historical Perspective* (Dundalk: Dundalgan Press, 1970), pp. 44–51; Hall, *Bank of Ireland*, pp. 15–29; Kelly, 'Harvests and Hardship', pp. 66–9; Cullen, *Economic History*, pp. 44–6.
67. *CJI*, iii, 267–8, 289; Griffin, 'Parliamentary Politics', pp. 102, 190–93.
68. Griffin, 'Parliamentary Politics', pp. 190–93; Johnston-Liik, *Irish Parliament*, vols. iii–vi, passim; D.W. Hayton and C. Jones (eds), *A Register of Parliamentary Lists, 1660–1761* (Leicester: University of Leicester, History Department, 1979), p. 139. The figures given in Table 8.2 and the calculations thereafter in the text differ by minus or plus one MP in certain calculations when compared with the figures detailed in an earlier consideration of this subject in C.I. McGrath, 'Parliament, People and other Possibilities', *Eighteenth-Century Ireland*, 17 (2002), pp. 164–5. The present calculations provide a corrected version of those earlier considerations.
69. NLI, MS 2256, pp. 67–9; Hall, *Bank of Ireland*, pp. 23–6.
70. Johnston-Liik, *Irish Parliament*, iii, 270–2, 316–18; iv, 371; vi, 21–2, 45–6, 216–17.
71. [Petitioners] to Lord Percival, 2 June 1720 (NLI, MS 2256, pp. 8–9); Griffin, 'Parliamentary Politics', pp. 108–10.
72. Petition to Grafton from George, Lord Forbes, and [Brabazon] Ponsonby [1720] (NLI, MS 2256, p. 11); Hall, *Bank of Ireland*, p. 17.
73. Commission and charter for a bank, 29 July 1721 (*CJI*, iii, pt. ii, pp. cciii–ccix).
74. Johnston-Liik, *Irish Parliament*, iv, 257–60, 417–18; L.M. Cullen, 'Landlords, Bankers and Merchants: The Early Irish Banking World, 1700–1820', in A.E. Murphy (ed.), *Economists and the Irish Economy from the Eighteenth Century to the Present Day* (Dublin: Irish Academic Press, 1984), pp. 32, 34.
75. McGrath, 'Revenue System', pp. 228–9.
76. Johnston-Liik, *Irish Parliament*, iii, 140–1, 214–15, 322–3, 377–81, 403–4; iv, 129–30,

284–6, 409–10, 417–18, 450–51; v, 62, 136–7, 190–91, 240–1, 337–8; vi, 41–2, 227–9, 233–4, 267–8, 276–7, 327, 379–80, 395–7, 435–6, 493–4, 562–3; Cullen, 'Bankers and Merchants', pp. 27, 29, 32, 34; T.W. Moody, F.X. Martin, and F.J. Byrne (eds), *A New History of Ireland*, ix, *Maps, Genealogies, Lists* (Oxford: Clarendon Press, 1984), p. 405.

77. It may also have been the case that other private bankers opposed the idea of a national bank mainly on grounds of commercial competition.
78. *Stat. Ire.*, v, 487–92.
79. Clayton to Mrs Charlotte Clayton, 2 Dec. 1730 (BL Add. MS 20102, ff. 138–9).
80. Dorset to [Newcastle], 8 Oct. 1731 (Nat. Arch., SP 63/394/93–4).
81. *CJI*, iv, 9–10.
82. *CJI*, iv, 22–5; app. pp. iii–v, xi–xiii.
83. Clayton to Mrs Clayton, 9 Nov. 1731 (BL Add. MS 20102, f. 152).
84. Dickson, *Financial Revolution*, pp. 48–9, 60–1, 63; Smith, 'Public Debts', pp. 729–33.
85. Clayton to Mrs Clayton, 9 Nov. 1731 (BL Add. MS 20102, ff. 152–4).
86. Newcastle to Dorset, 29 Nov. 1731; Dorset to Newcastle, 24 Dec. 1731 (Nat. Arch., SP 63/394/129, 145); minutes of the committee on Irish bills, 25 Nov. 1731 (Nat. Arch., PC 2/91, pp. 485–6); *CJI*, iv, 27–8, 38–41, 43.
87. *Stat. Ire.*, v, 487–92; Cullen, *Economic History*, pp. 46–9; D. Dickson, *New Foundations: Ireland 1660–1800* (Dublin: Irish Academic Press, 1987), p. 102.
88. *Stat. Ire.*, v, 487–92.
89. Clayton to Mrs Clayton, 2 Jan. 1732 (BL Add. MS 20102, ff. 158–60).
90. Walter Cary to Delafaye, 10 Dec. 1731 (Nat. Arch., SP 63/394/141–2); *Stat. Ire.*, v, 508–10.
91. Clayton to Mrs Clayton, 2 Jan. 1732 (BL Add. MS 20102, ff. 158–60).
92. Dorset to [Newcastle], 15 Nov. 1731 (Nat. Arch., SP 63/394/121–2).
93. *Stat. Ire.*, vi, 5–9, 175–80, 393–8, 483–9.
94. *CJI*, iv, 74–5, 76–8; app. pp. xxii, xxv, xxxvii–xli.
95. Coghill to Southwell, 20 Oct. 1733, 20 Nov. 1733 (BL Add. MS 21123, ff. 62, 66–7).
96. Dorset to Newcastle, 20 Nov. 1733 (Nat. Arch., SP 63/396/103).
97. *CJI*, iv, app. p. xxxvii.
98. Cary to Delafaye, 20 Nov. 1733 (Nat. Arch., SP 63/396/99–100).
99. Dorset to Newcastle, 20 Nov. 1733 (Nat. Arch., SP 63/396/103).
100. Cary to Delafaye, 20 Nov. 1733 (Nat. Arch., SP 63/396/99–100).
101. *CJI*, iv, app. pp. li–liii, lxxiii, cv–cvi, cxxxix–cxl.
102. *CJI*, iv, app. pp. xxii, xliii, li–lii, lx–lxi, lxxiii, lxxxi, cv–cvi, cxv, cxxxix–cxl, cl.
103. NLI, MS 694, pp. 1–76; Nat. Arch., SP 63/403/45, 49, 53–7, 61–3, 79; SP 63/404/70, 82, 98; PRONI, Wilmot papers, T3019/359.
104. Nat. Arch., SP 63/403/39–40, 45, 49, 53–7, 61–2; PRONI, Wilmot papers, T3019/239; *CJI*, iv, 341–6; app. p. clviii.
105. *CJI*, iv, 368–72; app. pp. cl–clii; Nat. Arch., SP 63/404/211–12, 223–4.
106. Devonshire to [Newcastle], 11 Nov. 1741 (Nat. Arch., SP 63/404/211–12).
107. Dickson, *New Foundations*, pp. 83–5; Cullen, *Economic History*, pp. 68–9; S.J. Connolly, *Religion, Law and Power: The Making of Protestant Ireland 1660–1760* (Oxford: Oxford University Press, 1992), p. 48.
108. Viscount Duncannon to Wilmot, 17 Nov. 1741 (PRONI, Wilmot papers, T3019/341); Nat. Arch., PC 2/97, pp. 20–5; SP 63/404/258.
109. *Stat. Ire.*, vi, 605–12; *CJI*, iv, app. p. clviii.
110. *CJI*, iv, 406, 408; app. pp. clvii–clviii, clx, clxx, ccxlviii–ccxlix; *Stat. Ire.*, vi, 643–50; Nat. Arch., PC 2/98, pp. 58–60, 64–7; PRONI, Wilmot papers, T3019/497, 510.
111. Nat. Arch., PC 2/98, pp. 269–73; SP 63/406/1, 3, 24, 30–1, 36–8, 41–4, 46–50, 52–3, 66–9, 71–2, 79, 81, 83, 85, 87, 89–92, 99–100, 109–11, 113, 121, 125, 127–8, 143, 149, 155–6; SP 63/407/12, 146–8, 152, 154; PRONI, Wilmot papers, T3019/503, 506, 532, 580, 609.
112. Nat. Arch., PC 2/99, pp. 182–201, 276–7; SP 63/408/68–70, 72–3, 96, 98–101, 106–8, 110–12, 116–18, 120, 130, 142–4, 147–9, 221–4, 239–41; SP 63/409/1–2, 120–25, 144, 147; PRONI, Wilmot papers, T3019/640, 647, 662, 665, 675, 681, 683, 687, 692; Ó Ciardha, *Jacobite Cause*, pp. 271–323; E. Magennis, *The Irish Political System 1740–1765: The Golden Age of the Undertakers* (Dublin: Four Courts Press, 2000), pp.

51–4; Dickson, *New Foundations*, pp. 85–7; Connolly, *Religion, Law and Power*, 245–7, 256–8; Dickson, *Financial Revolution*, pp. 216–28; Brewer, *Sinews of Power*, pp. 53–4.

113. Nat. Arch., SP 63/408/173–9, 181, 183–7, 193; PRONI, Wilmot papers, T3019/694; T3019/6455/54.
114. Chesterfield to Newcastle, 10 Oct. 1745 (Nat. Arch., SP 63/408/167); Nat. Arch., PC 2/99, pp. 246–7, 249–50; SP 63/408/169, 171–2, 221–4; *CJI*, iv, 449–56, 470.
115. Chesterfield to Newcastle, 31 Oct. 1745 (Nat. Arch., SP 63/408/196); Nat. Arch., SP 63/408/221–4; PRONI, Wilmot papers, T3019/699; *CJI*, iv, 452–8.
116. *CJI*, iv, 462–5.
117. Nat. Arch., PC 2/99, pp. 257–9, 264–5; PRONI, Wilmot papers, T3019/706; *CJI*, iv, 465–6, 471–5.
118. *Stat. Ire.*, vi, 702–10; vii, 6–15; PRONI, Wilmot papers, T3019/822.
119. TCD, MSS 7259–7266. For Clements, see A.P.W. Malcomson, *Nathaniel Clements: Government and the Governing Elite in Ireland, 1725–75* (Dublin: Four Courts Press, 2005); Johnston-Liik, *Irish Parliament*, iii, 425–30.
120. TCD, MSS 7259–7266.
121. *CJI*, iv, 453, 458; app. pp. ccxlviii–ccxlix, cclix.
122. *Stat. Ire.*, vi, 698–702, 810–17; vii, 6–15, 104–11; Nat. Arch., SP 63/411/49–55, 214–16.
123. *CJI*, iv, app. pp. clxvi, ccliv–cclvii, cclix, cclxxxii–cclxxxvii; vi, 127; app. pp. clxxii–clxxiii; *Stat. Ire.*, vii, 6–15, 104–11; Cullen, *Economic History*, chs. 3–4; Dickson, *New Foundations*, pp. 102–3; Kiernan, *History of the Financial Administration*, p. 160.
124. Nat. Arch., PC 2/102, pp. 363–4, 378–9, 383–5; PC 2/103, pp. 515–16, 518–19, 525, 546; SP 63/411/49–55, 214–16; SP 63/412/204, 206–7; SP 63/413/25–6, 103–4; BL Add. MS 35592, ff. 50–52, 85–6, 100–1, 109–10, 169–71, 173–4, 198–9, 200–1, 215–20; PRONI, Wilmot papers, T3019/2204, 2221; D. O'Donovan, 'The Money Bill Dispute of 1753', in T. Bartlett and D.W. Hayton (eds), *Penal Era and Golden Age: Essays in Irish History, 1690–1800* (Belfast: Ulster Historical Foundation, 1979), pp. 55–87.
125. *Common Sense*, pp. 1–76; BL Add. MS 35592, ff. 50–2, 215–20; NLI, MS 694, pp. 34–6.
126. *Stat. Ire.*, vii, 619–22, 801–7; ix, 7–17, 272–85, 489–503; x, 6–22, 71–87, 342–56, 647–62; xi, 13–29, 311–33, 353–72, 407–22; xii, 19–50; *CJI*, vii, 13, 95, 97–8, 108–10, 117–18, 147–9, 151–2; Magennis, *Political System*, pp. 133–43; F.G. James, *Ireland in the Empire, 1688–1770* (Cambridge, MA: Harvard University Press, 1973), pp. 259–61; R.V. Clarendon, *A Sketch of the Revenue and Finances of Ireland and of the Appropriated Funds, Loans and Debt of the Nation from their Commencement* (Dublin, 1791), app., p. xvi.

CHAPTER NINE

'Vested' Interests and Debt Bondage: Credit as Confessional Coercion in Colonial Ireland

SEÁN MOORE

Fools are more hard to conquer than persuade...
Because the fleece accompanies the Flock.
—John Dryden, *Absalom and Achitophel*

The Church of Ireland, a provincial branch of the Anglican communion, enjoyed a monopoly over ecclesiastical authority and property in eighteenth-century Ireland. Its status as the sole official church was patterned after the practice of the British state and was secured after the English Revolution of 1688 and the Treaty of Limerick in 1691. The Irish Parliament, to assure the loyalty of civil servants, passed acts requiring an oath swearing to the supremacy of the Church, a test of Dissenting Protestants' conformity to its articles of faith, and Penal Laws restricting Roman Catholic religious practice, property ownership, and legal rights. Though Church and Parliament were united in securing the dominance of the Anglo-Irish ruling caste, fissures between these clerical and lay *colóns* began to emerge over economic issues during the course of the following decades. Many of the clergy's complaints in this regard were against the Crown, focused on such issues as the latter's appropriation of the 'First Fruits and Twentieth Parts' of ministers' incomes and appointments of Englishmen rather than Anglo-Irishmen to Ireland's parishes and dioceses. The Church's main conflicts with the lay landed gentry of Parliament, however, were over finance, not property. The struggle over the proprietorship and value of tithes – the reduction in clerical income threatened by the laity's increasing use of land for pasturage rather than crops – has been one well-documented instance of that competition for revenue.[1] This essay, however, contends that ownership of the population's debts was a central aspect of the quarrel that has been overlooked in previous studies. Loans made by clergymen to the poor, I argue, were a form of debt bondage that not only enabled them to profit from the colonized majority of Ireland, but also to secure the latter's peonage through the conjoined exercises of material domination and ideological hegemony.

Ireland's mechanisms of private and public finance in this period were underdeveloped, especially when compared to those emerging in Britain. Philip O'Regan has asserted that 'Ireland was little affected by the changes in the financial system and outlook then occurring in England... A peripheral island without any central financial focus such as that supplied by the City of London in England, Ireland did not enjoy the level of economic, financial or political maturity conducive to such an evolution.' In this context, 'the almost feudal nature of its fiscal system' required an equally medieval social institution for the management of credit, namely the Church of Ireland. Since the Tudor era, it had accumulated 'enormous incomes derived from tithes and rents', and, in these primitive conditions, was the only organization possessing sufficient surplus capital to engage in lending on a large scale.[2]

Clerical lending was no new innovation, having formed the central economic basis for complaints against the Roman Catholic Church. The traditional view of the Protestant Reformation's material causation, advocated by Max Weber and others, was that it represented a triumph of capitalism over feudalism: a revolt against the anti-usury policies of the Vatican.[3] Recent scholars such as Robert Ekelund, however, have revised that view, arguing that the Catholic Church was already a monopolistic banker well before the sixteenth-century schisms.[4] Their work develops the arguments of R.H. Tawney, whose *Religion and the Rise of Capitalism* mapped the extent of ecclesiastical involvement in the debt market. Tawney regarded the Papacy as 'the greatest financial institution of the Middle Ages'. He provided evidence that there were frequent complaints that 'Priests... engage in trade and take usury' and that 'Cathedral chapters lend money at high rates of interest.'[5]

In his view, little changed after the Church of England had been established, as its clergy at all levels replaced their Catholic counterparts as creditors in the three kingdoms of England, Ireland, and Scotland. In an early modern economy still dominated by agrarian forms of capitalism, tenant farmers frequently borrowed money from the same lay or clerical landlord to whom they paid rent: '[T]he lender is often a monopolist – "a money master", a maltster or corn monger, "a rich priest", who is the solitary capitalist in a community of peasants and artisans. Naturally, he is apt to become their master.'[6] The Reformation, Tawney implies, may have been the product of a revolt against Rome's monopoly of debt by clergy seeking their own monopolies.

Tawney's notion that a master–slave relationship was often entailed by clerical credit resembles that of more recent critics of 'debt bondage', a term used to describe the twenty-first century forms of indentured servitude taking shape in Third World sweat-shops and the global sex trade. The concept, if not the term, has been in usage at least since the classical period. Edward Harris, in discussing whether Solon, the sixth-century BC archon of Athens, abolished debt-bondage, borrows the United Nations' definition of it as the 'status or condition arising from a pledge by a debtor of his personal services or those of a third person under his control as security for a debt'.[7] Debt bondage is not slavery because it is not the debtor's body that is owned, only the labour of that body, and only for the term of repayment of the debt.[8] Historians of pre-twentieth century Africa have explained this distinction by calling such debtors, or their proxies, 'pawns' within a 'pawnship' system for managing credit and labour. Toyin Falola and Paul Lovejoy write that 'Pawns themselves were not property and were not owned, although various authors sometimes refer to "masters" who "owned" pawns, as if they were slaves. In most instances, it would be more accurate to refer to "creditors" who "controlled" pawns.' Typically, 'the major victims of pawnship were destitute individuals who pawned themselves, children of the poor, social or religious outcasts, and domestic slaves'.[9] Though the trading classes in Africa often became pawns due to their own commercial debts, the great majority of these bondsmen and bondswomen were from more disenfranchised segments of the population.

Early modern Ireland, I argue, was a culture engaged in forms of pawnship in which indebted 'religious outcasts' provided a variety of services to their creditors, often their local Anglican clergyman. The content of those services, however, is not as important as their ideological effect: the binding of the debtor into a legal and social contract with the established church and the state of which it was a part. This essay discusses how the widespread existence of the practice was rendered visible only when it was challenged by the rise of more secular systems of public and private finance. The financial records of two clergymen, Jonathan Swift, Dean of St Patrick's Cathedral in Dublin, and William King, Archbishop of Dublin, demonstrate how Church of Ireland clergy were sceptical of the modernization of the country's credit practices yet proved themselves willing participants in that transformation.

I

The British Isles' traditional forms of lending came under pressure in the eighteenth century, as England began to experience a Financial Revolution that witnessed the centralization of public finance in the form of a national bank retailing the government's debts. Though Ireland lagged behind Britain in this modernizing trend, it too began to experiment. As Charles Ivar McGrath has indicated in an essay in this volume, the central innovation in Ireland's system of finance in this period was the establishment of a funded national debt in 1716, lent to the Treasury by Anglo-Irish Protestant members of the executive, legislative, and judicial branches of government. The immediate purpose of the loan was to raise supplemental army regiments for defense against the Jacobite invasion feared in those years, but over the long term it also was an investment in government securities that would be paid by future tax revenues.[10] Together with an attempt to structure this debt more formally by establishing a national Bank of Ireland in 1720–1, this development threatened existing credit institutions. The corpus of the bank controversy itself not only makes visible a colonial dimension to the bursting of the South Sea and Mississippi Bubbles in those years, but also provides evidence concerning the state of private credit relations in contemporary Ireland. By essentially having the government 'go public' with the eighteenth-century equivalent of an initial public offering (IPO) of shares in future taxes, the bank proposal's backers hoped to put Ireland's revenue, government debt, and currency system on a more sound footing. This project was considered in the Irish Parliament and contemporary pamphlet literature, but failed because its plan to lend its banknotes at 5 per cent interest threatened an Anglo-Irish Protestant identity increasingly based on the monopoly on lending at the higher rates of interest possessed by private creditors.

What vested interests feared was that by forming a central bank, Ireland would adopt the form of power-sharing between agrarian and commercial capitalists established when England had done the same in creating its bank. J.G.A. Pocock has discussed the political ideas surrounding this material arrangement, suggesting that Anglophone culture was formulating a new kind of republican ideology, one emerging from a compromise between 'two explicitly post-feudal ideals, one agrarian and the other commercial, one ancient and the other modern'.[11] Investment in government through the medium of a central bank and its monetary instruments, in this view, gave rise to the kind of participatory democracy characteristic of a joint-stock company, yet one in which landed property and commercial profit work hand-in-glove. In short, the state itself becomes represented in the image of such a company, yet one in which the stockholders profit from the commerce made possible by both credit (mobile property) and the surplus value that supported such an expansion of the scope of finance: the capital created by the greater consolidation, monopoly, and enclosure of land in the seventeenth and eighteenth centuries (immobile property). As Linda Colley has written, in Britain this relationship between the 'landed' and 'moneyed' was one in which the major joint-stock companies (mostly commercial men) subscribed to the National Debt in exchange for military intervention in markets by the government (mostly landed men).[12] It was for these reasons that Voltaire argued that England was exceptional, having 'established that wise and happy form of government where the prince is all-powerful to do good, and at the same time is restrained from committing evil; where the nobles are great without insolence or lordly power, and the people share in government without confusion'.[13] The fact that investment in Britain's public funds was open to all faiths and stations in life, and that there was no coercion to loan money to the government, was unique among European states.

Eighteenth-century Ireland, however, lacked a significant bourgeoisie, and the circumstances in which its national debt was established presents a much more clear-cut case of a 'landed class' that was also the 'moneyed class' of the nation. The restriction that public creditors to this fund had to be members of the Anglican faith suggests that its form of government was patterned after the old regimes of the Continent, not England. Anglo-Ireland was engaged in its own theorizing of a compromise between land and commerce, a debate that took the shape, in the work of William Molyneux and Jonathan Swift, of a 'landed' plea to British Crown prerogative and an objection to the 'moneyed' mercantilist interests of the British Parliament. Those established Anglo-Irishmen who had made loans to the Irish Treasury in 1716 did indeed constitute a republic of mutual interests. But due to the agrarian basis of their wealth and the country's colonial condition, these creditors were an exclusive coterie of landed men in whose hands the fortunes of the Anglican colonial state resided. Because Irish revenue measures had to originate in the exclusively Protestant parliament, Anglo-Irishmen's lending to the Treasury for such revenue was a crucial factor in the formation of Ireland's parliamentary autonomy vis-à-vis Britain. But their failure to incorporate other domestic constituencies into this coterie of investors guaranteed that their government would never obtain the level of assent and liberty of its English counterpart.

Understanding the political and economic conditions that shaped the Anglo-Irish 'Republic of Debt' and its accompanying restrictedly Anglican 'private' public sphere requires an investigation of the culture of credit in early eighteenth-century Ireland. I argue that these conditions can be explained in an analysis of Ireland's colonial version of what Karl Marx, in the fourth volume of *Capital*, would later call the dispute between early eighteenth-century political economists, who were apologists either for the 'rising industrial bourgeoisie' or the 'old-fashioned usurers'.[14] The subordination of the latter to the former, in Marx's view, was the precondition for modern capitalism to develop in countries like Britain. The pamphleteering over founding the Bank of Ireland in 1721 largely fell into these two theoretical camps, with lay and clerical 'old fashioned usurers' triumphing over a modernizing 'rising industrial bourgeoisie'. Ireland's inversion of Marx's conditions for industrial capital formation – the success of the 'old fashioned usurers' in defeating the bank and therefore the means to capitalize industry at this crucial stage in Ireland's development – can largely be blamed for the country's failure to compete with England and Continental Europe in the eighteenth century and after.

Part of the opposition to the central bank came from the urban bourgeoisie, members of a nascent private banking industry. According to F.G. Hall, these banks owed their existence to an Irish Parliamentary Act passed in 1709 (8 Anne c. 11 (Ir.)), which legalized the transferability of any notes issued by merchants, bankers, and other businesses.[15] The unethical practices of these new 'old fashioned usurers' were documented by Lady Molesworth in a letter to her son John in London of 17 May 1720:

> I believe most of our money of this kingdom is gone over to the South Sea stock, for I never saw it so hard to get in my life…They talk here of erecting a bank here, which mightily alarms our bankers. 'Twill make them more reasonable in their dealings with us, and for that reason they set themselves to oppose it all they can.[16]

Lady Molesworth not only describes the usurious rates of interest and insecure paper money practices of the private banks, but also their stake in preventing a rival national institution from setting up shop in Ireland. At the very least, she is hoping that the threat of the Bank of Ireland will place the Irish public in a position to negotiate with private Irish bankers for better rates of interest and security for paper credit. Pamphlets such as *A Letter to Henry Maxwell, Esq.*; *A Dialogue Between Mr. Freeport, a Merchant, and Tom Handy, A Trades-man, Concerning the Bank*; and *An Answer to a Book, Intitl'd, Reasons Offer'd for Erecting a Bank in Ireland* ridicule the high rates of interest charged by these small banks.[17] They suggest that the central bank's 5 per cent interest rates had the potential to undermine their business and intimate that their proprietors may have been bribing Members of Parliament to vote against establishing the central bank. This lobbying was not successful, as legislation to regulate Ireland's private banks was considered in the Irish Parliamentary session of 1721 alongside the bill to charter the national Bank of Ireland, though these measures probably would not have passed unless the more dire alternative of the Bank of Ireland were a possibility. This regulation was concerned with two issues: first, the payment of banknotes by bankers (that is, their redemption for gold and silver coin or other securities), which apparently had become quite dilatory in the cash-poor situation of post-South Sea Bubble Ireland; and second, a lowering of the legal rate of interest. 'An act for the better securing the payment of Bankers notes' (8 George I. C. 14 (Ir.)) had several provisions, including the right to sue bankers in court for the value of their scrip should they refuse or be unable to redeem it. This legislation was intended to correct the Irish banking industry's tendency to over-circulate banknotes beyond the gold and silver capital deposits that they had on hand. 'An act for reducing the interest of money to seven per cent' (8 George I. c.13 (Ir.)) was also passed, a measure that affected public and private credit transactions alike.[18]

Because such small banks had only been legal since 1709, however, they were not the main 'old fashioned usurers' with a stake in the outcome of the Bank of Ireland project. They were also more urban, affecting those in the cities and towns but not having as much influence in the country. The Anglican clergy had the most to lose because lending had been an integral component of their vocation for two centuries. But that calling's political purpose was the maintenance of the hegemony of their 'Constitution in Church and State', which depended on bonding the colonized population with the colonialist caste through debt obligations.

II

The clergy's opposition to the founding of a national bank reveals a deep structure of credit relations in eighteenth-century Ireland. The rhetoric emanating from Church of Ireland clergy may have been motivated not only by a fear that the Bank of Ireland's low interest loans would compete with the clergy's own lending practices. It was customary for individual clergymen to loan money at 8 per cent interest to borrowers from their parishes, an amount leading to the popular complaint throughout the British Isles that communities were 'being saddled with a vicar who took a penny in the shilling'.[19] This interest not only generated extra income for the clergy, but also gave them a measure of control over debtors in a population not entirely converted to the idea of English, and specifically Anglican, authority and privilege in Ireland. Christopher Fauske, in describing some of the controversy over the Bank of Ireland project, has noted that clergymen of the Church of Ireland were among those land-owning men who profited from private lending:

> One of the main arguments against the whole concept was that a central bank would concentrate money in the hands of a wealthy few, diminishing the influence of the cash-poor but land-rich, among whom would be numbered both a significant percentage of the bishops of the Church of Ireland and, crucially, many members of the lower house. Another complaint was that the low interest rates the bank would charge (about five per cent was the promise) threatened the rather more lucrative returns solvent landlords were getting from loaning money to their more impecunious peers.[20]

Though I do not agree with Fauske that lay and clerical landlords were opposing the Bank because they were 'cash-poor' (they did, after all, collect rents as well as the interest and principal from loans that they made), his suggestion that a large amount of private lending was taking place from these landlords to others is well-taken. The clergy, I argue, was engaged in 'clerical lending', and the more solvent lay landlords were involved in a similar practice. The Bank project's challenge to this culture of lending made visible how the 'Constitution in Church and State' and 'Protestant Interest' was maintained by the obligations generated by these loans, with clerical lending serving the Church portion of the arrangement and the lay landlord's credit the State portion. This problem gave rise among these 'old fashioned usurers' to a sense that the new national Bank would end their monopoly on lending and undermine a constitution partly built upon keeping most of the population in rent and debt slavery. Consequently, the Church felt obliged to moralize on the issue while the landed laity remained interested in disseminating fear that any change to the financial system would bring in the Pretender.[21]

The political necessity of debt bondage can be traced to its origins in moral discourse. The link between early modern concepts of morality and credit has been developed most thoroughly by Craig Muldrew in *The Economy of Obligation*. He says that in the century prior to the founding of public credit in England in 1694, there was a significant increase in the volume of what are more properly termed 'private credit' transactions. The power of the state was 'still much too weak' before the 1690s to establish both the central bank and the political economic theory necessary to develop public credit. The 'private' creditor relations of this earlier period built both trust and mistrust, creating a cult of reputation that linked one's creditworthiness with one's character: 'Credit as a currency of reputation was the means by which such trust was communicated beyond local face-to-face dealing between people who knew each other.' As a result, 'credit became a type of currency where a "propriety" or property of the self in terms of virtuous attributes, was circulated by word of mouth through the community'.[22] This 'private' paper credit therefore helped create an English 'imagined community' more effectively than other early modern written forms of property, such as literature, because of the overlapping layers of contractual obligation that bound individuals to each other exponentially.[23]

These observations take on more significance in early eighteenth-century Ireland in that this pre-1694 culture of private obligation –

and its corollary effects on notions of reputation and morality – become particularly charged by sectarian difference. Networks of lending dominated by clerical lenders would thus seem to involve both a moral obligation to the church of your lender as well as the monetary obligation. In the realm of 'private' credit, the private sphere was merged with the public sphere; and therefore household morality became a public concern, synthesizing creditworthiness with family and individual moral reputation. Access to credit, in short, could be enabled or jeopardized by one's religious preference inasmuch as that was a register of moral standing. For Muldrew,

> Trust had to be generated, communicated and negotiated by each household involved in the market, whose access to goods, wealth and to the social status and power conferred by wealth – such as office holding or patronage – was dependent on access to the continual circulation of credit within what I have chosen to term the 'serial sociability' of the credit economy. The result of this was that moral competition, in order to obtain credit, was often more characteristic than economic competition. Reputation, in the form of language, was produced and communicated for profit, and the potential effect of this production was continually evaluated by householders as they sought publicly to define their own reliable and virtuous personalities, and to be reassured about those of others with whom they did business. In this way, the virtues of middling householders were not the attitudes of a set 'class' of people, but rather the product of a continual attempt to maintain access to the circulation of credit.[24]

Here, virtue, in the commodified medium of language, is itself a form of commodity money that underwrites private paper credit. The personality – subjectivity – is thereby commodified while it becomes alienated and reified into a matrix of other circulating commodities. 'What mattered was not an internalized or autonomous self,' Muldrew writes, 'but the public perception of the self in relation to a communicated set of both personal and household virtues.'[25] Ireland's culture of 'clerical lending', in short, involved non-Church of Ireland borrowers in obligations to the Church of Ireland's community of credit, diminishing their ability to resist participation in the confessional state because individual reputation for obedience to the cleric was a register of continual access to the credit circulating within that community. Needless to say, the act of going to a Church of Ireland clergyman for a loan was necessary because the conditions of colonialism deprived non-Church of Ireland persons of the financial rewards of full participation in the state.

In the Bank controversy, the chief evidence that members of the Church of Ireland were lending to residents of their parishes (and therefore opposing the Bank of Ireland on the grounds that it would threaten their lending business) is contained in the satirical pro-Bank of Ireland pamphlet, *A Letter to Henry Maxwell, Esq*., published anonymously. The pamphlet masks itself as a critique of the Bank project from the position of Country ideology, which helps it to parody arguments against the Bank, identify its opponents, and put forward a pro-Bank agenda. The author reaches deeply into Irish culture to show how common private lending had become, accusing the Church of Ireland clergy and laity of supporting themselves by lending to the poorer Irish Dissenters and Catholics at the legal 8 per cent interest rate:

> ...it will manifestly appear upon Tryal, that many Persons in this Kingdom of the Laiety, and God knows how many of the Clergy, have great Sums of Money out at Interest at Eight per Cent, all which (if ever the Bank is set upon a right Foot, and People's Eyes are open to see the Security and Usefulness of it) must of Course lose above one Third of the interest they now flourish under; and who knows but such a Reduction from their Fortunes, may force some of them to lay down their Coaches and Chariots, and so the Vicar's Wife, as of old, must either trot to Church on Foot, or Ride with a Safeguard and Pillion behind his Reverence holding fast by the cannonical [*sic*] Girdle.[26]

If this assertion is true, then it would explain resistance to the Bank of Ireland, because as a lending institution it would upset the customary practices of lending that had grown up among the people, or at least between the well-heeled and those who needed money. This kind of monetary custom would have produced a communal unconscious and financial network dominated by 'old fashioned usurers' like Church of Ireland clergy in the very moment of the transaction – an unconscious that would be traumatized by new innovations like the Bank. It threatened the clergy's, and perhaps their own, lending schemes:

> Can you or any Man in his Senses, believe this [the 5 per cent interest of the Bank of Ireland] will not raise ill Blood in all the Eight *per Cent* Men, among which Number you cannot but know there are a great many Deans, Doctors and Priests (I shall never speak irreverently of the Lords in *Lawn*) who when they find themselves dispossest of their present Way of getting Wealth, will not fail in Season and out of Season, to raise up again the exploded Cry of the *Church's Danger*, there being allow'd in this Bank not only Papists, but Presbyterians and Quakers too, and you'l find they'l Treat this *Hydra* of a Bank with worse Language than they dare do the *Dragon* with Seven Heads, *Antichrist* or the *Whore of Babylon*, nay and probably draw in some Arguments by Head and Shoulders, to prove that setting the Poor on Work by taking away the Extortion of the Rich, is only Robbing *Peter* to pay *Paul*, or doing Evil that Good may come of it, and soon after say, that this pernicious Bank is a Bastard by Law, got by one Missisipi [*sic*] on the Body of a South-Sea Whore, and in its wicked Practice it is the very Sin against the Holy Ghost [for what wont an angry Priest say,][27] and then Lord have mercy upon all their Souls that are concerned in it.[28]

The satirist attributes to the Church of Ireland clergy good motivation for railing against the Bank of Ireland plan, and suggests that their rhetoric about the Bank setting up Catholics and Dissenters against the Church and the 'Constitution in Church in State' is cover for their more pecuniary interests. In his postscript, he hints that Swift's *Subscribers to the Bank Plac'd According to Their Order and Quality with Notes and Queries*, published at about this time, is an example of the defense-of-Church-lending-inspired rhetoric:

> To shew you that what I mention'd about the angry Priests is true, there is now a Paper of Scandal handed about by the Hawkers, as SWIFT as Lightning, that will blast your favourite Bank, tho' you love it as *David* did JONATHAN, tho' by the by, the Author is a little mistaken in Case of the Nobility, for all the Dukes and Marquesses of this Kingdom, except one, have nothing to say against the Bank; and 'tis hard to think such an inconsiderable Rabble as he makes the rest to be, can be able to devour and destroy 2,000,000 of People, had they as much Cruelty, and as good Stomacks as CANIBALLS.[29]

Though this passage has been used to identify Jonathan Swift as the author of that pamphlet, it also helps us locate him now as a target of this author's charges of predatory lending by clergy members. The bank would interfere with the custom of paying clergy in coin by replacing coin with paper currency.

Henry Maxwell, a proponent of the Bank, felt obliged to address the clergy because of this in his pamphlet *Reasons Offer'd for Erecting a Bank in Ireland; in a Letter to Hercules Rowley, Esq.* He links his theory that an increase in the volume of credit will improve demand for the produce of land with a benefit to the Church of Ireland clergy. He suggests that not only would their mission to supply the poor out of parish coffers be lifted by putting them to work in new manufactures, but that tithes will also be increased as more land will be tilled and less grazed. He says that

> The Restoring our Credit, Encreasing our Sock [*sic*], and in consequence of that, our Manufactures, will be the greatest Advantage the Clergy can receive; for the Tithe of an Acre of Flax or Hemp, is much more valuable than the Tithe of Corn of any kind . . . Thus the Clergy would have a double Advantage, as the Land now plowed would, by better Culture, become more fruitful, and as more Land would be broken up: And Land plowed is of more Advantage to the Clergy, than Land under Pasture, this relates to the Clergy in the Country: And in Cities and Towns, as they encreas'd, and fill'd with Inhabitants, the Clergy in them would plainly find their Account in that.[30]

More or less realistically, he sees the clergy as men interested in their account books, if only to fulfill their pastoral mission. Maxwell thus offers an incentive to the traditional intellectual defenders of the landed interest to consider the advantages of the Bank of Ireland scheme, suggesting that demand for Flax and Hemp – increased by low interest rates and the growth of the economy by reducing the cost of doing business, will reduce grazing, the principal element of the low-cost 'agistment' tithe on animal products. Clergy would be interested in that development because the tithe on crops would be higher, and the total take would be improved because of the need for a larger number of tillers of the soil. That demand would, accordingly, have the win-win effect of reducing unemployment. In short, Maxwell recognized that the anti-Bank of Ireland constitutional rhetoric was motivated by the pecuniary interests of 'clerical lenders' and the corollary control their loans gave them over an often disloyal body of borrowers in their parishes, most of whom did not belong to that Church.

III

The anonymous author of *A Letter to Henry Maxwell, Esq.* may have been indicting the clergy in general for lending at 8 per cent interest, though his particular target was Swift. His suggestion that Swift was an 'old-fashioned usurer' is supported by an early biographer, Patrick Delany. Delany, responding to Swift's first eulogist, John Boyle, the fifth Earl of Orrery, published *Observations upon Lord Orrery's Remarks on the Life and Writings of Dr. Jonathan Swift* in 1754, claiming that Swift's lending was part of his general charitable nature:

> After honesty, charity, I think, took up the next place in his heart. And that of his lending out a large sum of money in small portions, to honest, industrious, and necessitous tradesmen, was very conspicuous. He lent it out at a very small interest; and such as barely sufficed for a very moderate maintenance, or rather gratuity, to the person who kept the account of the disbursements and weekly payments.
>
> These payments he expected should be made out of the weekly profits of their trade, till the whole was repaid, within the compass of fifty weeks—This, my Lord, will, I believe, be allowed one of the most Christian, social, and well-judged charities, that ever was devised.
>
> It hath been, indeed, objected to it, that it was calculated to keep up his popularity with the weavers! But this, to my certain knowledge, is utterly false. For it was equally open to every other trade in the city: and required no other recommendation, than that of an honest, and necessitous industry.[31]

Swift may have been 'popular' with the weavers for his willingness to loan them money, but such an obligation would certainly help to keep Dissenters in awe of Church and State. Recent historians of Swift's finances have tended to support Delany's reading of Swift's loans as charity. Paul V. Thompson and Dorothy Jay Thompson, in their highly detailed reconstruction of Swift's finances, *The Account*

Books of Jonathan Swift, have summarized their study of his loans with an equally favorable view of his charity:

> The most remarkable and enlightened instance of Swift's benevolence, we might think today, would be his loans of money to people in need. The small amounts of 'industrious money' to tradespeople at low rates of interest began early; a possible instance is on 23 May 1703; 'Recd (and lent in part)'; the sums, under £10, are too small to have been more formal loans . . . The system was still in operation in his last days.[32]

Both Delany and the Thompsons, however, by taking an unproblematic view of Swift's loans, miss their larger function in building a community of obligation to the individual cleric making them and the colonialist Anglican Church and state for which he stands – a function that perhaps would go unnoticed if it were not challenged by the potential hegemony of the Bank of Ireland in 1720–1.

Perhaps Samuel Johnson was more accurate than Delany and the Thompsons when he wrote that Swift became unpopular because of this lending and his aggressive legal pursuit of defaulters. He suggests that Swift was not lending for charity's sake, but rather to keep up appearances:

> He [Swift] set aside some hundreds to be lent in small sums to the poor, from five shillings, I think, to five pounds. He took no interest, and only required that, at repayment, a small fee should be given to the accomptant; but he required that the day of promised payment should be exactly kept. A severe and punctilious temper is ill qualified for transactions with the poor; the day was often broken and the loan was not repaid. This might have been easily foreseen, but for this Swift had made no provision of patience or pity. He ordered his debtors to be sued. A severe creditor has no popular character; what then was likely to be said of him who employs the catchpoll under the appearance of charity? The clamour against him was loud and the resentment of the populace outrageous; he was therefore forced to drop his scheme and own the folly of expecting punctuality from the poor.[33]

Though Johnson differs from Delany on the question of whether Swift took interest, it is clear that these loans sometimes served as instruments by which to remind the poorest of his debtors of the coercive power of the confessional state.

Joseph McMinn has claimed that Swift's lending did not only extend to the weavers and other artisans living in the Liberties around St Patrick's, but also to Dublin artists. McMinn, another critic who prefers to see Swift's loans as charity, says that the Dean was especially helpful to dramatists. He documents the fact that Thomas Griffith, the actor and manager of Dublin's Smock Alley and Aungier Street Theatres, wrote to ask Swift for a loan to keep these theatres in business. The letter of 8 February 1736 reads: '[M]y last and only hope is fix'd on your generous Disposition, who sav'd a whole unhappy Nation from Destruction, will lend your supporting hand to defend me and my little State from Misery and Misfortune; and I will with utmost Gratitude repay it at my next Benefit, or in such other manner, as you shall please to direct.'[34] McMinn can find no evidence that Swift forwarded the loan on this occasion, but points to another that Swift did indeed make to the young, blind playwright Michael Clancy. Swift's letter to Clancy of 25 December 1737 reads:

> Some Friend of mine lent me a Comedy, which I am told was written by you: I read it carefully, and with much Pleasure, on Account both of the Characters, and the Moral. I have no Interest with the People of the Play-house, else I should gladly recommend it to them. I send you a small Present in such Gold as will not give you Trouble to change; for I much pity your Loss of Sight, which if it pleased God to let you enjoy, your other Talents might have been your honest Support, and have eased you of your present Confinement.[35]

McMinn says that Clancy replied immediately, sending the Dean tickets to the play.[36] It is clear, then, that Swift was a patron of the arts, if not in outright gifts, then in loans. In a situation in which artists had no real secular option for borrowing money to finance their projects, 'clerical lending' seems to have been the preferred form of credit.

Swift was by no means the only 'clerical lender' among the Anglican clergy. The correspondence of Archbishop King of Dublin bears witness to his lending and his legal maneuvers to recover bad debts. In a letter of 1 February 1723 to a tenant named Douglas, King complains that he cannot lend Douglas money to renew his lease because another tenant, Mr Moor, has not acknowledged receipt of a loan that King made to him for similar purposes. King says that Moor's bad debt has persuaded him to be cautious about lending money:

> So that I can't venture on a conveyance with any safety as to lending money. I have lost several summes that way and made a resolution never to lend any more than I designed to lose. I believe if you ask any lawier, he will be of Mr. Howard's opinion. Please to send Mr. Wilson to me and I will talk with him, and if any safe way can be thought of to help you, I will come into it.[37]

King was so afflicted with bad debtors in the 1720s that he wrote on several occasions of the cases he was pursuing in both Irish and English courts. The Declaratory Act of 1720 was particularly frustrating to him, because suits he had won against debtors in Irish courts were being appealed by defendants to English courts via 'Writs of Error', forms of appeal that suggested that the lower court was mistaken in its judgment. Writing Irish Lord Lieutenant Grafton on 11 December 1722, King points to how the Declaratory Act was interfering with Irish cases of debt:

> I beseech your grace to give me leave to represent the miserable condition of the subject of this Kingdom in respect of their properties. A poor man sues for a debt or claim, suppose, an 100 *ll* [one-hundred pounds sterling]. He gets judgment for it, his adversary brings a Writ of Error and it goes over to Great Britain. How long it must hang there, Your Grace will be able to judge by what you see in my cases, which have depended five or six years and had not your Grace been so kind as to interpose your interest, might for ought I know, have depended as much longer. But suppose that a determination shou'd be obtained in 3 or 4 terms, yet the cost is so extraordinary, that a man had better lose the principle [*sic*]. I assure your Grace that the two writs of Error, have already cost me about six hundred pounds ster. And how much more it may cost me, before I obtain a finall determination, I can't tell. Now if it be so difficult for me to bring on a cause there, who I thank God may pretend to some regard and interest there, how must it be with a poor man or a clergyman, who perhaps sues for twenty shill? Sure this is a matter, that deserves consideration and some remedy.[38]

The cost of litigation alone, King argues, makes pursuit of bad debtors in Ireland prohibitive, especially when their cases are appealed to English courts. In the case about which King is complaining, mistakes made in the composition of the writ itself led to mounting legal costs, as attorneys made no apologies for making those errors, but charged again to correct them. He complains to his English attorney Charles Sanderson that one of his suits for debt had been pending 'in the several courts for 20 years'.[39]

IV

It is clear, then, that clerical and lay Anglican-class lending was widespread and that litigation about Irish debt had important constitutional ramifications, if only because of the appeals process to England made possible by the Declaratory Act had a practical economic impact on Anglo-Irish culture. The practice of 'clerical lending' seems to have followed a pattern whereby Church of Ireland clergy in both urban and rural parishes collected rent and a tithe from inhabitants of their parishes – a tithe legally exacted upon Anglicans and non-Anglicans alike – from which clerics would accrue a capital fund. That fund seems to have formed a central account in the parish from which loans would be made to the locality at 8 per cent interest. Rent played much the same role for lay landlords, creating capital for a loan fund. The consequent indebtedness of the borrowers to the clerics, who were representatives of the colonialist state inasmuch as they represented the official state Church of Ireland, and to landlords in Parliament, enhanced the authority of the state through this obligation, and therefore helped to support the 'Constitution in Church and State'. The Bank of Ireland's proposed 5 per cent rate of interest, while threatening to damage the profits from the loan business of individual clergy of the Established Church and the lay landlords in Parliament, was probably more dangerous in its capacity to jeopardize the Anglo-Irish establishment's ability to obligate the population through the rent- and tithe-funded loan practice. By proposing a national paper credit and huge loan fund that would overwhelm this kind of control of the clergy over borrowers, the Bank of Ireland threatened a secularization of the Anglo-Irish Constitution. That secularization would greatly diminish the role of the Church in the state while also reducing the influence of the landed interest. The Church's and the landed men's fear of financial revolution, while a symptom of a general 'Country' fear of public credit and its institutions, can not be understood unless we recognise them as 'old fashioned usurers' who had a pecuniary and political stake in keeping residents of their parishes in the condition of debt-slaves.

Nonetheless, it is apparent that some clergy saw that the newly established national debt and the proposed Bank of Ireland might provide an opportunity to invest the rent, tithe, and interest funds that they had accumulated into a larger, secular project. For example, McGrath has identified three bishops and three rank-and-file ministers as among the subscribers to the 1716 loan and four bishops and eleven clergy to be among those investing in the Bank of Ireland scheme.[40] Swift himself may have invested £1200 in the debt with the deputy vice-treasurer John Pratt.[41] Given this evidence, it is possible that some clergy saw the opportunity to continue in their roles as 'old-fashioned usurers' while transitioning to the culture of the 'rising industrial bourgeoisie'. But the very limited number of clergy enrolled for the projects of the latter suggests that they continued to prefer their status as sole capitalists in their immediate environs.

NOTES

1. M.J. Bric, 'The Tithe System in Eighteenth-Century Ireland', *Proceedings of the Royal Irish Academy*, 86 (1986), pp. 271–88.
2. P. O'Regan, 'Accountability and Financial Control as "Patriotic" Strategies: Accomptants and the Public Accounts Committee in Late Seventeenth and Early Eighteenth Century Ireland', *Accounting Historians Journal*, 30/2 (2003), pp. 105–32; E. Brynn, 'Some Repercussions of the Act of Union on the Church of Ireland, 1801–1820', *Church History*, 40/3 (1971), pp. 284–96.
3. M. Weber, *The Protestant Ethic and the Spirit of Capitalism*, ed. A. Giddens, trans. T. Parsons (London: Harper Collins, 1991), p. 157.
4. R.B. Ekelund, Jr., R.F. Hebert, and R.D. Tollison (eds), 'An Economic Model of the Medieval Church: Usury as a Form of Rent Seeking', *Journal of Law, Economics, & Organization*, 5/2 (1989), pp. 325–7.
5. R.H. Tawney, *Religion and the Rise of Capitalism: A Historical Study* (London: Penguin, 1926), pp. 34–5.
6. Tawney, *Religion and the Rise of Capitalism*, p. 123.
7. E.M. Harris, 'Did Solon Abolish Debt-Bondage?', *Classical Quarterly*, 52/2 (2002), p. 417.
8. N. Stein, 'No Way Out', *Fortune*, 147/1 (2003), pp. 102–8; U. Biemann, 'Remotely Sensed: A Topography of the Global Sex Trade', *Feminist Review*, 80 (2005), pp. 180–93.
9. T. Falola and P.E. Lovejoy, 'Pawnship in Historical Perspective', in T. Falola and P.E. Lovejoy (eds), *Pawnship in Africa: Debt Bondage in Historical Perspective* (Boulder: Westview Press, 1994), pp. 3–4, 6.
10. See C.I. McGrath, '"The Public Wealth is the Sinew, the Life, of Every Public Measure": The Creation and Maintenance of a National Debt in Ireland, 1715–1745', in this volume.
11. J.G.A. Pocock, *Virtue, Commerce, and History: Essays on Political Thought and History, Chiefly in the Eighteenth Century* (Cambridge: Cambridge University Press, 1985), pp. 96, 109.
12. L. Colley, *Britons: Forging the Nation 1707–1837* (New Haven: Yale University Press, 1992), pp. 55–100.

13. Voltaire, *The Works of Voltaire: A Contemporary Version*, ed. J. Morley and T. Smollett, trans. W.F. Fleming (New York: E.R. Dumont, 1901), p. 4.
14. K. Marx, *Theories of Surplus Value: Volume IV of Capital*, trans. J. Cohen and S.W. Ryazanskaya, ed. S.W. Ryazanskaya and R. Dixon (Moscow: Progress Publishers, 1971), pt. 3, p. 467.
15. F.G. Hall, *The Bank of Ireland 1783–1946* (Dublin: Hodges Figgis, 1949), p. 3.
16. Lady Molesworth to John Molesworth, 17 May 1720, in *Historical Manuscripts Commission: Report on Manuscripts in Various Collections*, vol. 8 (London: HM Stationery Office, 1913), p. 287.
17. *A Letter to Henry Maxwell, Esq; Plainly Shewing the Great Danger that the Kingdom has Escaped, and the Great Inconveniencies, that Must of Necessity have Happen'd, if a Bank had been Establish'd in this Kingdom* (Dublin, 1721), pp. 8, 9. *A Dialogue between Mr. Freeport, a Merchant, and Tom Handy, a Trades-man, Concerning the Bank* (Dublin, 1721), recto (col. 1). Hercules Rowley, *An Answer to a Book, Intitl'd, Reasons Offer'd for Erecting a Bank in Ireland. In a Letter to Henry Maxwell, Esq.* (Dublin, 1721), pp. 29–30, 32–3.
18. *The Journals of the House of Commons of the Kingdom of Ireland, from the Eleventh Year of King James the First*, 2nd ed. (Dublin, 1763), iv, 710–11; iv, 866; *Journals of the House of Lords*, 8 vols. (Dublin, 1779–1800), ii, 734. *Commons*, iv, 873, 780, 800, 851; *Lords*, ii, 727. Hall, *Bank of Ireland*, p. 5.
19. Tawney, p. 131.
20. C. Fauske, *Jonathan Swift and the Church of Ireland* (Dublin: Irish Academic Press, 2002), p. 115.
21. It should be noted that George Berkeley, a Church of Ireland Bishop, differed from the majority of his colleagues by favouring a later national bank project in the 1730s. His enthusiasm for it, however, was not shared; the new initiative failed to gain any traction in the Parliamentary session of 1737–8. See G. Berkeley, *Queries Relating to a National Bank, Extracted from the Querist. Also the Letter Containing A Plan or Sketch of such Bank. Republished with Notes* (Dublin, 1737).
22. C. Muldrew, *The Economy of Obligation: The Culture of Credit and Social Relations in Early Modern England* (New York: St Martin's Press, 1998), pp. 99, 7, 156.
23. B. Anderson, *Imagined Communities: Reflections on the Origin and Spread of Nationalism* (London: Verso, 1983).
24. Muldrew, p. 151.
25. Muldrew, p. 156.
26. *A Letter to Henry Maxwell, Esq.*, p. 10.
27. Brackets in original.
28. *A Letter to Henry Maxwell, Esq.*, pp. 15–16.
29. *A Letter to Henry Maxwell, Esq.*, p. 19.
30. H. Maxwell, *Reasons Offer'd for Erecting a Bank in Ireland; in a Letter to Hercules Rowley, Esq.* (Dublin, 1721), pp. 58–9.
31. P. Delany, *Observations upon Lord Orrery's Remarks on the Life and Writings of Dr. Jonathan Swift* [1754] (New York: Garland, 1974), pp. 203–4.
32. P.V. Thompson and D. Jay Thompson, *The Account Books of Jonathan Swift* (Newark, DE: University Delaware Press, 1984), p. cxxvi.
33. S. Johnson, *The Lives of the Most Eminent English Poets; with Critical Observations on their Works*, ed. R. Lonsdale, 4 vols. (Oxford: Clarendon Press, 2006), iii, 206.
34. J. Swift, *The Correspondence of Jonathan Swift*, 5 vols, ed. H. Williams (Oxford: Clarendon Press, 1963–5), iv, 459, quoted in J. McMinn, 'Swift and Theatre', *Eighteenth-Century Ireland*, 16 (2001), p. 44.
35. *Correspondence of Jonathan Swift*, v, 81–2. Quoted in McMinn, p. 44.
36. McMinn, p. 44. *Correspondence of Jonathan Swift*, v, 83.
37. King to Douglas, 1 February 1723 (TCD MS 2537/70).
38. King to Grafton, 11 December 1722 (TCD MS 750/7/250).
39. King to Sanderson, 11 April 1723 (TCD MS 750/7/334).
40. See McGrath, Table 1.
41. E.M. Johnston-Liik, *History of the Irish Parliament 1692–1800: Commons, Constituencies and Statutes*, 6 vols. (Belfast: Ulster Historical Foundation, 2002), vi, 114.

CHAPTER TEN

The Failure of Berkeley's Bank: Money and Libertinism in Eighteenth-Century Ireland[1]

C. GEORGE CAFFENTZIS

Bishop George Berkeley devoted much of his thought during the first years of his bishopric to developing a theory of money and, crucially, to framing a proposal for a National Bank of Ireland that would be operated by the Irish legislature and hence would be truly 'national'. He published his theory and proposal in *The Querist* in three parts between 1735 and 1737. His anti-specieist theory of money has received some notoriety in the history of economic thought. But his Bank project did not fare as well. Just as Berkeley failed to realize his proposal for a College in the Bermudas a decade before, the energy and hope Berkeley invested in his Bank did not materialize either. The Bank like the college failed, but the Bank failed utterly: his College was discussed and even won approval in Westminster while his Bank proposal was never formally debated in the Irish Parliament.

Berkeley's misadventures in Bermuda have been the source of an enormous biographical and political literature,[2] but there have been few who have questioned why Berkeley's Bank never came about. This essay will study those social figures Berkeley identified as his Bank's main opponents and examine the political conjuncture in Ireland and England that doomed his proposal.

I *THE QUERIST*'S FAILURE

In an 'organizing' letter to Thomas Prior of 5 March 1737, we see Berkeley busily preparing a campaign for his National Bank proposal, which he began to elaborate in 1735. In the letter, he enclosed a brief abstract of the proposal to be printed in Dublin newspapers which he 'could wish were spread through the nation, that men may think on the subject against next [Parliamentary] session'. He was concerned about the timing of the publication: 'I would not have this letter made public sooner than a week after the publication of the Third Part of my *Querist,* which I have ordered to be sent to you.'[3] He travelled to Dublin in December 1737 to take his permanent seat as Bishop in the Irish House of Lords (for the first and only time in this capacity) during the 1737/8 session. Everything was readied for putting the National Bank and paper currency on the legislative agenda.

And then nothing. No bill concerning a National Bank was introduced in the 1737/8 session, and it was only a generation after his death, in 1783, that an institution named 'The Bank of Ireland' (whose operation substantially differed from his sketch) was chartered by the Irish Parliament. *The Querist* had failed, his Plan did not even have enough support to be put up and voted down. Berkeley left no report of the vicissitudes of his campaign. His surviving correspondence in the years after 1737/8 makes no reference to it. His only explicit statement on 'The Plan or Sketch of a National Bank' is in the 1750 'Advertisement by the Author' to a much revised text of *The Querist.* He wrote: 'it may be time enough to take again in hand [those queries dealing with a national bank] when the public shall seem disposed to make use of such an expedient'.[4] Berkeley had resigned himself to the failure of his 'expedient' by removing many of the queries dealing with the original purpose of the text.

Why had he so miscalculated the moment? He left us a few hints in his writings of that year: *The Irish Patriot or Queries upon Queries* and *Discourse addressed to Magistrates and Men in Authority Occasioned by the Enormous License and Irreligion of the Times.* Both have a decidedly un-Berkeleyan tone. The first, which was unpublished, is Swiftian in its irony, sarcasm, and pique. It seems to be a compilation of all the objections, rejections, retorts, and evasions he encountered in the endless dinner parties, social gatherings, and lobbying in the course of his campaign for the National Bank. The second, which was published in 1738 and had an immediate influence on events, is the most disjunctive and alarmist of all his writings. These are texts written in uncharacteristic anger against a motley crew of private bankers, 'Irish patriots', mercantilist foreign exchange managers, and Berkeley's bug-bears, the libertines – who, collectively, were responsible for the failure of his National Bank plan. Let us consider them in turn.

Private bankers had the most to lose from the establishment of Berkeley's bank and they probably fought it with all the considerable power at their disposal. As the sardonic Meta-Querist in *The Irish Patriot or Queries upon Queries* asks:

> 5. Whether it ought not to be considered that so long as private men skilled in the money-trade command our cash, they may to their great advantage traffic with the several species thereof? And whether this advantageous traffic may not be hurt by a national Bank?[5]

Unfortunately for Berkeley, private bankers were major players in the Irish economy by 1738 and formidable opponents. The history of Irish merchant banking began in 1719–21 with the founding of the La Touche & Kane bank and the house of Swift.[6] It was an auspicious debut: a mere decade later, banker's notes comprised about half of the Irish money supply. The bankers' influence was spread throughout Ireland, as banks appeared in a number of smaller centres, especially Cork, throughout the 1720 and 1730s, and many an indebted MP in the Commons or Lords was in his banker's pocket.

Bankers as a group were certainly vulnerable, for the Irish banking industry was largely unregulated and untested. They often issued bank notes excessively, and their reserve requirements were still determined by rules of thumb or limits of greed. Hence, the slightest 'shock', such as a rumour of failure or of a Jacobite invasion, could lead to panics and bank runs, ending with the bankers in bankruptcy or absconding. But private banks were indispensable to Ireland's specie-poor economy. Parliament demonstrated its vital interest in them throughout the 1730s by organizing payment to creditors, depositors, and note holders of suspended banks. Bankers and parliamentarians were apparently in each others' pockets.[7]

A National Bank would not only have crowded out private banks, it would have destroyed the special relationship with Parliament which private bankers coveted. Indeed, the Meta-Querist implied that they were themselves lobbying for a utopian bill that was similar to the Federal Deposit Insurance of the New Deal in the 1930s:

> 33. Whether, to remedy the fear of bankruptcies in private banks, and at the same time to avoid jobs and influence, it would not be the wisest way for the parliament to engage itself once for all to make good the deficiencies of all particular

> bankers, and whether this simple engagement may not do better than any new schemes whatsoever?[8]

Surely the existence of a National Bank, directly operated by Parliament, would have made this private banker's utopia impossible. Hence Berkeley's Bank would have met a wall of resistance in the highest financial circles of the capital city. Yet the 'moneyed interest' alone was not strong enough to destroy his plan.

Berkeley easily satirized private bankers' self-interest, but there was another type of critic who was much more of a wonder, the perverse 'Irish Patriot'. This Patriot responded to the final query of *The Querist* ('Whose fault is it if poor Ireland still continues poor?') with the first and last of *The Irish Patriot or Queries upon Queries:*

> 1. Whether riches, or even the appearance of riches, be not often dangerous to the liberties of a people?[9]
>
> 36. Whether it be not more prudent to yield to our fate, and possess our poverty in peace?[10]

The Meta-Querist, posing as a patriot, described the situation of the Anglo-Irish in the following query:

> 20. Whether there be not two ways of preserving a freedom and independence, either by being above oppression or below it?[11]

Since he despaired of being 'above' English Parliamentary oppression, the Patriot chose to remain far 'below' it – the lower the better, perhaps. For the poorer Ireland was, the more it could hinder the English (or the puppet Irish) government's 'exertions of it'.[12] If there were less industry, manufacture, and wealth, then there would be less opportunity for the British to tax, influence, and oppress. Hence the Irish Patriot took the role of Aesop's hungry but free wolf who scorned the well-fed dog's servitude with pride. Any project that might materially improve Ireland, like the National Bank project, was thus immediately suspicious. For is not 'the whole and sole duty of an Irish patriot . . . to nourish opposition, to guard against influence, and always to suspect the worst?'[13]

Such a rejectionist psyche was no figment of Berkeley's imagination. A previous effort to establish a Bank of Ireland in 1720/1 was stopped by such 'patriotic' reasoning. The Irish Patriots had not disappeared from the halls of Parliament or the streets of Dublin by 1737 and their arguments, though almost two decades old, still had a perverse charm. The 1720 Bank project was certainly flawed in Berkeley's eyes, but the opposition's objections had had nothing to do with his own criticisms (which were inscribed in his 'Plan or Sketch of a National Bank').[14] Hercules Rowley, a major opposition spokesman in the pamphlet war surrounding the earlier Bank project, replied to an exposition of its merits in his *An Answer to a Book, Intitl'd, Reasons Offer'd for Erecting a Bank in Ireland* (1721):

> if the intended *Bank* prove advantageous to us, by increasing our Trade and encouraging our Manufactures . . . and should in the least interfere with or hinder the Trade of *England*, then we may expect, they will procure a Repeal of the Charter; or, if that cannot be done, so cramp our Trade and discourage our Manufactures, as to render them impracticable . . . if it happens to impoverish us, and drain our little substance into *Great-Britain*, then indeed, we may be sure of a Continuation.[15]

Rowley's cynical, no-win reasoning touched a deep chord in Parliament, for after an auspicious beginning, the Bank faced surprising and decisive resistance in the Irish Parliament. The Bank proposal was defeated in the Commons by the vote of 150 *against* and 80 *for* in December 1721. The Commons then promulgated the following 'patriotic' address to the king:

> As this is a matter of unusual and national concern, your dutiful Commons took the same into their most serious consideration, and not finding any solid or good foundation for establishing a public bank, so as to be beneficial to the nation or even consistent with the welfare and liberties of it, think themselves obliged, in duty to your Majesty and justice to themselves and those which they represent, to offer their humble opinion to your Majesty that the establishing of any public bank in this Kingdom will be greatly prejudicial to your Majesty's service and of most dangerous and pernicious consequence to the welfare and liberty of the nation.[16]

The Commons even passed an open-ended resolution that put anyone attempting 'to solicit or endeavour to procure any Grant, or get the

Great Seal put to any Charter for erecting a public Bank in this Kingdom' in contempt of Commons and identified him as 'an enemy of his Country'. This ban technically placed even Berkeley's later efforts under a legal cloud.

But the 1720–1 Bank project and Berkeley's 1737–8 National Bank plan were defeated not only by perverse logic. Another element was the pervasive *a priori* suspicion against all monetary experiments in Europe which the Mississippi and South Sea Bubbles inspired after 1720. This was especially apparent in 1721, for the Irish Parliament debated the Bank of Ireland proposal just months after the Anglo-Irish gentry had lost a substantial amount of money in the Bubbles, while details of the British Parliamentary investigations of South Sea directors' frauds and bribes were the daily entertainment of Dublin. Jonathan Swift made this suspicion an essential aspect of the 'patriotic' opposition in many satiric pamphlets and poems aimed at paper money, Bank directors, and stock jobbing during the time. Thus he published the broadsheet, *The Bank Thrown Down*,[17] shortly after the defeat of the proposal, and brought together many of these themes:

> This Bank is to make us a New Paper Mill
> This Paper they say, by the Help of a Quill
> The whole Nations Pockets with Money will fill
> But we doubt that our Purses will quickly grow lank
> If nothing but Paper comes out of this Bank...
> Oh! then but see how the *Beggars* will Vapour,
> For Beggars have *Rags* and Rags will make Paper,
> And Paper makes Money, and what can be cheaper?...
> Those that dropt in the *South-Sea* discover'd this *Plank*,
> By which they might Swimmingly *land* on a Bank.[18]

The fear of Bubbles and ragged paper notes lived on long after the Bank proposal of 1720–1. Swift and many other 'patriotic' writers kept it strong throughout the 1720s and into the 1730s. For the generalized suspicion against 'monetary innovations' was compounded by a paranoia towards any device that might imitate the financial wizardry of the Walpolean state.

One consequence, however, of this politics of reaction was the steady decline of specie in Ireland's actual money supply. The suspicion of British intentions which drove the campaign to reject Wood's half-pence in 1724 also resulted in the increased use of cardboard tokens for small change and paper bank notes for large transactions. In their effort to have a mercantilist, 'sound' and hard money, Swift and his circle hastened the contrary result. Irish Patriots demanded specie for Ireland, both for its supposed economic indispensability and also because any substitute would mean reconciling themselves to a dependent status *vis-à-vis* England. Even though Swift's influence had waned in the mid-1730s, the financial attitudes he gave voice to were still very much in evidence. *The Querist* tried to overcome but could not unravel the Irish Patriot's labyrinth of resentments.

The private bankers, the gold bugs, and the Irish patriots were not the only opponents that Berkeley encountered (and complained of) in Dublin during 1737–8. There remained the libertines, and these were in Berkeley's estimation his most treacherous opponents: they did not present open arguments, but uttered insidious caveats and poisoned the ethical atmosphere upon which his National Bank depended.[19]

Berkeley's National Bank depended upon the public spirit of the legislature and its designated officials, none of whom individually should profit (or lose) from the Bank's activities. There ought to be no self-interest directing their decisions and actions. But could such a financial machine operate without a threat of corruption or the incentive to private gain? Berkeley clearly heard the cynics whispering:

> 26. Whether from all these things it doth not plainly follow that a national bank, as well as every other project for increasing the wealth of this kingdom, must in the event increase influence?
>
> 34. Whether it be possible to contrive any scheme for the public good which shall not suppose or require common honesty and common sense in the execution thereof; and whether this be not an unanswerable argument against all projectors?
>
> 35. Whether therefore it be not vain to talk of schemes for bettering our affairs?[20]

A successful National Bank would create wealth which would attract 'influence', and the national bankers' only defense from it would be 'common honesty' and 'common sense'.[21] But could these be adequate? Could the public trust its representatives and servants to protect the public good against 'influence'? The Mandevillean libertines, Berkeley argued, had subtly undermined any faith in the strength of public spirit and subverted the moral-theological foundation of any institution like Berkeley's Bank.[22] Money required trust (which must be rooted in religion, according to Berkeley) and libertinism, by attacking religion, destroyed Banking.

The libertines, therefore, had to be delegitimized and driven off the public stage. Berkeley's *Alciphron* and his writings on mathematics in 1734–5 took aim at these 'freethinkers', but by 1738, faced with his inability to get Parliament to consider the plan, Berkeley saw an opportunity to strike a mortal blow at '*the enormous License, and Irreligion of the Times*'. Hence his second work of the 1737/8 legislative session, *A Discourse addressed to Magistrates*.[23]

The opportunity arose ostensibly from the behaviour of members of a new Dublin 'society or club', the Blasters. An investigating committee had found that their leader, Peter Lens, a miniaturist painter, 'professes himself to be a votary of the Devil; that he hath offered up prayers to him, and publicly drank to the Devil's health; that he hath at several times uttered the most daring and execrable blasphemies against the sacred Name and Majesty of God'.[24] The Blasters were apparently not the only Satanist club operating in Dublin at the time. The Hellfire Club was even more notorious. It had been founded in 1735 by Lord Rosse and a portrait painter named James Worsdale, and included a number of young aristocrats and/or military officers like Lord Santry, Lord Irnham, and Colonel Henry Ponsonby. Stories of their satanic antics along with their sexual transgressions, public drunkenness, and violence against servants had already become legendary.[25]

Berkeley made one speech before Parliament during the only parliamentary session he ever attended. It did not, as we might have expected, introduce his plan for a National Bank, but rather it demanded legal action against the Blasters and other 'blasphemous' clubs. His jeremiad against them had a wider range, however, for libertinism rarely took the extravagant embodiment of a Lens, a Rosse or a Santry. Certainly, a Bishop of the Church of Ireland would naturally have been concerned that Anglo-Irish aristocrats could be open apostates, but pure satanism was a minor phenomenon in Ireland, as it was in France. Hell-raising rakes, demonic Don Juans, and neo-satanic Blasters were not to be taken seriously, since their very existence revealed the diminishing power of the Devil both in the social imagination and in the legal code. After all, James I's draconian witchcraft statute of 1604 had been repealed by the British Parliament in 1731 and the traditional symptoms of demonic presence were quickly becoming medicalized.[26]

These clubs might have been laboratories for a new type of sociality, mentality, and sexuality. Berkeley, however, represented the Blasters as a 'symptom of the madness of our times':

> Blasphemy against God is a great crime against the State. But that a set of men should, in open contempt of the laws, make this very crime their profession, distinguish themselves by a peculiar name [Blasters], and form a distinct Society, whereof the proper and avowed business shall be to shock all serious Christians by the most impious and horrid blasphemies, uttered in the most public manner: this surely must alarm all thinking men. It is a new thing under the sun reserved for our worthy times and country.[27]

That is, the Blasters subvert the moral-theological foundation of human behaviour and reduce trust in the state and mutual obligations among the public. Was it fair to identify a Peter Lens with the luminaries of freethought, deism, and masonry? Hardly. But Berkeley's use of a politically charged synecdoche in the *Discourse* allows him to identify the true target of these remarks (the deistic followers of Mandeville and Shaftesbury, his main antagonists in *Alciphron*, freethinkers like Collins, anticlericalists like Toland, atheists, and freemasons) with the most extravagant *outré* element of the clerical opposition. Berkeley knew, of course, that deism and satanism were logical contraries, for the former recognized God without the Devil while the latter recognized the Devil without God. Socially, however, this synecdoche had a point, for there was a new and paradoxical social creature gestating outside the circle of the family, the firm, the state or the Church: the club. The club was private, but it was not the home; it was public, but it was not the state; it was inward, but it was not the church; it was associative, but it was not social. The club was increasingly the place where new notions and principles of actions were being discussed, debated, and put into action. Indeed, Berkeley had helped form one such society during his sojourn in Rhode Island in 1728–31 and he had participated in the progress of the Dublin Society, largely animated by his editor, Samuel Madden, and by his collaborator, Thomas Prior. These clubs and semi-secret societies, however, by being outside of the eye of Church and State, could easily degenerate into a confusing diabolical mixture of rationalist discussion and satanic inspiration.

After all, an organization most similar to the club was the witches' coven mentioned so often in Continental witch-trial transcripts. Berkeley called on the magistrates to investigate the inner workings of these gatherings of 'the better sort' in order to protect the 'outworks' of the state.[28]

Berkeley's sense of alarm was growing, not because of the jocular antics of the rakes and hell-raisers of Dublin, but because he could see in the wider network of new deistic and freethinking clubs the intellectual source both of the material attack on the Church (the *tithe of agistment* crisis during 1734/5) and of the indifference his National Bank plan faced despite all the work done by Prior, Madden, and the Dublin Society. He wanted, of course, to crush the immediate 'symptom' of 'the license and Irreligion of the times', and that was easily done. Laws against blasphemy existed and a short campaign in the House of Lords against 'Kneller's bastard', Peter Lens, proved adequate to drive him from Ireland and to dissolve the Blasters. But Berkeley was after larger game.

That is why the *Discourse* was not simply the Country-party, High-Church jeremiad that the 1721 *Essay* had been, but rather marked the arrival of a major terminological revolution in his work. The simple ontological division of ideas and spirits which proved central to the anti-abstractionist and anti-materialist arguments of the early works opened now to a revalued realm of mediating terms like 'notion', 'principle', 'belief', 'opinion', and 'prejudice'. 'Prejudice' of course, was the most surprising revision, for 'prejudice' had often in his earlier writings been a short-hand term for 'false doctrine', as, for example, in this capsule theory of learning he proposed after comparing belief in infinitesimals with transubstantiation:

> Ancient and rooted prejudices do often pass into principles: and those propositions which once obtain the force and credit of a principle, are not only themselves, but likewise whatever is deducible from them, thought privileged from all examination.[29]

Similarly, 'opinion' had been synonymous with an ill-considered but popular position:

> But let us examine the received opinion. It is said extension is a mode or accident of matter, and that matter is the substratum that supports it.[30]

> From the opinion that spirits are to be known after the manner of an idea or sensation, have risen many absurd and heterodox tenets . . . [31]

Consider also the most conspicuous use of this sense of the word in the *Treatise*:

> It is indeed an opinion strangely prevailing amongst men, that houses, mountains, rivers, and in a word all sensible objects have an existence natural or real, distinct from their being perceived by the understanding.[32]

'Notion' had already been revalued in the decisive 1732–4 period, that is, between the first edition of *Alciphron* and the second edition of the *Treatise* and the third edition of the *Dialogues*. For in 1712–13 'notion' was used as interchangeable with 'idea', but by the 1734 revisions, 'notion' was used in contrast with 'idea' as a way of *speaking about* speaking about spirits (finite or infinite). For the young Berkeley had used his simple ontological dichotomy between inactive ideas and active spirits to great effect, but this dichotomy led to an apparent dilemma. If spirits are not ideas, how can they be known or even spoken about if words refer only to ideas?

There is now a substantial literature on the transformation of the notion of notion in the later Berkeley, and we can see that this revaluation parallels the revaluation of algebra over geometry and the rhetoric of questions and hints over proofs and conclusions.[33] But a similar transformation of terms like 'opinion', 'belief', 'principle' and 'prejudice' has not been much commented on, even though both transformations arose from Berkeley's need for a social vocabulary that would not only allow for the bare existence of other minds, but also help him formulate methods for their 'taming':

> Man is an animal formidable both from his passions and his reason; his passions often urging him to great evils, and his reason furnishing means to achieve them. To tame this animal, and make him amenable to order, to inure him to a sense of justice and virtue, to withhold him from ill courses by fear, and encourage him in his duty by hopes; in short, to fashion and model him for society, hath been the aim of civil and religious institutions, and in all times the endeavour of good and wise men.[34]

This taming process required that 'good principles be propagated in the mind', 'a certain system of salutary notions, a prevailing set of opinions...embraced rather by the memory than the judgment... these are prejudices; inasmuch as they are therefore neither less useful nor less true, although their proofs may not be understood by all men'. The notions, opinions, principles, and prejudices one 'embraces' determine one's action, for, Berkeley claims, 'such as arc men's notions, such will be their deeds'. Thus the freethinkers' attempt to criticize 'prejudices' as unconsidered and probably false opinions, is itself prejudiced (in a pejorative sense): 'the difference between prejudices and other opinions doth not consist in this; that the former are false and the latter true; but in this, that the former are taken on trust and the latter acquired by reasoning'.[35]

Moreover, every moral precept cannot be the product of reasoning; there must be prejudices taken on trust and faith, since the 'bulk of mankind' cannot be philosophers. Here Berkeley opposes the 'twofold philosophy' of his antagonists, such as Toland and Collins (who divide the human race into the credulous, superstitious mob, filled with false prejudices, and the intellectual elite arriving at reasoned conclusions) by pointing out that prejudices and reasoned conclusions can have the same propositional content.[36] The freethinkers' utopian impulse to found a rational morality without religious notions, opinions, beliefs, principles, and prejudices invites catastrophe. Such a rational civil society would quickly become an uncivil monstrosity, since the freethinkers have not provided for the inner religious 'prejudices' that would curb vice and spur worthy conduct.

No actually existing monarchical, hierarchical society can survive without obedience; and obedience cannot be assured simply by the fear of punishment of a Hobbesian state, since Leviathan's multiple eyes cannot peer into the 'inward ways of thinking, which at times will break out and shew themselves paramount to all laws and institutions whatsoever'.[37] To obey is not a simple, self-evident matter, since obedience must proceed from a rule of selection of principles to be obeyed. That rule, Berkeley claims, can only be provided by religion. He laid out the terrain of this new social vision (which had been concretized in *The Querist*) through the use of an analogy.[38] The series 'God–Nature–Industry' is analogous to the series 'God–Principles and Divine Impressions–Government'. God provides in the language of nature 'materials for food and raiment', but human industry is necessary to transform these materials so that 'mankind may not perish with cold and hunger'. Analogously, God influences human minds 'by instinct, by the light of nature, by his declared will', and these 'Divine impressions' (paralleling the sensations) provide the material for salvation, but they must be cultivated and encouraged by human government. One can no more expect fields of ripe wheat in autumn without labour (even though the seeds, soil, and weather were in perfect combination) than one can expect to have tame humans without careful governing (even though each person has within all the necessary principles, instincts, and reason for perfection).

Religion is at the intersection of the divine and human government; hence it is both inevitable and indispensable. Here again Berkeley takes a deistic intellectual gambit (the insistence on examining the notion of religion in general and of 'religions' as a range of objects for comparative study instead of a fixation on the uniqueness of Christianity), outdoes it, and turns it against its creators.[39] He examines the writings and behaviour of Roman, Greek, Babylonian, Persian, Chinese, Islamic, French, and English authorities (including the 'very unsuspected writer', James Harrington) and finds a fundamental agreement on the need for governmental support and protection for religion and morality.[40]

The Blasters and other authors of 'atheistical blasphemy' openly subvert 'a religious awe and fear of God, being . . . the centre that unites, and the cement that connects all human society'. Hence they are responsible for the consequences of filling Ireland with 'highwaymen, house-breakers, murderers, fraudulent dealers, perjured witnesses, and every other pest of society'.[41] Clearly, if the magistrates do not legally punish and 'put out of countenance' those who display open contempt for God, then they undermine their own dignity and authority. Moreover, the aristocrats and rich merchants who either participated in or are entertained by deistical-satanic sallies prepared the stage for their own destruction:

> One thing it is evident they do not know; to wit, that while they rail at prejudice, they are undoing themselves: they do not comprehend (what hath been before hinted) that their whole figure, their political existence, is owing to certain vulgar prejudices, in favour of birth, title, or fortune, which add nothing of real worth either to mind or body, and yet cause the most worthless person to be respected.[42]

Berkeley was not above playing with the Blasters' fire and brimstone, as we can see here, but with an ironic Enlightenment twist. In the peroration of his *Discourse* he draws an extended parallel between political economy and morality:

> The morals of a people are in this like their fortunes; when they feel a national shock, the worst doth not show itself immediately. Things make a shift to subsist for a time on the credit of old notions and dying opinions.[43]

But as that credit declined and that accumulated fortune dwindled, a new generation, grown up in a climate of satanist pranks and freethinking sophistries, would create an 'age of monsters' incapable of regenerating the lost credit and fortune of the land – unless, of course, magistrates (from the king down to 'the petty constable') recognize that their authority is derived from God and 'manfully' protect it from blasphemers.

Berkeley's *Discourse* and his speech before the House of Lords were effective in that the 'Report from the Lords' Committees for Religion' resolved on the prosecution of Peter Lens, directing 'the Judges in their several circuits to charge the magistrates to put the laws in execution against immorality and profane cursing and swearing and gaming, and to inquire into atheistical and blasphemous clubs'.[44] Moreover, as a result of the Parliamentary agitation, the atmosphere surrounding the 'atheistical and blasphemous clubs' turned hostile. The fate of Lord Santry, who was almost hanged for the killing of a porter a few months later, made it clear that membership in such clubs could strip one of the normal protections that came with title and fortune. The atmosphere was further poisoned by the Dublin publication in 1738 of *The Irish Blasters: or, The Votaries of Bacchus* (largely a translation of a part of the 39th Book of Livy's *Histories*) which told in blood-curdling detail of the campaign of a Roman magistrate to destroy a secret Bacchic society. The author of the pamphlet hoped that 'the Christian Magistrate may be spirited up by the Example of a Roman . . . and that the infamous Society of Men, known by the Title of BLASTERS, may as successfully be punished as the Roman Bacchanalians'.[45] Berkeley could be gratified insofar as he helped to make the life of a Dublin Satanist/deist/atheist/freemason club rather uncomfortable. But this was a small reward: his revenge on this underworld did not so affect the moral-political climate as to make his project for a National Bank a reality.

II THE ILL-STARRED CONJUNCTURE: ENGLISH PATRIOTS AND WALPOLE

Private bankers, Irish Patriots, 'hard currency' reactionaries, and Dublin libertines managed to keep Berkeley's National Bank from being given a serious airing in the Irish Parliament of 1737/8. The weight of this opposition was substantial, but not necessarily decisive. For Berkeley's project was not only dependent upon Anglo-Irish events and prejudices; he had Country-Party allies in England whose support could be adequate to force consideration of his proposal whatever the opposition in Dublin, but only on condition that these allies had taken over Parliamentary power from Walpole *and* were interested in changing the place of Ireland in the colonial system.[46] The Excise Crisis of 1733 gave Berkeley hope that the Walpolean path to accumulation could be terminated, but the election that followed was not encouraging. The Walpole administration slowly recovered its poise and was to rule until 1742. By the time Berkeley published the last installment of *The Querist* in 1737, Alexander Pope had begun his own retreat, feeling the threat of a libel suit from a Walpole ministry now on the offensive. In 1737 a playhouse licensing act passed Parliament requiring plays to be approved by the Lord Chamberlain, a definite sign of danger for the literary opposition. In July 1738 Pope published the last of his Satires and ended with these lines:

> Yes, the last pen for freedom let me draw,
> When truth stands trembling on the edge of law;
> Here, last of Britons! let your names be read;
> Are none, none living? let me praise the dead,
> And for that cause which made your fathers shine,
> Fall by the votes of their degenerate line.[47]

The Irish Parliamentary session of 1737–8, however, began in a climate of new crisis for the Walpole regime. In July of 1737 Frederick, Prince of Wales, set up an independent court and offered himself as the figurehead of the anti-Walpole opposition. This was important, since the opposition could not be 'Jacobite-baited' while it was under his protection. Then, in November of 1737, Queen Caroline died. Her death was taken by many to be potentially disastrous for Walpole, since Caroline had been considered to be essential in mediating between the king and Walpole.[48]

These events allowed the Opposition to stage a remarkable revival, but held little promise for Berkeley's National Bank. The death of the 'Philosopher Queen' was as damaging to Berkeley's political prestige as it was to Walpole's political management. Caroline, as Princess of Wales, had been the instigator of the Leibniz–Clarke correspondence and organized a weekly philosophy seminar to which Berkeley had been often invited throughout the 1720s when he was in London. Berkeley was able to secure high office in the Church of Ireland on his return to London after the collapse of the Bermuda Project due only to Caroline's patronage.[49] Caroline's evident concern for Berkeley's career would have given added aura to his political proposals, including that of the National Bank, if only because of her value to Walpole. If she was persuaded by *The Querist*'s hints, then her support might have been enough for Walpole to relax his instinctual hostility toward any 'innovations' in Ireland.[50] Her death stripped Berkeley's proposal of potential royal support.

Matters degenerated in other ways also. By the time Berkeley had gone to Dublin to begin his campaign for an Irish National Bank, the new imperial, anti-Spanish thrust of the Walpolean opposition was apparent to all sophisticated observers. Berkeley's alarm in March 1737 over rumours of a split in the royal family between Frederick and the king, undoubtedly intensified by the turn of events in July, was quite justified. For Berkeley's National Bank campaign and his 'de-linking' economic strategy ironically needed Walpole's foreign policy of peace with the Catholic state powers of the Continent, especially Spain and France. Berkeley's project required a more autonomous Anglo-Irish ruling class which was less dependent upon English military force to crush an indigenous revolt. But it was almost an axiom of Irish history that whenever there was war with Catholic (and often pro-Jacobite) Spain or France, the probability of invasion, 'priestly agitation', and generalized tension increased.[51] The Patriot opposition's demands for war immediately sent a message to the Irish Parliament to be prepared for domestic unrest. War would also mean the reduction of the army's presence in Ireland, which was the visible defence against a native Irish uprising. Berkeley's plan to launch a more autonomous course for Ireland in the midst of an imperial war fever, generated by Berkeley's own allies in London, would have caused an immediate dissonance in the Irish Parliament about the political consequences of the National Bank.

The 1737–8 economy was also problematic for Berkeley's inward-looking strategy of national disengagement. Whatever the results of the 'kingdom/colony' debate in political matters, Ireland was economically one part of the British colonial system and more than one half of Ireland's imports and export went directly to Britain.[52] Inevitably, an Anglo-Spanish war would bring embargoes on the profitable Irish trade with Spain and France, directives to fill war-related needs, and greater taxation.[53] *The Querist*'s image of an Ireland surrounded by a wall of brass and tending its own monetary garden could not help but weaken in the midst of a Patriotic war. Ironically, it was Walpole's conciliatory foreign policy that would have been crucial to the success of Berkeley's plan, and it was this policy that proved to be Walpole's 'weak link'. When it broke, Walpole fell, but so did Berkeley's Bank.

A few years after his failure, Berkeley defended his hopes and utopias at the moment of crisis which the opposition had been trying to provoke for almost two decades: Walpole's fall from power in early 1742. To his friend Gervais in Dublin he wrote:

> I find by your letter, the reigning distemper at the Irish Court is disappointment. A man of less spirits and alacrity would be apt to cry out, *Spes et fortuna valete,* &c., but my advice is, never to quit your hopes. Hope is often better than enjoyment. Hope is often the cause as well as the effect of youth. It is certainly a very pleasant and healthy passion. A hopeless person is deserted by himself; and he who forsakes himself is soon forsaken by friends and fortune.[54]

To John Percival's son, a Westminster MP in the midst of negotiations concerning the constitution of a post-Walpole ministry, he wrote:

> Utopian schemes (I grant) are not suited to the present times, but a scheme the most perfect *in futuro* may take place in idea at present. The model or idea cannot be too perfect though perhaps it may never be perfectly attained in fact. Things though not adequate to a rule, will yet be less crooked for being, even clumsily, applied to it. And though no man hits the mark, they who come nearest merit applause.[55]

These Platonic and Christian sentiments constitute an *apologia pro vita sua* for Berkeley's National Bank and currency campaign. He clearly did not see the 1742 post-Walpole world as any more congenial to his 'utopian' idea than that of 1737–8. He kept his hopes, however, although after the great frost and famine of 1740, when the bodies of frozen children littered the Irish roads, he abandoned his Bank and turned to his next utopia of social transformation: tar-water.[56]

NOTES

1. An earlier version of this essay appeared in *Eighteenth-Century Ireland*, 12 (1997).
2. See, e.g., D. Berman, *George Berkeley: Idealism and the Man* (Oxford: Clarendon Press, 1994), ch. 5.
3. A.A. Luce and T.E. Jessop (eds), *The Works of George Berkeley Bishop of Cloyne*, 9 vols. (London: Thomas Nelson and Sons, 1948–57), viii, 244–5 (hereafter, *Works*).
4. Reprinted in J. Johnston, *Bishop Berkeley's Querist in Historical Perspective* (Dundalk: Dundalgan Press, 1970), p. 124. Johnson reprints *The Querist* in all of its versions.
5. Berkeley, *Works*, vi, 189–90; Johnston, *Berkeley's Querist*, p. 210.
6. See L.M. Cullen, 'Landlords, Bankers and Merchants: The Early Irish Banking World, 1700–1820', in A.E. Murphy (ed.), *Economists and the Irish Economy from the Eighteenth Century to the Present Day* (Dublin: Irish Academic Press, 1984), pp. 26–30. In Berkeley's correspondence with his lawyer, Thomas Prior, throughout the 1720s and '30s, we find him, like many other absentee landlords and clerics, asking Prior to carry on his financial affairs through the banking firm of Swift and Co.
7. F.G. Hall, *The Bank of Ireland 1783–1946* (Dublin: Hodges Figgis, 1949), pp. 1–29.
8. Berkeley, *Works*, vi, 192; Johnston, *Berkeley's Querist*, p. 212.
9. Berkeley, *Works*, vi, 189; Johnston, *Berkeley's Querist*, p. 210.
10. Berkeley, *Works*, vi, 192; Johnston, *Berkeley's Querist*, p. 213.
11. Berkeley, *Works*, vi, 191; Johnston, *Berkeley's Querist*, p. 211.
12. Berkeley, *Works*, vi, 191; Johnston, *Berkeley's Querist*, p. 211 (query 21).
13. Berkeley, *Works*, vi, 191; Johnston, *Berkeley's Querist*, p. 212 (query 28).
14. The Bank of Ireland's structure was modelled on that of the Bank of England. It was essentially a private corporate bank, owned by subscribers who put up the initial capital, but its main customer was to be the Irish government. Berkeley's bank was to be owned and managed by the Government and was similar to the *Banque Royale* of France. For more details on the aborted 1720–1 Bank of Ireland, see Hall, *Bank of Ireland*. Berkeley wrote in a 'Plan or Sketch of a National Bank': 'We have had, indeed, Schemes of private Association formerly proposed, which some may Mistake for National Banks. But it doth not appear, that any Scheme of this Nature was ever proposed in these Kingdoms'. Johnston, *Berkeley's Querist*, p. 208.
15. H. Rowley, *An Answer to a Book, Intitl'd, Reasons Offer'd for Erecting a Bank in Ireland* (Dublin, 1721), p. 5, quoted in Johnston, *Berkeley's Querist*, p. 47.
16. Quoted in Hall, *Bank of Ireland*, p. 20.
17. Reproduced as a plate in Hall, facing p. 26.
18. J. Swift, *Poetical Works*, ed. H. Davis (London: Oxford University Press, 1967), pp. 221–2.
19. For a discussion of freethinkers as constituting an anticlerical, instead of a crypto-atheistic, movement see J.A.I. Champion, *The Pillars of Priestcraft Shaken: The Church of England and its Enemies, 1660–1730* (Cambridge: Cambridge University Press, 1992). Libertinism enters into the story under a Mandevillean and rakish guise.
20. Berkeley, *Works*, vi, 191–2; Johnston, *Berkeley's Querist*, pp. 212–13.
21. 'Influence' was a popular political term of the day, borrowed from the dictionary of the occult and transformed, via Newtonian physics, into the glossary of Walpolean politics, i.e., the effecting of events at a distance by hidden or screened forces.
22. A similar debate concerning the prerequisites of a monetary society has broken out in the field of economic sociology in the last two decades; see R. Swedberg, 'Major Traditions of Economic Sociology', *Annual Review of Sociology*, 17 (1990), pp. 251–76; and M. Granovetter and R. Swedberg, *The Sociology of Economic Life* (Boulder, CO: Westview Press, 1992).
23. The full title reads: *A Discourse addressed to Magistrates and Men in Authority.*

Occasioned by the enormous License, and Irreligion of the Times (Dublin, 1738). A Cork edition and London edition appeared in the same year, with second editions in Dublin and London, also in 1738.

24. From 'A report from the Lords' Committees for Religion, appointed to examine into the causes of the present notorious immorality and profaneness', printed in Berkeley, *Works*, vi, 197. The 'Report' was delivered by the Earl of Granard, 10 March 1737.
25. See L.C. Jones, *The Clubs of the Georgian Rakes* (New York: Columbia University Press, 1942), pp. 51–3 and 64–79; J.T. Gilbert, *A History of the City of Dublin*, 3 vols. (Dublin, 1854–9), iii, 251–7; A. Peter, *Sketches of Old Dublin* (Dublin: Sealy, Bryers and Walker, 1907), pp. 277–83; M. Craig, *Dublin 1660–1860* (London: The Cresset Press, 1952), pp. 154–5.
26. On the end of the witch-hunt see K. Thomas, *Religion and the Decline of Magic* (New York: Charles Scribner's Sons, 1971), pp. 570–83; J.B. Russell, *A History of Witchcraft: Sorcerers, Heretics and Pagans* (London: Thames and Hudson, 1980), pp. 122–37. For a classic story of the confrontation of a satanic aristocrat like Rosse and a modernizing bourgeois like Samuel Madden (*The Querist*'s 'editor'), see Jones, *Clubs*, pp. 65–6.
27. Berkeley, *A Discourse addressed to Magistrates*, in *Works*, vi, 218–19.
28. For the club as the seed of 'civil society', see J. Habermas, *The Structural Transformation of the Public Sphere* (Cambridge, MA: MIT Press, 1989). On the roles of Madden and Prior in the formation and operation of the first phase of the Dublin Society see T. de Vere White, *The Story of the Royal Dublin Society* (Tralee: The Kerryman Ltd., 1955), pp. 1–32. It can be observed that 'the worse sort' were similarly creating new social spaces in this period. The workers' combinations, pirate utopias, and maroon villages created a rhizome of communication and revolt throughout the British Atlantic and Caribbean. See R.W. Malcolmson, 'Workers' Combinations in Eighteenth-Century England', in M. Jacob and J. Jacob (eds), *The Origins of Anglo-American Radicalism* (London: George Allen & Unwin, 1984), pp.149–61; M. Rediker, *Between the Devil and the Deep Blue Sea* (Cambridge: Cambridge University Press, 1987); P.L. Wilson, *Pirate Utopias* (New York: Autonomedia, 1995).
29. Berkeley, *Treatise*, para. 124, in *Works*, ii.
30. Berkeley, *Treatise*, para. 16.
31. Berkeley, *Treatise*, para. 137.
32. Berkeley, *Treatise*, para. 4.
33. For a sampling of the literature, see A.D. Woozley, 'Berkeley's Doctrine of Notions and Theory of Meaning', in W. Doney (ed.), *Berkeley on Abstraction and Abstract Ideas* (New York: Garland Press, 1989), pp. 253–60; D. Flage, *Berkeley's Doctrine of Notions: A Reconstruction Based on his Theory of Meaning* (New York: St Martin's Press, 1987), passim; R.G. Muehlmann, *Berkeley's Ontology* (Indianapolis: Hackett Publishing Co., 1992), pp. 235–40; G. Caffentzis, 'Algebraic Money: Berkeley's Philosophy of Mathematics and Money', *Berkeley Studies*, 18 (2007), pp. 3–23.
34. Berkeley, *A Discourse addressed to Magistrates*, in *Works*, vi, 202.
35. Berkeley, *A Discourse addressed to Magistrates*, in *Works*, vi, 203–5.
36. For a sophisticated discussion of the deists' 'twofold philosophy', see P. Harrison, *'Religion' and the Religions in the English Enlightenment* (Cambridge: Cambridge University Press, 1990), pp. 85–92.
37. Berkeley, *A Discourse addressed to Magistrates*, in *Works*, vi, 202.
38. Berkeley increasingly relied on analogical reasoning as he developed his social and theological thought. Analogy was used in the 'solution' to the 'other minds' problem as well as in the determination of God's attributes. Thus in *Alciphron* (Dialogue 4) he criticized the 'negative theology' of his Anglo-Irish colleagues Archbishop King and Bishop Peter Browne. See Berman, *George Berkeley*, pp. 140–4.
39. See Harrison, *'Religion' and the Religions in the English Enlightenment*, pp. 139–46. John Toland's writings were a source of this 'gambit': see S.H. Daniel, *John Toland: His Methods, Manners, and Mind* (Kingston and Montreal: McGill-Queen's University Press, 1984), pp. 21–4.
40. Berkeley, *A Discourse addressed to Magistrates*, in *Works*, vi, 213–15.
41. Berkeley, *A Discourse addressed to Magistrates*, in *Works*, vi, 219.
42. Berkeley, *A Discourse addressed to Magistrates*, in *Works*, vi, 216.
43. Berkeley, *A Discourse addressed to Magistrates*, in *Works*, vi, 221.

44. Berkeley, *Works*, vi, 198.
45. See W.H. McGowan, 'Did Berkeley Write *The Irish Blasters?*', *Berkeley Newsletter*, no. 6 (1982/3), pp. 1–4.
46. It was for that reason that Berkeley arranged for the simultaneous publication of the three parts of *The Querist* in England with the help of Sir John Percival, Earl of Egmont. On Thursday, 27 May 1736, Percival wrote in his Diary, 'I also send Bishop Berkeley's second part of Queries to Mr. Richardson to be printed'. *Manuscripts of the Earl of Egmont. Diary of Viscount Percival afterwards First Earl of Egmont*, 3 vols. (London: His Majesty's Stationery Office, 1920–3), iii, 275.
47. A. Pope, 'Epilogue to the Satires: Dialogue II' (ll. 248–53), in P. Rogers (ed.), *Alexander Pope: Selected Poetry* (Oxford: Oxford University Press, 1994), pp. 127–8.
48. H.T. Dickson, *Walpole and the Whig Supremacy* (London: The English Universities Press, 1973), pp. 69–70.
49. See J. Stock, 'An Account of the Life of George Berkeley' (1776), in D. Berman (ed.), *George Berkeley: Eighteenth-Century Responses*, 2 vols. (New York: Garland Publishing, 1989), i, 35–6; A.A. Luce, *The Life of George Berkeley Bishop of Cloyne* (London: Nelson, 1949), pp. 155–8.
50. See D. Hayton, 'Walpole and Ireland', in J. Black (ed.), *Britain in the Age of Walpole* (New York: St Martin's Press, 1984), pp. 95–119.
51. See D. Dickson, *New Foundations: Ireland 1660–1800* (Dublin: Helicon, 1987), p. 85.
52. See L.M. Cullen, *Anglo-Irish Trade: 1660–1800* (Manchester: Manchester University Press, 1968), p. 45.
53. War goes to the heart of mercantilism as a 'system of power' which forces 'economic policy into the service of power as an end in itself'. E.F. Heckscher, *Mercantilism*, 2 vols, trans. M. Shapiro, rev. ed., ed. E.F. Söderlund (London: George Allen & Unwin, 1955), ii, 17. Therefore war is the primary act of the state, as Colbert aphorized: 'Trade is the source of finance and finance is the vital nerve of war' (quoted in Heckscher, ii, 17). For a classic discussion of mercantilism as a system of power, see Heckscher, ii, 13–49. The development of the eighteenth-century debate between mercantilist *machtpolitik* and the irenic potentialities of capitalist development is traced in A.O. Hirschman, *The Passions and the Interests: Political Arguments for Capitalism before its Triumph* (Princeton: Princeton University Press, 1977), pp. 48–66. A discourse that incorporates the argument that 'money-making' is a non-violent activity in the context of the slave trade and genocide in the Americas must have a large gullet.
54. 2 February 1742, *Works,* viii, 259–60.
55. 28 March 1742, *Works,* viii, 262.
56. The Irish *famine* of 1740, like most other *famines,* had an epidemic phase and Berkeley tried to deal with fevers, dysentery, and diarrhoea through the application of various remedies. He found tar-water the most effective and in 1744 he wrote *Siris: A Chain of Philosophical Inquiries concerning the Virtues of Tar-water and Divers Subjects Connected Together and Arising One from Another.*

CHAPTER ELEVEN

The Suspension of Cash Payments and Ireland's Narrative Economy: The Contexts of Maria Edgeworth's 'National' Novels

KEVIN BARRY

> 'I have been in the wrong in our argument', continued the Sultan, turning to his vizier. 'I acknowledge that the histories of Saladin, the Lucky, and Murad, the Unlucky, favour your opinion, that prudence has more influence than chance, in human affairs.... Henceforward, let Murad, the Unlucky, be named Murad, the Imprudent: let Saladin preserve the surname he merits, and be henceforth called Saladin, the Prudent'.
>
> (Maria Edgeworth, 'Murad the Unlucky', *Popular Tales*, 1804)

From 1797 to 1825 – the era of the suspension of cash payments and the £1 paper note – important differences in ideas of credit, paper, and specie emerged between Ireland, England, and Scotland. These differences prompted not only an array of formal economic analyses and interventions in the public press, but also stimulated the work of one of Ireland's leading writers of fiction, Maria Edgeworth, whose tales and novels registered a lived experience and generated a new narrative economy that defines her construction of the 'national' novel. In the context of fiction, in other words, a complex political-economic reality was represented, mediating alternative economic and cultural developments in an Irish setting.

The structural distinctiveness of Ireland's case has been traced in the work of economic historians: with the suspension of gold payments, or (in modern terms) the abandonment of the gold standard, the Dublin pound, and London pound floated against other currencies and against each other; from 1799 to 1803 the Dublin pound depreciated by up to 10 per cent against London; a drain of silver to England favored a proliferation of private banks and a widespread issue of small notes in Munster and Leinster; the North of Ireland exempted itself, retained a metal pound and eschewed paper currencies; the Ulster pound appreciated in value against both Dublin and London, and earned the praise of bullionists for behaving as they wished to predict a metal pound would do.[1]

The complexity and confusion of different circulating media was registered in contemporary newspaper opinion and also notably in the Irish tales of Maria Edgeworth. Edgeworth was well placed to observe and analyse the Irish economy locally at work. Her membership of a landlord class, her Enlightenment commitments, her work with her father on political economy, the geographical location of her fictions in the northern regions of the Irish midlands – all these conditions inform the perspectives of her narratives. Her Irish fiction prioritizes a detailed representation and analysis of the workings of new processes of credit, exchange, and debt. These Irish fictions display a domestic and political economy quite unlike those of Britain. In effect, Edgeworth's Irish tales constitute a defense of paper credit in general and, finally, of the paper money of a national bank. In opposition to the consensus amongst her English contemporaries, Edgeworth distrusts the 'gold standard' of specie, and of guinea coins in particular. During the first decades of the nineteenth century Edgeworth's defense of paper instruments of credit is remarkable because the structure of her moral argument is grounded upon a distrust of gold and of commodity money. English commentators identify honesty and prudence with specie, and with the convertibility on demand of paper into gold. The riddle of Edgeworth's Irish tales is that, contrary to English norms, they are a corrosive exposé of processes of manipulation whereby the gold standard, usually in the form of guinea coins, exerts a brutal and immediate power to expropriate, perplex, defraud, and seduce.

In order to understand the peculiar moral economy of Edgeworth's fiction, this essay is divided into two sections. The first section examines the ideological contradictions within London's suspension of cash payments and analyses the different responses to this crisis in Britain and Ireland. These contradictions derive from eighteenth-century economic thought, and from London's reaction both to colonial experiment with paper currencies and to the *assignats* of the revolution in France. The second section locates Edgeworth's construction in Ireland of a distinctive narrative economy that foregrounds a local machinery of credit, articulates the management of its confusions, and passes new judgements on the moral values implicit in coin and paper.

I: LONDON'S SUSPENSION OF CASH PAYMENTS AND ITS CONTEXTS

1797 in Eighteenth-Century Monetary Thought

On 26 February 1797 William Pitt secured an Order in Council instructing the Bank of England, at its own request, to suspend cash payments. A French fleet had appeared off the Irish coast. At Fishguard a handful of men had landed from a French frigate. In this mood of alarm the reserves of the country banks and of the Bank of England were drained. Before 26 February a bank note issued by the Bank, or by one of the many independent country banks, could be exchanged on demand for silver or gold coin. After 26 February the Bank would only exchange paper for paper. The promise to pay, inscribed on the note, became a promise to pay promises with promises. The Government immediately suspended its own law against paper notes of less than £5 in value.[2] According to Sir Francis Baring, the inconvertible paper resulted in 'a prodigious influx of gold and silver, whilst the panic has subsided, and confidence is generally restored'. In March 1797 the Bank Restriction was extended from England to Ireland.[3]

Cash payments remained suspended until 1821. In 1825 the £1 note was again abolished.[4] The London Government's attempt also to forbid in Scotland the issue of small notes failed under the withering satire of Sir Walter Scott writing his *Thoughts on the Proposed Change of Currency* (1826) in the assumed persona of Malachi Malagrowther.[5] In the words of one commentator, 'It is probably not an exaggeration to say that the small notes scare was the most sharply contested issue of Scottish national rights of the entire nineteenth century. The very act of issuing banknotes in Scotland thus became charged with a unique national significance.'[6] By contrast, so strong was the English bullionist antipathy to a paper currency that the Bank of England, for its part, would not again issue a pound note until 1928. In 1826, John Wilson Croker (an Irishman writing in the guise of an Englishman) defended the English prejudice against paper in his counterblast to Walter Scott's defense of the customary tradition in Scotland of widespread paper credit and small banknotes: 'Such a system is specious, and even splendid, but is it *solid*? In England, we think *not* – nay, we think that experience has *proved* that it is not.'[7]

By the demon of analogy, Croker's proof derives not from the experience of banking but from the building of Fonthill Abbey, that fantastic expression of wealth by William Beckford, the author of *Vathek*, and the son of a Jamaican merchant who had become Lord Mayor of London. Croker ridicules the extravagant construction, which collapsed in 1825:

> Nothing was more splendid, nothing could look more solid; it had stood many winters, and had weathered tremendous gales; it wore the character, too, of antiquity, and allied itself harmoniously with the lower and more solid parts of the domestic residence; but, *mole ruit suâ*,[8] and in one night, in weather of no unusual violence, the wonder of Wiltshire was levelled to the dust.
>
> We, in England, have (I hope in good time), seen the danger of this extravagant overbuilding, and we are anxious to exchange for the *solidity* of a metallic foundation, the airy and precarious pinnacles which a paper currency had enabled us to raise our commercial fabric.
>
> I confess that I cannot see any real, or essential difference between England and Scotland on this point.[9]

Few Englishmen had a good word to say for widespread paper credit. Any ideology in its favour had been a colonial or a revolutionary invention. In Scotland in 1705, two years before the union with England, John Law of Lauriston near Edinburgh had published his '*Proposal for Supplying the Nation with Money*': a paper currency, notionally backed by Scotland's stock of land, to stimulate prosperity.[10] Earlier, in Boston in 1691, Cotton Mather had ridiculed those for whom the word 'paper' was a scandal, arguing that 'the *Nature of Mony*... is but a *Counter* or *Measure* of mens Proprieties'.[11] Such proposals, necessitated by a colony's lack of precious metal (or in the words of the Boston banker Thomas Hancock, the debtor and creditor finding themselves 'out of the limits of the circulation of money')[12] lay behind later eighteenth-century defenses of a national paper money – what the Scottish political economist, Sir James Steuart, called a 'pure ideal money'.[13] A handful of texts, of which the Irish philosopher George Berkeley's *The Querist* (1735–7) remains the most famous, argued that money derives not from wealth but from need. Berkeley proposed the relief of Irish economic depression and poverty through a paper currency issued from a national bank. His proposal for a currency of paper tokens derived from colonial experience during his residence at Rhode Island.[14] A remarkably small number of pamphlets supplemented these arguments by Law, Berkeley, and Steuart about the power of paper to liquidate real property;[15] its dynamic effect upon the unemployed;[16] its weakening of the influence of despotic ministries;[17] its congruence with republican liberty;[18] its perpetual recirculation, like a 'great fountain', paying off the national debt.[19]

Berkeley proposed that paper money could be understood as the most advanced means of exchange. *The Querist* asks:

> 445. Whether in the rude original of society the first step was not the exchanging of commodities; the next a substituting of metals by weight as the common medium of circulation; after this the making use of coin; lastly, a further refinement by the use of paper with proper marks and signatures? And whether this, as it is the last, so it be not the greatest improvement?[20]

The Querist, with its rhetorical structure anticipating the disbelief of its readers, was indirectly translated into revolutionary France through the Scottish political economist and fellow champion of John Law's colonial experiment with paper money, Sir James Steuart. Steuart's *Principles of Political Economy* appeared in 1767 and was re-published several times before the end of the eighteenth century. In 1789 a French translation appeared in Paris. Steuart at certain moments bears comparison with Berkeley, and writes of a pure ideal money, proposing an ideal of civic interdependence, and emphasizing the relation of paper to consent and to public opinion. Furthermore, Steuart extensively identifies metals of intrinsic value with landed property and proposes that paper, by contrast, 'melts down' such property and redistributes wealth away from a landed aristocracy. Like Berkeley he emphasizes the value to a poor economy of a paper currency. The innovative model for both Steuart and Berkeley is that man of 'superior genius', John Law,[21] whose writings first appeared in collected form in Paris in 1790.[22]

PAPER CREDIT IN THE AMERICAN AND FRENCH REVOLUTIONS

The *assignat* of the Revolution (*hypothéqué sur les domaines nationaux*) melted down the lands of the Church and of the *émigrés*, on the principles of a land-bank underwriting a paper currency, as had been proposed in Scotland by Law and in Ireland by Berkeley. In 1793 the idealization of the *assignats* by Jacques-Louis David, in his painting of the death of Marat, follows in this tradition. The painting represents money not as a sign of wealth, but as a form of asceticism, benevolence, and need. The *assignat* note lies on the bare box and Marat's last letter, lying there with the money, indicates that it is to be enclosed as recompense to a needy widow of the Revolution. T.J. Clark has drawn attention to the importance of this painting by David in its coming to terms with an idea of money: 'the root form of representation in bourgeois society'. By frankly recognizing money in its paper form, David has achieved one of those moments of lucidity, when painting recognizes the nature of signs in general, their demand for interpretation, their social function, and their irreducible contingency.[23]

Paper money, in the form of *assignats*, had been both the enabling credit and one of the virtuous emblems of the French Revolution. 'Avilissons l'or et l'argent, traînons dans la boue ces dieux de la monarchie,' urged Joseph Fouché in October 1793. For Ramel de Nogaret, 'Les assignats ont fait la Révolution, ils ont renversé le trône et fondé la République.'[24]

The revolution in France was not the first to be financed by a paper currency. In America the colonies from Virginia to Massachusetts had each experimented with several kinds of money: with wampum or shells suggested to them by the native Americans, with re-worked playing-cards and, most extensively in the South, with tobacco as a legal tender and the outlawing of all payments in gold or silver. Pennsylvania had first issued paper money in 1723, and in 1729 Benjamin Franklin published his *Modest Enquiry into the Nature and Necessity of a Paper Currency*. The London government in 1751 and more extensively in 1764 forbade its American colonies from making bills of credit legal tender. When the Continental Congress of 1775 defiantly printed its own notes ('Continentals'), it thereby declared America's independence from London.[25]

Trust in paper money invoked a new idea of virtue. The Continental Congress had resolved in 1776 that

> any person who shall hereafter be so lost to all virtue and regard for his country, as to refuse to receive said bills in payment...shall be deemed, published and treated as an enemy in this country and precluded from all trade or intercourse with the inhabitants of these Colonies.[26]

Virtue could now be defined not as dependence upon property and independence from the power of the state, but as interdependence among citizens, or between citizens and government, through the public credit of the nation. It is precisely this virtue of interdependence that Walter Scott was to celebrate in his defense of Scottish banknotes in 1826. The emission and acceptance of paper money brings into being an imagined community, internally dependent upon itself. The first Continentals were inscribed with the title 'The United Colonies', and it is on these banknotes in 1777 that the title 'The United States' was published for the first time.

1797 AND THE BRITISH DEBATE ABOUT THE FRENCH REVOLUTION

The suspension of cash payments in 1797, however, had abruptly placed English credit at the level of the incredible. The wording of the Order in Council asserted that it is 'indispensably necessary for the public service that the Directors of the Bank of England should forbear issuing any cash in payment... for maintaining the means of circulation and supporting the public and commercial credit of the kingdom at this important conjuncture'.[27] English contempt for the American and French systems of paper credit threatened to undermine the Order in Council. In retrospect, Pitt judged it to be the most difficult decision of his political life.[28] The English opposition, in the persons of Fox and Sheridan, revelled in the confusion.

The colonial and revolutionary idea of virtue, not propertied independence but national and civic interdependence, now entered the metropole. Within some dozen years the government press could confirm that inconvertible paper

> offers the Government a most indestructible support because it makes the daily bread of every individual depend substantially

> on the safety of government, whereas money, which can be hoarded, separates the individual from the public safety.[29]

The shock of contradiction was extreme. Before 1797 the rhetoric of English economic thought had been resolutely opposed to the popular diffusion of paper credit. After 1797 that rhetoric continued in force while in practice credit expanded and paper money was the only issue of the Bank of England. The period of the Bank Restriction provoked an intense flurry of denunciatory pamphlets that appeared from February 1797 through the debates and recommendations of the Bullion Committee, the most famous discussion about money and its management, which reported in 1810. The Bullion Committee recommended that paper again be made immediately convertible with metal, in effect with gold. The Government, still at war with France, refused the Committee's advice, at least in the medium term. Several orthodoxies of classical economics were established by the Committee: that inflation depends upon the money supply; that the money supply must be restricted; that, in the words of the contemporary economist, David Ricardo, 'a currency, to be perfect, should be absolutely invariable in value'.[30] Ricardo argued, as others such as Sir John Sinclair had earlier done, that inconvertible paper would fluctuate wildly, and the only restriction could and must be the conversion of paper into metal, as Sinclair put it, 'at a moments [*sic*] notice, according to the pleasure of the holder'.[31] For Ricardo, the signifier must not be detached from its signified, but must always be prepared to re-present, to be exchanged for, the signified. But, as long as the Bank suspended cash payments, the signifier acquired both an indefinite and an inconvertible reality.

We should then not be surprised at the overwhelming consensus in England against paper money among those on the left and those on the right, and among those who changed political positions from one side to the other. The counter-revolutionary Edmund Burke was against it and so was his radical opponent Thomas Paine; the plain-spoken William Cobbett, in prison for seditious libel, was against it, and so was the secretary for Foreign Affairs, George Canning; the rabid defender of the landed aristocracy, Lord King, was against it, and so was the mercurial opponent of the old order, Percy Bysshe Shelley. Cobbett himself, in his *Paper against Gold and Glory against Prosperity* (1815), noticed the otherwise strange fact that Burke, Paine, and the future prime minister, Lord Liverpool, agreed with each other on this question alone:

> all opposed to each other as to every other question; each one hating the other two, and each one hating the other one: yet all as agreeing harmoniously as their bones would now agree, if they happened to be tumbled together; all agreeing as to these principles respecting paper-money.[32]

The power of the rhetoric directed against the French *assignats* in Burke's *Reflections upon the Revolution in France* had maximized the ideological weight against paper and in favour of specie:

> Is there a debt which presses them? – Issue *assignats*. Are compensations to be made, or a maintenance decreed to those whom they have robbed of their freehold in their office, or expelled from their profession? – *Assignats*. Is a fleet to be fitted out? – *Assignats*. If sixteen millions sterling of these *assignats*, forced on the people, leave the wants of the state as urgent as ever – issue, says one, thirty millions sterling of *assignats* – says another, issue fourscore millions more of *assignats*.[33]

Burke died in 1797 but had just enough time to seize the opportunity, after the February suspension, privately to damn Pitt's decision and also to condemn the new issue of £1 notes that the suspension required. So powerful was Burke's authority that when in 1825 George Canning rose in the House of Commons to announce the abolition of small notes, in an atmosphere of high emotion, he quoted from one of the last letters of the dying Burke, condemning the introduction of paper notes.[34]

II: IDEOLOGIES OF PAPER AND SPECIE IN IRELAND AFTER 1797

There is, therefore, considerable irony in events in Ireland in Spring of 1797. The United Irishmen and their radical newspaper the *Northern Star* found themselves opposed to the introduction of a paper currency, even though such paper currencies had enabled the American and French revolutions upon which they modelled their republican ideals. In the issues that immediately preceded its forced closure in May by government militia, the *Northern Star* devoted as many column inches to the suspension of cash payments as to almost any other controversy. The extension of the Bank Restriction from England to Ireland in March 1797 provoked the immediate mock advertisement of a Grand National Exhibition in which William Pitt would figure as 'the Sieur Pittachio' and his cabinet as 'the Fantoccini Figures' in

> the *new* [theatrical] Piece of the BANK NOTE . . . In the course of the Piece will be presented a new Scene, designed by the SIEUR . . . called *The Paper-Mill at Work*. After the Play will be performed A Farce called, THE COMMITTEE; *Written* and *cast* by the Sieur himself, . . . The whole [to] conclude with a new, grand, *Burlesque* Ballet Called, THE REPORT, Designed by the Sieur. . . A twenty-shilling Note will admit four to the Boxes, or ten to the Gallery.[35]

It then becomes a matter of practice, and for some a matter of honour, in Ulster *not* to accept paper money. The *Northern Star* ridiculed the Marquis of Hillsborough who 'some days ago posted up a paper in Hillsborough and Lisburn, proposing not only to receive his rents in national notes, but to encourage his own market town by discounting them for any person who should make any purchase there'. The *Northern Star* gleefully remarked that 'The whole country was about to run upon him. But he prudently withdrew his too benevolent promise. Would he would as speedily retract every error of his life.' A majority of the advertisers in the *Northern Star* declared that they would only take ready cash or guineas, although one, Richard Fulton of Lisburn, advertised that he would take Dublin bank notes for goods sold and pay out 'some Money' for goods bought by him during what he called 'these times of public calamity'. Nevertheless the *Northern Star* cried out in the tones of William Cobbett against those who would 'substitute the bayonet for the law – the dungeon for justice – paper for gold'.[36]

This rhetoric against paper was to include in Ireland the resources of sectarian theology. An anonymous contributor to *Walker's Hibernian Magazine* attacked the new paper economy in September 1799 in terms of the Protestant and Catholic dispute about transubstantiation and the real presence of God in a wafer of bread. Transubstantiation constituted a 'badge of spiritual tyranny' and 'slavery', an indication that Catholics were 'bankrupt in understanding' as a result of their 'juggling leaders', who deprived them of 'reason and common sense':

> Luckily, we have shaken off this creed, and indeed most other religious creeds and prejudices. It is enough for us to swallow

> the political transubstantiation of civil property: And yet our infatuation seems to fall little short of the Roman Catholics, when we can really believe the wealth and power of a nation to be truly and substantially exprest and represented by *scraps of paper*; which are so far from being property, that they signify nothing...
>
> ...And although we should be ready to laugh at the sly priest, who putting the wafer into our mouths, cries, *hoc est corpus*; yet we have no suspicion of the state juggler, who putting some flimsy bits of paper into our hands, tells us one is a freehold estate, a second a manor, a third a town-house, and a fourth a pipe of wine...
>
> ...In truth, we live in a mere enchanted island, and an individual may almost doubt from the strong propensity there is now towards paper, whether he is himself made of any better materials....We have heard of the Golden, Silver, and Iron ages of the poets; the present, to mark its frivolity, may be called the *Paper Age*.[37]

An argument that paper money is a crypto-Catholic fetish is a peculiarly refined example of what is a common Christian unease with money in general.[38] The anonymous and sceptical contributor to *Walker's Hibernian Magazine* provocatively mocks the fact that the idealization of flimsy paper notes is logically continuous with pious reverence for the wafer of the Eucharist.

Between 1797 and 1810, when Ireland divided North and South on the issue of a paper currency, both regions remained, like England, rhetorically committed to a preference for specie over paper. However, whereas in the South banknotes quickly replaced specie and private banks sprang up in numbers outside Dublin, in the North coins and guineas remained the predominant medium of exchange. Ulster landlords would only accept rents in coin, and trade generally avoided paper money. The Ulster 'metal' pound developed a strongly positive rate of exchange against the Dublin 'paper' pound, and the 'Course of Exchange', a bi-weekly report with several publishers during this period, displayed the rate of exchange and quarterly average between Dublin and Belfast. Rates of exchange were also quoted between London, Belfast, Dublin, and Newry.[39] The appreciation of the Ulster pound and the depreciation of the Dublin pound had peaked in 1803. The British Parliament then established a Committee of enquiry into the Irish Pound charged with establishing the cause of depreciation. This Irish Committee served as a dry run for the more famous Bullion Committee of 1810. Both were equally committed to a Bullionist theory. Depreciation of the Irish pound was attributed to an excessive issue of paper by the Bank of Ireland in Dublin and to a proliferation of private banking in the South.[40]

John Carr's *The Stranger in Ireland*, a travel account published in London and Philadelphia in 1806, offers the following description of 'the nature of the currency of Ireland, which consists', he said:

> 1st. Of a copious effusion of paper, from a guinea note to several thousand pounds.
>
> 2d. English guineas, seldom seen out of the north of Ireland, worth one pound two shillings and nine-pence Irish each.
>
> 3d. Dollars worth five shillings and fivepence Irish each.
>
> 4th. Silver bank tokens of six shillings Irish each.
>
> 5th. Silver bank tokens called tenpenny and fivepenny pieces, worth so much Irish each.
>
> 6th. Hogs, or shillings, sometimes called thirteens, worth thirteen pence Irish each.
>
> 7th. Pigs, or testers, worth sevenpence Irish each.
>
> 8th. Penny, half-penny, and farthing pieces, a very recent and handsome coinage. – For reasons which will hereafter appear, as long as any difference of exchange continues above par, it will be adviseable for those who visit Ireland, either to draw on England if they are known, or to take over guineas.[41]

Cormac Ó Gráda comments on the distinctive complexity of these accommodations that the 'dollar mentioned above would have been minted in Mexico or Spain. The six-shilling bank tokens were also dollars, overstruck by the Bank of Ireland. Nor is the list above exhaustive; sometimes, more exotic foreign coins were employed, and copper tokens were issued locally, as by mine-owners at Cronebane near Arklow. The ability of the public to master all this confusion should not be underestimated.'[42] Maria Edgeworth's Irish tales register the unequal mastery of this confusion by tenant, agent, and landlord. Following this money trail, she analyses the interplay of material and moral life in Ireland. The distinctive narrative form of her Irish fiction provides readers with a sense of the lived reality of monetary experience, as well as a contemporary moral perspective on these transactions.

MARIA EDGEWORTH AND IRISH CURRENCIES

Maria Edgeworth writes from the point of view of an enlightened and reformist member of the landlord class. Hostile to absenteeism and to the growth in the power and influence of middlemen, Edgeworth does not conceal from the reader her higher gentry affiliations.[43] Those affiliations do not coincide, however, with landed hostilities to industry and commerce. Indeed, even before the publication of *Castle Rackrent* (1800) it was a matter of regret to Edgeworth that this most distinctly 'landed' of her novels did not include 'a sense of Ireland's economic possibilities'.[44] Louis Cullen has mapped those possibilities in his study of landlords, bankers, and merchants of this period in Ireland and his work serves to locate Edgeworth amongst the local and conflicting ideologies within which she lived and wrote. Cullen proposes that the northern landlords' demand to be paid rent in guinea coins was an archaic insistence by a conservative gentry opposed to economic innovations and to a society of credit and commerce.[45] Edgeworth's vilification of this practice, extending it as the does to the more southerly middlemen and agents of her fictional estates, indicates how her range of sympathies include new economic energies and experimentation.

Edgeworth's analytic narratives deconstruct ideologies that favour specie. Again and again a climactic moment of these narratives is a cascade of guinea coins. The master of this moment of exchange is neither tenant nor landlord, but the middleman. It is his mastery of specie that determines Edgeworth's distrust of gold and her criticism of its immediate power to expropriate, perplex, defraud, and seduce. Consider the following passage towards the end of *Castle Rackrent*, in which the narrator Thady Quirk describes how his son Jason (agent of the Rackrents and holder of the golden fleece) reduced the landlord, Sir Condy, to the status of tenant:

> 'I have only three words to say, and those more of consequence to you, Sir Condy, than me. You are a little cool, I observe, but I hope you will not be offended at what I have brought here in my pocket," – and he pulls out two long rolls, and showers down golden guineas upon the bed. 'What's this? (said Sir Condy) it's long since' – but his pride stops him – 'All these are your lawful property this minute, Sir Condy, if you please,' said Jason. – 'Not for nothing, I'm sure, (said Sir Condy, and laughs a little) – nothing for nothing, or I'm under a mistake with you,

> Jason.' – 'Oh, Sir Condy, we'll not be indulging ourselves in any unpleasant retrospects, (says Jason) it's my present intention to behave, as I'm sure you will, like a gentleman in this affair. – Here's two hundred guineas, and a third I mean to add, if you should think proper to make over to me all your right and title to those lands that you know of.' – 'I'll consider of it,' said my master; and a great deal more, that I was tired listening to, was said by Jason, and all that, and the sight of the ready cash upon the bed worked with his honor; and the short and long of it was, Sir Condy gathered up the golden guineas and tied up in a handkerchief, and signed some paper Jason brought with him as usual, and there was an end of the business; Jason took himself away, and my master turned himself round and fell asleep again.[46]

The malignant suddenness of this episode acts to present implicitly a defense of the slower rhythm of time that credit allows but which Jason refuses. It is this suddenness that the immediacy of the gold coin precipitates: an instant of social revolution, the momentous re-expropriation of the Rackrent title and land.

In *The Absentee* (1812), the use of guinea coins retains the same perverse power, now more complex and systematic. In the local economy of the absentee estate the agent, as in the North of Ireland, will accept from tenants only guinea coins in payment of rent. The tenants are constrained to purchase guinea coins, and it is from the agent that they must buy them. The agent's sale and resale of guinea coins works toward the depreciation of all other circulating media and imperils the resources of the tenants. Here the operation of unequal power is downward from agent to tenant, rather than upward as in *Castle Rackrent*. *The Absentee*, published as it was in 1812, coincides with the bringing into force, both in the North and in the South, of a law that made Bank of Ireland notes legal tender. A consequence of this law, as one contemporary newspaper noted, was that 'all transactions for the buying and selling of guineas must surely be clandestine'.[47] It is precisely these clandestine transactions that facilitate the expropriation of tenants' holdings in *The Absentee*. The novel's hero, Lord Colambre, enters his hometown disguised as a copper-mining engineer in order to detect the malpractice of his father's agent 'St Dennis'. There he sees the agent call 'to a man on the other side of the street, who had evidently been waiting for him; he went under a gateway with this man, and gave him a bag of guineas'. Lord Colambre follows this man with the bag of guineas into the public house 'where a new scene presented itself to his view':

> The man to whom St Dennis gave the bag of gold was now selling this very gold to the tenants, who were to pay their rent next day at the castle.
>
> The agent would take nothing but gold. The same guineas were bought and sold several times over, to the great profit of the agent and loss of the poor tenants; for, as the rents were paid, the guineas were resold to another set...
>
> The higgling for the price of the gold; the time lost in disputing about the goodness of the notes, among some poor tenants, who could not read or write, and who were at the mercy of the man with the bag in his hand; the vexation, the useless harrassing of all, who were obliged to submit ultimately – Lord Colambre saw, and all this time he endured the smell of tobacco and whiskey, and of the sound of various brogues, the din of men wrangling, brawling, threatening, whining, drawling, cajoling, cursing, and every variety of wretchedness.
>
> 'And, is this my father's town of Clonbrony?' thought Lord Colambre. 'Is this Ireland?'[48]

Lord Colambre, the novel makes clear to its readers, is a man of virtue and also a paper money man. It is paper notes that he carries in his purse; it is in paper that he states his value; and it is paper that he gives in gift to those he most wishes to assist. His father, Lord Clonbrony, mired in debt, is perforce a guineas man: indeed it is a specie-based complicity of absentee landlord and agent that our hero Lord Colambre must resist by managing the long future that his young age makes available to him, in order to raise new credit, as he tells his father, 'to free you from this man'.[49]

The narrative of currencies, property, and debt in *The Absentee* is supplemented with a rhetoric that privileges paper over coin. The women are marginal to the plot but, no less than the men, the text must free women of virtue from the immediate taint of gold. The heiress Miss Broadhurst is rescued from allegations that she is a 'golden Venus' amid golden apples and golden girdles, and revealed to be a plainspoken intelligence who has 'besides 100,000*l.* in the funds, a clear landed property of 10,000*l.* per annum'. Miss Broadhurst therefore is constructed to disappoint those greedy for coin and to win Colambre's and the reader's appreciation for her clear perception that her fortune makes love difficult at the best of times, and quite impossible if she presents herself 'blazing at the opera': 'I have the misfortune to be an heiress,' she declares, because 'Hearts are to be won only by radiant eyes.'[50] It is not the glitter of gold but the intellectual structures upon which credit depends that have worked to construct the virtuous character of Miss Broadhurst:

> Her father made his immense fortune by the power and habit of constant, bold, and just calculation. The power and habit, which she had learned from him, she applied on a far larger scale; with him, it was confined to speculations for the acquisition of money; with her, it extended to the attainment of happiness. He was calculating and mercenary – she was estimative and generous.[51]

The heroine of *The Absentee* also exists within a rhetoric that ameliorates the character of credit ('estimative' is so much kinder than 'calculating') and that privileges paper over specie. The names of characters in Maria Edgeworth often function emblematically (Jason, St Dennis, Old Nick) and the name of the heroine of *The Absentee*, Grace Nugent ('God give you Grace'), is one device among many that distance her from the immediate taint of gold. The over-determination of paper, not only as currency but also as the bearer of credit and signature, pervades the texture of the novel.[52] Grace herself is born and reborn amidst its folds. Suspected of being an illegitimate child, she must await the belated discovery of her wealth, legitimate status, and new identity as Grace Reynolds, an identity that depends upon a paper certificate, itself mislaid but protected within dense layers of paper, of newsprint, and an ambassador's journal, within which yet more papers remain, and finally one signed and sealed and discovered: the marriage certificate of her parents:

> At last, when they had opened, as they thought, every paper; and, wearied and in despair, were just on the point of giving up the search; Lord Colambre spied a bundle of old newspapers at the bottom of a trunk.
>
> 'They are only old Vienna Gazettes, I looked at them,' said Sir James.
>
> Lord Colambre, upon this assurance, was going to throw them into the trunk again, but observing that the bundle had

> not been untied, he opened it, and within side of the newspapers he found a rough copy of the ambassador's journal, and with it the packet, directed to Ralph Reynolds, sen., Esq., Old Court, Suffolk, per favour of his excellency earl *****, – a note on the cover, signed O'Halloran, stating when received by him, and the date of the day when delivered to the ambassador – seals unbroken.[53]

THE ECONOMY OF PAPER AND THE 'NATIONAL' NOVEL

The prudent care of paper, the good management of one's credit, the investment of wealth 'in the funds', constitute the possibility of virtue for men and women of substance in Maria Edgeworth's fiction. The paper money and the paper credit that she supports is that of stable, usually national, banking institutions. In the rhetorical texture of her fiction almost all paper is promising. This promise remains constant even into the writing of *Ormond* (1817). In that novel the downturn of the Irish economy after the Napoleonic wars is made all the worse by the collapse of under-capitalized private banks, in particular that of Ormond's guardian Sir Ulick. Yet Edgeworth is in no way panicked into a diatribe against banking. The main loss that *Ormond* records is a short-term loss of public trust. The gain is a timely lesson in prudence for the novel's eponymous hero who will rescue those at risk of immiseration. Edgeworth ensures that Sir Ulick's defrauding of rich and poor alike in no way compromises the virtues of prudent banking. For Ormond to make safe his own inheritance two things only are required: prudent management of his own signature, and the proper caution of his Dublin bankers.[54]

In contradiction of her affiliations with Edmund Burke, and in spite of the findings of the Bullion Committee (1810) and its Irish precursor, the *Report of the Committee on the Circulating Paper, Specie and the Current Coin of Ireland* (1804), Edgeworth maintains a unique refusal to trust a world of coin and commodity money, and her novels remain persuaded of the relative virtue of paper, of credit, and of the signature. It is coin that facilitates the mutual corruption of landlords and agents in *The Absentee* (1812). In that novel it is a complex layering of paper and signatures that establishes truth in the relationship between Grace Nugent, her past, and her future in Ireland with Lord Colambre. In *Ormond* (1817) the prudent management of paper credit serves, even under stress, as an indicator of virtue.

Maria Edgeworth's Irish tales, given this context of domestic and political economy, are quite different from her English novels. Edgeworth's English fiction corresponds to the patterns found in the majority of English women novelists at the turn of the eighteenth and nineteenth centuries. It has been recognized that during the first decades of the nineteenth century a change takes place in English fiction about women's status in domestic economies, a change from relatively passive and anxious uncertainties to their management of consumer power.[55] Edgeworth's *Belinda* (1801) catches that change as the heroine of the novel learns to move assuredly within a world of wealth that she must control with prudence and virtue. It is true that this novel is spectacular in its juxtaposition of the registers of affection and of economy. Belinda's aunt warns her to avoid the imprudence of 'a poor girl, who, after spending not only the interest, but the solid capital of her small fortune in dress, and frivolous extravagance, fails in her matrimonial expectations, (as many do merely from not beginning to speculate in time)'.[56] The reader, even from the first pages of the narrative, is provoked by the mobility of terms from two distinct domains and temporalities of risk: the exchanges of finance and of courtship. Beyond the economy of marriage the novel engages a complex sympathy for Belinda's corrupt mentor, Lady Delancourt, who admits to having lovers in abundance: 'I had been used to see the men about me lick the dust – for it was gold dust.' The novel's heroine, Belinda, adjusts her future to cope with a speculative world and to maintain her principled caution against 'matches of interest, convenience, and vanity'.[57]

All this chimes well with Edward Copeland's conclusions in his study of English women novelists writing about money:

> After 1800, money finds a far less anxious place in the women's novel. Women's fiction abandons, bit by bit, its narrative of economic victimization to embrace a narrative of economic empowerment, a fictional world in which women assertively participate in the economy as managers of the domestic budget.... Readers of Jane Austen will recognize the difference in economic emphasis immediately: the contrast between the relatively passive voice of the Dashwood women in *Sense and Sensibility* and the assertive, outspoken words of Anne Elliot, Lady Russell, and Mrs. Croft in *Persuasion*.[58]

These patterns common to Edgeworth and Austen match the plot frequencies of the lesser-known writers of fiction for the *Lady's Magazine* in which, from 1800 onwards, the responsible woman, capable housekeeper, wife to a bad husband, supplant the passive 1790s heroine rescued by marriage.[59]

The Irish Edgeworth constructs quite another world. For Edgeworth's Irish novels analyse the machinery and the intimate technicalities of debt, investment, and exchange. Edgeworth constructs narrative relationships that tie money's material form of coin or paper (or its immaterial form, linking feudal and credit economies, of a man's word or signature) to virtue, mischance, and prudence. These relationships constitute the primary rhetoric of her narratives of land tenure, uncertainty, debt, trust, and risk. The Irish novels have most in common then, not with the English story *Belinda*, but with Edgeworth's analytic Oriental fable *Murad the Unlucky* (1804) and with her revisionist novel *Harrington* (1817). *Harrington*, published and bound together with *Ormond*, is a novel in defense of mercantile Jews, a deliberate corrective by Edgeworth herself to her earlier anti-Semitic prejudice, detected both in *Castle Rackrent* and in *The Absentee*, which she later judged to be marred by their Shylock-and-Jessica figuration of Jews. Throughout the revisionist account in *Harrington* of Jewish political economy and Protestant anti-Semitism, and citing in her own support Lessing's *Nathan the Wise* and Edmund Malone's evidence that the original story of *The Merchant of Venice* had not pitted Jew against Christian, Maria Edgeworth asserts the dignity of those whose wanderings upon the earth required, and whose intelligence enabled, the invention of paper credit.[60]

Marilyn Butler memorably explains how Edgeworth's contemporaries praised her as the founder of the 'national' novel because they detected in her work the 'discovery how to draw a modern society with all its parts functioning in their real-life relation to one another'. Butler asserts that the distinctive method of the Irish tales is Edgeworth's new ability to arrange her fictions so that social and economic realities become more central than any individual character is allowed to be.[61] *Castle Rackrent*, *The Absentee*, and *Ormond* are less concerned with individual women and men, and more concerned to expose the workings of a distinct economy within which men and women may live and make practical decisions. The distinctive form of Edgeworth's Irish novels derives from a local and remarkable economic complexity, foregrounds its machinery, analyses in detail its confusions, and passes judgement on the unequal mastery of its constituent elements of paper and coin. In this her Irish novels display an extraordinary modernity that recognizes how political and social structures, and the virtues of independent citizenship, are now constituted by acts of fictional representation.

NOTES

1. F.W. Fetter, *The Irish Pound 1797–1826: A Reprint of the Report of the Committee of 1804 of the British House of Commons on the Condition of the Irish Currency, with selections from the Minutes of Evidence Presented to the Committee* (London: George Allen & Unwin, 1955), pp. 123–9; L.M. Cullen, 'Landlords, Bankers and Merchants: The Early Irish Banking World, 1700–1820', in A.E. Murphy (ed.), *Economists and the Irish Economy from the Eighteenth Century to the Present Day* (Dublin: Irish Academic Press, 1984), pp. 40–43; C. Ó Gráda, *Ireland: A New Economic History, 1780–1939* (Oxford: Clarendon Press, 1994), pp. 46–62.
2. Sir J. Clapham, *The Bank of England: A History*, 2 vols. (Cambridge: Cambridge University Press, 1944), i, 271–2.
3. Sir F. Baring, *Observations on the Establishment of the Bank of England and on the Paper Circulation of the Country* (London, 1797), pp. 68–9; *Third Report of the Committee of Secrecy* (London, 1797), p. 71.
4. Y. Beresiner and C. Narbeth, *The Story of Paper Money* (Newton Abbot: David and Charles, 1973), p. 28; Clapham, i, 271–2; ii, 1–74.
5. Sir W. Scott, *Thoughts on the Proposed Change of Currency*; and J.W. Croker, *Two Letters on Scottish Affairs*, intro. by D. Simpson and A. Wood (Shannon: Irish University Press, 1972).
6. D. Blaazer, 'Sterling Identities', *History Today*, 52/1 (2002), p. 17.
7. Croker, *Two Letters*, pp. 45–6.
8. Quoting Horace, *Odes* 3.4.65: *Vis consili expers mole ruit sua* (Force without wisdom falls by its own weight).
9. Croker, *Two Letters*, pp. 46–7.
10. J. Law, *Money and Trade Considered, with a Proposal for Supplying the Nation with Money* (Edinburgh, 1705), pp. 59–61.
11. C. Mather, *Some Considerations on the Bills of Credit now Passing in New-England* (1691), reprinted in *Colonial Currency Reprints 1682–1751*, 4 vols., ed. A. McFarland Davis (Boston: Prince Society, 1910–11), i, 189–90.
12. Quoted in W.T. Baxter, *The House of Hancock: Business in Boston 1724–1775* (Cambridge, MA: Harvard University Press, 1945), p. 16.
13. Sir J. Steuart, *An Inquiry into the Principles of Political Oeconomy* [1767], 2 vols., ed. A.S. Skinner (Edinburgh and London: Oliver & Boyd, 1966), ii, 421. See also W. Hixson, *Triumph of the Bankers: Money and Banking in the Eighteenth and Nineteenth Centuries* (Westport, CT: Praeger, 1993), p. 49.
14. J. Johnston, *Bishop Berkeley's Querist in Historical Perspective* (Dundalk: Dundalgan Press, 1970). Johnston reprints *The Querist* in its various editions.
15. Steuart, ii, 461, 534–7.
16. Johnston, *Berkeley's Querist*, pp. 126–7.
17. [W. Anderson], *The Iniquity of Banking: or, Bank Notes proved to be Injurious to the Public* (London, 1797), pp. 37–40, 62–4.
18. *An Essay on the Theory of Money* (London, 1771), pp. 17, 21–2.
19. E. Tatham, *A Letter to the Right Honourable William Pitt, Chancellor of the Exchequer, on the National Debt* ([Oxford], 1795), pp. 12–18.
20. Johnston, *Berkeley's Querist*, p. 162.
21. Steuart, ii, 478.
22. J. Law, *Oeuvres*, trans. E. de Sénovert (Paris, 1790); A.E. Murphy, 'John Law and the *assignats*', in G. Faccarello and P. Steiner (eds), *La pensée économique pendant la Révolution française: 1789–1799* (Grenoble: Presses Universitaires de Grenoble, 1990), pp. 431–81.

23. T.J. Clark, *Farewell to an Idea: Episodes from a History of Modernism* (New Haven: Yale University Press, 1999), pp. 10, 15–53.
24. Quoted in M. Bruguière, '*Assignats*', in F. Furet and M. Ozouf (eds), *Dictionnaire critique de la Révolution française* (Paris: Flammarion, 1988), p. 468.
25. A. Gallatin, *A Sketch of the Finances of the United States* (New York, 1796), pp. 87–9.
26. Quoted in J.K. Galbraith, *Money: Whence it Came, where it Went* (Boston: Houghton Mifflin, 1975), p. 59.
27. Quoted in E. Cannan, *The Paper Pound of 1797–1821* (London: P.S. King & Son, 1919), p. xi.
28. J. Ehrman, *The Younger Pitt: The Consuming Struggle* (London: Constable, 1996), pp. 5–7.
29. *Morning Post*, 14 September 1810.
30. D. Ricardo, *The Works and Correspondence of David Ricardo*, 11 vols. ed. P. Sraffa (Cambridge: Cambridge University Press, 1951–73), iv, 58. Quoted in Galbraith, *Money*, p. 37.
31. Sir J. Sinclair, *Letters Written to the Governor and Directors of the Bank of England* (London, 1797), p. 27.
32. W. Cobbett, *Paper against Gold and Glory against Prosperity*, 2 vols. (London, 1815), i, 185.
33. E. Burke, *Reflections on the Revolution in France: A Critical Edition*, ed. J.C.D. Clark (Stanford: Stanford University Press, 2001), p. 403.
34. T.W. Copeland et al. (eds), *The Correspondence of Edmund Burke*, 10 vols. (Cambridge: Cambridge University Press, 1958–78), ix, 269–70.
35. *Northern Star*, no. 540, 20–24 March 1797.
36. *Northern Star*, no. 543, 31 March–3 April 1797; no. 544, 4–7 April 1797.
37. *Walker's Hibernian Magazine*, September 1799, pp. 190–1.
38. M. Shell, *Art and Money* (Chicago: University of Chicago Press, 1995), pp. 7–8.
39. Fetter, *Irish Pound*, p. 129.
40. Fetter, *Irish Pound*, pp. 74, 123–4.
41. J. Carr, *The Stranger in Ireland; or, A Tour in the Southern and Western Parts of that Country, in the Year 1805* (London, 1806), p. 25.
42. Ó Gráda, *Ireland*, p. 48.
43. M. Edgeworth, *Tales of Fashionable Life*, 6 vols. (London, 1812), vi, 7–34.
44. M. Butler, *Maria Edgeworth, a Literary Biography* (Oxford: Clarendon Press, 1972), p. 357.
45. Cullen, 'Landlords, Bankers and Merchants', pp. 40–43.
46. [M. Edgeworth], *Castle Rackrent, an Hibernian Tale* (London, 1800), pp. 166–8.
47. Quoted in Ó Gráda, *Ireland*, p. 62.
48. Edgeworth, *Tales of Fashionable Life*, vi, 199–201.
49. Edgeworth, *Tales of Fashionable Life*, vi, 203–4, 236, 252.
50. Edgeworth, *Tales of Fashionable Life*, v, 255–7, 278–9.
51. Edgeworth, *Tales of Fashionable Life*, v, 381–2.
52. Edgeworth, *Tales of Fashionable Life*, vi, 180–92, 236.
53. Edgeworth, *Tales of Fashionable Life*, vi, 371–2.
54. M. Edgeworth, *Ormond*, ed. Claire Connolly (Harmondsworth: Penguin, 2000), pp. 280–81.
55. E. Copeland, *Women Writing about Money: Women's Fiction in England, 1790–1820* (Cambridge: Cambridge University Press, 1995), p. 61.
56. M. Edgeworth, *Belinda*, ed. E. Ní Chuilleanáin (London: Dent, 1993), p. 4.
57. Edgeworth, *Belinda*, pp. 32, 127.
58. Copeland, *Women Writing about Money*, p. 61.
59. Copeland, *Women Writing about Money*, pp. 61–3.
60. M. Edgeworth, *Harrington* (London, 1817), pp. 235–9; E. Malone (ed.), *The Plays and Poems of William Shakespeare,* 11 vols. (London, 1790), iv, 4n.
61. Butler, *Maria Edgeworth*, pp. 334–6.

Bibliography

Manuscripts

Bodleian Library:
MS Gough Somerset 7
MS Locke b. 3

British Library:

Add. MS 20102	Sundon Correspondence
Add. MS 21122	Southwell MSS
Add. MS 21123	Southwell MSS
Add. MS 35592	Hardwicke Papers

National Archives, London:

SP 63/	State Papers, Ireland
PC 2/	Privy Council Register

National Library of Ireland:

MS 694	'Some observations on the taxes paid by Ireland to support the government'
MS 2256	Bank of Ireland

Public Record Office of Northern Ireland:

T3019/	Wilmot Papers

Trinity College Dublin:

MSS 7259–7266	Clements MSS
MSS 750/1–8; 750/13–14; 2537/70	Correspondence of Archbishop King

Primary Sources

Accounts of Net Public Income and Expenditure of Great Britain and Ireland, 1688–1800 (London, 1869) [HC 1868–69 (366) xxxv.1, 483].

Anderson, J. *Observations on the Means of Exciting a Spirit of National Industry Chiefly Intended to Promote Agriculture, Commerce, Manufactures and Fisheries of Scotland* (Edinburgh, 1777).

[Anderson, W.], *The Iniquity of Banking: or, Bank Notes proved to be Injurious to the Public* (London, 1797).

Arnould, A.-M. *De la balance du commerce et des relations commerciales extérieures de la France dans toutes les parties du globe, particulièrement à la fin du règne de Louis XIV*, 2 vols. (Paris, 1791).

Bailyn, B. (ed.). *Pamphlets of the American Revolution, 1750–1776* (Cambridge, MA: Harvard University Press, 1965).

Barbon, N. *A Discourse Concerning Coining the New Money lighter. In Answer to Mr. Lock's Considerations about raising the Value of Money* (London, 1696).

Baring, Sir F. *Observations on the Establishment of the Bank of England and on the Paper Circulation of the Country* (London, 1797).

Berkeley, G. *A Discourse addressed to Magistrates and Men in Authority. Occasioned by the enormous License, and Irreligion of the Times* (Dublin, 1738).

— *Queries Relating to a National Bank, Extracted from the Querist. Also the Letter Containing A Plan or Sketch of such Bank. Republished with Notes* (Dublin, 1737).

— *Siris: A Chain of Philosophical Inquiries concerning the Virtues of Tar-water and Divers Subjects Connected Together and Arising One from Another* (Dublin and London, 1744).

— *The Works of George Berkeley Bishop of Cloyne*, ed. A.A. Luce and T.E. Jessop, 9 vols. (London: Thomas Nelson and Sons, 1948–57).

Brock, W.R. (ed). *The Federalist* (London: Dent, 2000).

Burke, E. *The Correspondence of Edmund Burke*, 10 vols., ed. T.W. Copeland, B. Lowe, P. Marshall, and J.A. Woods (Cambridge: Cambridge University Press, 1958–78).

— *Reflections on the Revolution in France: A Critical Edition*, ed. J.C.D. Clark (Stanford: Stanford University Press, 2001).

Burns, R. *The Canongate Burns*, ed. A. Noble and P.S. Hogg (Edinburgh: Canongate, 2001).

Calendar of State Papers, Colonial Series: America and the West Indies, 1706–1708, June [vol. 23], ed. C. Headlam (London: HM Stationery Office, 1916).

Calendar of State Papers, Colonial Series: America and the West Indies, 1724–1725 [vol. 34], ed. C. Headlam (London: HM Stationery Office, 1936).

Carr, J. *The Stranger in Ireland; or, A Tour in the Southern and Western Parts of that Country, in the Year 1805* (London: Richard Phillips, 1806).

Chalmers, G. *Arrangements with Ireland Considered* (London, 1785).

— *An Estimate of the Comparative Strength of Great-Britain, during the Present and Four Preceding Reigns; and of the Losses of her Trade from every War since the Revolution. A New Edition, Corrected, and Improved; with a Dedication to Dr. James Currie, the Reputed Author of 'Jasper Wilson's Letter.'* (1794; New York: Augustus M. Kelley, 1969).

— *The Life of Thomas Pain, with a Review of his Writings; Particularly of Rights of Man, Parts First and Second. By Francis Oldys, A.M. of the University of Philadelphia*, 5th ed. (London, 1792).

Clarendon, R.V. *A Sketch of the Revenue and Finances of Ireland and of the Appropriated Funds, Loans and Debt of the Nation from their Commencement* (Dublin, 1791).

Cobbett, W. *Paper against Gold and Glory against Prosperity*, 2 vols. (London, 1815).

— *Peter Porcupine in America: Pamphlets on Republicanism and the Revolution*, ed. D.A. Wilson (Ithaca: Cornell University Press, 1994).

Colquhoun, P. *A Treatise on the Wealth, Power and Resources of the British Empire, in every Quarter of the World, including the East Indies: The Rise and Progress of the Funding System Explained; With Observations on the National Resources for the beneficial Employment of a redundant Population, and for rewarding the Military and Naval Officers, Soldiers, and Seamen for their Services to their Country during the late War. Illustrated by Copious Statistical Tables, constituted on a New Plan, and Exhibiting a collected View of the different subjects discussed in this Work*, 2nd ed. (London, 1815).

Common Sense: in a Letter to a Friend. To which is prefixed an Explanatory Preface. By the Author of Ireland in Tears (London, 1755).

Considerations upon the Act of Parliament, whereby a Duty is laid of six Pence Sterling per Gallon on Molasses, and five Shillings per Hundred on Sugar of Foreign Growth, imported into any of the British Colonies (Boston, 1764), repr. in B. Bailyn (ed.), *Pamphlets of the American Revolution, 1750–1776* (Cambridge, MA: Harvard University Press, 1965), pp. 361–77.

Croker, J.W. *Two Letters on Scottish Affairs* [1828] [facsimile published with Sir W. Scott, *Thoughts on the Proposed Change of Currency*], intro. by D. Simpson and A. Wood (Shannon: Irish University Press, 1972).

Davenant, C. *Two Manuscripts by Charles Davenant*, ed. A.P. Usher (Baltimore: Johns Hopkins Press, 1942).

Delany, P. *Observations upon Lord Orrery's Remarks on the Life and Writings of Dr. Jonathan Swift* [1754] (New York: Garland, 1974).

A Dialogue between Mr. Freeport, a Merchant, and Tom Handy, a Trades-man, Concerning the Bank (Dublin, 1721).

Edgeworth, M. *Belinda*, ed. E. Ní Chuilleanáin (London: Dent, 1993).

— *Castle Rackrent, an Hibernian Tale* (London, 1800).

— *Harrington* (London, 1817).

— *Ormond*, ed. Claire Connolly (Harmondsworth: Penguin, 2000).

— *Tales of Fashionable Life*, 6 vols. (London, 1812).

Edinburgh Annual Register for 1823 (Edinburgh and London, 1824).

An Essay on the Theory of Money (London, 1771).

Fauquier, Francis. *The Official Papers of Francis Fauquier, Lieutenant Governor of Virginia, 1758–1768*, 3 vols, ed. G. Reese (= *Virginia Historical Society. Documents*, vols. 14–16) (Charlottesville: University Press of Virginia, 1980–83).

Fetter, F.W. *The Irish Pound 1797–1826: A Reprint of the Report of the Committee of 1804 of the British House of Commons on the Condition of the Irish Currency, with selections from the Minutes of Evidence Presented to the Committee* (London: George Allen & Unwin, 1955).

Franklin, B. *A Modest Enquiry into the Nature and Necessity of a Paper-Currency* (Philadelphia, 1729).

— *The Papers of Benjamin Franklin*, ed. L.W. Labaree et al. (New Haven: Yale University Press, 1959–).

Gallatin, A. *A Sketch of the Finances of the United States* (New York, 1796).

Hamilton, A. *The Papers of Alexander Hamilton*, 27 vols., ed. H.C. Syrett (New York: Columbia University Press, 1961–87).

Historical Manuscripts Commission: Report on Manuscripts in Various Collections, vol. 8 (London: HM Stationery Office, 1913).

Hopkins, S. *The Rights of Colonies Examined* (Providence, RI, 1765), repr. in B. Bailyn (ed.), *Pamphlets of the American Revolution, 1750–1776* (Cambridge, MA: Harvard University Press, 1965).

Horace, *Odes and Epodes,* ed. Niall Rudd (Cambridge, MA: Harvard University Press, 2004).

Hume, D. *Essays, Moral, Political and Literary*, ed. E.F. Miller (Indianapolis: Liberty Fund, 1985).

— *A Treatise of Human Nature*, 2nd ed., ed. L.A. Selby-Bigge and P.H. Nidditch (Oxford: Clarendon Press, 1978).

Hutcheson, F. *A System of Moral Philosophy*, 2 vols. [1755]. Rpt. with an introduction by D. Carey (Bristol: Thoemmes Press, 2000).

Jefferson, T. *Notes on the State of Virginia*, ed. F. Shuffelton (Harmondsworth: Penguin, 1999).

Johnson, S. *The Lives of the Most Eminent English Poets; with Critical Observations on their Works*, 4 vols., ed. Roger Lonsdale (Oxford: Clarendon Press, 2006).

The Journals of the House of Commons of the Kingdom of Ireland, 21 vols. 3rd ed. (Dublin, 1796–1800).

Journals of the House of Lords, 8 vols. (Dublin, 1779–1800).

Labaree, L.W. (ed.). *Royal Instructions to British Colonial Governors, 1670–1776*, 2 vols. (New York: D. Appleton & Co, 1935).

Law, J. *Money and Trade Considered, with a Proposal for Supplying the Nation with Money* (Edinburgh, 1705).

— *Oeuvres*, trans. E. de Sénovert (Paris, 1790).

Law, R. (ed.). *Correspondence from the Royal African Company's Factories at Offra and Whydah on the Slave Coast of West Africa in the Public Record Office, London 1678–1693* (Edinburgh: Centre of African Studies, Edinburgh University, 1989).

— *Correspondence of the Royal African Company's Chief Merchants at Cabo Corso Castle with William's Fort, Whydah, and the Little Popo Factory, 1727–1728* (Madison: African Studies Program, University of Wisconsin-Madison, 1991).

— *The English in West Africa, 1681–1683: The Local Correspondence of the Royal African Company of England, 1681–1699, Part 1* (Oxford: Oxford University Press, 1997).

— *Further Correspondence of the Royal African Company of England Relating to the 'Slave Coast', 1681–1699* (Madison: African Studies Program, University of Wisconsin-Madison, 1992).

A Letter to Henry Maxwell, Esq; Plainly Shewing the Great Danger that the Kingdom has Escaped, and the Great Inconveniencies, that Must of Necessity have Happen'd, if a Bank had been Establish'd in this Kingdom (Dublin, 1721).

Locke, J. *The Correspondence of John Locke*, 8 vols. ed. E.S. de Beer (Oxford, 1976–89).

— *An Essay concerning Human Understanding*, corr. ed., ed. P.H. Nidditch (Oxford: Clarendon Press, 1979).

Lowndes, W. *A Report Containing an Essay for the Amendment of the Silver Coins* (London, 1695).

Macaulay, T.B. *The History of England from the Accession of James II* [1848], 2 vols. (London: Longmans, Green, 1903).

Madison, J. *Notes of Debates in the Federal Convention of 1787 Reported by James Madison*. Bicentennial Edition (New York: Norton, 1987).

Malone, E. (ed.). *The Plays and Poems of William Shakspeare*, 11 vols. (London, 1790).

Mather, C. *Some Considerations on the Bills of Credit now Passing in New-England* (1691), reprinted in *Colonial Currency Reprints 1682–1751*, 4 vols., ed. A. McFarland Davis (Boston: Prince Society, 1910–11).

Maxwell, H. *Reasons Offer'd for Erecting a Bank in Ireland; in a Letter to Hercules Rowley, Esq*. (Dublin, 1721).

McFarland Davis, A. (ed.). *Colonial Currency Reprints 1682–1751*, 4 vols. (Boston: Prince Society, 1910–11).

McIlwaine, H.R. (ed.). *Journals of the House of Burgesses of Virginia* [1619–93, 1695–1706, 1710–15, 1718, 1727–34, 1736–40, 1742–49, 1752–58, 1762–76], 13 vols., (Richmond, VA: The Colonial Press, 1905–15).

Morning Post, 14 September 1810.

Mun, T. *England's Treasure by Forraign Trade* (London, 1664).

The Northern Star, no. 540, 20–24 March 1797; 543, 31 March–3 April 1797; no. 544, 4–7 April 1797.

Paine, T. *The Complete Writings of Thomas Paine*, 2nd ed., 2 vols. ed. P.S. Foner (New York: Citadel Press, 1969).

— *Public Good* (Philadelphia, 1780).
Percival, J., Earl of Egmont. *Manuscripts of the Earl of Egmont. Diary of Viscount Percival afterwards First Earl of Egmont*, 3 vols. (London: His Majesty's Stationery Office, 1920–23).
Playfair, W. *A General View of the Actual Force and Resources of France, in January, MDCCXCIII* (London, 1793).
— *An Inquiry into the Permanent Causes of the Decline and Fall of Powerful and Wealthy Nations, Illustrated by Four Engraved Charts. Designed to Shew how the Prosperity of the British Empire may be Prolonged* (London, 1805).
Pope, A. 'Epilogue to the Satires: Dialogue II', in P. Rogers (ed.), *Alexander Pope: Selected Poetry* (Oxford: Oxford University Press, 1994).
Price, R. *Observations on the Nature of Civil Liberty* (London, 1776; repr. Charlestown, SC: 1776).
A Proposal of Special Advantage to this Nation and Posterity (London, 1672).
Reasons for Regulating the Coin, and reducing the Interest; with a Scheme for paying part of the National Debt without burthening Ireland ([Dublin], 1731).
Reflections on the National Debt; with Reasons for Reducing the Legal Interest; and against a Public Loan. With some Advice to the Electors of Members of Parliament ([Dublin], 1731).
A Reply to the Defence of the Bank: Setting forth the Unreasonableness of their Slow Payments (London, 1696).
Ricardo, D. *The Works and Correspondence of David Ricardo*, 11 vols. ed. P. Sraffa (Cambridge: Cambridge University Press, 1951–73).
Rowley, H. *An Answer to a Book, Intitl'd, Reasons Offer'd for Erecting a Bank in Ireland. In a Letter to Henry Maxwell, Esq.* (Dublin, 1721).
Royal African Company 'Fourth Charter', *Collections of the Virginia Historical Society*, new ser., 6 (1887), pp. 37–53.
Ruffhead, O. (ed.). *The Statutes at Large, from Magna Charta, to the End of the Last Parliament, 1761* [*and continued to the 20th Year of the Reign of George III, inclusive*], 13 vols. (London, 1763–80).
Scott, Sir W. *Thoughts on the Proposed Change of Currency* [1828] [facsimile published with J.W. Croker, *Two Letters on Scottish Affairs*], intro by A. Wood and D. Simpson (Shannon: Irish University Press, 1972).
Shaw, W.A. *Select Tracts and Documents Illustrative of English*

Monetary History 1626–1730 (1896; London: George Hardin, 1935).
Simmons, R.C. and Thomas, P.D.G. (eds). *Proceedings and Debates of the British Parliaments Respecting North America, 1754–1783*, 6 vols. (Millwood, NY: Kraus International, 1982–87).
Sinclair, Sir J. *History of the Public Revenue of the British Empire*, 3rd ed., 3 vols. (1803–4; New York: Augustus M. Kelley, 1966).
— *Letters Written to the Governor and Directors of the Bank of England* (London, 1797).
— *The Speech of the Rt. Hon. Sir John Sinclair, Bart. on the Subject of the Bullion Report, in the House of Commons* (London, 1811).
Smith, A. *An Inquiry into the Nature and Causes of the Wealth of Nations*, ed. R.H. Campbell and A.S. Skinner, 2 vols. (Oxford: Clarendon Press, 1982).
— *An Inquiry into the Nature and Causes of the Wealth of Nations*, 3 vols., ed. W. Playfair [1805] (London: Pickering & Chatto, 1995).
— *Lectures on Jurisprudence*, ed. R.L. Meek, D.D. Raphael, and P.G. Stein (Oxford: Clarendon Press, 1978).
Smith, P.H. (ed.). *Letters of Delegates to Congress, 1774–1789*, 25 vols. (Washington, DC: Library of Congress, 1976–98).
The Statutes at Large Passed in the Parliaments Held in Ireland, 20 vols. (Dublin, 1763–1801).
Steuart, Sir J. *Inquiry into the Principles of Political Economy* [1767], 2 vols. ed. A.S. Skinner (Chicago: University of Chicago Press / Edinburgh and London: Oliver & Boyd, 1966).
Stock, J. 'An Account of the Life of George Berkeley' (1776), in D. Berman (ed.), *George Berkeley: Eighteenth-Century Responses*, 2 vols. (New York: Garland Publishing, 1989).
Swift, J. *The Correspondence of Jonathan Swift*, 5 vols. ed. H. Williams (Oxford: Clarendon Press, 1963–65).
— *Poetical Works*, ed. H. Davis (London: Oxford University Press, 1967).
Tatham, E. *A Letter to the Right Honourable William Pitt, Chancellor of the Exchequer, on the National Debt* ([Oxford], 1795).
The Journals of the House of Commons of the Kingdom of Ireland, from the Eleventh Year of King James the First, 2nd ed. (Dublin, 1763).
Third Report of the Committee of Secrecy (London, 1797).
Vance, H. *An Inquiry into the Nature and Uses of Money* (Boston,

1740), in A. McFarland Davis (ed.) *Colonial Currency Reprints 1682–1751*, 4 vols. (Boston: Prince Society, 1910–11).
Walker's Hibernian Magazine.
Witherspoon, J. *An Annotated Edition of Lectures on Moral Philosophy by John Witherspoon*, ed. J. Scott (Newark, DE: University of Delaware Press, 1982).
— *Essay on Money, as a Medium of Commerce; with Remarks on the Advantages and Disadvantages of Paper admitted into general Circulation* (Philadelphia, 1786).
— *The Works of the Rev. John Witherspoon*, 4 vols. (Philadelphia, 1800–1802).
Yeats, G.D. ['Iatros']. *A Biographical Sketch of the Life and Writings of Patrick Colquhoun, Esq., LL.D.* (London, 1818).
Young, A. *The Example of France a Warning to Britain* (London, 1793).

Secondary Sources

Alberts, R.C. *The Golden Voyage: The Life and Times of William Bingham, 1752–1804* (Boston: Houghton-Mifflin, 1969).
Aldridge, A.O. 'Why Did Thomas Paine Write on the Bank?', *Proceedings of the American Philosophical Society*, 93/4 (1949), pp. 309–15.
Allan, D. *Virtue, Learning and the Scottish Enlightenment: Ideas of Scholarship in Early Modern Scotland* (Edinburgh: Edinburgh University Press, 1993).
Anderson, B. *Imagined Communities: Reflections on the Origin and Spread of Nationalism* (London: Verso, 1983).
Appleby, J.O. *Economic Thought and Ideology in Seventeenth-Century England* (Princeton: Princeton University Press, 1978).
— 'Locke, Liberalism, and the Natural Law of Money', *Past & Present*, 71 (1976), pp. 43–69.
Armitage, D. *The Ideological Origins of the British Empire* (Cambridge: Cambridge University Press, 2000).
— 'The Scottish Vision of Empire: Intellectual Origins of the Darien Venture', in J. Robertson (ed.), *A Union for Empire: Political Thought and the British Union of 1707* (Cambridge: Cambridge University Press, 1995), pp. 97–118.
Barrow, T.C. *Trade and Empire: The British Customs Service in Colonial America 1660–1775* (Cambridge, MA: Harvard University Press, 1967).

Bartlett, T. *The Fall and Rise of the Irish Nation: The Catholic Question, 1690–1830* (Dublin: Gill & Macmillan, 1992).

— '"This famous island set in a Virginian sea": Ireland in the British Empire, 1690–1801', in W.R. Louis and P.J. Marshall (ed.), *The Oxford History of the British Empire, Volume II, The Eighteenth Century* (Oxford: Oxford University Press, 2001), pp. 253–75.

Baxter, W.T. *The House of Hancock: Business in Boston 1724–1775* (Cambridge, MA: Harvard University Press, 1945).

Beer, G.L. *The Origins of the British Colonial System, 1578–1660* (1908; repr. Gloucester, MA: P. Smith, 1959).

Beresiner, Y. and Narbeth, C. *The Story of Paper Money* (Newton Abbot: David and Charles, 1973).

Berman, D. *George Berkeley: Idealism and the Man* (Oxford: Clarendon Press, 1994).

Biemann, U. 'Remotely Sensed: A Topography of the Global Sex Trade', *Feminist Review*, 80 (2005), pp. 180–93.

Bin Wong, R. 'The Search for European Differences and Domination in the Early Modern World: A View from Asia', *The American Historical Review*, 107/2 (2002), pp. 447–69.

Blaazer, D. 'Sterling Identities', *History Today*, 52/1 (2002), pp. 12–18.

Blake, B. and Callaway, J. *Paper Money of Ireland* (Sutton, Surrey: Pam West, 2009).

Böttcher, N. 'Cuba and the Thirteen Colonies During the North American War of Independence', in H. Pietschmann (ed.), *Atlantic History: History of the Atlantic System, 1580–1830* (Göttingen: Vandenhoeck & Ruprecht, 2002), pp. 481–95.

Bowen, H.V. 'The Bank of England during the Long Eighteenth Century, 1694–1820', in R. Roberts and D. Kynaston (eds), *The Bank of England: Money, Power and Influence 1694–1994* (Oxford: Clarendon Press, 1995), pp. 1–18.

Braddick, M.J. *The Nerves of State: Taxation and the Financing of the English State, 1558–1714* (Manchester: Manchester University Press, 1996).

Breen, T.H. *Tobacco Culture: The Mentality of the Great Tidewater Planters on the Eve of the Revolution* (Princeton: Princeton University Press, 1985).

Brewer, J. *The Sinews of Power: War, Money and the English State, 1688–1783* (London: Routledge, 1989).

Bric, M.J. 'The Tithe System in Eighteenth-Century Ireland', *Proceedings of the Royal Irish Academy*, 86 (1986), pp. 271–88.

Broadie, A. *The Scottish Enlightenment: The Historical Age of the Historical Nation* (Edinburgh: Birlinn Press, 2001).
Brooke, J.L. *The Heart of the Commonwealth: Society and Political Culture in Worcester County, Massachusetts, 1713–1861* (Cambridge: Cambridge University Press, 1989).
Brown, M.L. 'William Bingham, Agent of the Continental Congress, in Martinique', *Pennsylvania Magazine of History and Biography*, 61 (1937), pp. 54–87.
Bruguière, M. '*Assignats*', in F. Furet and M. Ozouf (eds), *Dictionnaire critique de la Révolution française* (Paris: Flammarion, 1988), pp. 462–72.
Brynn, E. 'Some Repercussions of the Act of Union on the Church of Ireland, 1801–1820', *Church History*, 40/3 (1971), pp. 284–96.
Burkholder, M.A. and Johnson, L.L. *Colonial Latin America*, 2nd ed. (New York: Oxford University Press, 1994).
Burns, R.E. *Irish Parliamentary Politics in the Eighteenth Century*, 2 vols. (Washington, DC: Catholic University of America Press, 1989–90).
Buron, E. 'Statistics on Franco-American Trade', *Journal of Economic and Business History*, 4 (1931–32), pp. 571–80.
Butler, M. *Maria Edgeworth, a Literary Biography* (Oxford: Clarendon Press, 1972).
Caffentzis, G. 'Algebraic Money: Berkeley's Philosophy of Mathematics and Money', *Berkeley Studies*, 18 (2007), pp. 3–23.
— *Clipped Coins, Abused Words, and Civil Government: John Locke's Philosophy of Money* (New York: Automedia, 1989).
— 'Fiction or Counterfeit? David Hume's Interpretations of Paper and Metallic Money', in C. Wennerlind and M. Schabas (eds), *David Hume's Political Economy* (London: Routledge, 2008), pp. 146–67.
Cain, P.J. and Hopkins, A.G. *British Imperialism: Innovation and Expansion* (London: Longman, 1993).
Cannan, E. *The Paper Pound of 1797–1821* (London: P.S. King & Son, 1919).
Carruthers, B.G. *City of Capital: Politics and Markets in the English Financial Revolution* (Princeton: Princeton University Press, 1996).
Challis, C.E. 'Lord Hastings to the Great Silver Recoinage, 1464–1699', in C.E. Challis (ed.), *A New History of the Royal Mint* (Cambridge: Cambridge University Press, 1992), pp. 179–397.

Champion, J.A.I. *The Pillars of Priestcraft Shaken: The Church of England and its Enemies, 1660–1730* (Cambridge: Cambridge University Press, 1992).

Chaudhuri, K.N. *Trade and Civilization in the Indian Ocean: An Economic History from the Rise of Islam to 1750* (Cambridge: Cambridge University Press, 1985).

Checkland, S.G. *Scottish Banking: A History* (Glasgow: Collins, 1975).

Clapham, Sir J. *The Bank of England: A History*, 2 vols. (Cambridge: Cambridge University Press, 1944).

Clark, J.C.D. *English Society, 1660–1832: Religion, Ideology and Politics during the Ancien Regime* (Cambridge: Cambridge University Press, 2000).

Clark, S. *Paisley: A History* (Edinburgh: Mainstream, 1988).

Clark, T.J. *Farewell to an Idea: Episodes from a History of Modernism* (New Haven: Yale University Press, 1999).

Clemens, P.G.E. *The Atlantic Economy and Colonial Maryland's Eastern Shore: From Tobacco to Grain* (Ithaca: Cornell University Press, 1980).

Colley, L. *Britons: Forging the Nation 1707–1837* (New Haven: Yale University Press, 1992).

Connolly, S.J. 'The Defence of Protestant Ireland, 1660–1760', in T. Bartlett and K. Jeffery (eds), *A Military History of Ireland* (Cambridge: Cambridge University Press, 1996), pp. 231–46.

— *Religion, Law and Power: The Making of Protestant Ireland 1660–1760* (Oxford: Oxford University Press, 1992).

Copeland, E. *Women Writing about Money: Women's Fiction in England, 1790–1820* (Cambridge: Cambridge University Press, 1995).

Craig, M. *Dublin 1660–1860* (London: The Cresset Press, 1952).

Crowley, J.E. *The Privileges of Independence: Neomercantilism and the American Revolution* (Baltimore: Johns Hopkins University Press, 1993).

Cullen, L.M. *Anglo-Irish Trade: 1660–1800* (Manchester: Manchester University Press, 1968).

— *An Economic History of Ireland since 1660*, 2nd ed. (London: B.T. Batsford, 1987).

— 'Landlords, Bankers and Merchants: The Early Irish Banking World, 1700–1820', in A.E. Murphy (ed.), *Economists and the Irish Economy from the Eighteenth Century to the Present Day* (Dublin: Irish Academic Press, 1984), pp. 25–44.

Curtin, P.D. *Cross-Cultural Trade in World History* (Cambridge: Cambridge University Press, 1984).

— *Economic Change in Precolonial Africa: Senegambia in the Era of the Slave Trade* (Madison: University of Wisconsin Press, 1975).

— *The Rise and Fall of the Plantation Complex: Essays in Atlantic History* (Cambridge: Cambridge University Press, 1990).

— 'The West African Coast in the Era of the Slave Trade', in P. Curtin, S. Feierman, L. Thompson and J. Vansina, *African History: From Earliest Times to Independence*, 2nd ed. (London: Longman, 1995).

Dale, R. *The First Crash: Lessons from the South Sea Bubble* (Princeton: Princeton University Press, 2004).

Dalzell, F.A.B. 'Taxation with Representation: Federal Revenue in the Early Republic' (PhD thesis, Harvard University, 1993).

Daniel, S.H. *John Toland: His Methods, Manners, and Mind* (Kingston and Montreal: McGill-Queen's University Press, 1984).

Davies, K.G. *The North Atlantic World in the Seventeenth Century* (Minneapolis: University of Minnesota Press, 1974).

— *The Royal African Company* (London: Longman, 1957).

Davis, R. 'English Foreign Trade, 1660–1700', *Economic History Review*, 7 (1954–55), pp. 150–66.

De Vere White, T. *The Story of the Royal Dublin Society* (Tralee: The Kerryman Ltd., 1955).

Devine, T.M. 'Colonial Commerce and the Scottish Economy, c.1730–1815', in L.M. Cullen and Smout, T.C. (eds), *Comparative Aspects of Scottish and Irish Economic and Social History 1600–1900* (Edinburgh: John Donald, 1977), pp. 177–90.

— 'Irish and Scottish Development Revisited', in T.M. Devine, *Clearance and Improvement: Land, Power and People in Scotland, 1700–1900* (Edinburgh: John Donald, 2006), pp. 27–41.

— 'The Modern Economy: Scotland and the Act of Union', in T.M. Devine, C.H. Lee, and G.C. Peden (eds), *The Transformation of Scotland: The Economy since 1700* (Edinburgh: Edinburgh University Press, 2005), pp. 13–33.

— *The Scottish Nation, 1700–2000* (London: Allen Lane, 1999).

Dickerson, O.M. *The Navigation Acts and the American Revolution* (Philadelphia: University of Pennsylvania Press, 1951).

Dickson, D. *New Foundations: Ireland 1660–1800* (Dublin: Helicon, 1987).

Dickson, H.T. *Walpole and the Whig Supremacy* (London: The English Universities Press, 1973).

Dickson, P.G.M. *The Financial Revolution in England: A Study in the Development of Public Credit, 1688–1756* (London: Macmillan, 1967; reprinted, Aldershot: Ashgate, 1993).

Doerflinger, T.M. *A Vigorous Spirit of Enterprise: Merchants and Economic Development in Revolutionary Philadelphia* (Chapel Hill: University of North Carolina Press, 1986).

Dorfman, J. *The Economic Mind in American Civilization*, 2 vols. (New York, 1946).

Dow, A. and Dow, S. (eds). *A History of Scottish Economic Thought* (London: Routledge, 2006).

Downing, N.W. 'Transatlantic Paper and the Emergence of the American Capital Market', in W.M. Goetzmann and K.G. Rouwenhorst (eds), *The Origins of Value: The Financial Innovations that Created Modern Capital Markets* (Oxford: Oxford University Press, 2005), pp. 271–98.

Durey, M. *Transatlantic Radicals and the Early American Republic* (Lawrence, KS: University Press of Kansas, 1997).

Edling, M.M. *A Revolution in Favor of Government: Origins of the U.S. Constitution and the Making of the American State* (New York: Oxford University Press, 2003).

— '"So immense a power in the affairs of war": Alexander Hamilton and the Restoration of Public Credit', *William and Mary Quarterly*, 3rd ser., 64/2 (2007), pp. 287–326.

Edling M.M. and Kaplanoff, M.D. 'Alexander Hamilton's Fiscal Reform: Transforming the Structure of Taxation in the Early Republic', *William and Mary Quarterly*, 3rd ser., 61/4 (2004), pp. 713–44.

Egerton, D., Games, A., Landers, J.G., Lane, K., Wright, D.R. *The Atlantic World: A History, 1400–1888* (Wheeling, IL: Harlan Davison, 2007).

Egnal, M. *A Mighty Empire: The Origins of the American Revolution* (Ithaca: Cornell University Press, 1988).

Ehrman, J. *The Younger Pitt: The Consuming Struggle* (London: Constable, 1996).

Ekelund, Jr., R.B., Hebert, R.F. and Tollison, R.D. (eds). 'An Economic Model of the Medieval Church: Usury as a Form of Rent Seeking', *Journal of Law, Economics, & Organization*, 5/2 (1989), pp. 307–31.

Elkins, S. and McKitrick, E. *The Age of Federalism: The Early American Republic, 1788–1800* (New York: Oxford University Press, 1993).

Eltis, D. *The Rise of African Slavery in the Americas* (Cambridge: Cambridge University Press, 2000).

Eltis, D., Behrendt, S.D., Richardson, D. and Klein, H.S. (eds). *The Trans-Atlantic Slave Trade: A Database on CD–Rom* (Cambridge: Cambridge University Press, 1999).

Eltis, W. 'John Locke, the Quantity Theory of Money and the Establishment of a Sound Currency', in M. Blaug et al., *The Quantity Theory of Money: From Locke to Keynes and Friedman* (Cheltenham: Edward Elgar, 1995), pp. 4–26.

Ernst, J. *Money and Politics in America, 1755–1775* (Chapel Hill: University of North Carolina Press, 1973).

Fairlie, S. 'Dyestuffs in the Eighteenth Century', *Economic History Review*, 17 (1964–65), pp. 488–510.

Falola, T. and Lovejoy, P.E. 'Pawnship in Historical Perspective', in T. Falola and P.E. Lovejoy (eds), *Pawnship in Africa: Debt Bondage in Historical Perspective* (Boulder: Westview Press, 1994), pp. 1–26.

Fauske, C. *Jonathan Swift and the Church of Ireland* (Dublin: Irish Academic Press, 2002).

Fay, C.R. 'Locke versus Lowndes', *Cambridge Historical Journal*, 4/2 (1933), pp. 143–55.

Feavearyear, Sir A. *The Pound Sterling: A History of English Money*, 2nd ed. rev. E.V. Morgan (Oxford: Clarendon Press, 1963).

Fechner, R.J. 'The Godly and Virtuous Republic of John Witherspoon', in H. Cravens (ed.), *Ideas in America's Cultures: From Republic to Mass Society* (Ames, IA: Iowa State University Press, 1982), pp. 7–25.

— 'The Moral Philosophy of John Witherspoon and the Scottish-American Enlightenment' (PhD thesis, University of Iowa, 1974).

Ferguson, E.J. *The Power of the Purse: A History of American Public Finance, 1776–1790* (Chapel Hill: University of North Carolina Press, 1961).

Ferguson, N. *The Cash Nexus: Money and Power in the Modern World, 1700–2000* (London: Allen Lane, 2001).

Fetter, F.W. *Development of British Monetary Orthodoxy 1797–1875* (Cambridge, MA: Harvard University Press, 1965).

Finkelstein, A. *Harmony and the Balance: An Intellectual History of Seventeenth-Century English Economic Thought* (Ann Arbor: University of Michigan Press, 2000).

Finlay, C.J. *Hume's Social Philosophy: Human Nature and Commercial Sociability in A Treatise of Human Nature* (London: Continuum, 2007).

— 'Hume's Theory of Civil Society', *The European Journal of Political Theory*, 3/4 (2004), pp. 369–91.

Flage, D. *Berkeley's Doctrine of Notions: A Reconstruction Based on his Theory of Meaning* (New York: St Martin's Press, 1987).

Forbes, D. *Hume's Philosophical Politics* (Cambridge: Cambridge University Press, 1975).

Galbraith, J.K. *Money: Whence it Came, where it Went* (Boston: Houghton Mifflin, 1975).

Galenson, D. *Traders, Planters, and Slaves: Market Behavior in Early English America* (Cambridge: Cambridge University Press, 1986).

Gilbart, J.W. *The History, Principles, and Practice of Banking*, rev. A.S. Michie, 2 vols. (London: G. Bell & Sons, 1882).

Gilbert, J.T. *A History of the City of Dublin*, 3 vols. (Dublin, 1854–59).

Goebel, D.B. 'The "New England Trade" and the French West Indies, 1763–1774: A Study in Trade Policies', *William and Mary Quarterly*, 3rd ser., 20 (1963), pp. 331–72.

Goodwin, J. *Greenback: The Almighty Dollar and the Invention of America* (New York: Henry Holt and Company, 2003).

Granovetter, M. and Swedberg, R. *The Sociology of Economic Life* (Boulder, CO: Westview Press, 1992).

Griffin, J. 'Parliamentary Politics in Ireland during the Reign of George I' (MA thesis, UCD, 1977).

Griffiths, Sir P. *A Licence to Trade: The History of English Chartered Companies* (London: E. Benn, 1974).

Guy, A.J. 'The Irish Military Establishment, 1660–1776', in T. Bartlett and K. Jeffery (eds), *A Military History of Ireland* (Cambridge: Cambridge University Press, 1996), pp. 211–30.

Habermas, J. *The Structural Transformation of the Public Sphere* (Cambridge, MA: MIT Press, 1989).

Hall, F.G. *The Bank of Ireland 1783–1946* (Dublin: Hodges Figgis, 1949).

Hamilton, H. *The English Brass and Copper Industries to 1800* (London: Longman, 1926).

Hammond, B. *Banks and Politics in America from the Revolution to the Civil War* (Princeton: Princeton University Press, 1957).

Harper, L.A. *The English Navigation Laws: A Seventeenth-Century Experiment in Social Engineering* (New York: Columbia University Press, 1939).

Harris, E.M. 'Did Solon Abolish Debt-Bondage?', *Classical Quarterly*, 52/2 (2002), pp. 415–30.

Harrison, P. *'Religion' and the Religions in the English Enlightenment* (Cambridge: Cambridge University Press, 1990).

Hayton, D.W. 'Anglo-Irish Attitudes: Changing Perceptions of National Identity among the Protestant Ascendancy in Ireland, ca. 1690–1750', *Studies in Eighteenth-Century Culture*, 17 (1987), pp. 145–57.

— 'Walpole and Ireland', in J. Black (ed.), *Britain in the Age of Walpole* (New York: St Martin's Press, 1984), pp. 95–119.

Hayton, D.W. and Jones, C. (eds). *A Register of Parliamentary Lists, 1660–1761* (Leicester: University of Leicester, History Department, 1979).

Heckscher, E.F. *Mercantilism*, 2 vols. trans. M. Shapiro, rev. ed., ed. E.F. Söderlund (London: George Allen & Unwin, 1955).

Heslip, R. 'Brass Money', in W.A. Maguire (ed.), *Kings in Conflict: The Revolutionary War in Ireland and its Aftermath 1689–1750* (Belfast: The Blackstaff Press, 1990), pp. 122–35.

Higman, B.W. 'The Sugar Revolution', *The Economic History Review*, n.s. 53/2 (2000), pp. 213–36.

Hirschman, A.O. *The Passions and the Interests: Political Arguments for Capitalism before its Triumph* (Princeton: Princeton University Press, 1977).

Hixson, W. *Triumph of the Bankers: Money and Banking in the Eighteenth and Nineteenth Centuries* (Westport, CT.: Praeger, 1993).

Hoppit, J. 'Checking the Leviathan, 1688–1832', in D. Winch and P.K. O'Brien (eds), *The Political Economy of British Historical Experience, 1688–1914* (Oxford: Oxford University Press for The British Academy, 2002), pp. 267–94.

Horsefield, J.K. *British Monetary Experiments 1650–1710* (Cambridge, MA: Harvard University Press / London: G. Bell and Sons, 1960).

— 'The Duties of a Banker. II: The Effects of Inconvertibility', in T.S. Ashton and R.S. Sayers (eds), *Papers in English Monetary History* (Oxford: Clarendon Press, 1953), pp. 16–36.

Houghton, J.W. *Culture and Currency: Cultural Bias in Monetary Theory and Politics* (Boulder, CO: Westview Press, 1991).

Howe, D.W. 'John Witherspoon and the Transatlantic Enlightenment', in S. Manning and F.D. Cogliano (eds), *The Atlantic Enlightenment* (Aldershot: Ashgate, 2008), pp. 61–79.

Hummel, J.R. 'The Monetary History of America to 1789: A Historiographical Essay', *Journal of Libertarian Studies*, 2/4 (1978), pp. 373–89.

Jacob, M. and Jacob, J. (eds). *The Origins of Anglo-American Radicalism* (London: George Allen & Unwin, 1984).

James, F.G. *Ireland in the Empire, 1688–1770* (Cambridge, MA: Harvard University Press, 1973).

Johnston, J. *Bishop Berkeley's Querist in Historical Perspective* (Dundalk: Dundalgan Press, 1970).

Johnston-Liik, E.M. *History of the Irish Parliament 1692–1800: Commons, Constituencies and Statutes*, 6 vols. (Belfast: Ulster Historical Foundation, 2002).

Jones, D.W. *War and Economy in the Age of William III and Marlborough* (Oxford: Basil Blackwell, 1988).

Jones, L.C. *The Clubs of the Georgian Rakes* (New York: Columbia University Press, 1942).

Kelly, J. 'Harvests and Hardship: Famine and Scarcity in Ireland in the Late 1720s', *Studia Hibernica*, 26 (1992), pp. 65–105.

Kelly, P.H. 'General Introduction: Locke on Money', in Kelly (ed.) *Locke on Money*, 2 vols. (Oxford, 1991), pp. 1–109.

— '"Monkey" Business: Locke's "College" Correspondence and the Adoption of the Plan for the Great Recoinage of 1696', *Locke Studies*, 9 (2009), pp. 139–65.

— 'Perceptions of Locke in Ireland in the Eighteenth Century', *Proceedings of the Royal Irish Academy*, 89, section C (1989), pp. 17–35.

— 'The Politics of Political Economy in Mid-Eighteenth-Century Ireland', in S.J. Connolly (ed.), *Political Ideas in Eighteenth-Century Ireland* (Dublin: Four Courts Press, 2000), pp. 105–29.

Kidd, C. *Subverting Scotland's Past: Scottish Whig Historians and the Creation of an Anglo-British Identity, 1689–c.1830* (Cambridge: Cambridge University Press, 1993).

Kiernan, T.J. *History of the Financial Administration of Ireland to 1817* (London: P.S. King & Son, 1930).

Killinger III, C.L. 'The Royal African Slave Trade to Virginia, 1689–1713' (MA thesis, College of William and Mary, 1969).

Kleer, R.A. '"Fictitious Cash": English Public Finance and Paper Money, 1689–97', in C.I. McGrath and C. Fauske (eds), *Money, Power, and Print: Interdisciplinary Studies on the Financial Revolution in the British Isles* (Newark: University of Delaware Press, 2008), pp. 70–103.

— '"The ruine of Diana": Lowndes, Locke, and the Bankers', *History of Political Economy*, 36/3 (2004), pp. 533–56.

Klein, M.A. 'The Impact of the Atlantic Slave Trade on the Societies of the Western Sudan', *Social Science History*, 14/2 (1990), pp. 231–53.

Klingman, D. 'The Significance of Grain in the Development of the Tobacco Colonies', *Journal of Economic History*, 29 (1969), pp. 268–78.

Knorr, K.E. *British Colonial Theories 1570–1850* (1944; London: Frank Cass, 1963).

Kramnick, I. 'The "Great National Discussion": The Discourse of Politics in 1787', *The William and Mary Quarterly*, 3rd ser., 45/1 (1988), pp. 3–32.

Lamb, J. *Preserving the Self in the South Seas, 1680–1840* (Chicago: University of Chicago Press, 2001).

Lansing Collins, V. *President Witherspoon: A Biography*, 2 vols. (Princeton: Princeton University Press, 1925).

Law, R. 'The Gold Trade of Whydah in the Seventeenth and Eighteenth Centuries', in D. Henige and T.C. McCaskie (eds), *West African Economic and Social History: Studies in Memory of Marion Johnson* (Madison: African Studies Program, University of Wisconsin-Madison, 1990), pp. 105–18.

— *The Slave Coast of West Africa, 1550–1750* (Oxford, 1991).

Lee, C.H. 'The Establishment of the Financial Network', in T.M. Devine, C.H. Lee, and G.C. Peden (eds), *The Transformation of Scotland: The Economy since 1700* (Edinburgh: Edinburgh University Press, 2005), pp. 100–27.

Lewis, J.A. 'Anglo-American Entrepreneurs in Havana: The Background and Significance of the Expulsion of 1784–1785', in J.A. Barbier and A.J. Kuethe (eds), *The North American Role in the Spanish Imperial Economy, 1760–1819* (Manchester: Manchester University Press, 1984), pp. 112–26.

Li, M.-H. *The Great Recoinage of 1696 to 1699* (London: Weidenfeld and Nicolson, 1963).

Luce, A.A. *The Life of George Berkeley Bishop of Cloyne* (London: Nelson, 1949).

Magennis, E. *The Irish Political System 1740–1765: The Golden Age of the Undertakers* (Dublin: Four Courts Press, 2000).

— 'Whither the Irish Financial Revolution?: Money, Banks and Politics in Ireland in the 1730s', in C.I. McGrath and C. Fauske (eds), *Money, Power, and Print: Interdisciplinary Studies on the Financial Revolution in the British Isles* (Newark: University of Delaware Press, 2008), pp. 189–207.

Malcomson, A.P.W. *Nathaniel Clements: Government and the*

Governing Elite in Ireland, 1725–75 (Dublin: Four Courts Press, 2005).
Mann, B.H. *Republic of Debtors: Bankruptcy in the Age of American Independence* (Cambridge, MA: Harvard University Press, 2002).
Marcuzzo, M.C. and Rosselli, A. *Ricardo and the Gold Standard: The Foundations of the International Money Order* (London: Macmillan, 1986).
Marshall, P.J. (ed.). *The Eighteenth Century* (Oxford: Oxford University Press, 1998).
Martin, G. 'Commercial Relations between Nantes and the American Colonies during the War of Independence', *Journal of Economic and Business History*, 4 (1931–32), pp. 812–29.
Marx, K. *Theories of Surplus Value: Volume IV of Capital*, trans. J. Cohen and S.W. Ryazanskaya, ed. S.W. Ryazanskaya and R. Dixon (Moscow: Progress Publishers, 1971).
McCusker, J.J. 'The Current Value of English Exports, 1697–1800', *William and Mary Quarterly*, 3rd ser., 28 (1971), pp. 607–28.
McCusker, J.J. and Menard, R.R. *The Economy of British America, 1607–1789. With Supplementary Bibliography* (Chapel Hill: University of North Carolina Press, 1991).
McGowan, W.H. 'Did Berkeley Write *The Irish Blasters?*', *Berkeley Newsletter*, no. 6 (1982/83), pp. 1–4.
McGrath, C.I. 'Central Aspects of the Eighteenth-Century Constitutional Framework in Ireland: The Government Supply Bill and Biennial Parliamentary Sessions, 1715–82', *Eighteenth-Century Ireland*, 16 (2001), pp. 9–34.
— 'The Irish Experience of "Financial Revolution" 1660–1760', in C.I. McGrath and C. Fauske (eds), *Money, Power, and Print: Interdisciplinary Studies on the Financial Revolution in the British Isles* (Newark: University of Delaware Press, 2008), pp. 157–88.
— 'The Irish Revenue System: Government and Administration, 1689–1702' (PhD thesis, University of London, 1997).
— *The Making of the Eighteenth-Century Irish Constitution: Government, Parliament and the Revenue, 1692–1714* (Dublin: Four Courts Press, 2000).
— 'Parliament, People and other Possibilities', *Eighteenth-Century Ireland*, 17 (2002), pp. 157–66.
McGrath, C.I. and Fauske, C. (eds). *Money, Power, and Print: Interdisciplinary Studies on the Financial Revolution in the British Isles* (Newark: University of Delaware Press, 2008).

McMinn, J. 'Swift and Theatre', *Eighteenth-Century Ireland*, 16 (2001), pp. 35–46.

McNally, P. *Parties, Patriots and Undertakers: Parliamentary Politics in Early Hanoverian Ireland* (Dublin: Four Courts Press, 1997).

Meyer, J. 'Les difficultés du commerce Franco-Americain vues de Nantes (1776–1790)', *French Historical Studies*, 11/2 (1979), pp. 159–83.

Miller, P.N. *Defining the Common Good: Empire, Religion and Philosophy in Eighteenth-Century England* (Cambridge: Cambridge University Press, 1994).

Moody, T.W., Martin, F.X. and Byrne, F.J. (eds). *A New History of Ireland*, ix, *Maps, Genealogies, Lists* (Oxford: Clarendon Press, 1984).

Morgan, E.S. 'Colonial Ideas of Parliamentary Power', *William and Mary Quarterly*, 3rd ser., 5 (1948), pp. 311–41, repr. in J.P. Greene (ed.), *The Reinterpretation of the American Revolution* (New York: Harper & Row, 1968), pp. 151–81.

Morgan, K. 'Mercantilism and the British Empire, 1688–1815', in D. Winch and P.K. O'Brien (eds), *The Political Economy of British Historical Experience, 1688–1914* (Oxford: Oxford University Press for The British Academy, 2002), pp. 165–91.

Muehlmann, R.G. *Berkeley's Ontology* (Indianapolis: Hackett Publishing Co., 1992).

Muldrew, C. *The Economy of Obligation: The Culture of Credit and Social Relations in Early Modern England* (New York: St Martin's Press / Basingstoke: Macmillan, 1998).

Murphy, A.E. *The Genesis of Macroeconomics: New Ideas from Sir William Petty to Henry Thornton* (Oxford: Oxford University Press, 2009).

— 'John Law and the *assignats*', in G. Faccarello and P. Steiner (eds), *La pensée économique pendant la Révolution française: 1789–1799* (Grenoble: Presses Universitaires de Grenoble, 1990), pp. 431–81.

— 'John Law and the Scottish Enlightenment', in A. Dow and S. Dow (eds), *A History of Scottish Economic Thought* (London: Routledge, 2006), pp. 9–26.

— *John Law: Economic Theorist and Policy-Maker* (Oxford: Clarendon Press, 1997).

Murphy, A.L. *The Origins of English Financial Markets: Investment and Speculation before the South Sea Bubble* (Cambridge: Cambridge University Press, 2009).

Nash, G.B. *The Urban Crucible: Social Change, Political*

Consciousness, and the Origins of the American Revolution (Cambridge, MA: Harvard University Press, 1979).

Nash, R.C. 'Irish Atlantic Trade in the Seventeenth and Eighteenth Centuries', *William and Mary Quarterly*, 3rd ser., 42/3 (1985), pp. 329–56.

— 'The Organization of Trade and Finance in the British Atlantic Economy, 1600–1830', in P.A. Coclanis (ed.), *The Atlantic Economy during the Seventeenth and Eighteenth Centuries: Organization, Operation, Practice, and Personnel* (Columbia: University of South Carolina Press, 2005), pp. 95–151.

Neal, L. *The Rise of Financial Capitalism: International Capital Markets in the Age of Reason* (Cambridge: Cambridge University Press, 1990).

Nettels, C. 'British Policy and Colonial Money Supply', *The Economic History Review*, 3/2 (1931), pp. 219–45.

— 'The Origins of Paper Money in the English Colonies', *Economic History*, 3, no. 9 (1934), pp. 35–56.

Newell, M.E. *From Dependency to Independence: Economic Revolution in Colonial New England* (Ithaca: Cornell University Press, 1998).

North, D.C. and Weingast, B.R. 'Constitutions and Commitment: The Evolution of Institutions Governing Public Choice in Seventeenth-Century England', *Journal of Economic History*, 49 (1989), pp. 803–32.

Nuxoll, E.M. *Congress and the Munitions Merchants: The Secret Committee of Trade during the American Revolution, 1775–1777* (New York: Garland, 1985).

Ó Ciardha, É. *Ireland and the Jacobite Cause, 1685–1766: A Fatal Attachment* (Dublin: Four Courts Press, 2002).

Ó Gráda, C. *Ireland: A New Economic History, 1780–1939* (Oxford: Clarendon Press, 1994).

O'Brien, P.K. 'Fiscal Exceptionalism: Great Britain and its European Rivals from Civil War to Triumph at Trafalgar and Waterloo', in D. Winch and P.K. O'Brien (eds), *The Political Economy of British Historical Experience, 1688–1914* (Oxford: Oxford University Press for The British Academy, 2002), pp. 245–65.

— 'Merchants and Bankers as Patriots or Speculators? Foreign Commerce and Monetary Policy in Wartime, 1793–1815', in J.J. McCusker and K. Morgan (eds), *The Early Modern Atlantic Economy* (Cambridge: Cambridge University Press, 2000), pp. 250–77.

— 'The Political Economy of British Taxation, 1660–1815', *Economic History Review*, 2nd ser., 41/1 (1988), pp. 1–32.

— 'Public Finance in the Wars with France, 1793–1815', in H.T. Dickinson (ed.), *Britain and the French Revolution, 1789–1815* (Basingstoke: Macmillan, 1989), pp. 164–87.

O'Brien, P.K. and Hunt, P.A. 'England, 1485–1815', in R. Bonney (ed.), *The Rise of the Fiscal State in Europe, c.1200–1815* (Oxford: Oxford University Press, 1999), pp. 53–101.

O'Donovan, D. 'The Money Bill Dispute of 1753', in T. Bartlett and D.W. Hayton (eds), *Penal Era and Golden Age: Essays in Irish History, 1690–1800* (Belfast: Ulster Historical Foundation, 1979), pp. 55–87.

O'Regan, P. 'Accountability and Financial Control as "Patriotic" Strategies: Accomptants and the Public Accounts Committee in Late Seventeenth and Early Eighteenth Century Ireland', *Accounting Historians Journal*, 30/2 (2003), pp. 105–32.

O'Shaughnessy, A.J. *An Empire Divided: The American Revolution and the British Caribbean* (Philadelphia: University of Pennsylvania Press, 2000).

Ohlmeyer, J. and Ó Ciardha, É. (eds). *The Irish Statute Staple Books, 1596–1687* (Dublin: Dublin City Council, 1998).

Papenfuse, E.C. 'An Uncertain Connection: Maryland's Trade with France during the American Revolution, 1778–1783', in C. Fohlen and J. Godechot (eds), *La révolution américaine et l'Europe* (Paris: CNRS, 1979), pp. 243–64.

Perkins, E.J. *American Public Finance and Financial Services, 1700–1815* (Columbus, OH: Ohio State University Press, 1994).

Peter, A. *Sketches of Old Dublin* (Dublin: Sealy, Bryers and Walker, 1907).

Phillips, M.S. *Society and Sentiment: Genres of Historical Writing in Britain, 1740–1820* (Princeton: Princeton University Press, 2000).

Phillipson, N.T. 'The Scottish Enlightenment', in R. Porter and M. Teich (eds), *The Enlightenment in National Context* (Cambridge: Cambridge University Press, 1981), pp. 19–40.

Pincus, S. *1688: The First Modern Revolution* (New Haven: Yale University Press, 2009).

Pitman, F.W. *The Development of the British West Indies, 1700–1763* (New Haven: Yale University Press, 1917).

Pittock, M.G.H. 'John Law's Theory of Money and its Roots in Scottish Culture', *Proceedings of the Antiquarian Society of Scotland*, 133 (2003), pp. 391–403.

Pocock, J.G.A. *The Machiavellian Moment: Florentine Political Thought and the Atlantic Republican Tradition* (Princeton: Princeton University Press, 1975).

— *Political Thought and History: Essays on Theory and Method* (Cambridge: Cambridge University Press, 2009).

— 'Standing Army and Public Credit: The Institutions of Leviathan', in D. Hoak and M. Feingold (eds), *The World of William and Mary: Anglo-Dutch Perspectives on the Revolution of 1688–89* (Stanford: Stanford University Press, 1996), pp. 87–103.

— *Virtue, Commerce, and History: Essays on Political Thought and History, Chiefly in the Eighteenth Century* (Cambridge: Cambridge University Press, 1985).

Pomeranz, K. 'Political Economy and Ecology on the Eve of Industrialization: Europe, China, and the Global Conjuncture', *The American Historical Review*, 107/2 (2002), pp. 425–46.

Porter, R. and Teich, M. (eds). *The Enlightenment in National Context* (Cambridge: Cambridge University Press, 1981).

Poterba, J.M. 'Annuities in Early Modern Europe', in W.M. Goetzmann and K.G. Rouwenhorst (eds), *The Origins of Value: The Financial Innovations that Created Modern Capital Markets* (Oxford: Oxford University Press, 2005), pp. 207–24.

Pressnell, L.S. *Country Banking in the Industrial Revolution* (Oxford: Clarendon Press, 1956).

Price, J.M. *Capital and Credit in British Overseas Trade: The View from the Chesapeake, 1700–1776* (Cambridge, MA: Harvard University Press, 1980).

— *France and the Chesapeake: A History of the French Tobacco Monopoly, 1674–1791, and of Its Relationship to the British and American Tobacco Trades*, 2 vols. (Ann Arbor: University of Michigan Press, 1973).

Quinn, S. 'Gold, Silver, and the Glorious Revolution: Arbitrage between Bills of Exchange and Bullion', *Economic History Review*, 44/3 (1996), pp. 473–490.

— 'Goldsmith-Banking: Mutual Acceptance and Interbanker Clearing in Restoration London', *Explorations in Economic History*, 34/4 (1997), pp. 411–32.

Rediker, M. *Between the Devil and the Deep Blue Sea* (Cambridge: Cambridge University Press, 1987).

Redish, A. *Bimetallism: An Economic and Historical Analysis* (Cambridge: Cambridge University Press, 2000).

Reynolds, D.E.F. 'Ammunition Supply in Revolutionary Virginia',

Virginia Magazine of History and Biography, 70 (1965), pp. 56–77.

Richards, R.D. *The Early History of Banking in England* (London: P.S. King & Son, 1929).

— 'The Exchequer Bill in the History of English Governmental Finance', *Economic History*, 3, no. 11 (1936), pp. 193–211.

— 'The First Fifty Years of the Bank of England', in J.G. Van Dillen (ed.), *History of the Principal Public Banks* (The Hague: Martinus Nijhoff, 1934), pp. 219–30.

— 'The Lottery in the History of English Government Finance', *Economic History*, 3, no. 9 (1934), pp. 57–76.

Robertson, J. 'Introduction', in Andrew Fletcher, *Political Works*, ed. J. Robertson (Cambridge: Cambridge University Press, 1997), pp. ix–xxx.

— 'The Scottish Enlightenment at the Limits of the Civic Tradition', in I. Hont and M. Ignatieff (eds), *Wealth and Virtue: The Shaping of Political Economy in the Scottish Enlightenment* (Cambridge: Cambridge University Press, 1983), pp. 137–78.

— 'Universal Monarchy and the Liberties of Europe: David Hume's Critique of an English Whig Doctrine', in N. Phillipson and Q. Skinner (eds), *Political Discourse in Early Modern Britain* (Cambridge: Cambridge University Press, 1993), pp. 349–73.

Robertson, J. (ed.). *A Union for Empire: Political Thought and the British Union of 1707* (Cambridge: Cambridge University Press, 1995).

Rogers Taylor, G. 'Wholesale Commodity Prices at Charleston, 1732–1791', *Journal of Economic and Business History*, 4 (1932), pp. 356–77.

Roseveare, H. *The Financial Revolution 1660–1760* (London: Longman, 1991).

Russell, J.B. *A History of Witchcraft: Sorcerers, Heretics and Pagans* (London: Thames and Hudson, 1980).

Ryder, M. 'The Bank of Ireland, 1721: Land, Credit and Dependency', *Historical Journal*, 25 (1982), pp. 557–82.

Sargent, T.J. and Velde, F.R. *The Big Problem of Small Change* (Princeton: Princeton University Press, 2002).

Saville, R. *Bank of Scotland: A History 1695–1995* (Edinburgh: Edinburgh University Press, 1996).

Schnurmann, C. *Atlantische Welten: Engländer und Niederländer im amerikanisch-atlantischen Raum 1648–1713* (Cologne: Böhlau Verlag, 1998).

Schumpeter, J.A. *A History of Economic Analysis* (1954; New York: Oxford University Press, 1986).

Scott, W.R. *The Constitution and Finance of English, Scottish, and Irish Joint Stock Companies to 1720*, 3 vols. (Cambridge, MA: Harvard University Press, 1910–12).

Scribner, R.L. (ed.). *Revolutionary Virginia: The Road to Independence*, 7 vols. in 8 (Charlottesville: University of Virginia Press, 1973–83).

Shell, M. *Art and Money* (Chicago: University of Chicago Press, 1995).

Shepherd, J.F. and Walton, G.M. *Shipping, Maritime Trade and the Economic Development of Colonial North America* (Cambridge: Cambridge University Press, 1972).

Sherman, R.B. *Roger Sherman: Signer and Statesman* (Philadelphia: University of Pennsylvania Press, 1938).

Skinner, Q. *Liberty before Liberalism* (Cambridge: Cambridge University Press, 1997).

— *Visions of Politics III: Hobbes and Civil Science* (Cambridge: Cambridge University Press, 2002).

Sosin, J.M. *Agents and Merchants: British Colonial Policy and the Origins of the American Revolution, 1763–1775* (Lincoln, NE: University of Nebraska Press, 1965).

Stein, N. 'No Way Out', *Fortune*, 147/1 (2003), pp. 102–8.

Stephenson, O.W. 'The Supply of Gunpowder in 1776', *American Historical Review*, 30/2 (1924–25), pp. 271–81.

Sterne Randall, W. *Alexander Hamilton: A Life* (New York: HarperCollins, 2003).

Sullivan, K. *Maryland and France, 1774–1789* (Philadelphia: University of Pennsylvania Press, 1936).

Swedberg, R. 'Major Traditions of Economic Sociology', *Annual Review of Sociology*, 17 (1990), pp. 251–76.

Tawney, R.H. *Religion and the Rise of Capitalism: A Historical Study* (London: Penguin, 1926).

Thomas, K. *Religion and the Decline of Magic* (New York: Charles Scribner's Sons, 1971).

Thomas, P.D.G. *British Politics and the Stamp Act Crisis: The First Phase of the American Revolution 1763–1767* (Oxford: Oxford University Press, 1975).

Thompson, P.V. and Thompson, D.J., *The Account Books of Jonathan Swift* (Newark, DE: University Delaware Press, 1984).

Thornton, J. *Africa and Africans in the Making of the Atlantic*

World, 1400–1800, 2nd ed. (Cambridge: Cambridge University Press, 1998).

Truxes, T.M. *Irish-American Trade, 1660–1783* (Cambridge: Cambridge University Press, 1988).

— 'London's Irish Merchant Community and North Atlantic Commerce in the Mid-Eighteenth Century', in D. Dickson, J. Parmentier, and J. Ohlmeyer (eds), *Irish and Scottish Mercantile Networks in Europe and Overseas in the Seventeenth and Eighteenth Centuries* (Gent: Academia Press, 2007), pp. 271–309.

Tuck, R. *The Rights of War and Peace: Political Thought and the International Order from Grotius to Kant* (Oxford: Oxford University Press, 1999).

US Bureau of the Census, *Historical Statistics of the United States: Colonial Times to 1970*, 2 vols. (Washington, DC: USGPO, 1975).

Valenze, D. *The Social Life of Money in the English Past* (Cambridge: Cambridge University Press, 2006).

Van Brock, L. *The Currency of the American Colonies, 1700–1764: A Study in Colonial Finance and Imperial Relations* (New York: Arno Press, 1975).

Ver Steeg, C.L. *Robert Morris: Revolutionary Financier. With an Analysis of his Earlier Career* (Philadelphia: University of Pennsylvania Press, 1954).

— 'Stacey Hepburn and Company: Enterprisers in the American Revolution', *South Carolina Historical Magazine*, 55/1 (1954), pp. 1–5.

Vickers, D.W. *Studies in the Theory of Money, 1690–1776* (1959; New York: Augustus M. Kelley, 1968).

Victory, I. 'The Making of the 1720 Declaratory Act', in G. O'Brien (ed.), *Parliament, Politics and People: Essays in Eighteenth-Century Irish History* (Dublin: Irish Academic Press, 1989), pp. 9–29.

Voltaire, *The Works of Voltaire: A Contemporary Version*, ed. J. Morley and T. Smollett, trans. W.F. Fleming (New York: E.R. Dumont, 1901).

Watt, D. *The Price of Scotland: Darien, Union and the Wealth of Nations* (Edinburgh: Luath Press, 2007).

Weber, M. *The Protestant Ethic and the Spirit of Capitalism*, ed. A. Giddens, trans. T. Parsons (London: Harper Collins, 1991).

Wellenreuther, H. *Ausbildung und Neubildung: Die Geschichte Nordamerikas vom Ausgang des 17. Jahrhunderts bis zum Ausbruch der Amerikanischen Revolution 1775* (Münster and Hamburg: Lit Verlag, 2001).

— *Von Chaos und Krieg zu Ordnung und Frieden: Der Amerikanischen Revolution erster Teil, 1775–1783* (Münster and Hamburg: Lit Verlag, 2006).

Wennerlind, C. *Casualties of Credit: The English Financial Revolution, 1620–1720* (Cambridge, MA: Harvard University Press, forthcoming).

— 'Credit-Money as the Philosopher's Stone: Alchemy and the Coinage Problem in Seventeenth-Century England', *History of Political Economy*, supplement to vol. 35 (2003), pp. 234–61.

— 'The Link between David Hume's *Treatise of Human Nature* and His Fiduciary Theory of Money', *History of Political Economy*, 33/1 (2001), pp. 139–60.

Wennerlind, C. and Schabas, M. (eds). *David Hume's Political Economy* (London: Routledge, 2008).

Whitaker, T.K. 'Origins and Consolidation, 1783–1826', in F.S.L. Lyons (ed.), *Bank of Ireland 1783–1983: Bicentenary Essays* (Dublin: Gill and Macmillan, 1983), pp. 11–29.

White, E.N. 'France and the Failure to Modernize Macroeconomic Institutions', in M.G. Bordo and R. Cortés-Conde (eds), *Transferring Wealth and Power from the Old to the New World: Monetary and Fiscal Institutions in the 17th through the 19th Centuries* (Cambridge: Cambridge University Press, 2001), pp. 59–99.

Whiting, J.R.S. *Trade Tokens: A Social and Economic History* (Newton Abbot: David and Charles, 1971).

Wilson, P.L. *Pirate Utopias* (New York: Autonomedia, 1995).

Wood, J.H. *A History of Central Banking in Great Britain and the United States* (Cambridge: Cambridge University Press, 2005).

Woozley, A.D. 'Berkeley's Doctrine of Notions and Theory of Meaning', in W. Doney (ed.), *Berkeley on Abstraction and Abstract Ideas* (New York: Garland Press, 1989), pp. 253–60.

Wordie, J.R. 'Deflationary Factors in the Tudor Price Rise', *Past & Present*, 154/1 (1997), pp. 32–70.

Wright, D.R. *The World and a Very Small Place in Africa* (London: M.E. Sharpe, 1997).

Wright, R.E. *Hamilton Unbound: Finance and the Creation of the American Republic* (Westport, CT: Greenwood, 2002).

Index